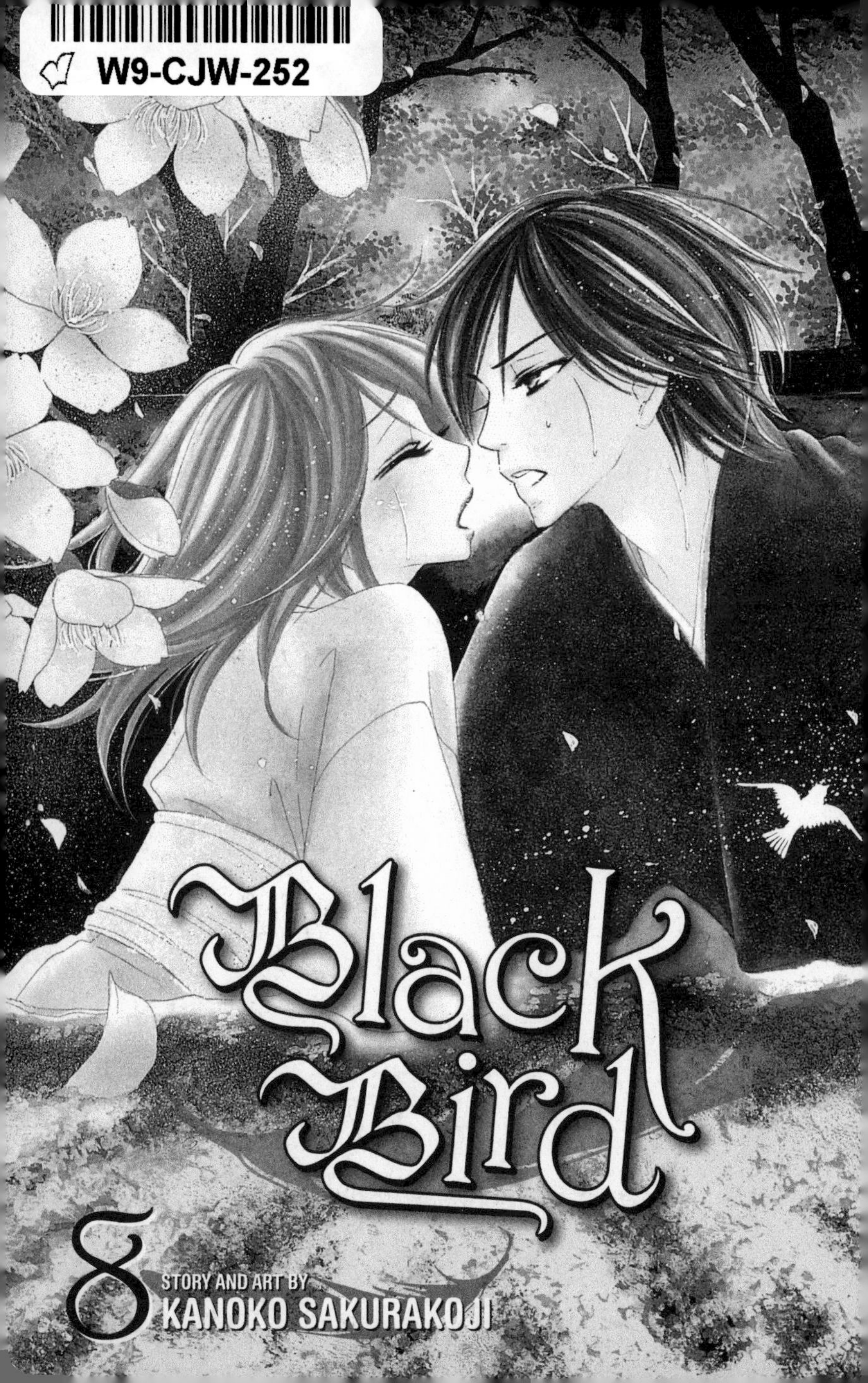
Black Bird
8
STORY AND ART BY
KANOKO SAKURAKOJI

Black Bird

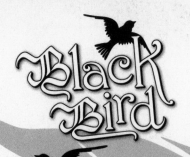

CONTENTS

CHARACTERS

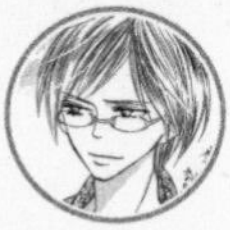

TADANOBU KUZUNOHA
Kyo's close friend since childhood. Current leader of the Kitsune clan.

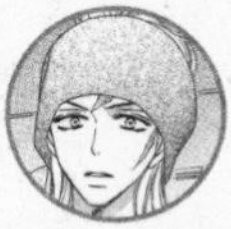

RAIKOH WATANABE
Like Misao, he can see demons and spirits. However, he refuses to believe that humans and demons can live in harmony, and uses his abilities to destroy them.

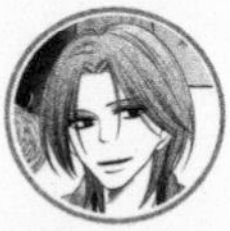

SHO USUI
Kyo's older bother and a ex-member of the Eigh Daitengu, where he wa also known as Sojo. His attempted coup failed, and his whereabouts ar currently unknown.

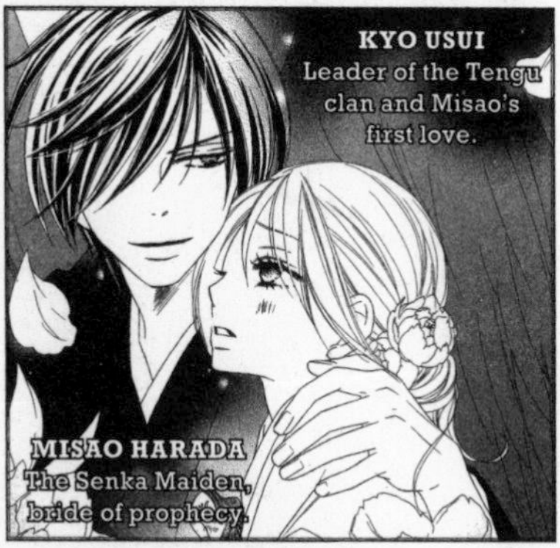
KYO USUI
Leader of the Tengu clan and Misao's first love.
MISAO HARADA
The Senka Maiden, bride of prophecy.

THE EIGHT DAITENGU
Kyo's bodyguards. Their names designate their official posts.

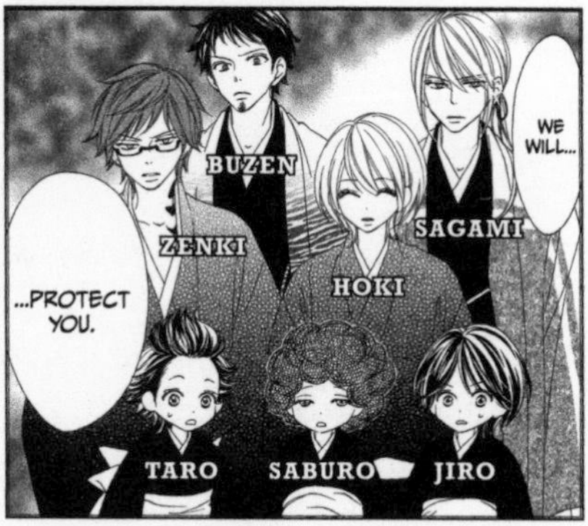
WE WILL...
...PROTECT YOU.
BUZEN
SAGAMI
ZENKI
HOKI
TARO
SABURO
JIRO

STORY THUS FAR
Misao can see spirits and demons, and her childhood sweetheart Kyo has been protecting her since she was little.

"Someday, I'll come for you, I promise." Kyo reappears the day before Misao's 16th birthday to tell her, "Your 16th birthday marks 'open season' on you." She is the Senka Maiden, and if a demon drinks her blood, he is granted a long life. If he eats her flesh, he gains eternal youth. And if he makes her his bride, his clan will prosper...And Kyo is a *tengu*, a crow demon, with his sights firmly set on her.

But no one knows if Misao, a human, will survive being bedded by a demon, so Kyo decides to wait until they can discover the truth.

One day Misao's father brings home a young man named Raikoh, who bears the scars from a demon attack he suffered as a child. As a result, Raikoh holds a deep hatred for demons. Raikoh immediately recognizes that Kyo is a demon, and warns Misao that if she doesn't end their relationship, he will exorcise Kyo.

Because Misao is a human, Kyo hesitates to use his power against another human. And then Misao discovers that the only way for Kyo to withstand the threat of exorcism and have enough power to fight Raikoh without injuring anyone is to bed her!

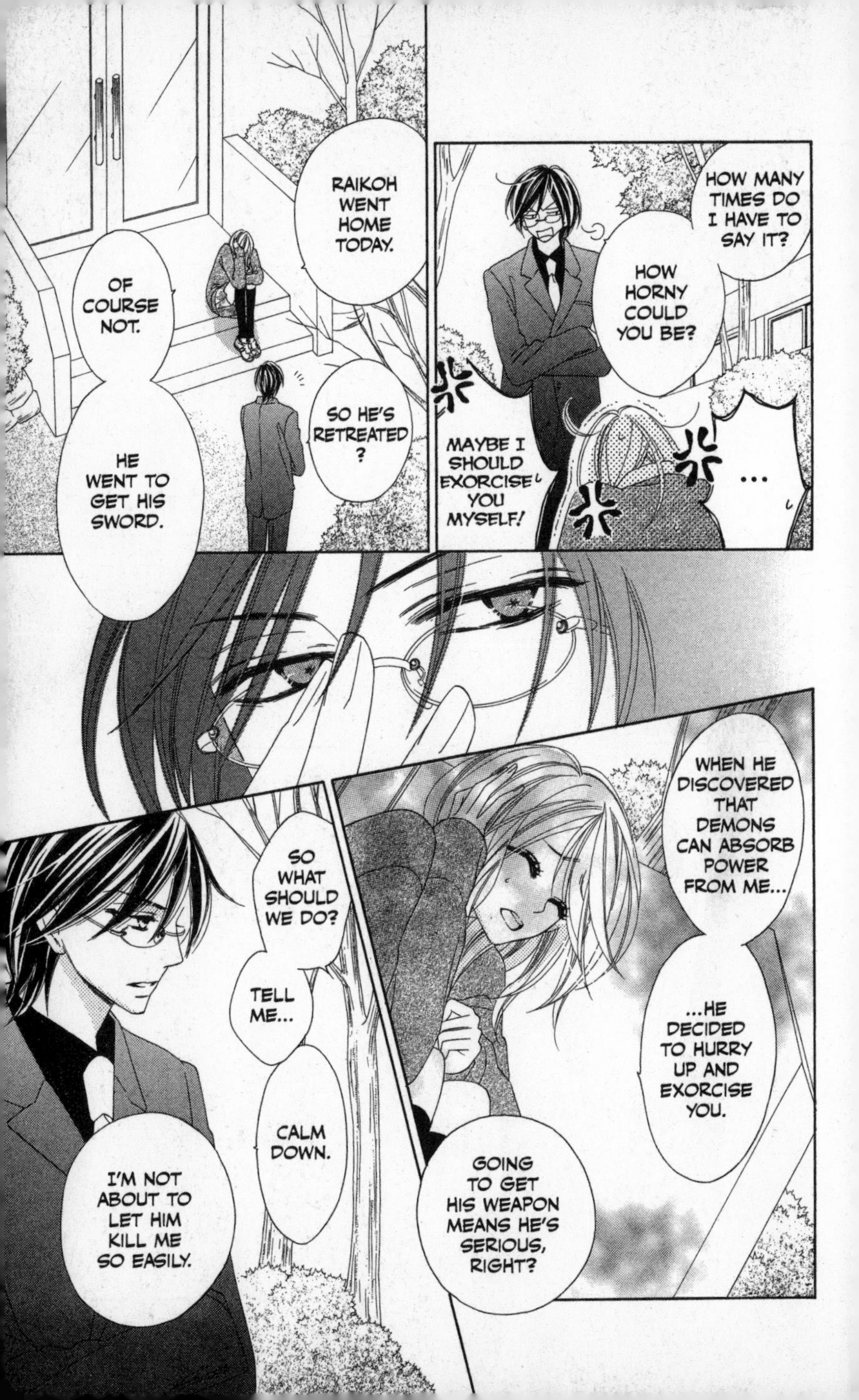
HOW MANY TIMES DO I HAVE TO SAY IT?
HOW HORNY COULD YOU BE?
...
MAYBE I SHOULD EXORCISE YOU MYSELF!
RAIKOH WENT HOME TODAY.
SO HE'S RETREATED?
OF COURSE NOT.
HE WENT TO GET HIS SWORD.
WHEN HE DISCOVERED THAT DEMONS CAN ABSORB POWER FROM ME...
...HE DECIDED TO HURRY UP AND EXORCISE YOU.
GOING TO GET HIS WEAPON MEANS HE'S SERIOUS, RIGHT?
SO WHAT SHOULD WE DO?
TELL ME...
CALM DOWN.
I'M NOT ABOUT TO LET HIM KILL ME SO EASILY.

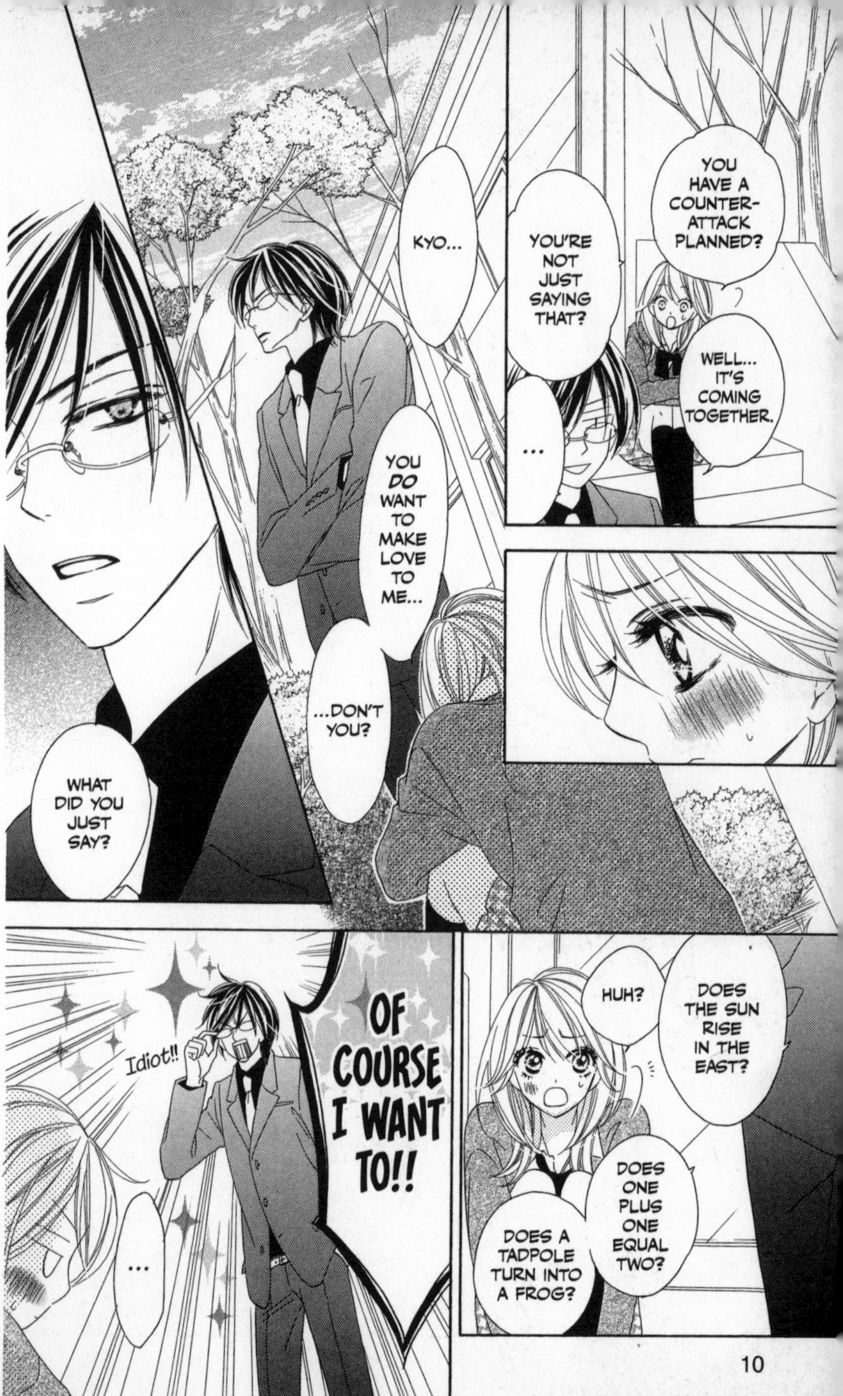
YOU HAVE A COUNTER-ATTACK PLANNED?
YOU'RE NOT JUST SAYING THAT?
WELL... IT'S COMING TOGETHER.
...
KYO...
YOU *DO* WANT TO MAKE LOVE TO ME...
...DON'T YOU?
WHAT DID YOU JUST SAY?
DOES THE SUN RISE IN THE EAST?
HUH?
DOES ONE PLUS ONE EQUAL TWO?
DOES A TADPOLE TURN INTO A FROG?
OF COURSE I WANT TO!!
Idiot!!
...

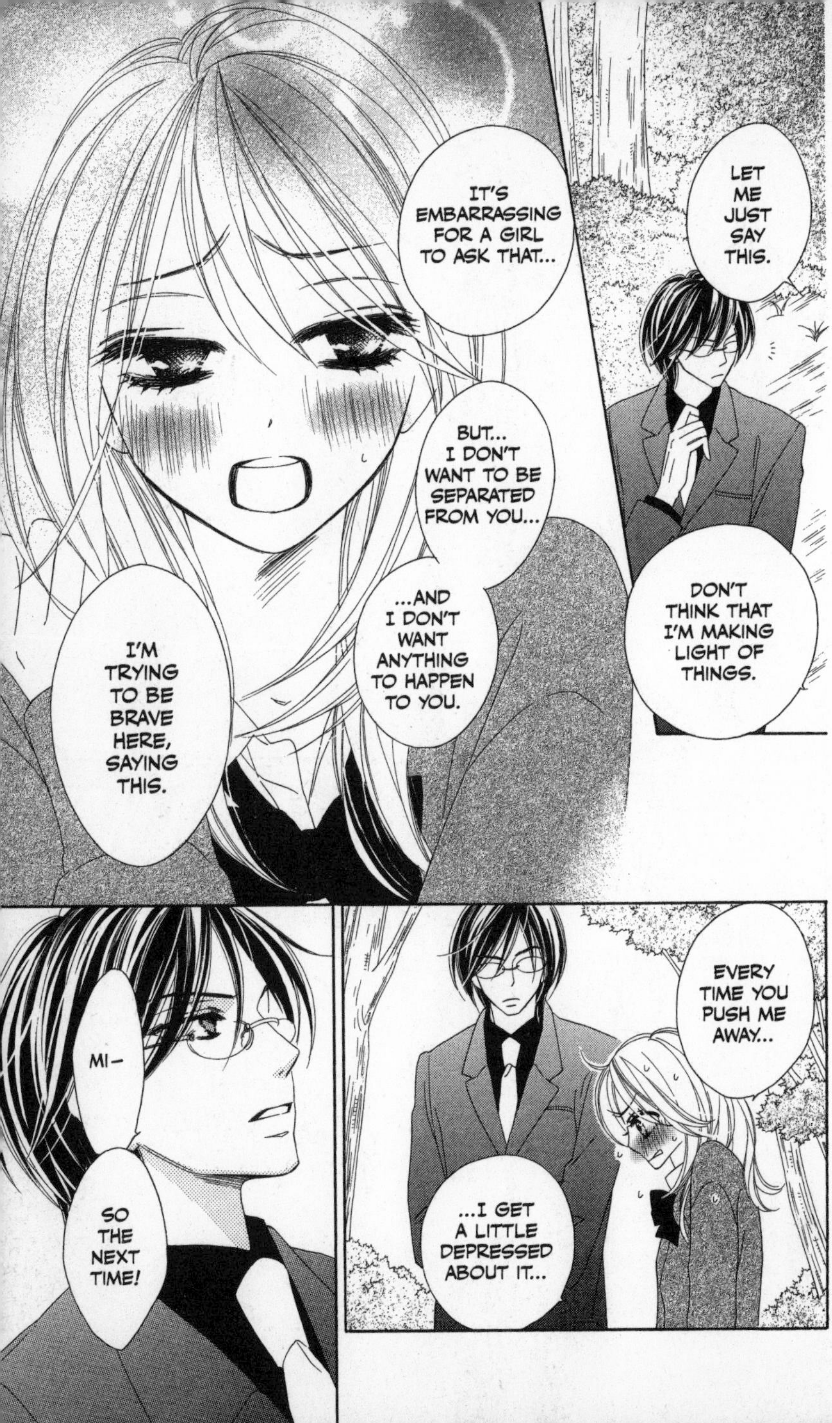
LET ME JUST SAY THIS.
DON'T THINK THAT I'M MAKING LIGHT OF THINGS.
IT'S EMBARRASSING FOR A GIRL TO ASK THAT...
BUT... I DON'T WANT TO BE SEPARATED FROM YOU...
...AND I DON'T WANT ANYTHING TO HAPPEN TO YOU.
I'M TRYING TO BE BRAVE HERE, SAYING THIS.
EVERY TIME YOU PUSH ME AWAY...
...I GET A LITTLE DEPRESSED ABOUT IT...
MI–
SO THE NEXT TIME!

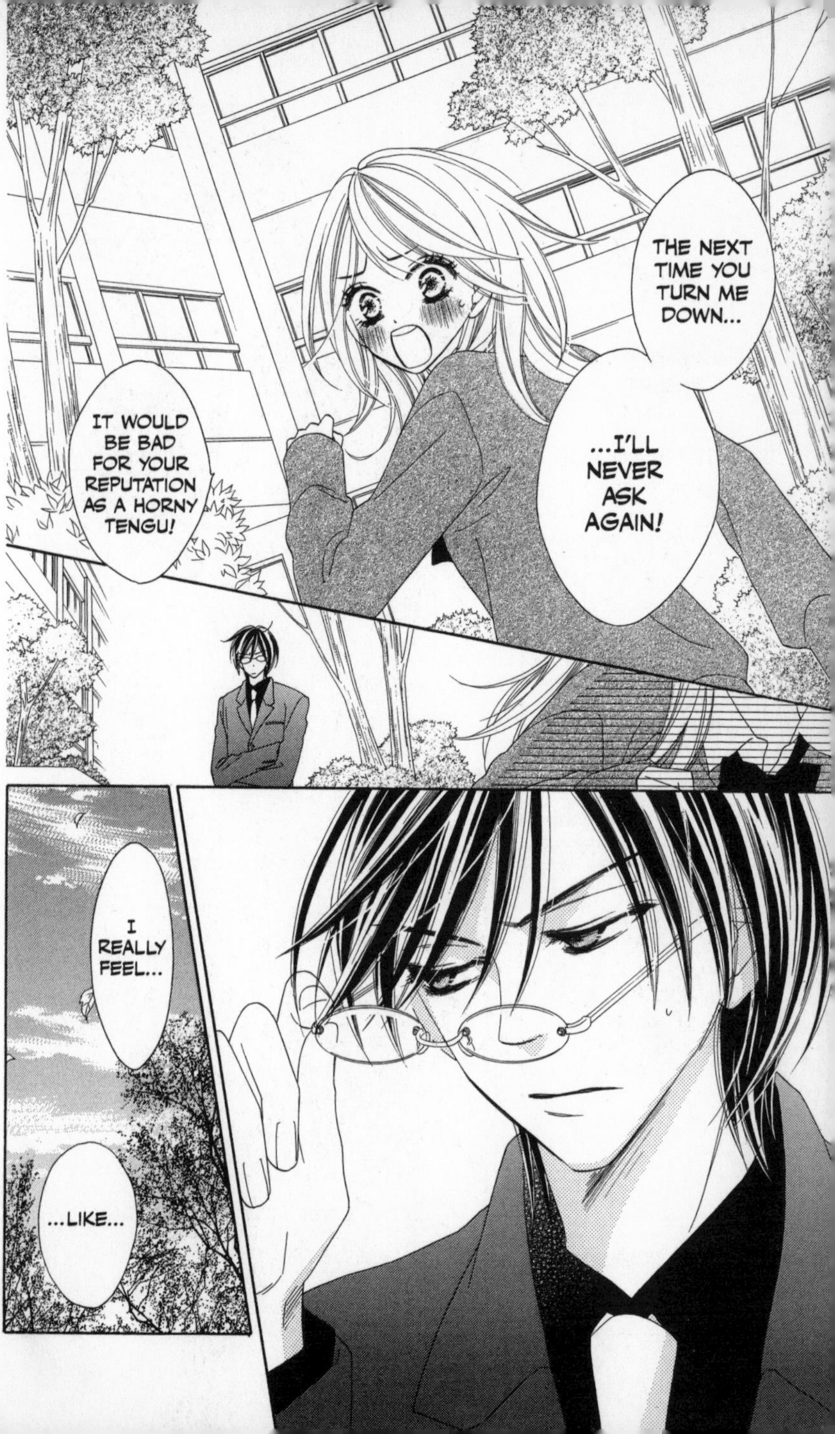
THE NEXT TIME YOU TURN ME DOWN...
...I'LL NEVER ASK AGAIN!
IT WOULD BE BAD FOR YOUR REPUTATION AS A HORNY TENGU!
I REALLY FEEL...
...LIKE...

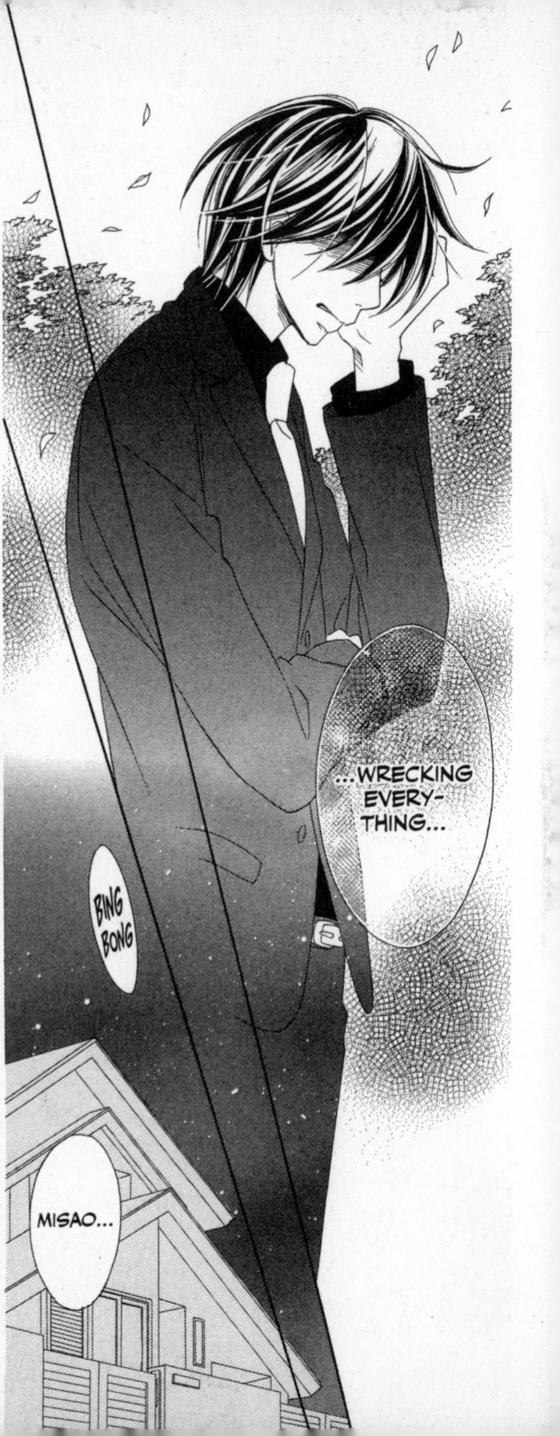
...WRECKING EVERY-THING...
BING BONG
MISAO...

Hello, everyone. This is Kanoko Sakurakoji.

Black Bird is already at volume 8.

I just realized that this is my twentieth graphic novel, and I'm feeling a little faint.

I've been able to come this far thanks to all of you!

Each chapter in this volume begins with an illustration that originally ran in color♥, so I've written little comments on their motifs on the following page. Of course, most of them are flowers.

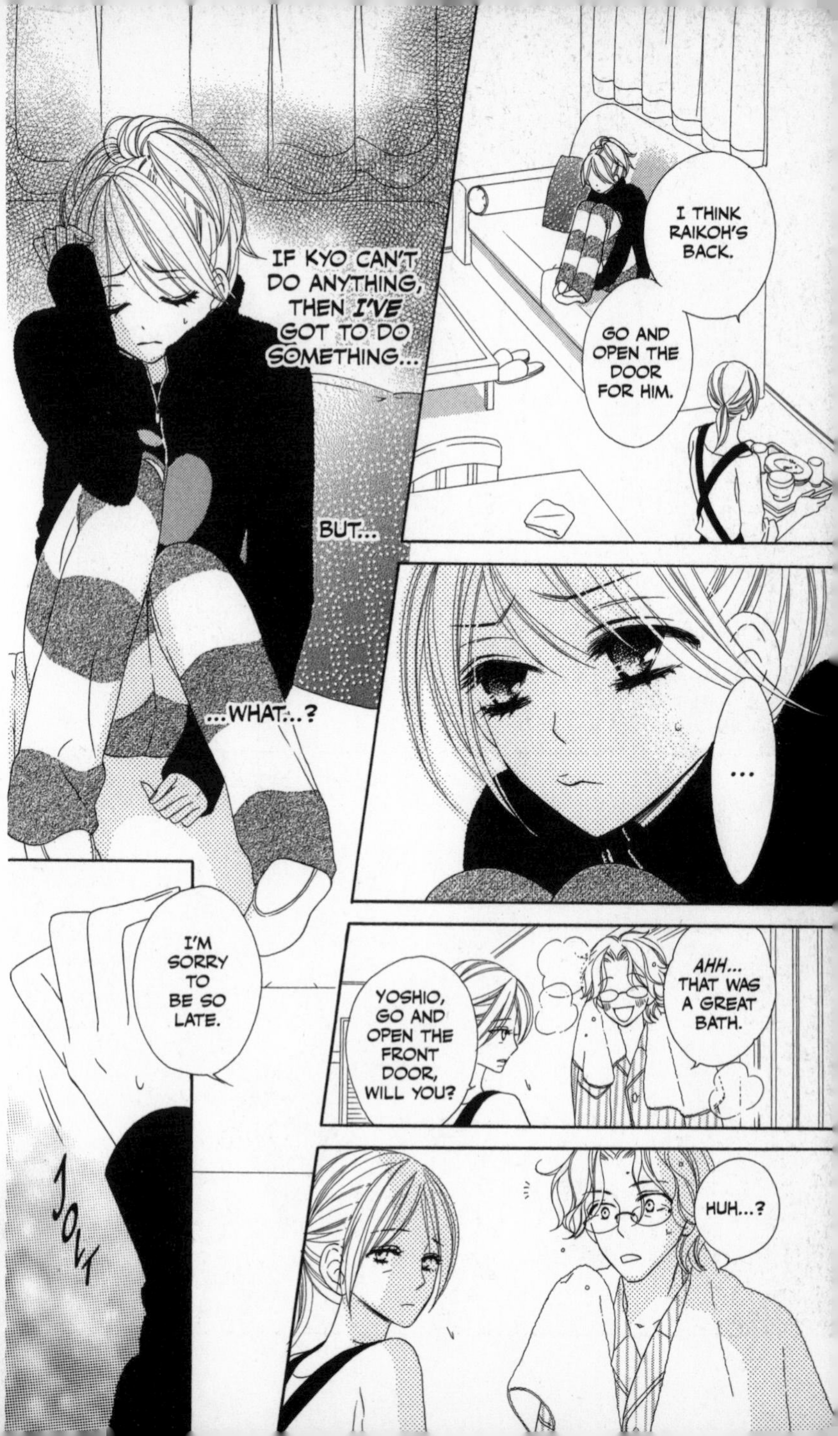
I THINK RAIKOH'S BACK.
GO AND OPEN THE DOOR FOR HIM.
...
IF KYO CAN'T DO ANYTHING, THEN *I'VE* GOT TO DO SOMETHING...
BUT...
...WHAT...?
AHH... THAT WAS A GREAT BATH.
YOSHIO, GO AND OPEN THE FRONT DOOR, WILL YOU?
HUH...?
I'M SORRY TO BE SO LATE.
JOLT

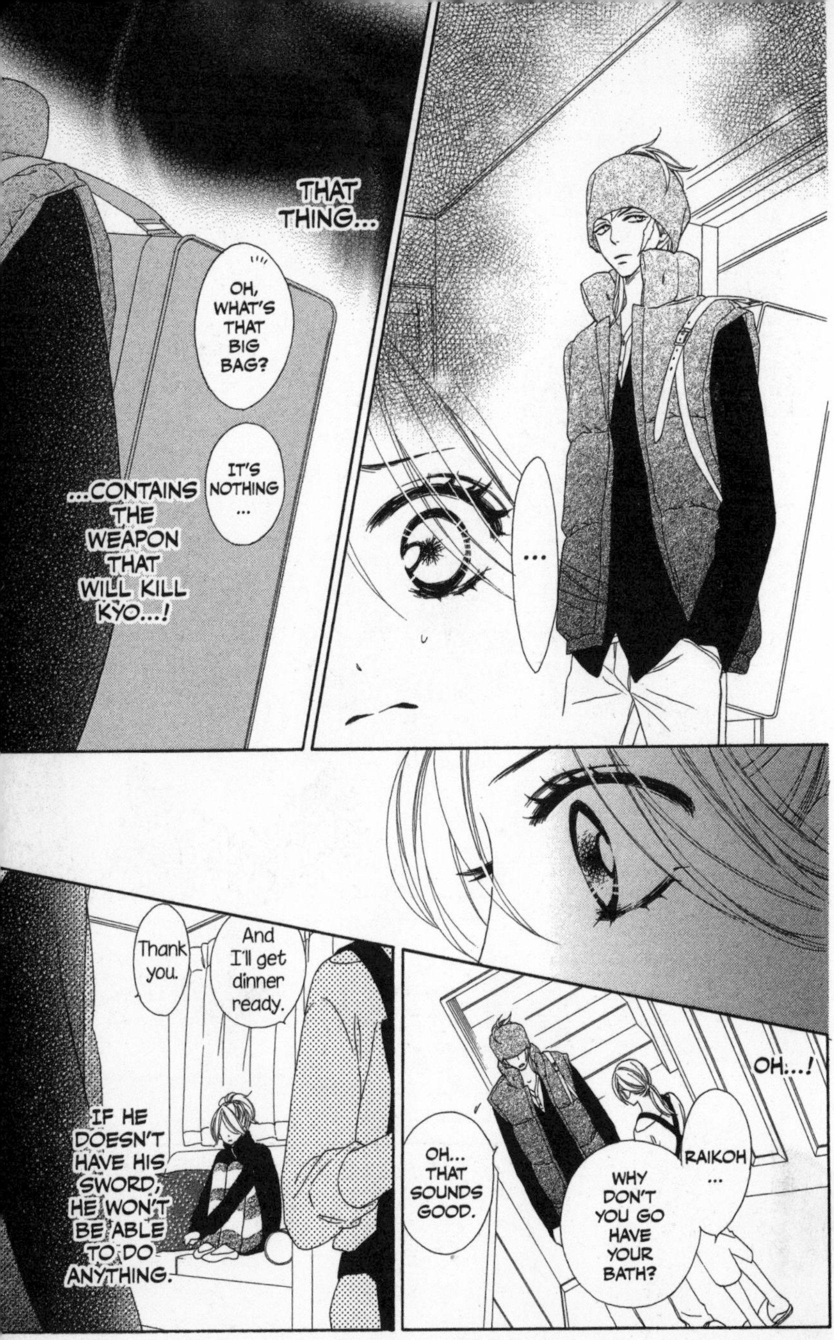
...
THAT THING...
OH, WHAT'S THAT BIG BAG?
IT'S NOTHING...
...CONTAINS THE WEAPON THAT WILL KILL KYO...!
OH...!
RAIKOH...
WHY DON'T YOU GO HAVE YOUR BATH?
OH... THAT SOUNDS GOOD.
And I'll get dinner ready.
Thank you.
IF HE DOESN'T HAVE HIS SWORD, HE WON'T BE ABLE TO DO ANYTHING.

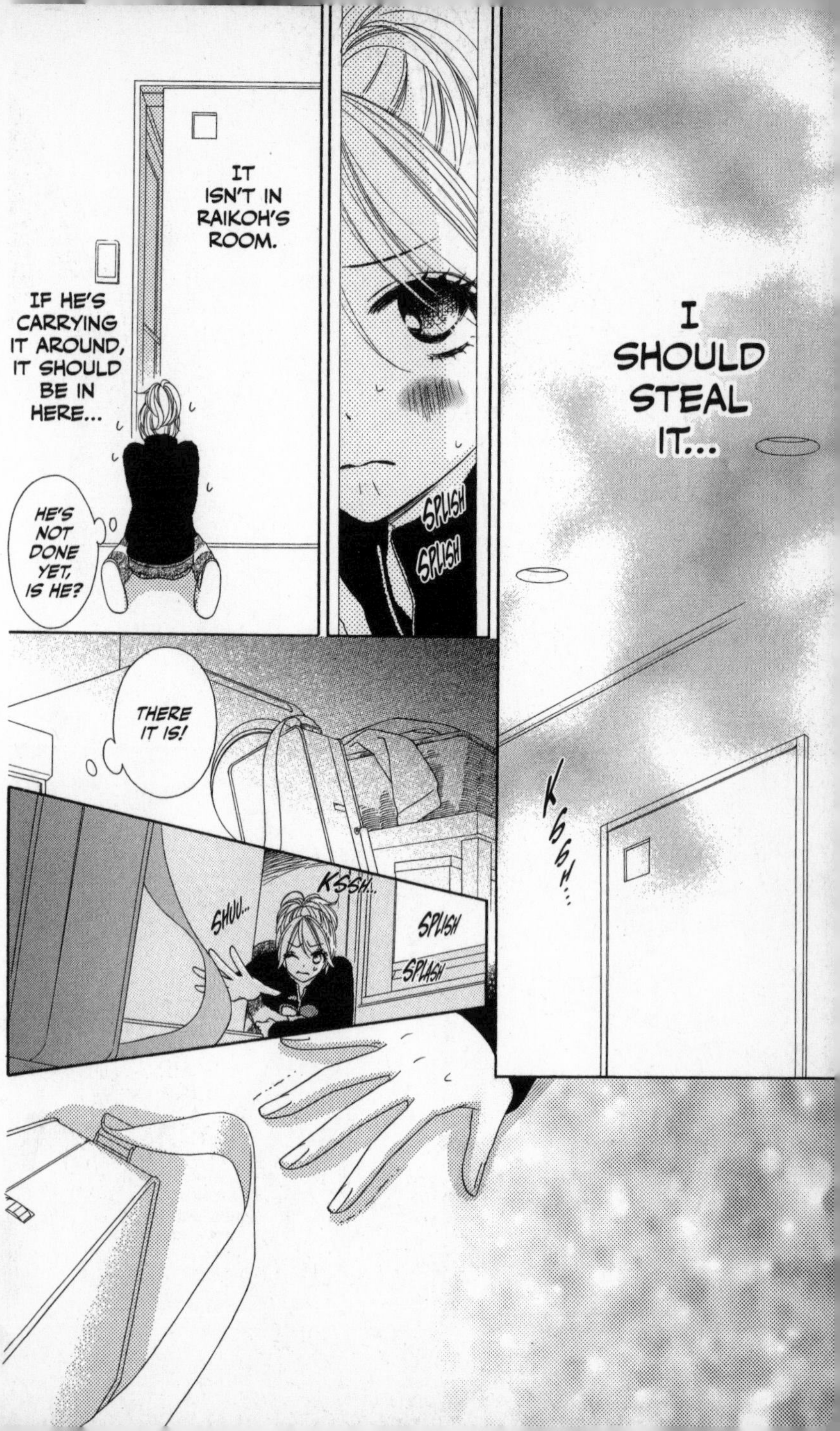
I SHOULD STEAL IT...
KSSH...
SPLISH
SPLISH
IT ISN'T IN RAIKOH'S ROOM.
IF HE'S CARRYING IT AROUND, IT SHOULD BE IN HERE...
HE'S NOT DONE YET, IS HE?
THERE IT IS!
KSSH...
SPLISH
SPLASH
SHUU...

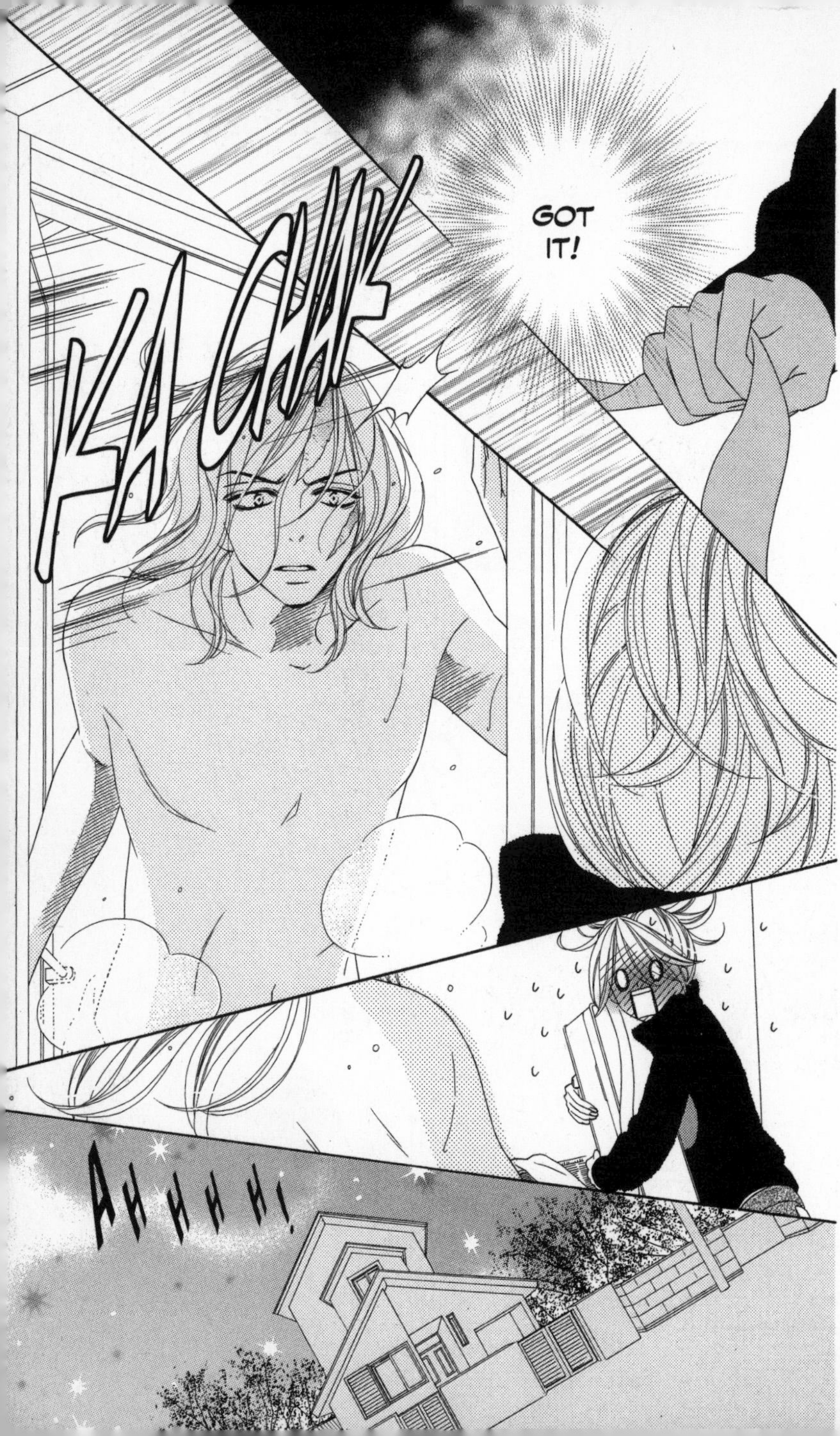
GOT IT!
KA CHAK
AHHHH!

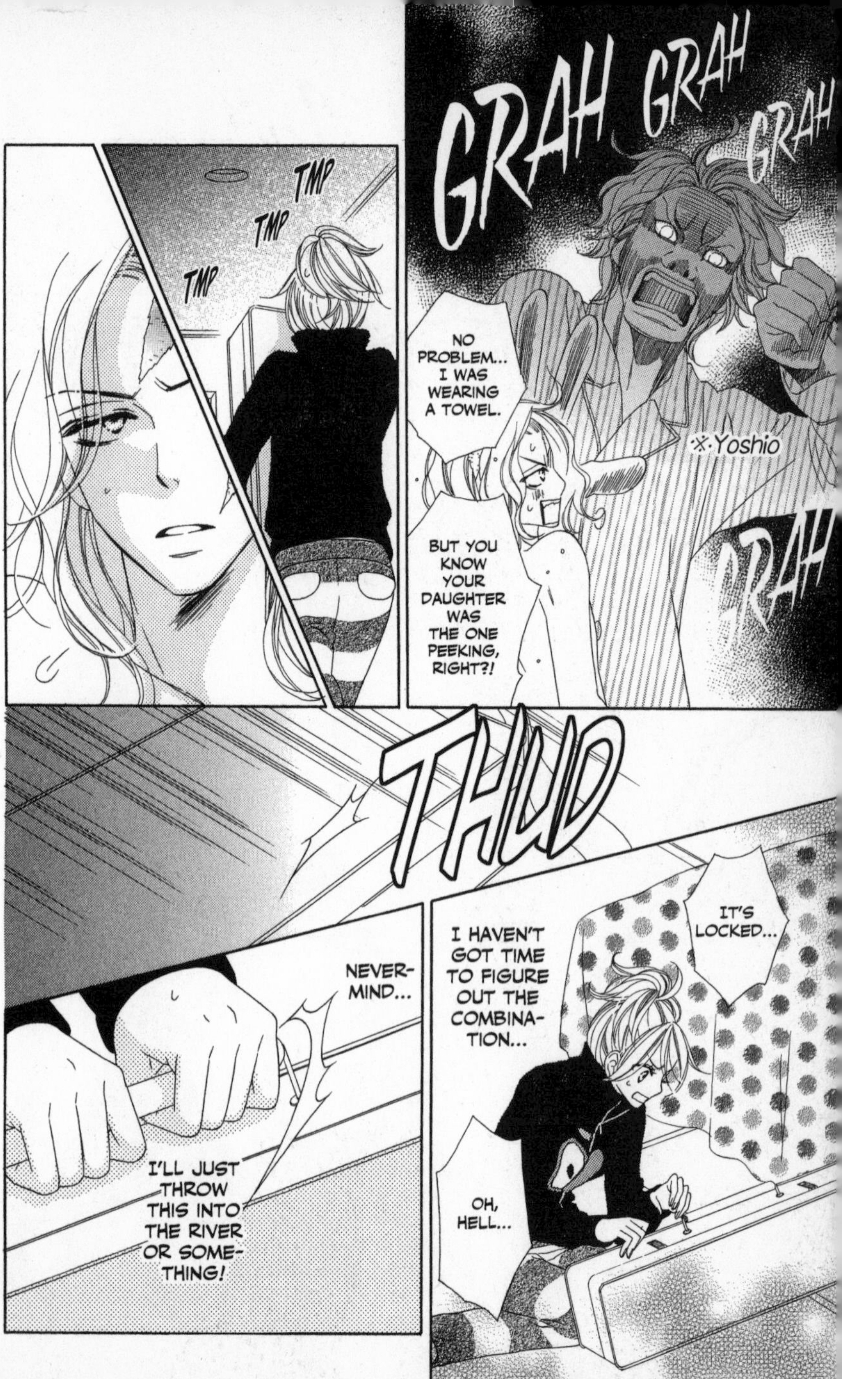
GRAH GRAH GRAH
NO PROBLEM... I WAS WEARING A TOWEL.
※Yoshio
BUT YOU KNOW YOUR DAUGHTER WAS THE ONE PEEKING, RIGHT?!
GRAH
TMP TMP TMP
THUD
IT'S LOCKED...
I HAVEN'T GOT TIME TO FIGURE OUT THE COMBINA-TION...
OH, HELL...
NEVER-MIND...
I'LL JUST THROW THIS INTO THE RIVER OR SOME-THING!

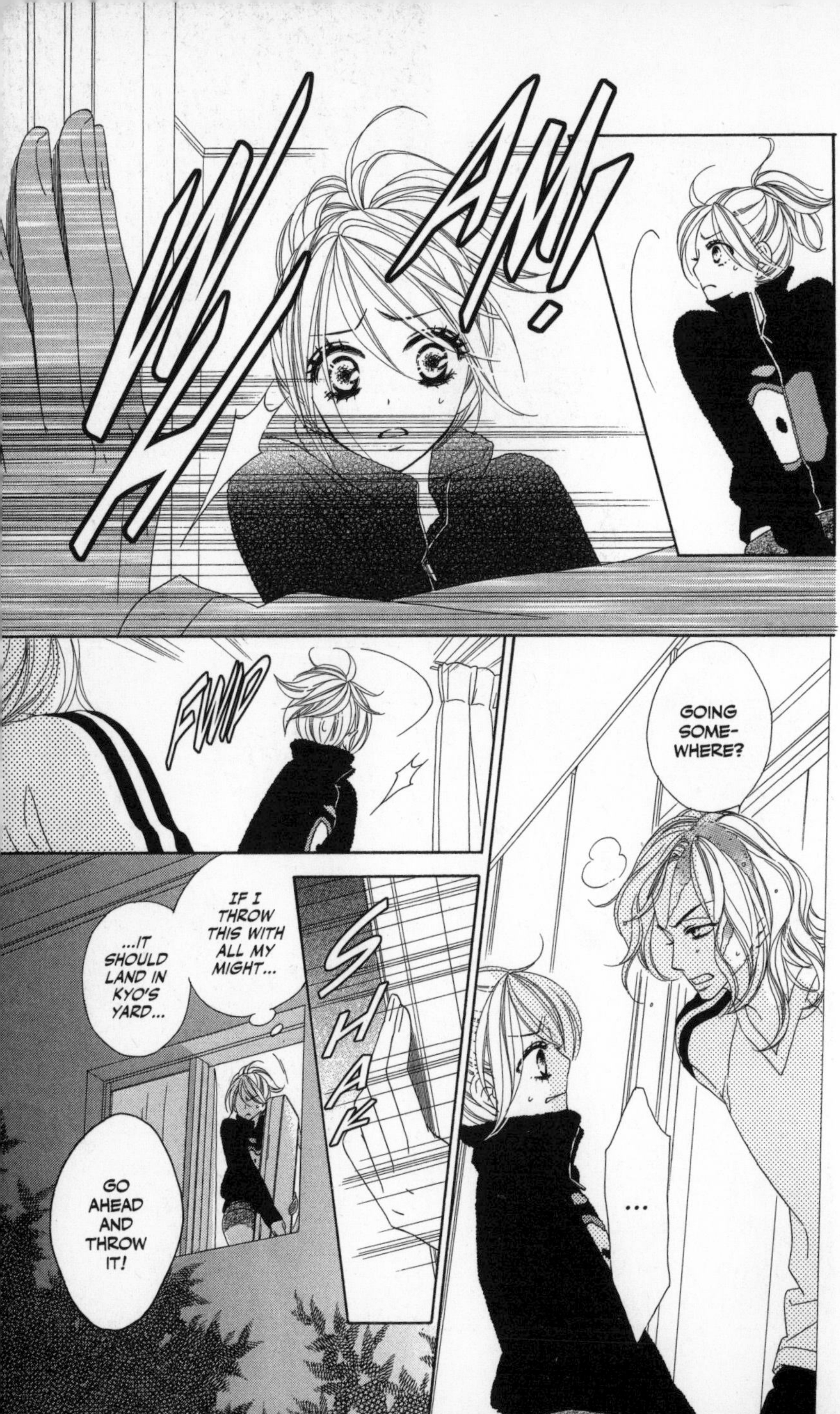
WHAM!
GOING SOME-WHERE?
...
FWIP
SHAK
IF I THROW THIS WITH ALL MY MIGHT...
...IT SHOULD LAND IN KYO'S YARD...
GO AHEAD AND THROW IT!

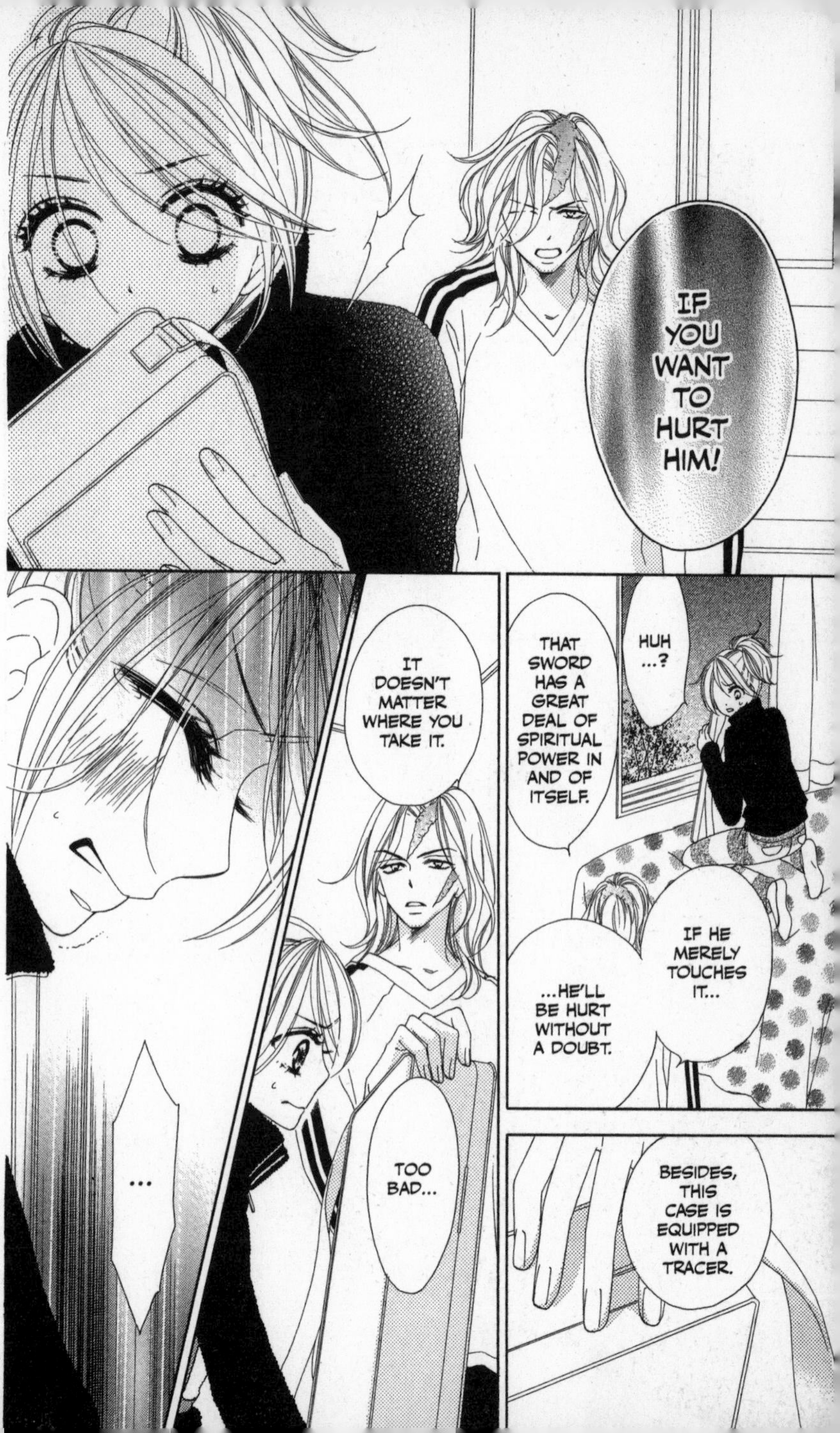
IF YOU WANT TO HURT HIM!
HUH ...?
THAT SWORD HAS A GREAT DEAL OF SPIRITUAL POWER IN AND OF ITSELF.
IF HE MERELY TOUCHES IT...
...HE'LL BE HURT WITHOUT A DOUBT.
BESIDES, THIS CASE IS EQUIPPED WITH A TRACER.
IT DOESN'T MATTER WHERE YOU TAKE IT.
TOO BAD...
...

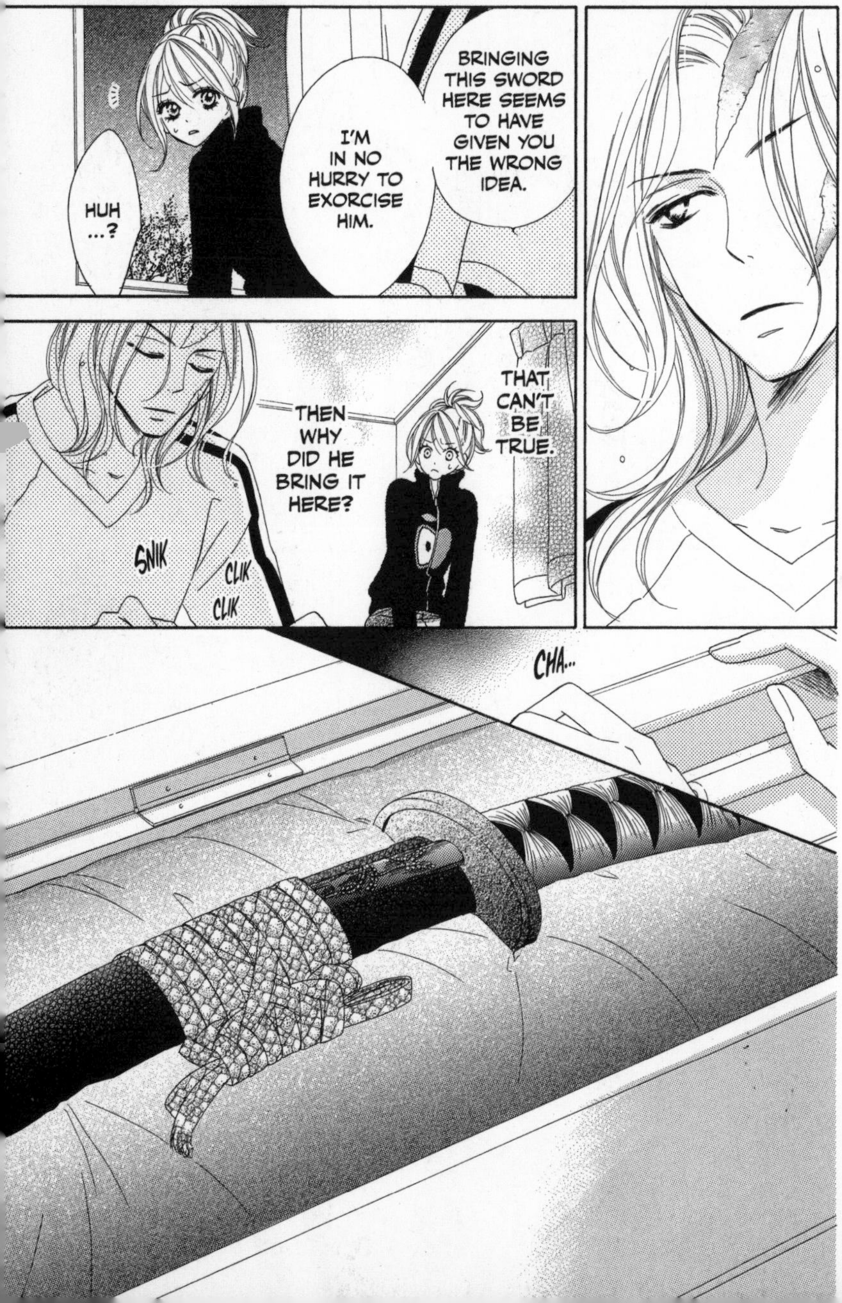
BRINGING THIS SWORD HERE SEEMS TO HAVE GIVEN YOU THE WRONG IDEA.
I'M IN NO HURRY TO EXORCISE HIM.
HUH ...?
THAT CAN'T BE TRUE.
THEN WHY DID HE BRING IT HERE?
CLIK
CLIK
SNIK
CHA...

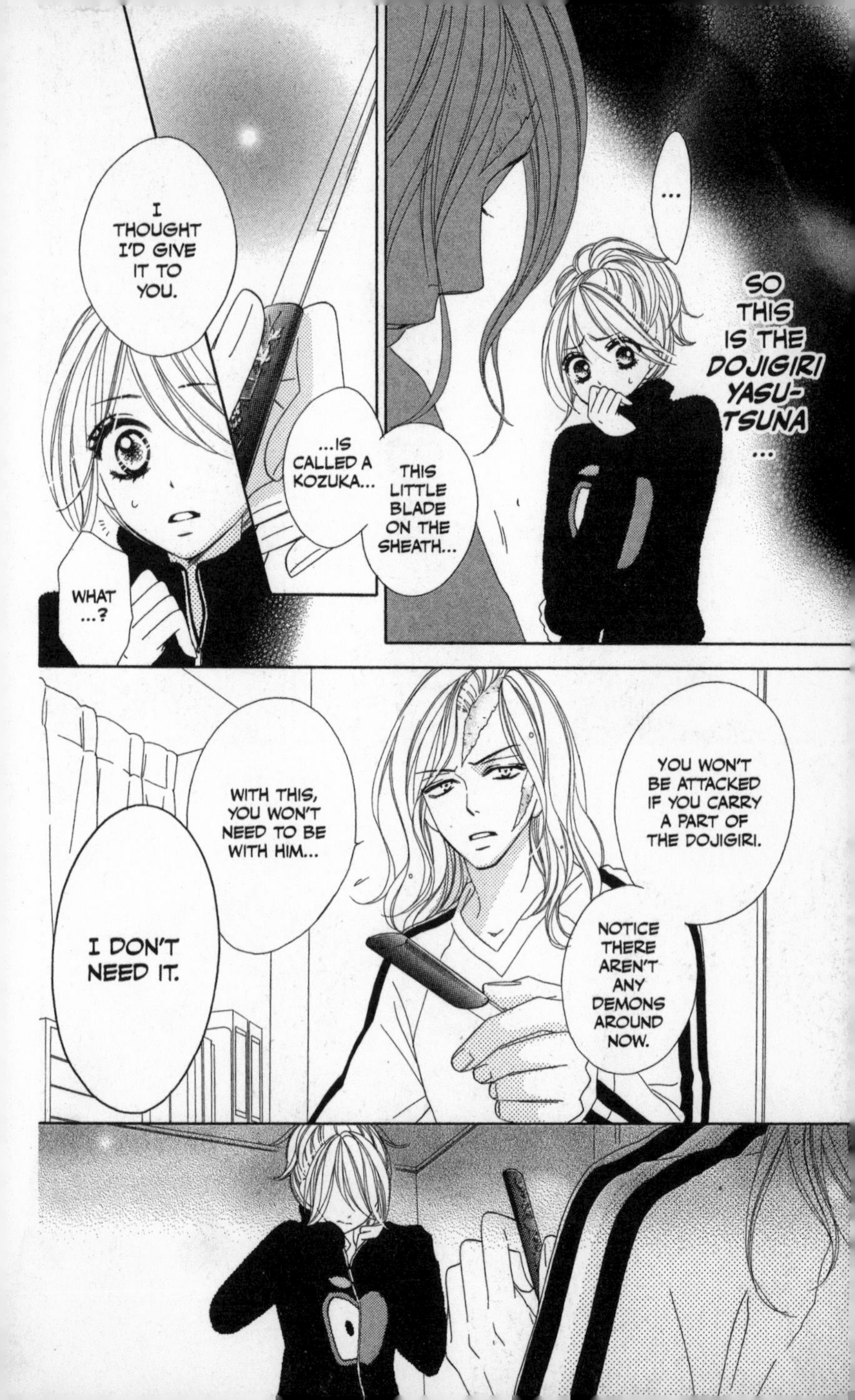
...
SO THIS IS THE DOJIGIRI YASU-TSUNA...
THIS LITTLE BLADE ON THE SHEATH...
...IS CALLED A KOZUKA...
I THOUGHT I'D GIVE IT TO YOU.
WHAT...?
YOU WON'T BE ATTACKED IF YOU CARRY A PART OF THE DOJIGIRI.
NOTICE THERE AREN'T ANY DEMONS AROUND NOW.
WITH THIS, YOU WON'T NEED TO BE WITH HIM...
I DON'T NEED IT.

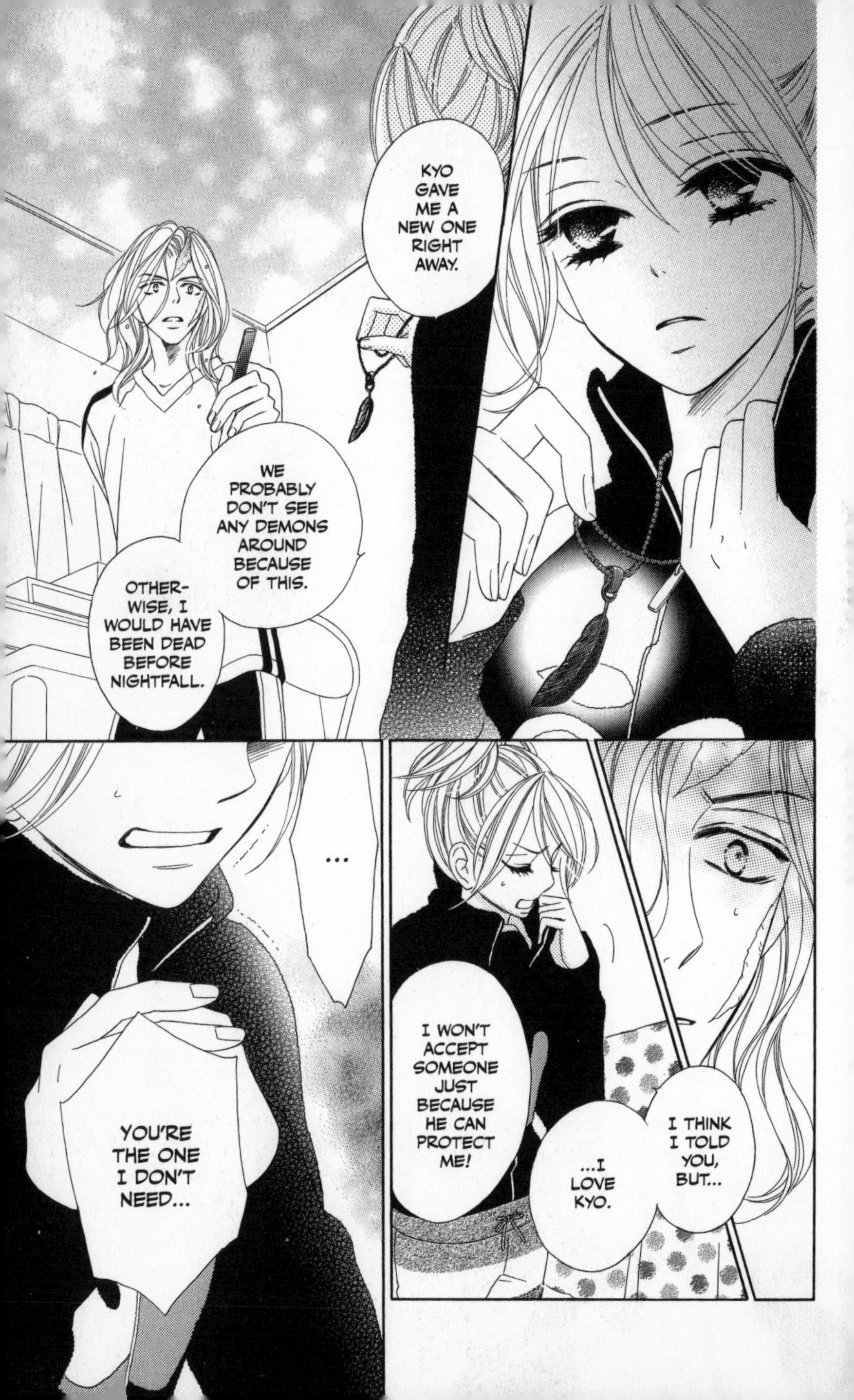
KYO GAVE ME A NEW ONE RIGHT AWAY.
WE PROBABLY DON'T SEE ANY DEMONS AROUND BECAUSE OF THIS.
OTHER-WISE, I WOULD HAVE BEEN DEAD BEFORE NIGHTFALL.
I THINK I TOLD YOU, BUT...
...I LOVE KYO.
I WON'T ACCEPT SOMEONE JUST BECAUSE HE CAN PROTECT ME!
...
YOU'RE THE ONE I DON'T NEED...

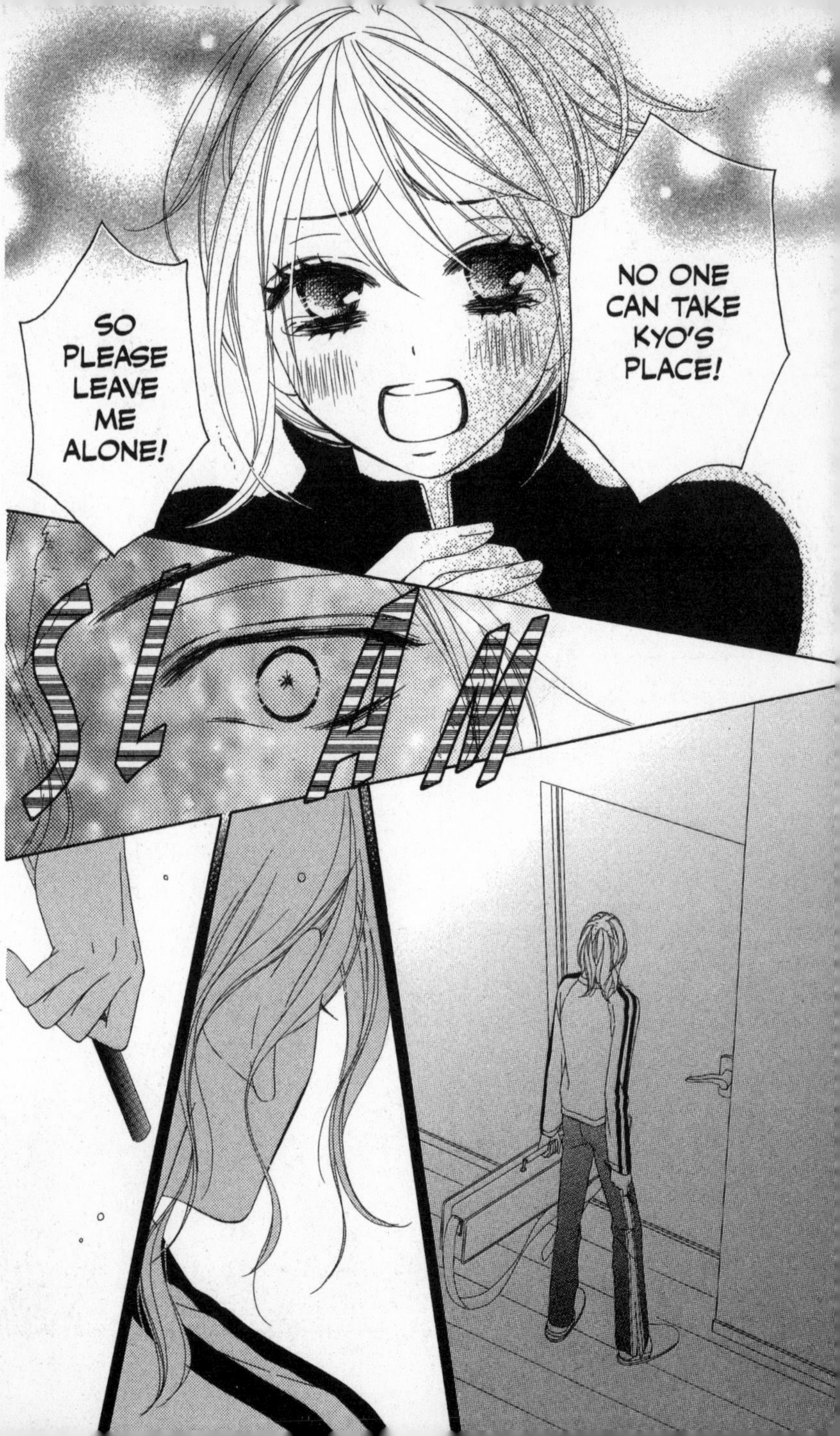
NO ONE CAN TAKE KYO'S PLACE!
SO PLEASE LEAVE ME ALONE!
SLAM

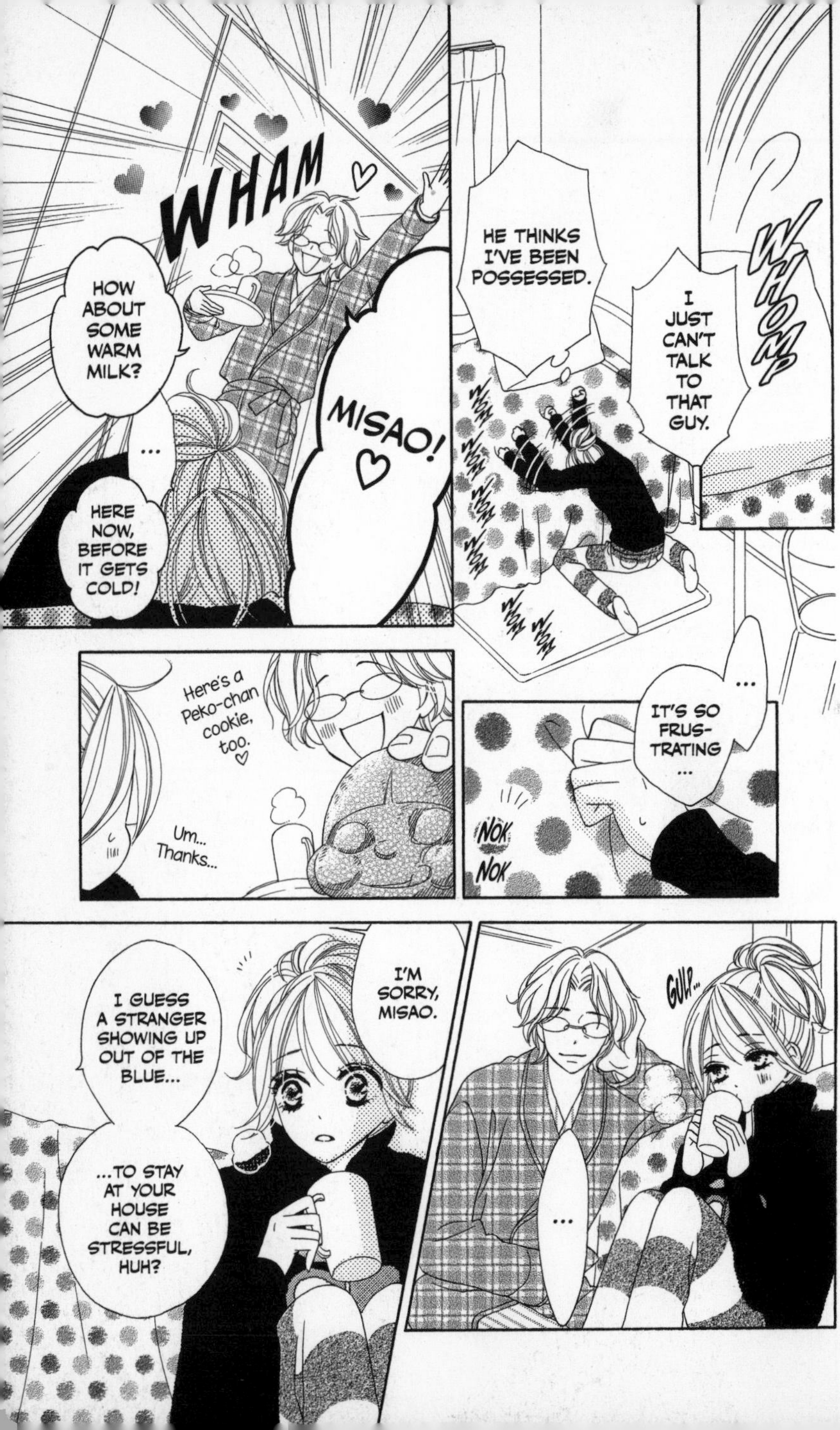
WHOMP
HE THINKS I'VE BEEN POSSESSED.
I JUST CAN'T TALK TO THAT GUY.
MISAO! ♡
WHAM ♡
HOW ABOUT SOME WARM MILK?
...
HERE NOW, BEFORE IT GETS COLD!
...
IT'S SO FRUS-TRATING...
NOK NOK
Here's a Peko-chan cookie, too. ♡
Um... Thanks...
GULP...
...
I'M SORRY, MISAO.
I GUESS A STRANGER SHOWING UP OUT OF THE BLUE...
...TO STAY AT YOUR HOUSE CAN BE STRESSFUL, HUH?

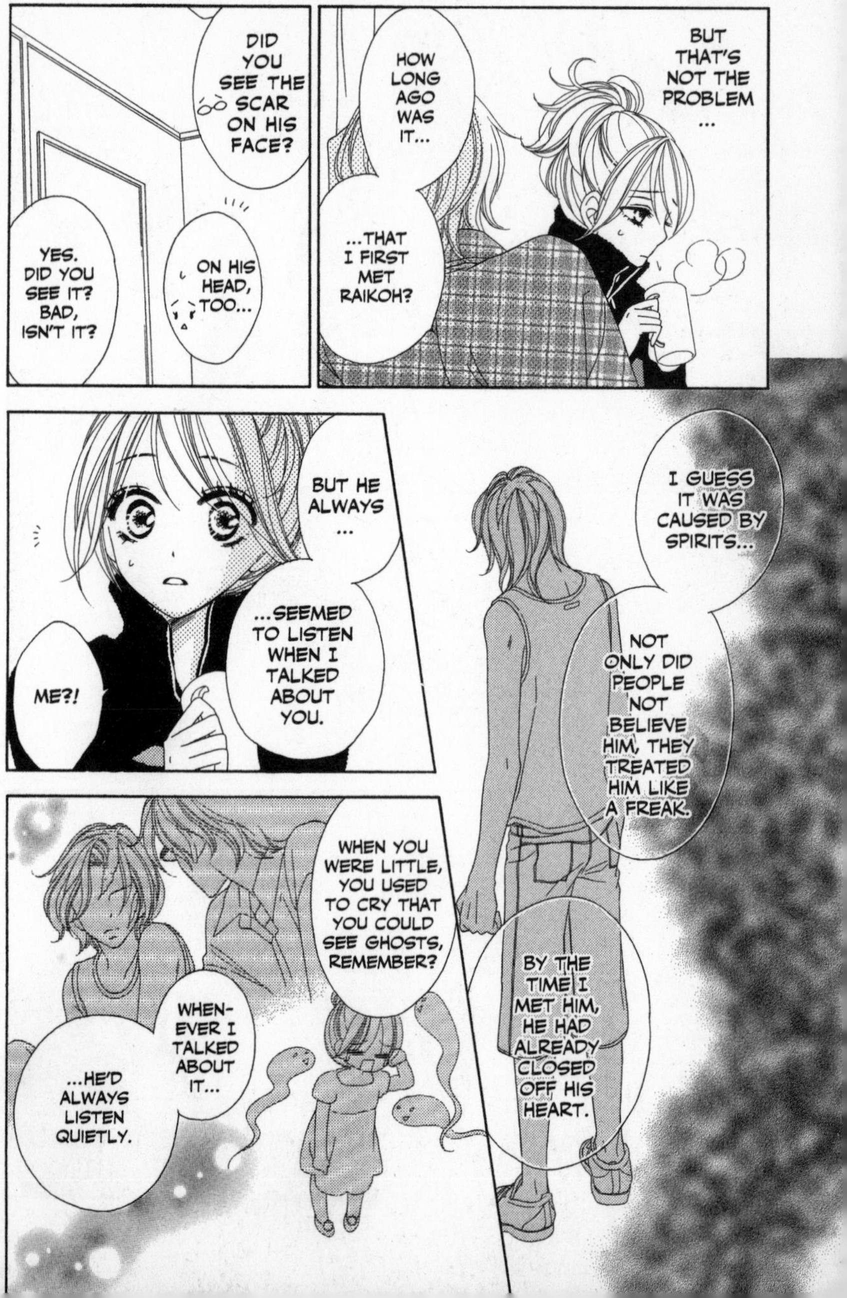
BUT THAT'S NOT THE PROBLEM ...
HOW LONG AGO WAS IT...
...THAT I FIRST MET RAIKOH?
DID YOU SEE THE SCAR ON HIS FACE?
ON HIS HEAD, TOO...
YES. DID YOU SEE IT? BAD, ISN'T IT?
I GUESS IT WAS CAUSED BY SPIRITS...
NOT ONLY DID PEOPLE NOT BELIEVE HIM, THEY TREATED HIM LIKE A FREAK.
BY THE TIME I MET HIM, HE HAD ALREADY CLOSED OFF HIS HEART.
BUT HE ALWAYS ...
...SEEMED TO LISTEN WHEN I TALKED ABOUT YOU.
ME?!
WHEN YOU WERE LITTLE, YOU USED TO CRY THAT YOU COULD SEE GHOSTS, REMEMBER?
WHEN-EVER I TALKED ABOUT IT...
...HE'D ALWAYS LISTEN QUIETLY.

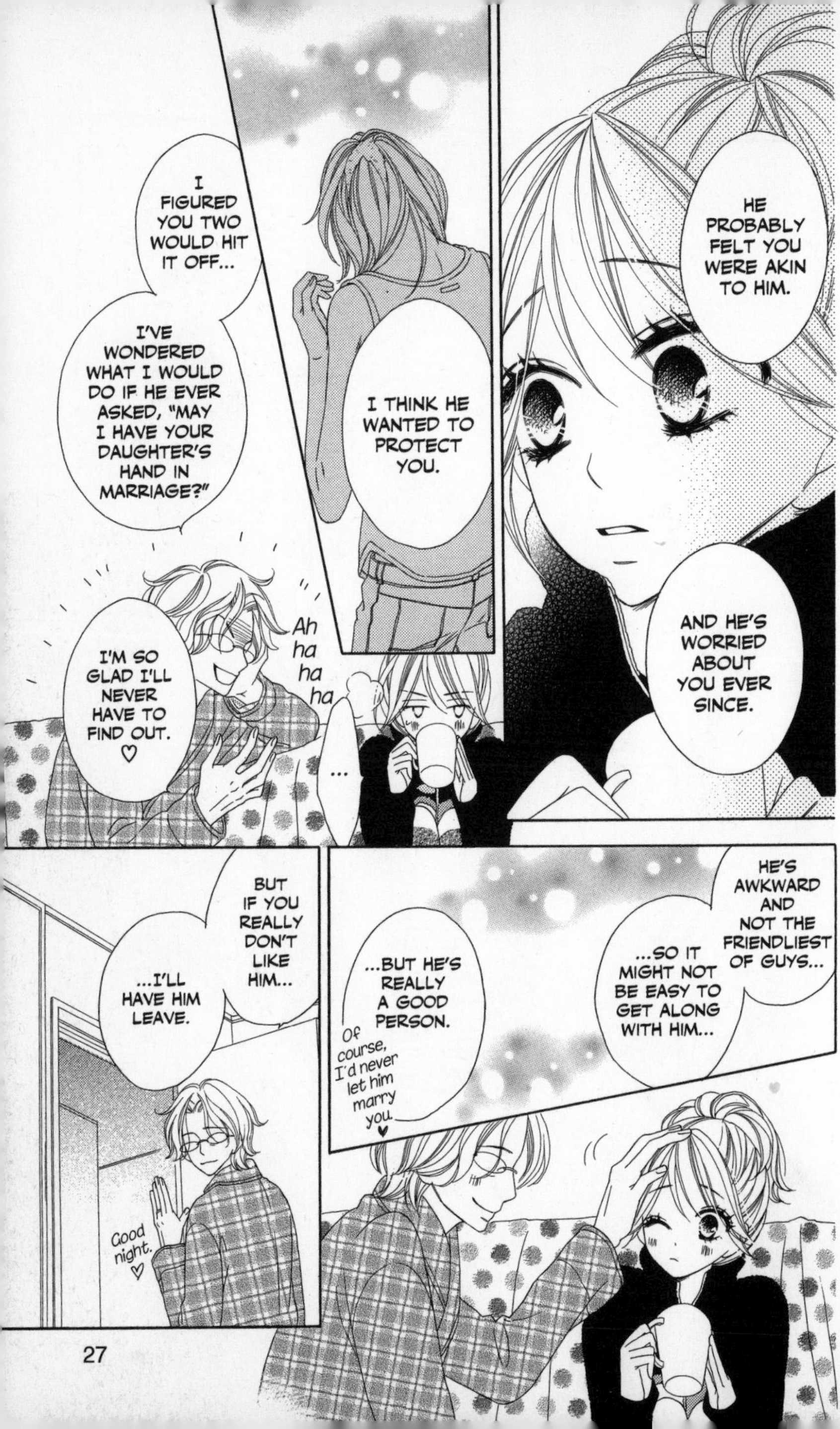
HE PROBABLY FELT YOU WERE AKIN TO HIM.
AND HE'S WORRIED ABOUT YOU EVER SINCE.
I THINK HE WANTED TO PROTECT YOU.
I FIGURED YOU TWO WOULD HIT IT OFF...
I'VE WONDERED WHAT I WOULD DO IF HE EVER ASKED, "MAY I HAVE YOUR DAUGHTER'S HAND IN MARRIAGE?"
I'M SO GLAD I'LL NEVER HAVE TO FIND OUT. ♡
Ah ha ha ha
...
HE'S AWKWARD AND NOT THE FRIENDLIEST OF GUYS...
...SO IT MIGHT NOT BE EASY TO GET ALONG WITH HIM...
...BUT HE'S REALLY A GOOD PERSON.
Of course, I'd never let him marry you. ♥
BUT IF YOU REALLY DON'T LIKE HIM...
...I'LL HAVE HIM LEAVE.
Good night. ♡

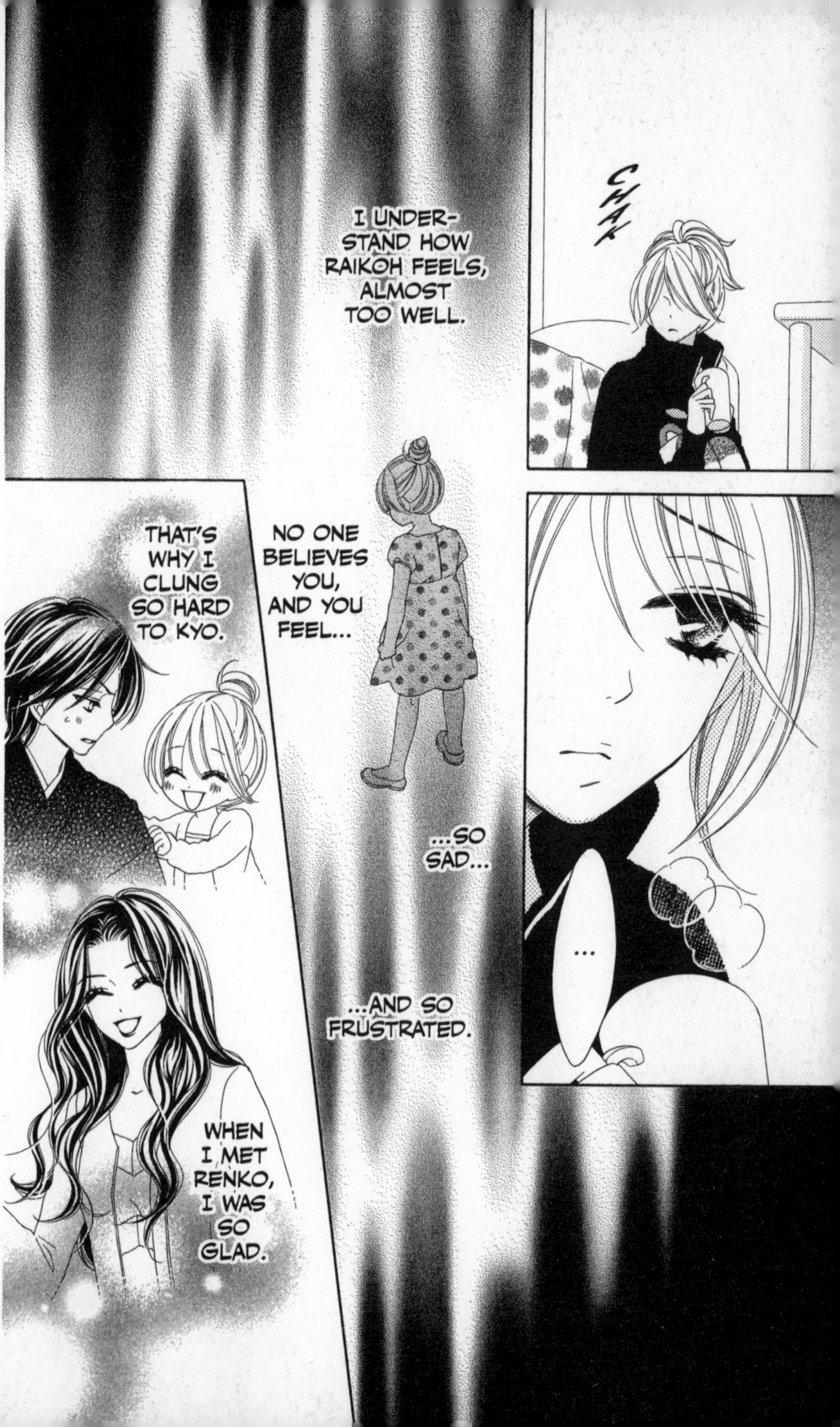
CHAK
I UNDERSTAND HOW RAIKOH FEELS, ALMOST TOO WELL.
...
NO ONE BELIEVES YOU, AND YOU FEEL...
...SO SAD...
...AND SO FRUSTRATED.
THAT'S WHY I CLUNG SO HARD TO KYO.
WHEN I MET RENKO, I WAS SO GLAD.

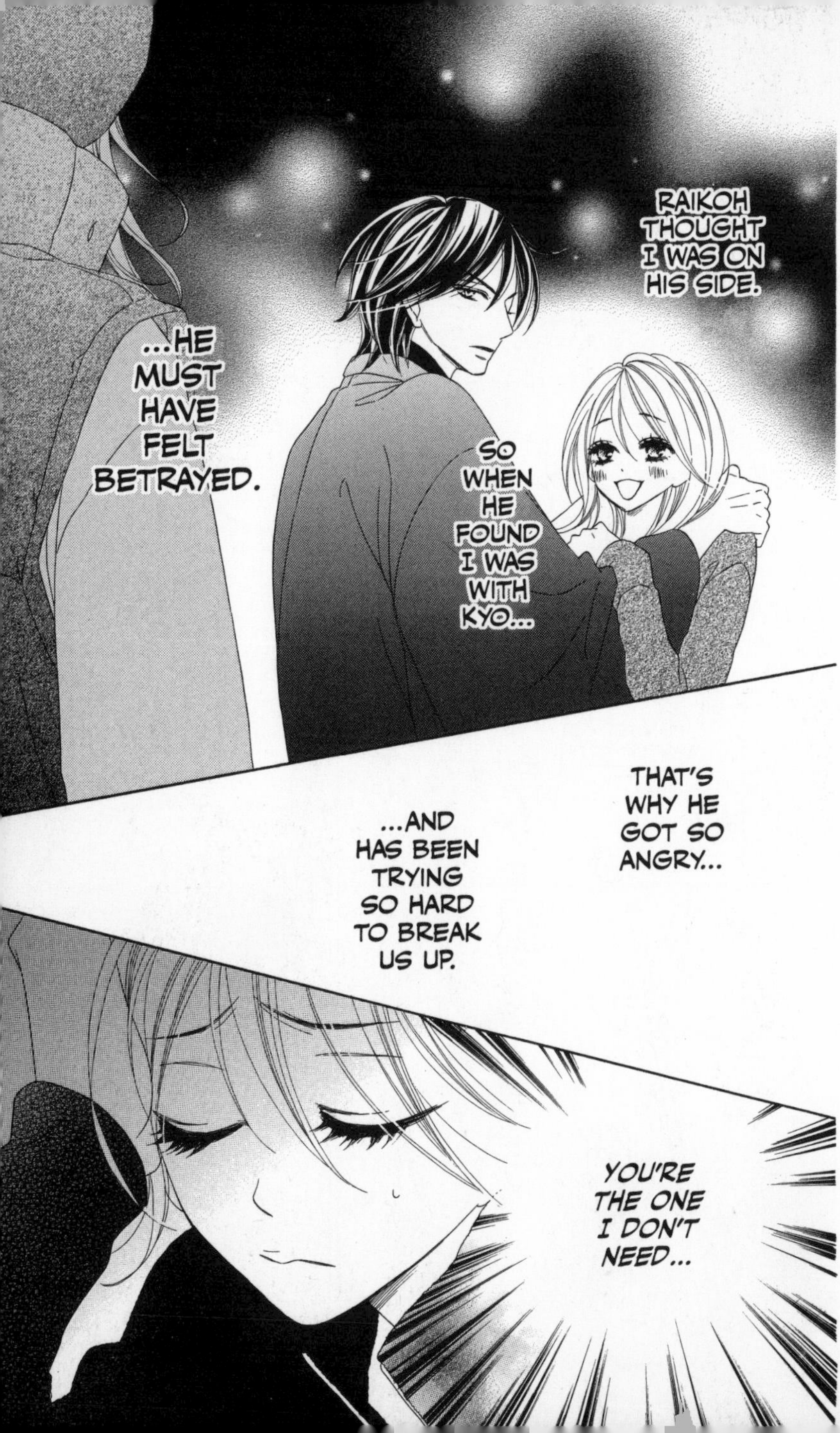
RAIKOH THOUGHT I WAS ON HIS SIDE.
SO WHEN HE FOUND I WAS WITH KYO...
...HE MUST HAVE FELT BETRAYED.
THAT'S WHY HE GOT SO ANGRY...
...AND HAS BEEN TRYING SO HARD TO BREAK US UP.
YOU'RE THE ONE I DON'T NEED...

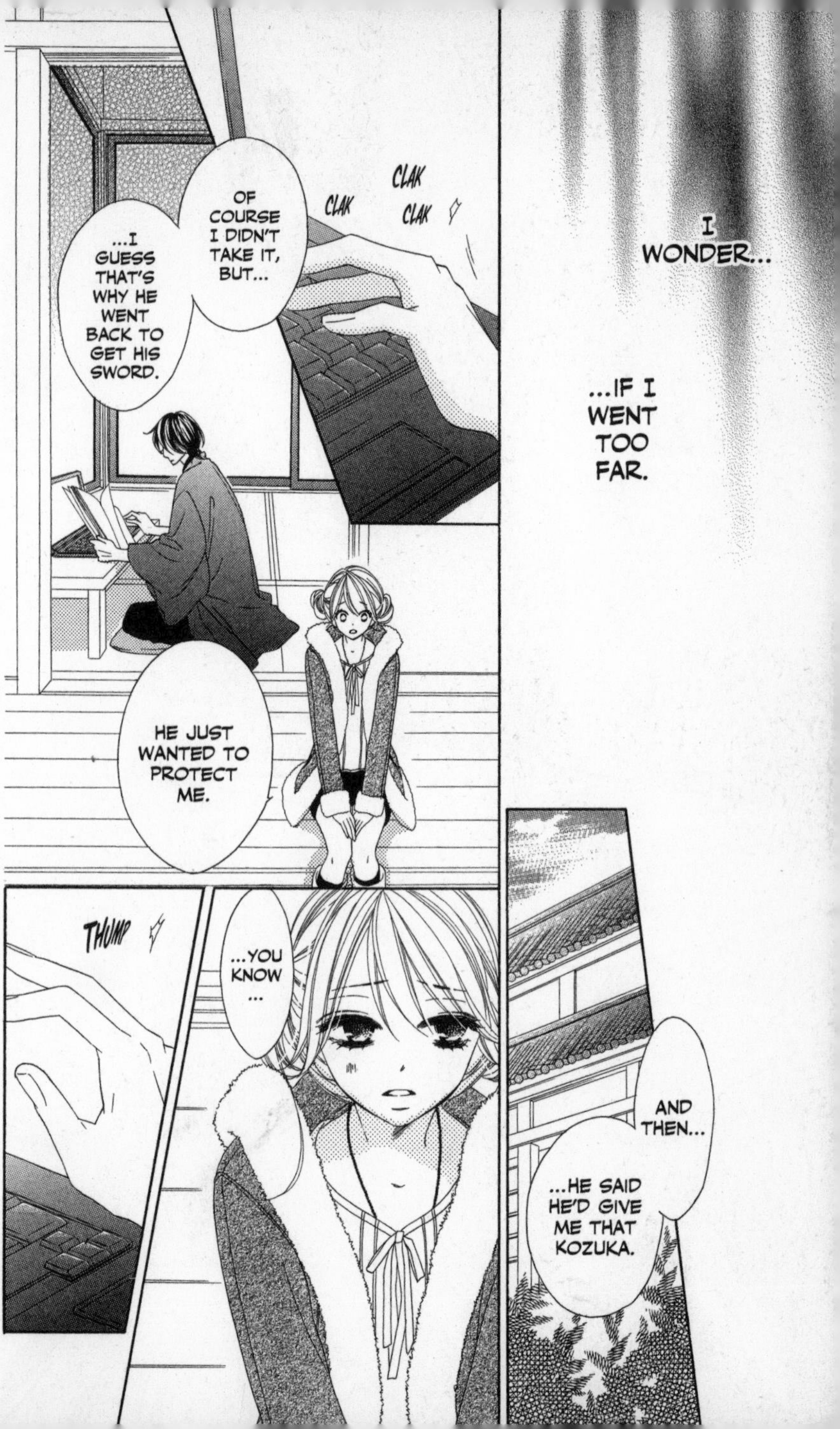
I WONDER...
...IF I WENT TOO FAR.
CLAK
CLAK
CLAK
OF COURSE I DIDN'T TAKE IT, BUT...
...I GUESS THAT'S WHY HE WENT BACK TO GET HIS SWORD.
HE JUST WANTED TO PROTECT ME.
AND THEN...
...HE SAID HE'D GIVE ME THAT KOZUKA.
...YOU KNOW...
THUMP

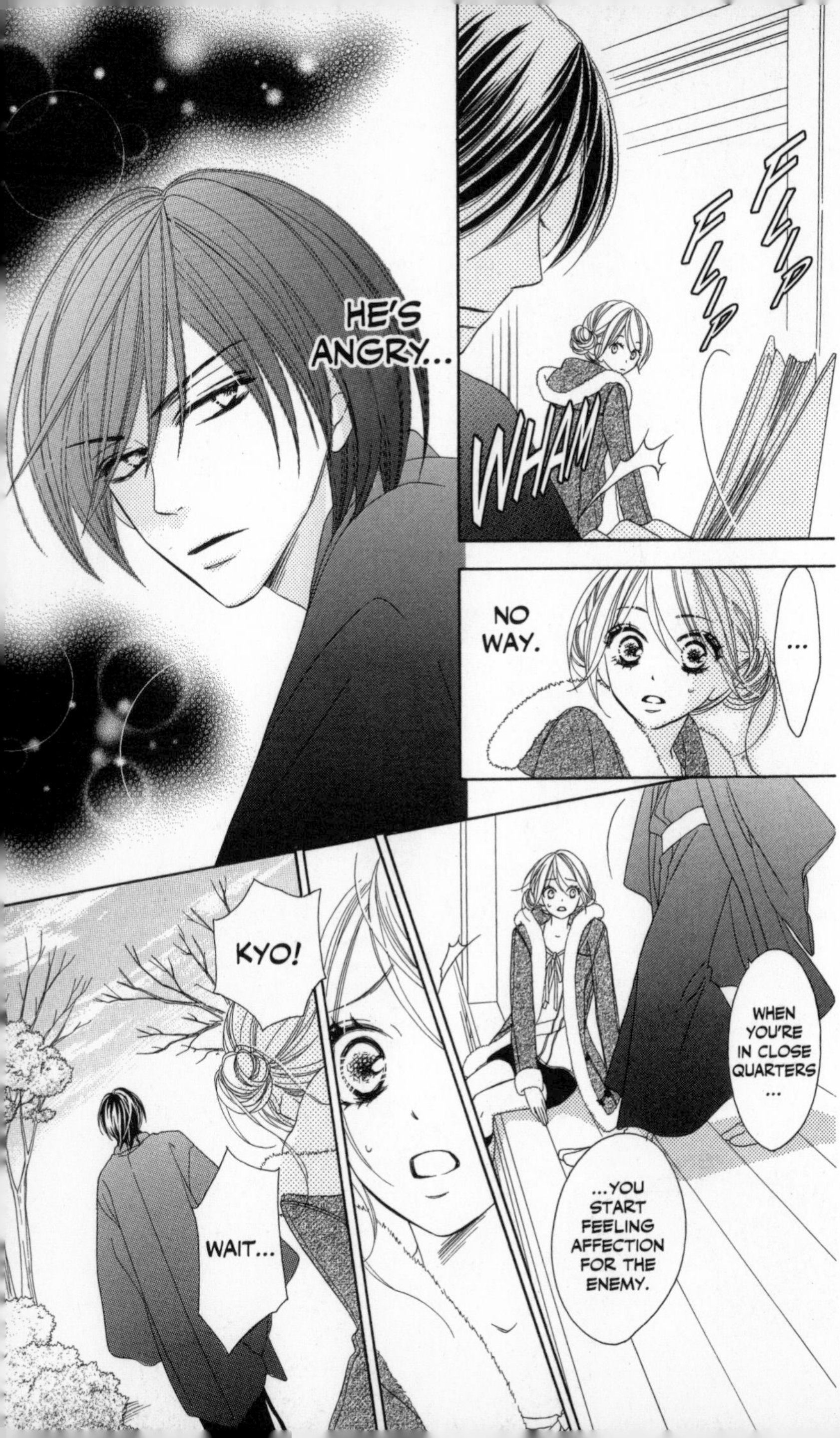
FLIP FLIP
WHAM
...
NO WAY.
HE'S ANGRY...
WHEN YOU'RE IN CLOSE QUARTERS...
...YOU START FEELING AFFECTION FOR THE ENEMY.
KYO!
WAIT...

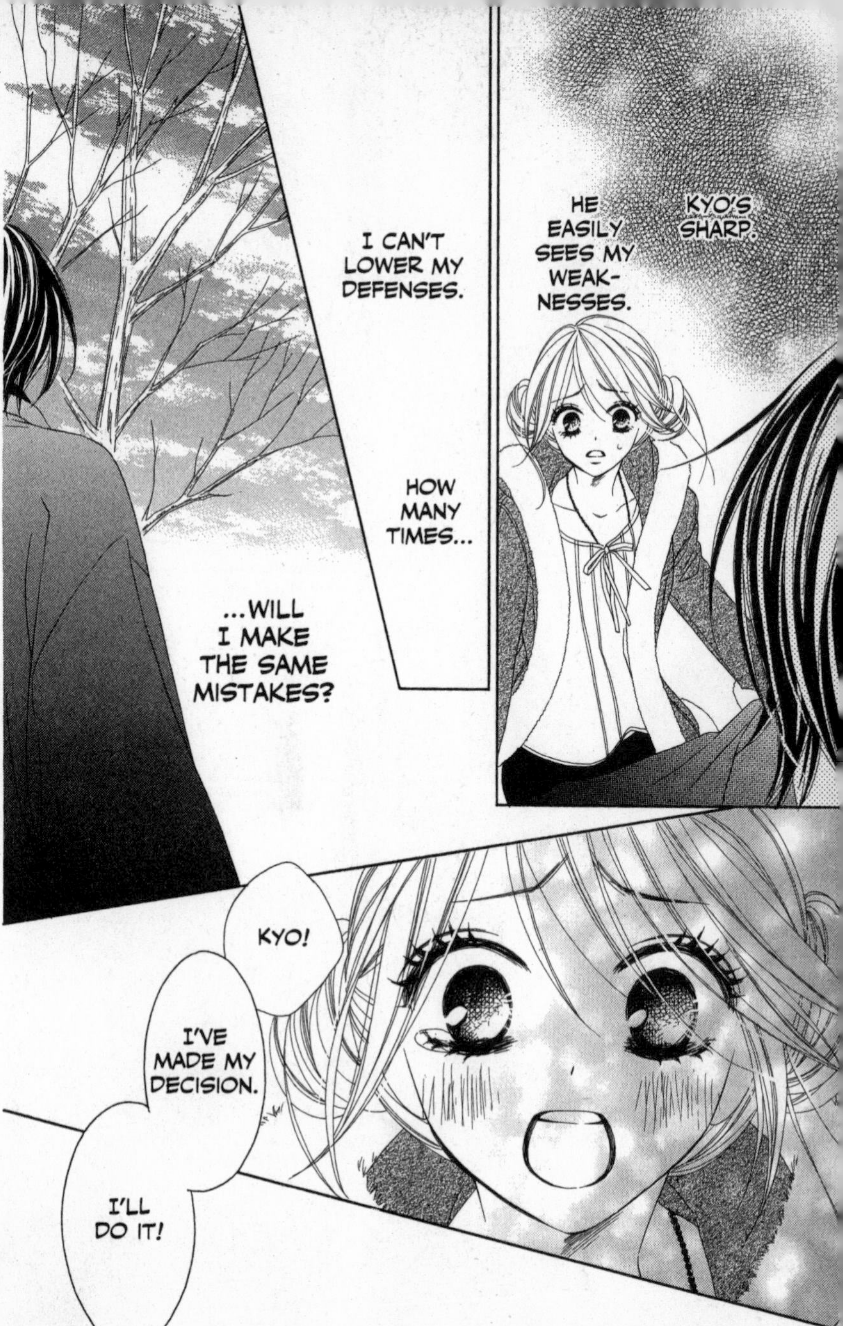
KYO'S SHARP.
HE EASILY SEES MY WEAK-NESSES.
I CAN'T LOWER MY DEFENSES.
HOW MANY TIMES...
...WILL I MAKE THE SAME MISTAKES?
KYO!
I'VE MADE MY DECISION.
I'LL DO IT!

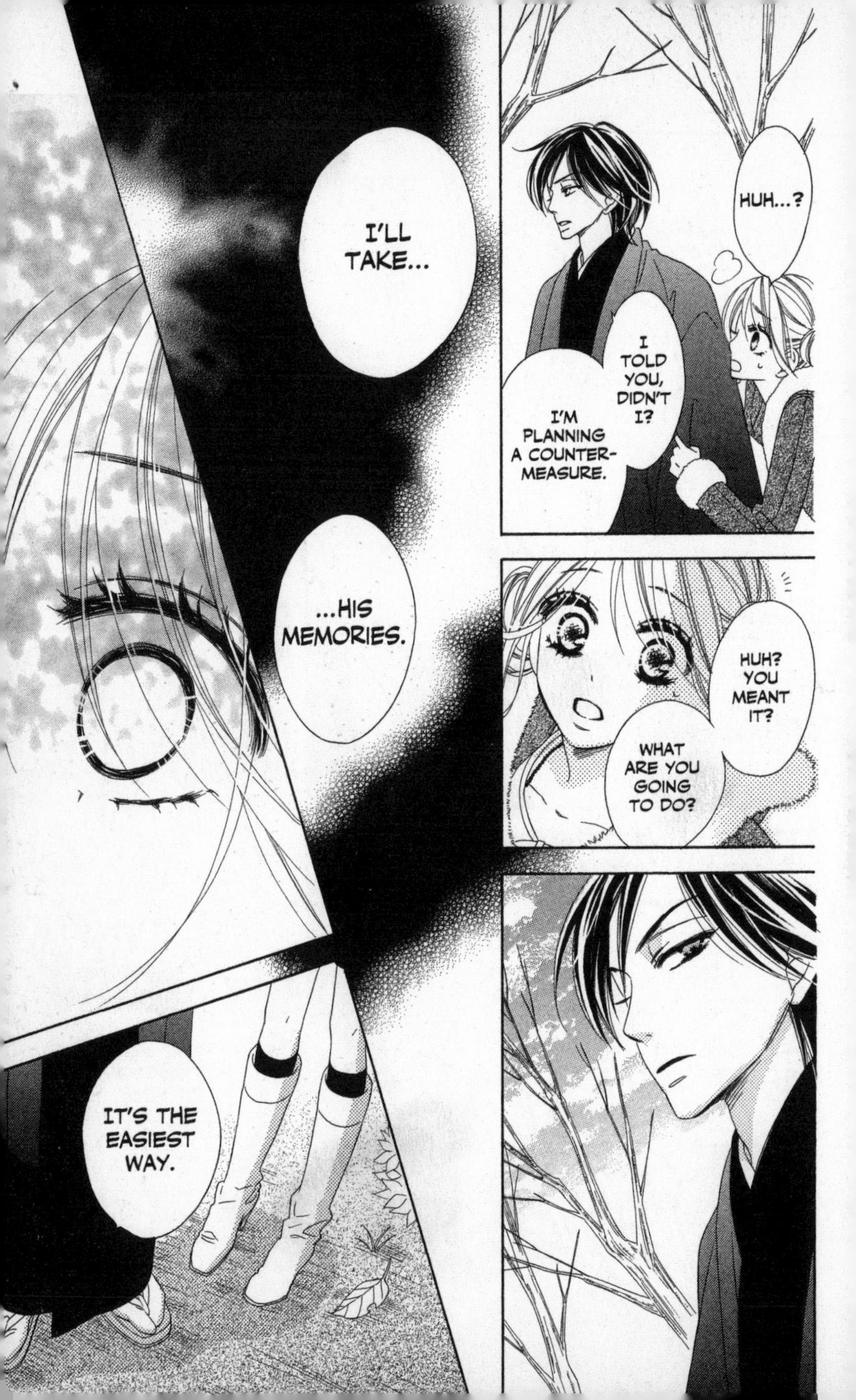
HUH...?
I TOLD YOU, DIDN'T I?
I'M PLANNING A COUNTER-MEASURE.
HUH? YOU MEANT IT?
WHAT ARE YOU GOING TO DO?
I'LL TAKE...
...HIS MEMORIES.
IT'S THE EASIEST WAY.

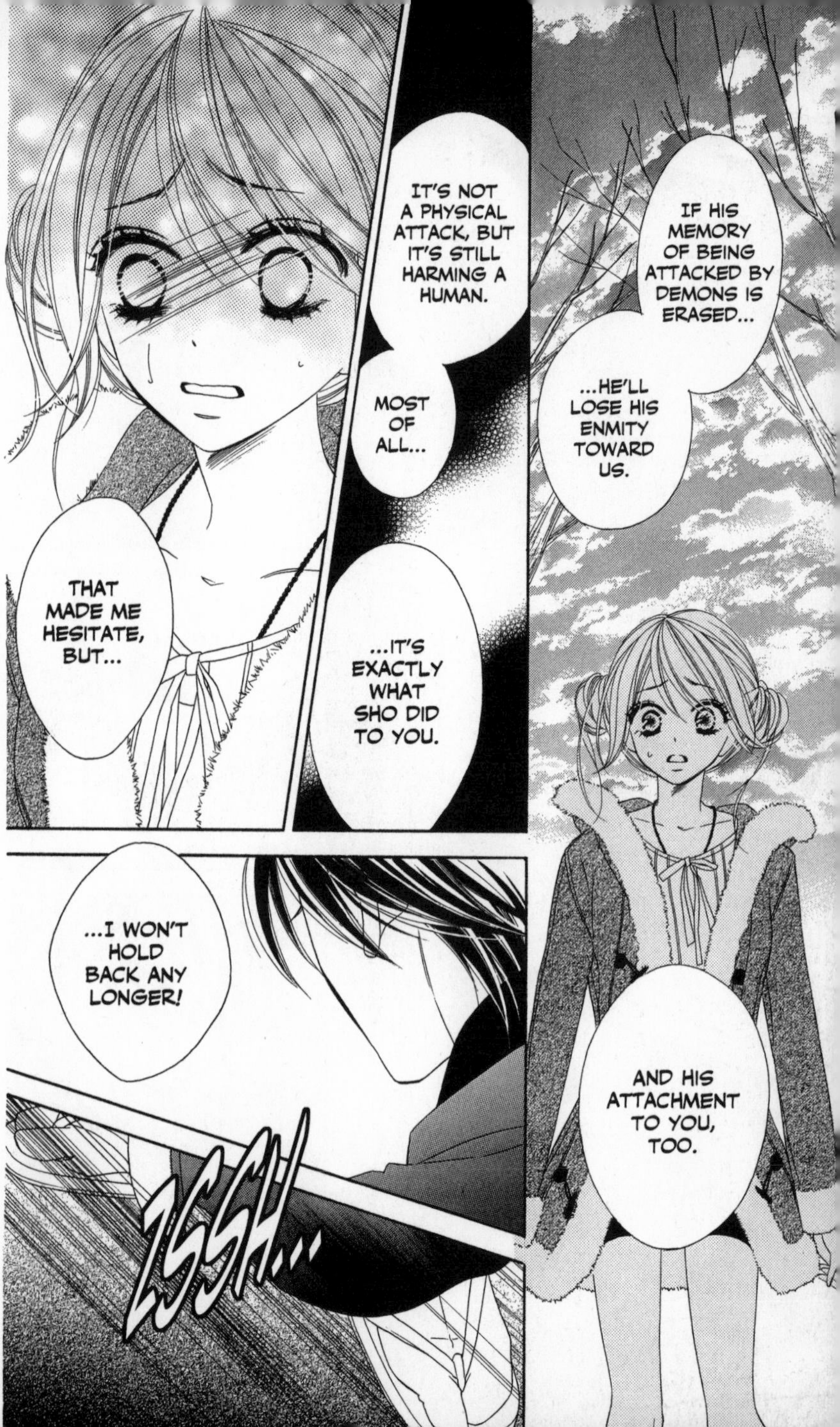
IF HIS MEMORY OF BEING ATTACKED BY DEMONS IS ERASED...
...HE'LL LOSE HIS ENMITY TOWARD US.
AND HIS ATTACHMENT TO YOU, TOO.
IT'S NOT A PHYSICAL ATTACK, BUT IT'S STILL HARMING A HUMAN.
MOST OF ALL...
...IT'S EXACTLY WHAT SHO DID TO YOU.
THAT MADE ME HESITATE, BUT...
...I WON'T HOLD BACK ANY LONGER!
ZSSH...

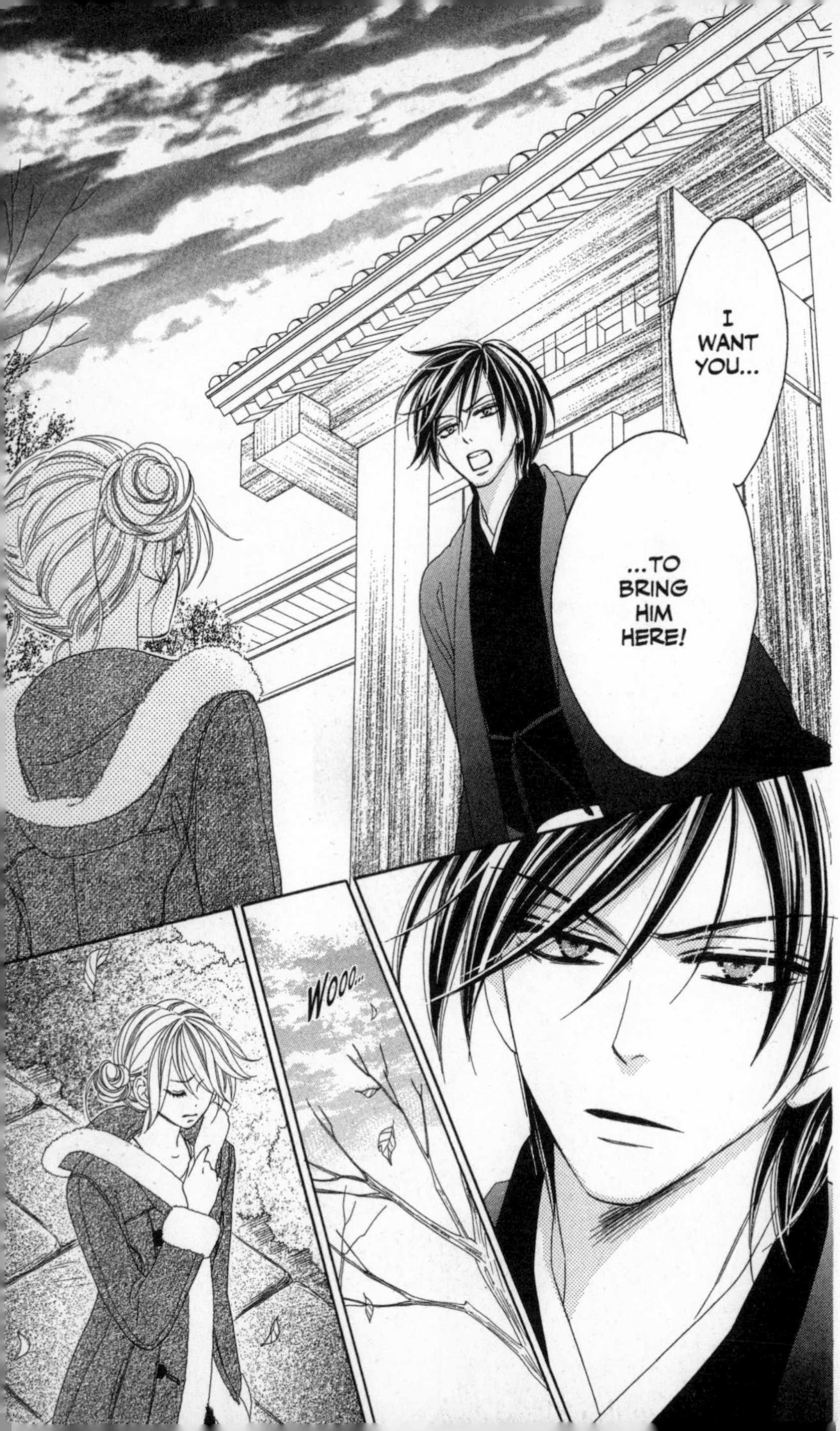
I WANT YOU...
...TO BRING HIM HERE!
WOOO...

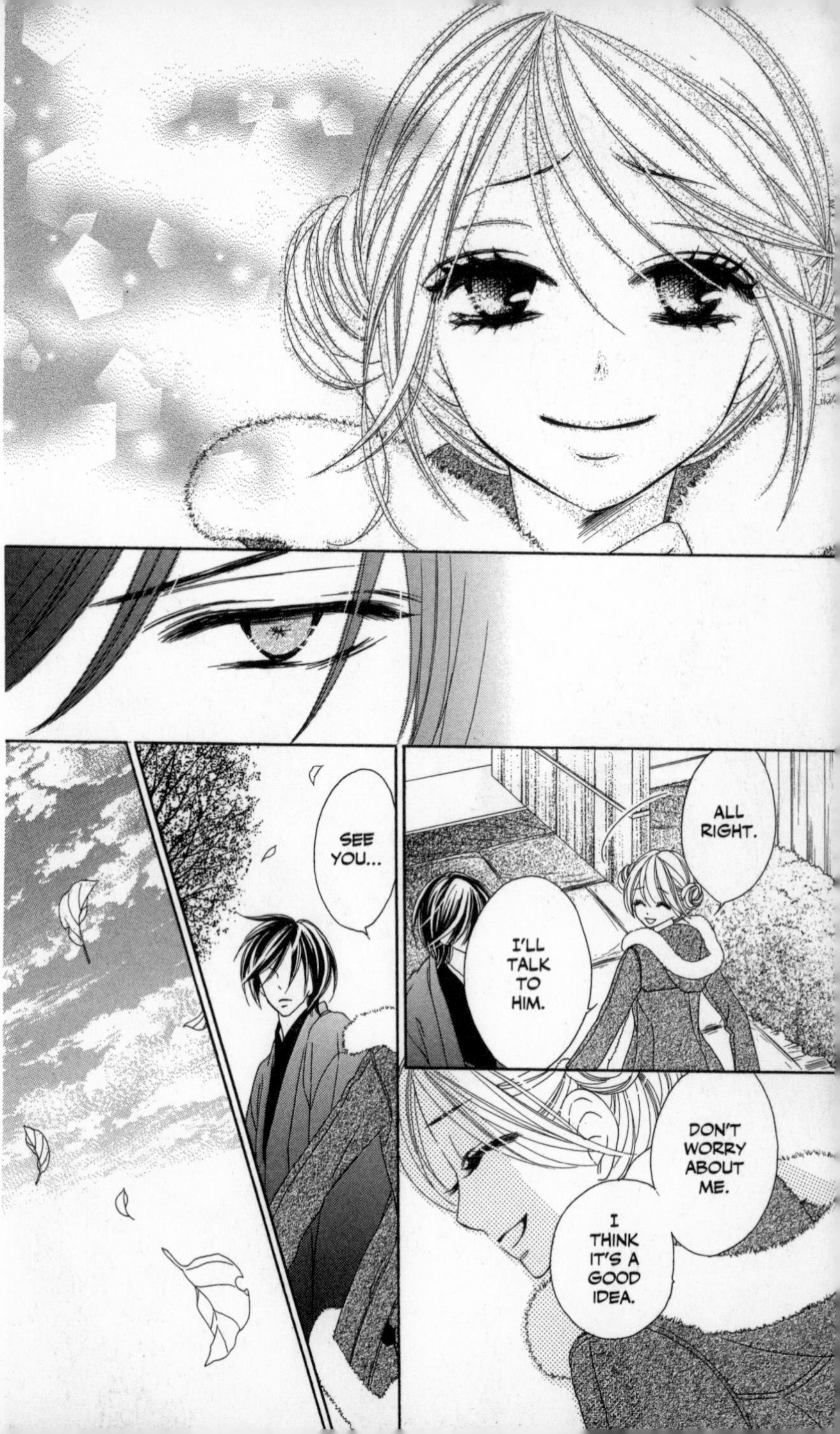
ALL RIGHT.
I'LL TALK TO HIM.
DON'T WORRY ABOUT ME.
I THINK IT'S A GOOD IDEA.
SEE YOU...

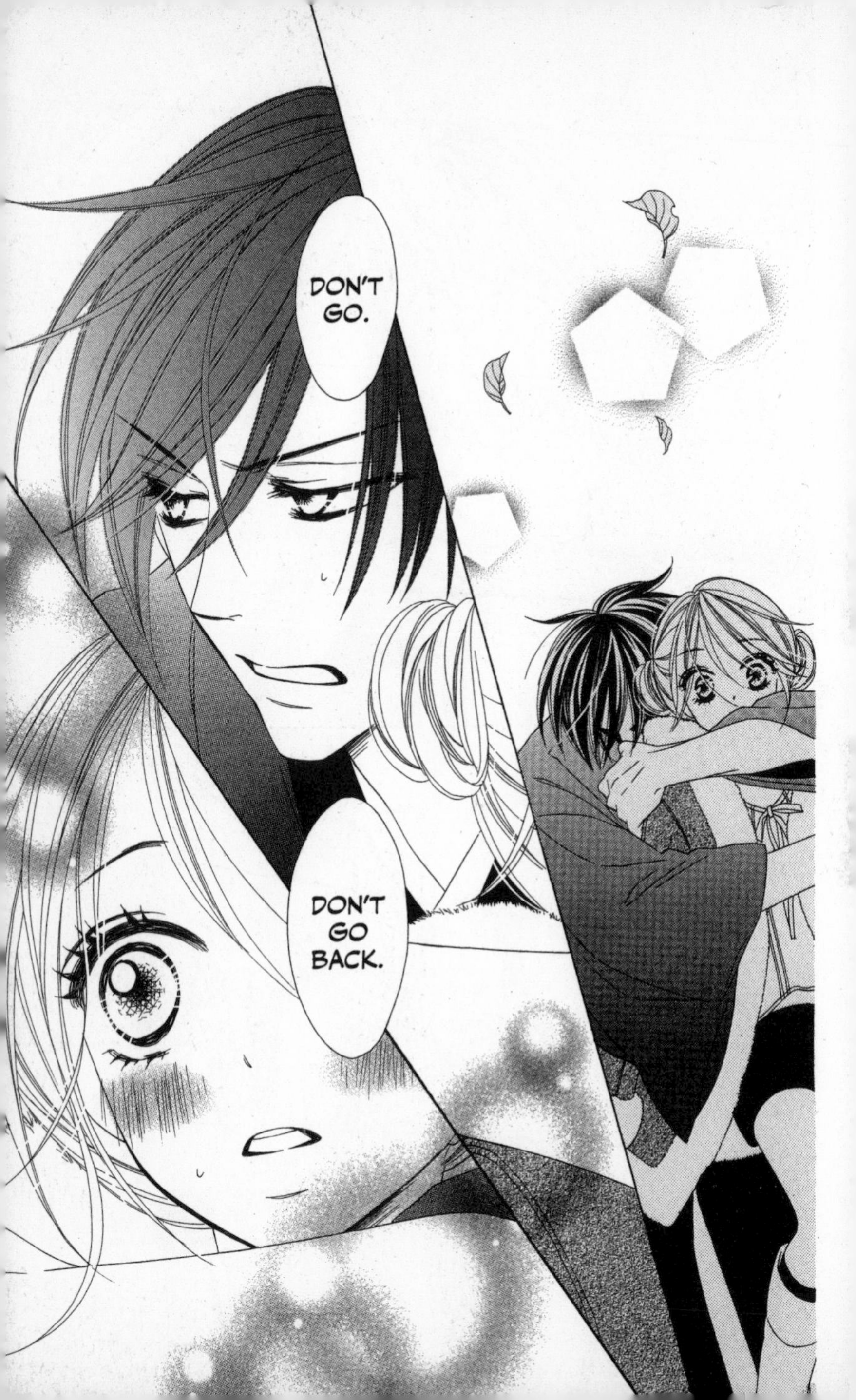
DON'T GO.
DON'T GO BACK.

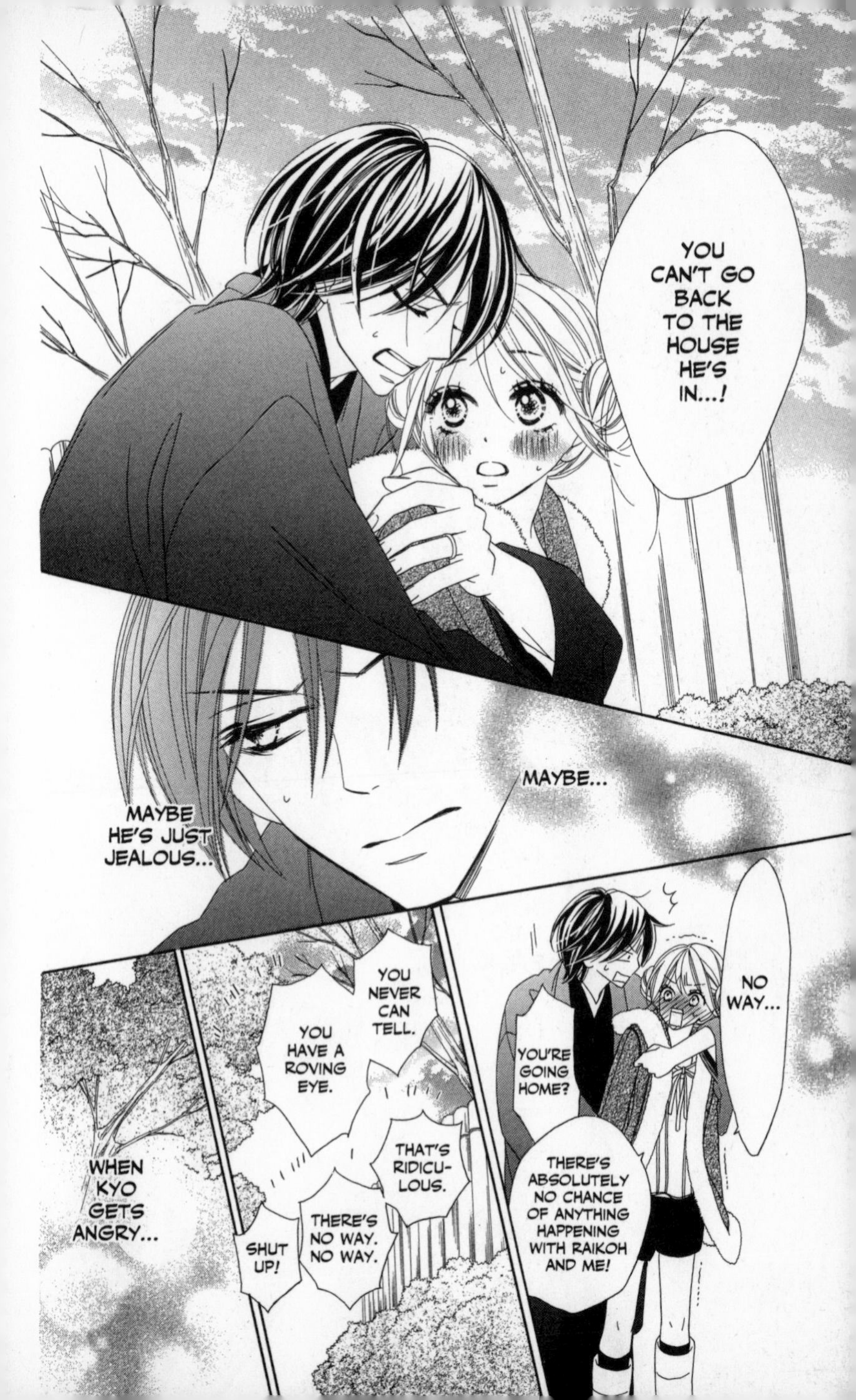
YOU CAN'T GO BACK TO THE HOUSE HE'S IN...!
MAYBE...
MAYBE HE'S JUST JEALOUS...
NO WAY...
YOU'RE GOING HOME?
THERE'S ABSOLUTELY NO CHANCE OF ANYTHING HAPPENING WITH RAIKOH AND ME!
YOU NEVER CAN TELL.
YOU HAVE A ROVING EYE.
THAT'S RIDICULOUS.
THERE'S NO WAY. NO WAY.
SHUT UP!
WHEN KYO GETS ANGRY...

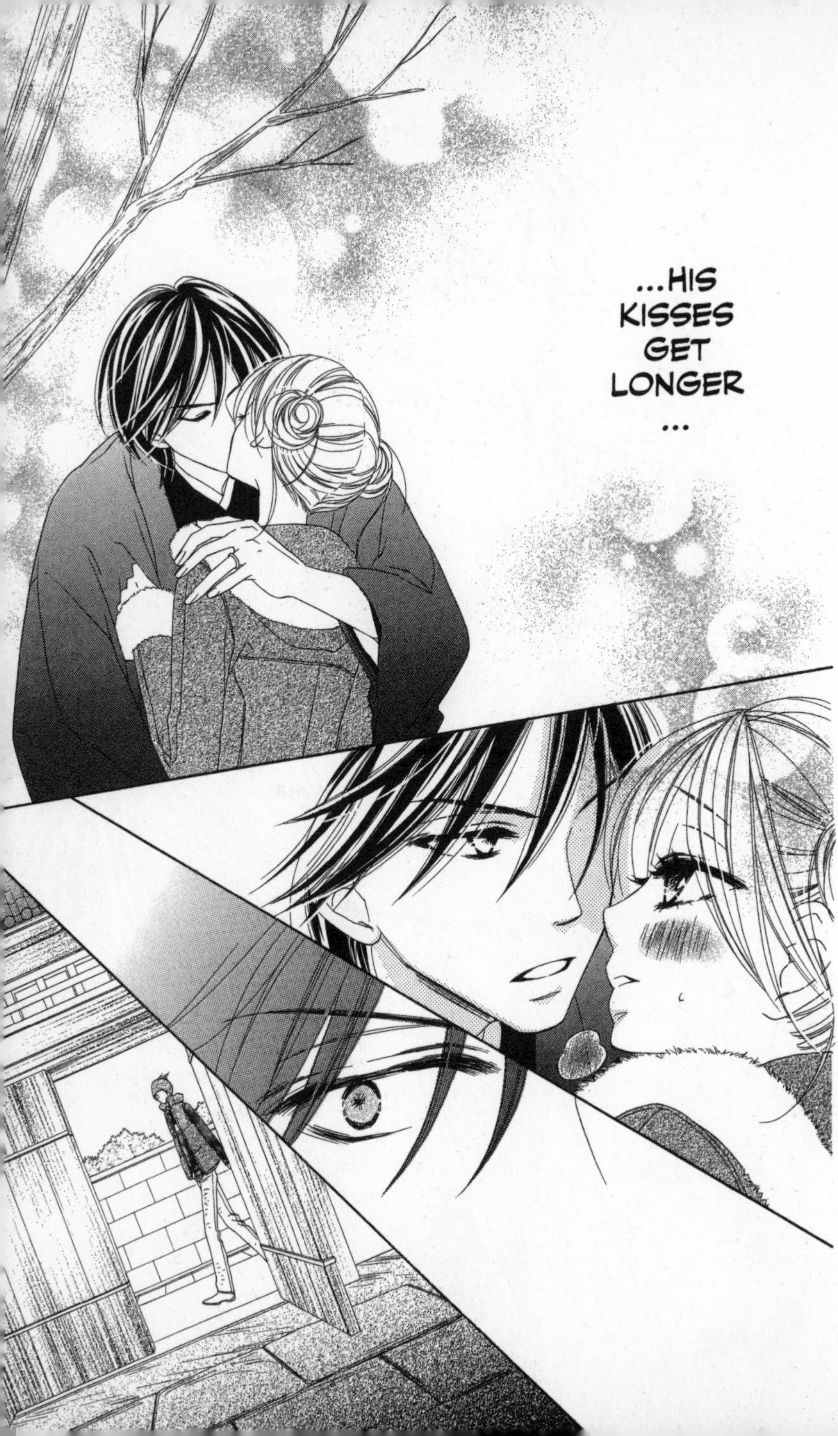
...HIS KISSES GET LONGER ...

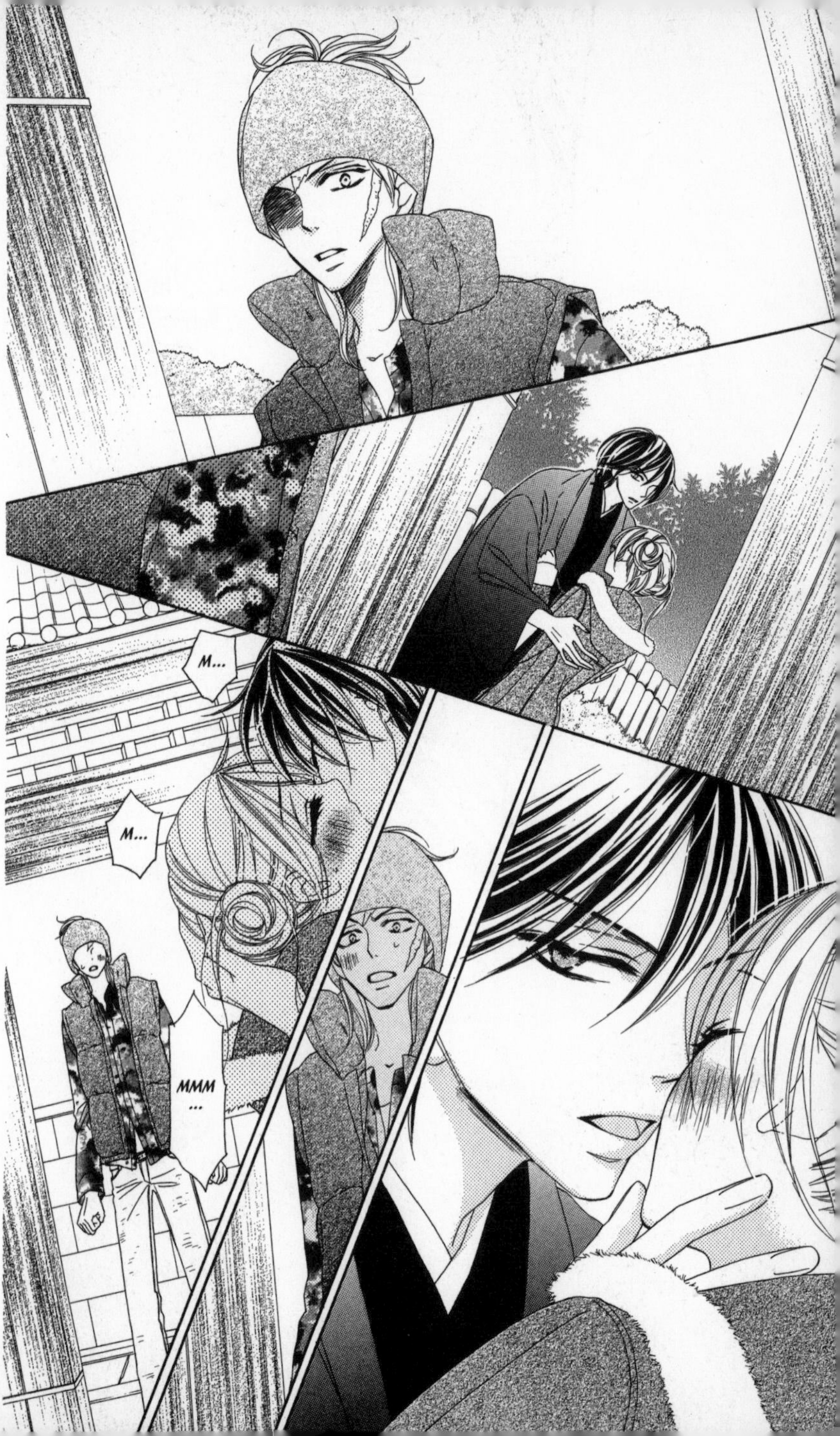
M...
M...
MMM
...

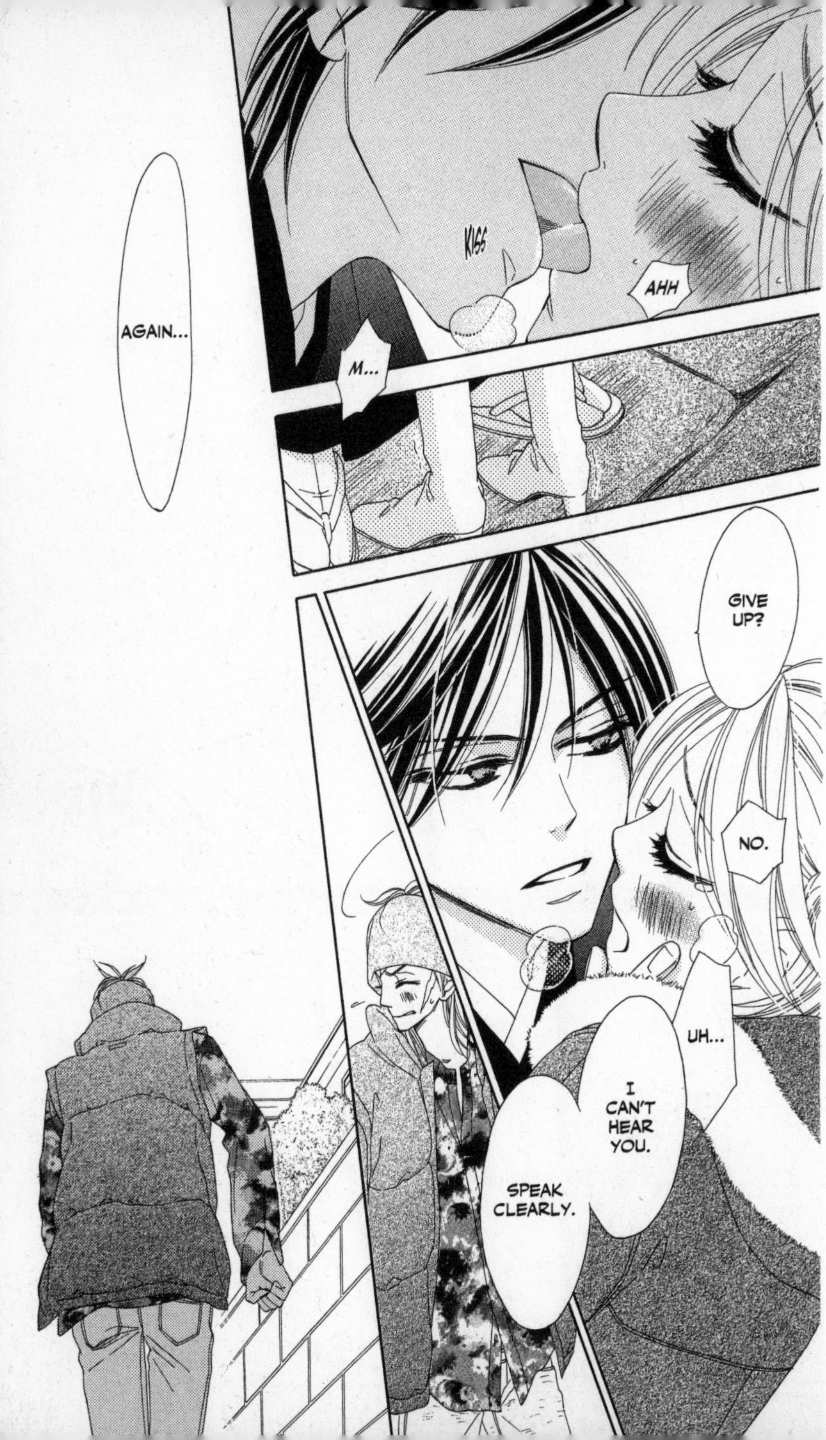
KISS
AHH
M...
GIVE UP?
NO.
UH...
I CAN'T HEAR YOU.
SPEAK CLEARLY.
AGAIN...

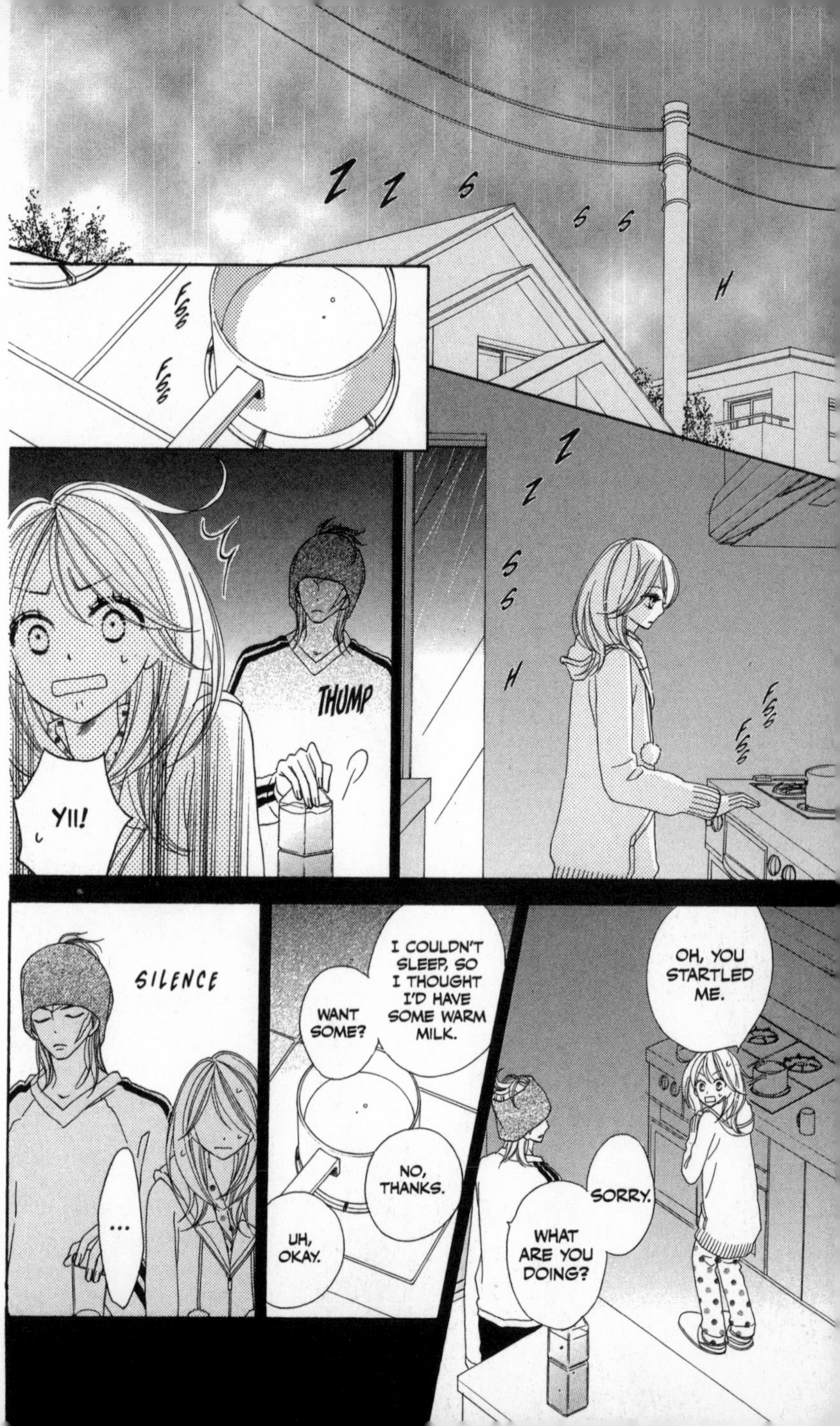
ZZSSSH
ZZSSH
FSS
FSS
FSS
FSS
THUMP
YII!
OH, YOU STARTLED ME.
SORRY.
WHAT ARE YOU DOING?
I COULDN'T SLEEP, SO I THOUGHT I'D HAVE SOME WARM MILK.
WANT SOME?
NO, THANKS.
UH, OKAY.
SILENCE
...

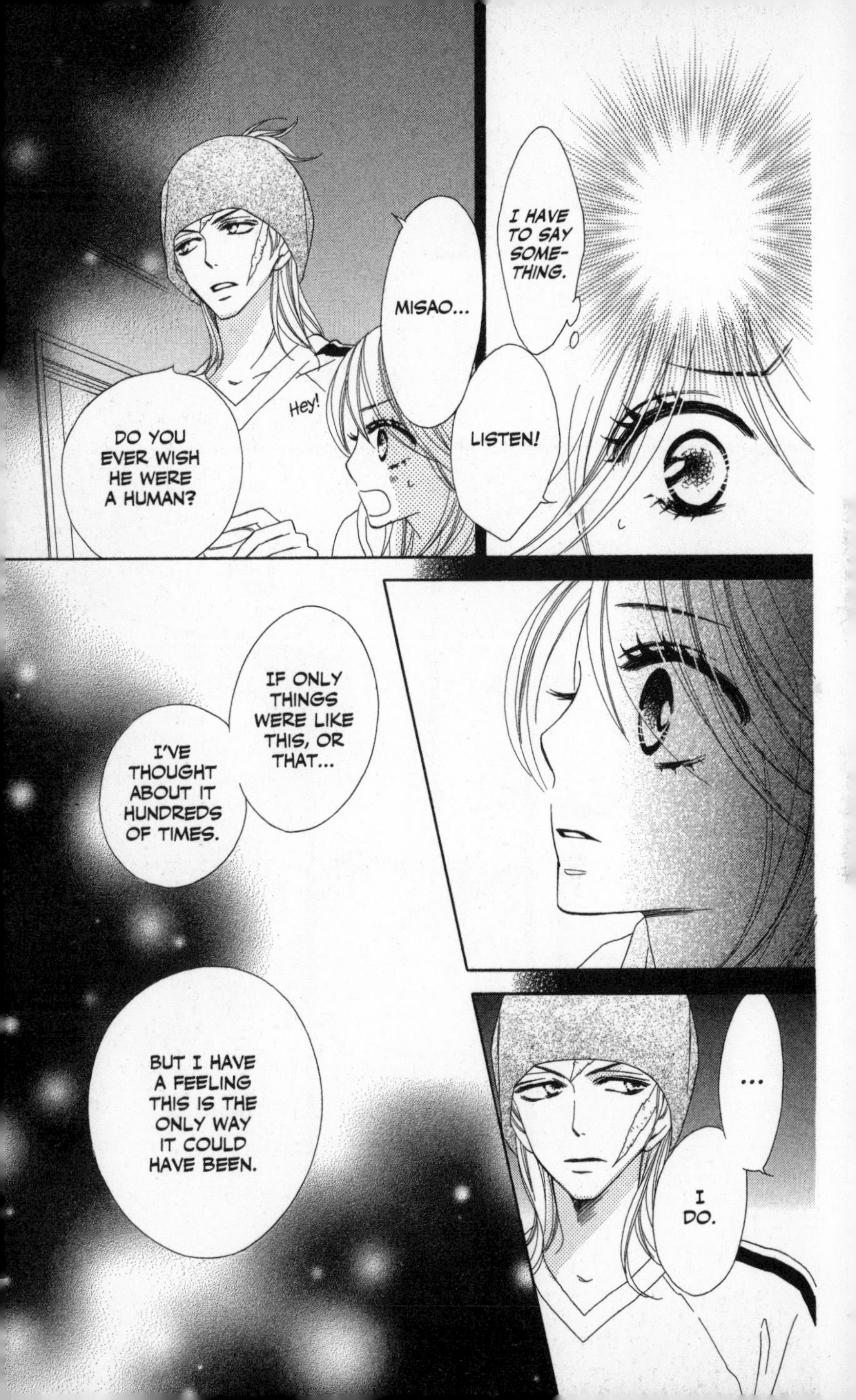
I HAVE TO SAY SOME-THING.
LISTEN!
MISAO...
Hey!
DO YOU EVER WISH HE WERE A HUMAN?
IF ONLY THINGS WERE LIKE THIS, OR THAT...
I'VE THOUGHT ABOUT IT HUNDREDS OF TIMES.
BUT I HAVE A FEELING THIS IS THE ONLY WAY IT COULD HAVE BEEN.
...
I DO.

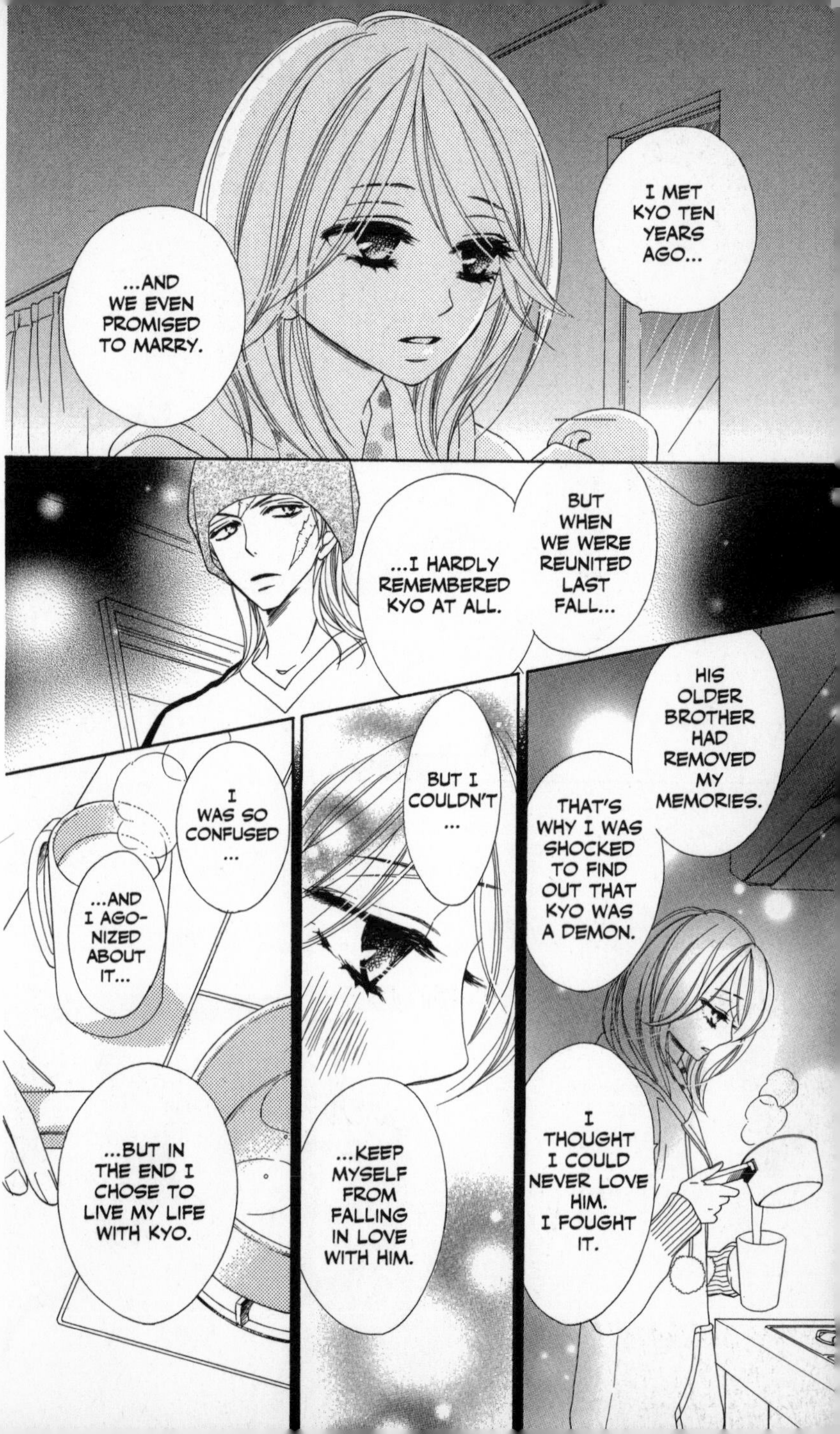
I MET KYO TEN YEARS AGO...
...AND WE EVEN PROMISED TO MARRY.
BUT WHEN WE WERE REUNITED LAST FALL...
...I HARDLY REMEMBERED KYO AT ALL.
HIS OLDER BROTHER HAD REMOVED MY MEMORIES.
THAT'S WHY I WAS SHOCKED TO FIND OUT THAT KYO WAS A DEMON.
I THOUGHT I COULD NEVER LOVE HIM. I FOUGHT IT.
BUT I COULDN'T ...
...KEEP MYSELF FROM FALLING IN LOVE WITH HIM.
I WAS SO CONFUSED ...
...AND I AGO-NIZED ABOUT IT...
...BUT IN THE END I CHOSE TO LIVE MY LIFE WITH KYO.

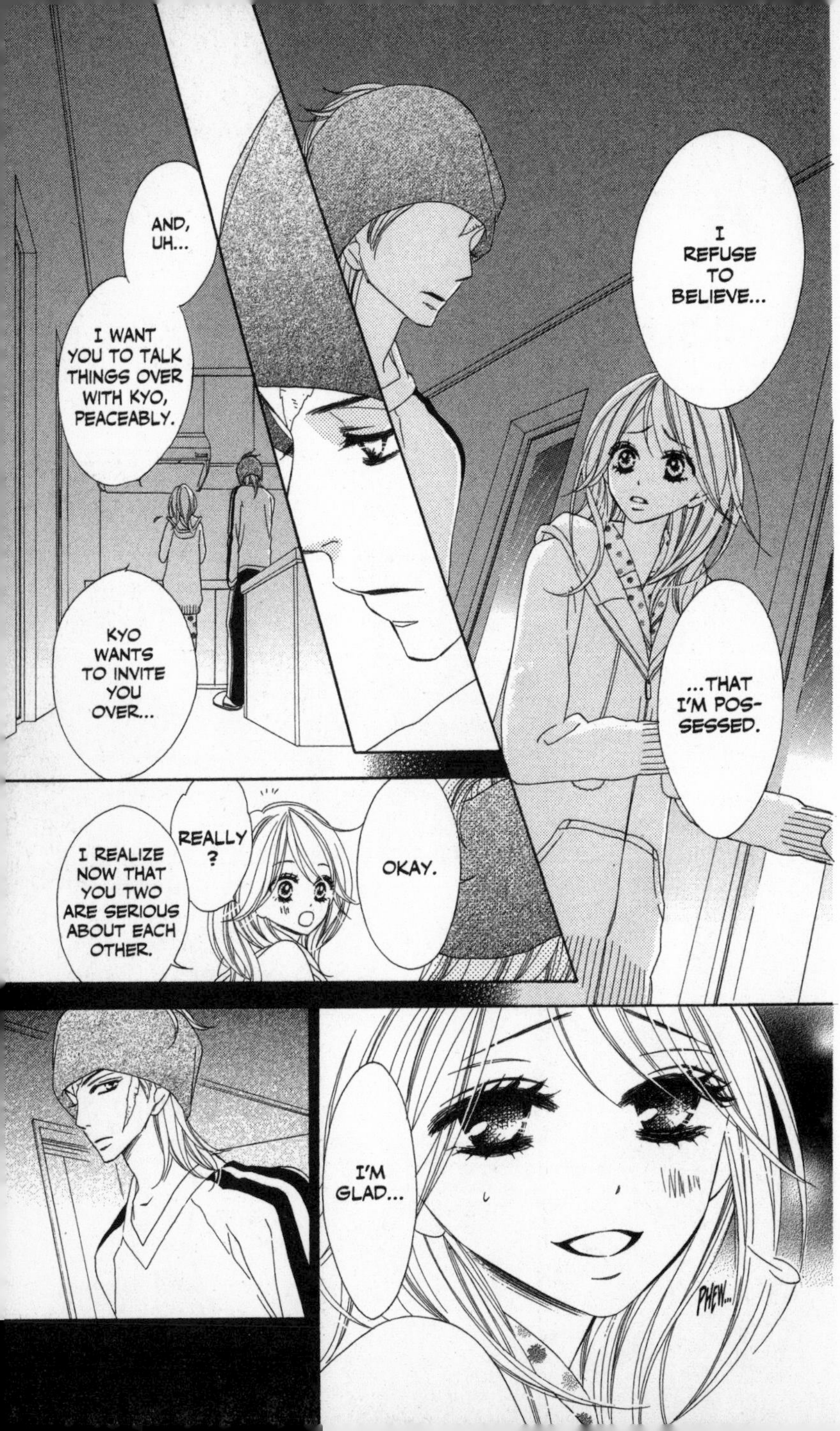
I REFUSE TO BELIEVE...
...THAT I'M POS-SESSED.
AND, UH...
I WANT YOU TO TALK THINGS OVER WITH KYO, PEACEABLY.
KYO WANTS TO INVITE YOU OVER...
OKAY.
REALLY?
I REALIZE NOW THAT YOU TWO ARE SERIOUS ABOUT EACH OTHER.
I'M GLAD...
PHEW...

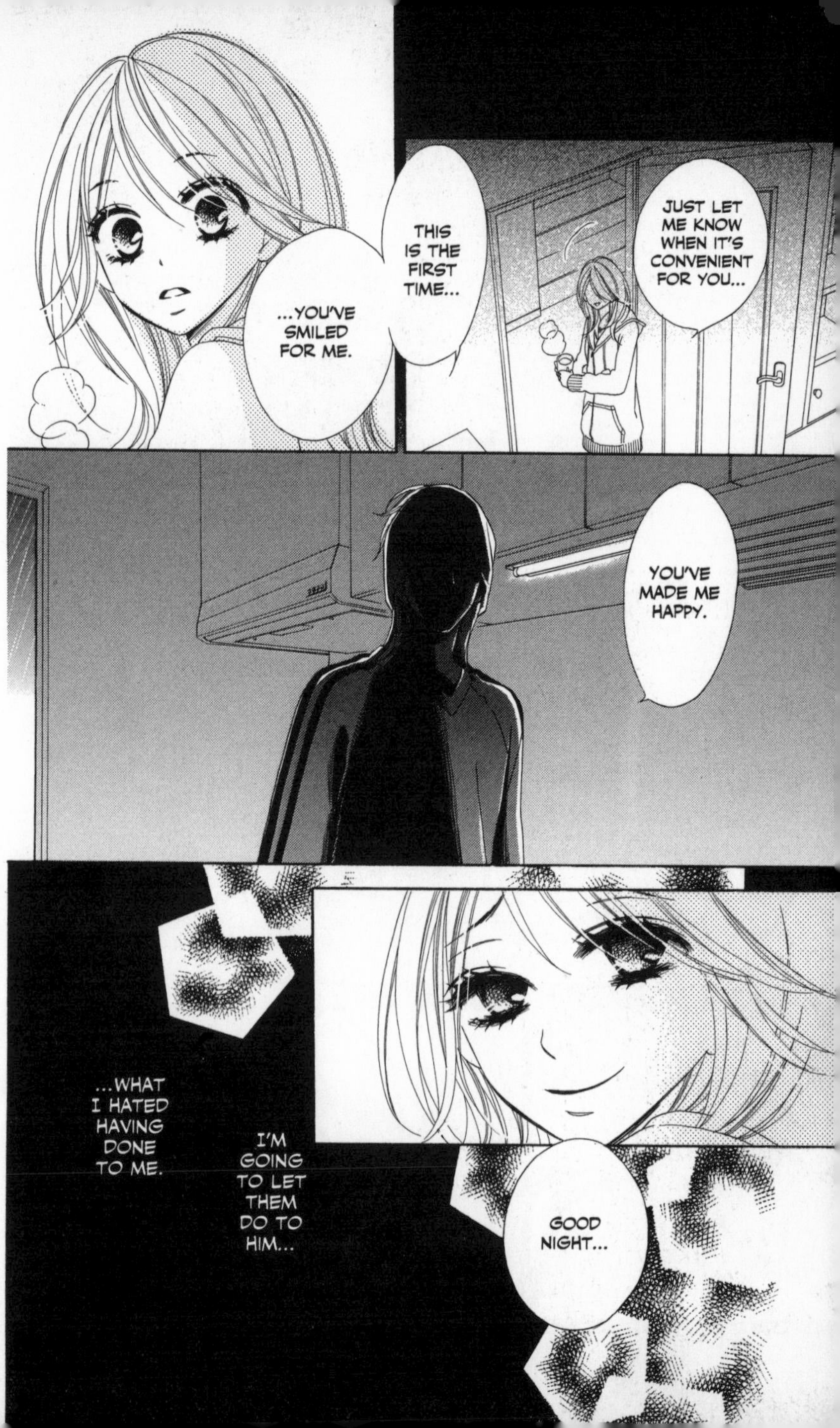

JUST LET ME KNOW WHEN IT'S CONVENIENT FOR YOU...
THIS IS THE FIRST TIME...
...YOU'VE SMILED FOR ME.
YOU'VE MADE ME HAPPY.
GOOD NIGHT...
I'M GOING TO LET THEM DO TO HIM...
...WHAT I HATED HAVING DONE TO ME.

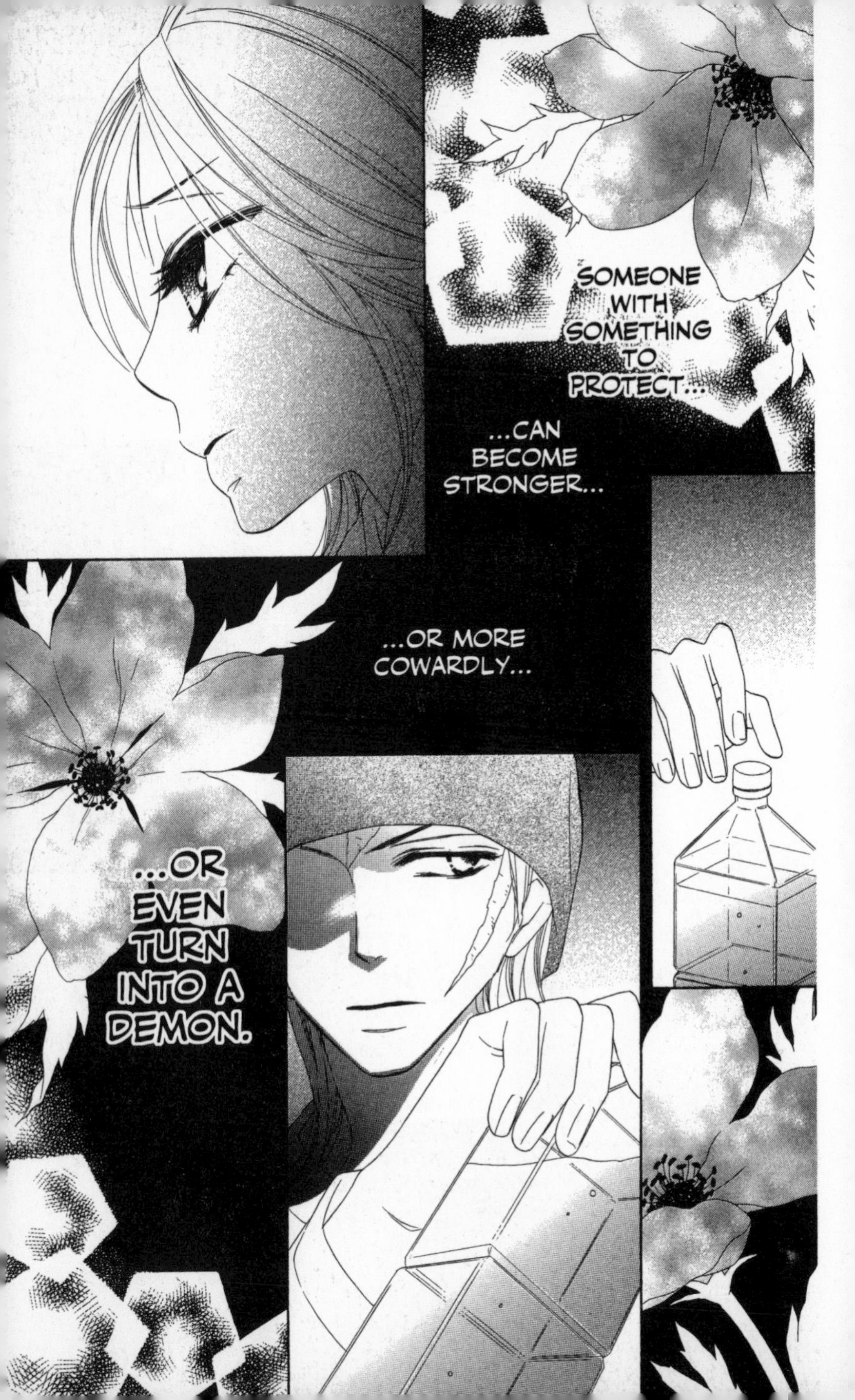
SOMEONE WITH SOMETHING TO PROTECT...
...CAN BECOME STRONGER...
...OR MORE COWARDLY...
...OR EVEN TURN INTO A DEMON.

Illustration Request Number Eleven

"Firemen"

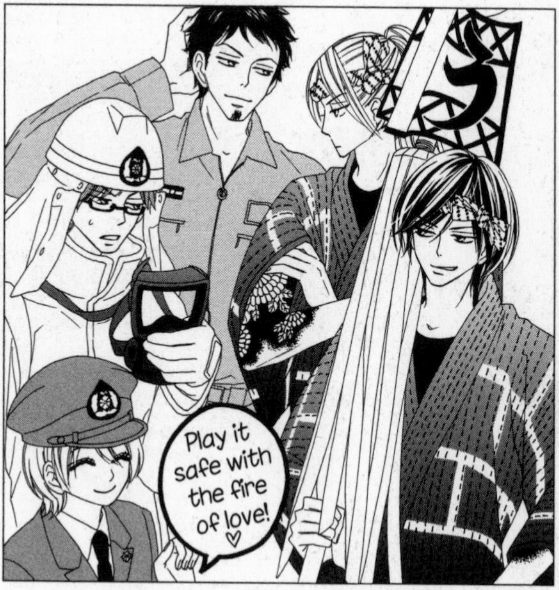
Play it safe with the fire of love! ♡

I drew some historical and modern firemen.

Buzen is a rescue worker in orange.

The standard bearer was always the handsomest of the crew♥, so here it's Kyo... For now.

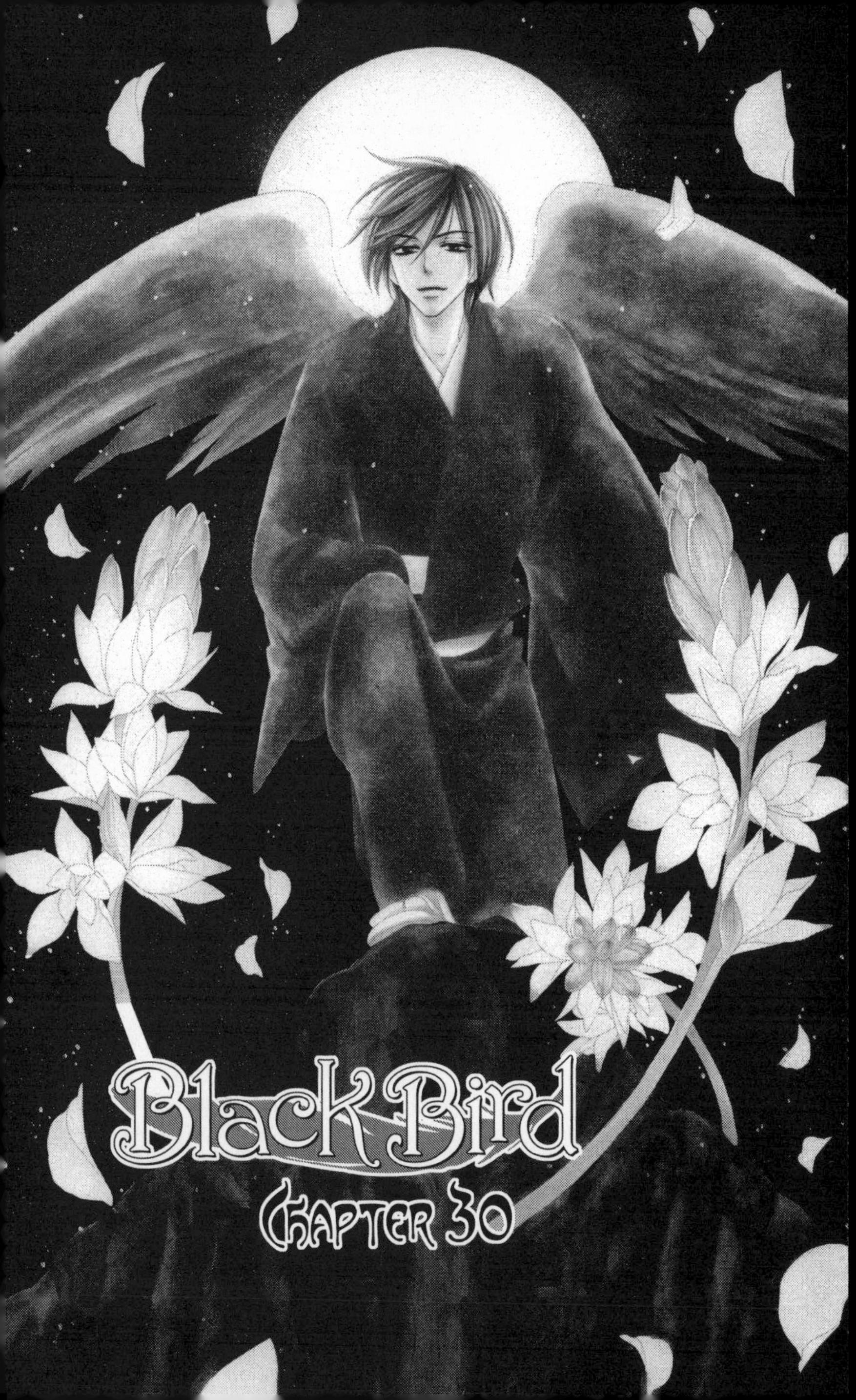
Black Bird
Chapter 30

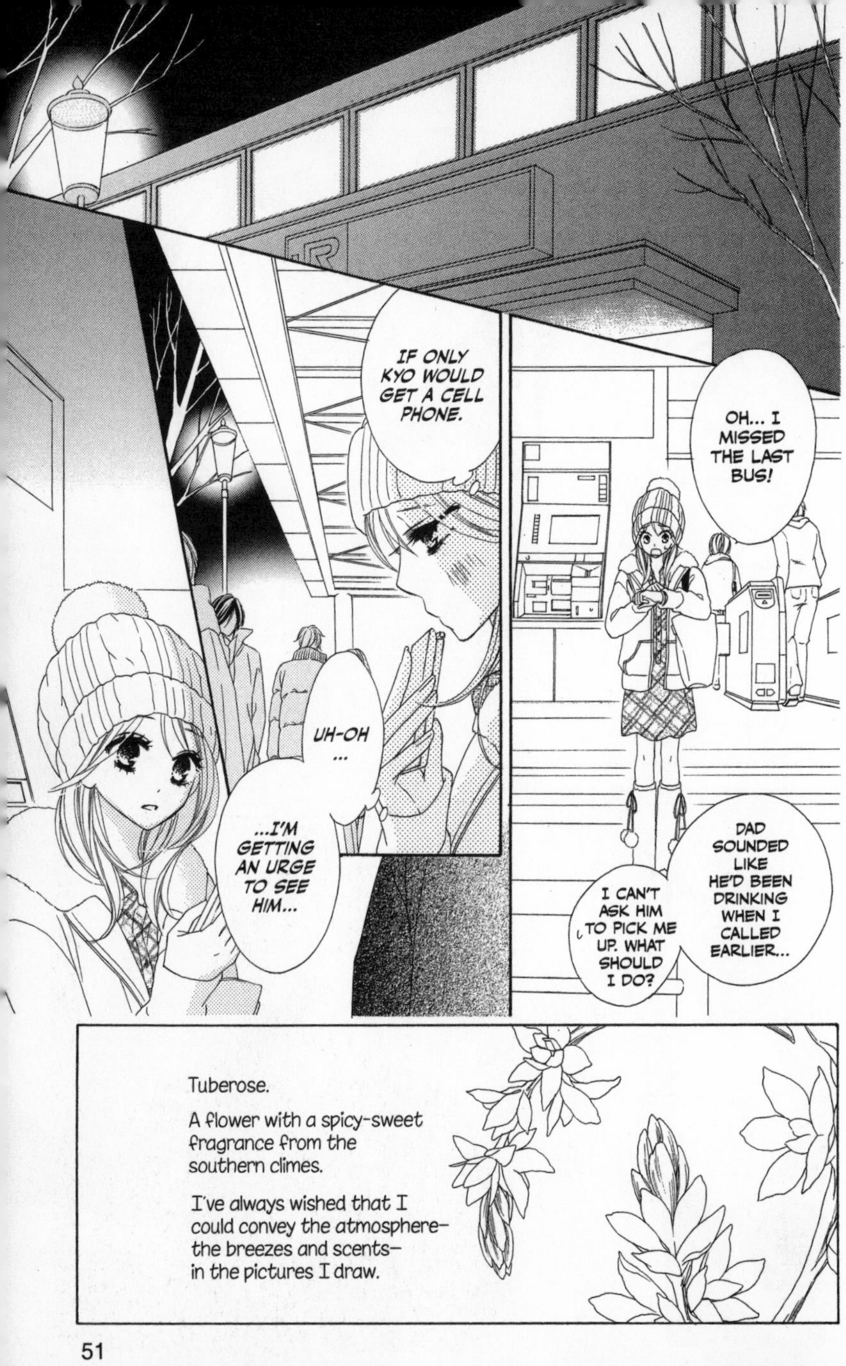
OH... I MISSED THE LAST BUS!
DAD SOUNDED LIKE HE'D BEEN DRINKING WHEN I CALLED EARLIER...
I CAN'T ASK HIM TO PICK ME UP. WHAT SHOULD I DO?
IF ONLY KYO WOULD GET A CELL PHONE.
UH-OH ...
...I'M GETTING AN URGE TO SEE HIM...
Tuberose.
A flower with a spicy-sweet fragrance from the southern climes.
I've always wished that I could convey the atmosphere–the breezes and scents–in the pictures I draw.

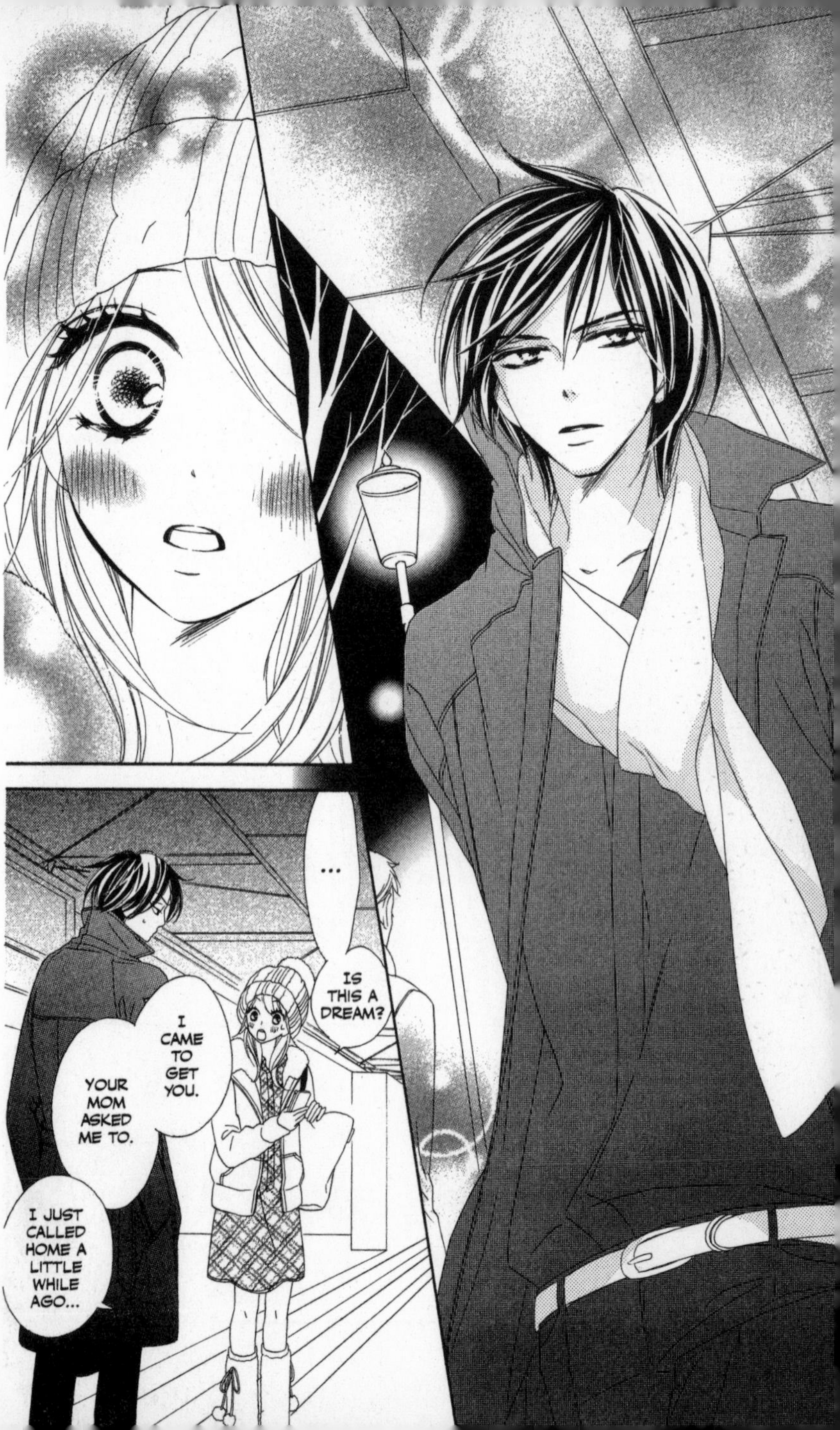
...
IS THIS A DREAM?
I CAME TO GET YOU.
YOUR MOM ASKED ME TO.
I JUST CALLED HOME A LITTLE WHILE AGO...

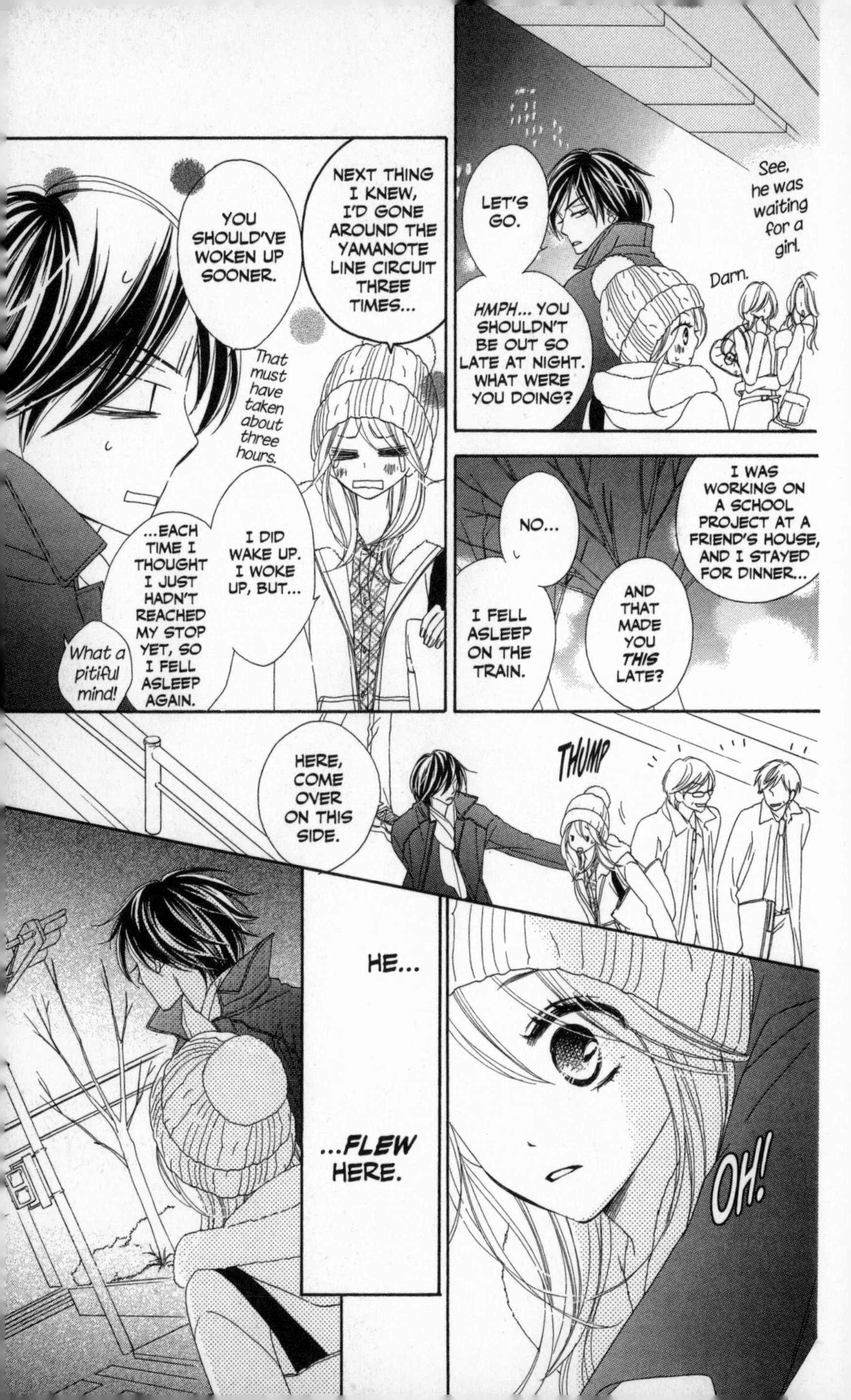
See, he was waiting for a girl.
Darn.
LET'S GO.
HMPH... YOU SHOULDN'T BE OUT SO LATE AT NIGHT. WHAT WERE YOU DOING?
I WAS WORKING ON A SCHOOL PROJECT AT A FRIEND'S HOUSE, AND I STAYED FOR DINNER...
NO...
AND THAT MADE YOU THIS LATE?
I FELL ASLEEP ON THE TRAIN.
NEXT THING I KNEW, I'D GONE AROUND THE YAMANOTE LINE CIRCUIT THREE TIMES...
YOU SHOULD'VE WOKEN UP SOONER.
That must have taken about three hours.
I DID WAKE UP. I WOKE UP, BUT...
...EACH TIME I THOUGHT I JUST HADN'T REACHED MY STOP YET, SO I FELL ASLEEP AGAIN.
What a pitiful mind!
THUMP
HERE, COME OVER ON THIS SIDE.
OH!
HE...
...FLEW HERE.

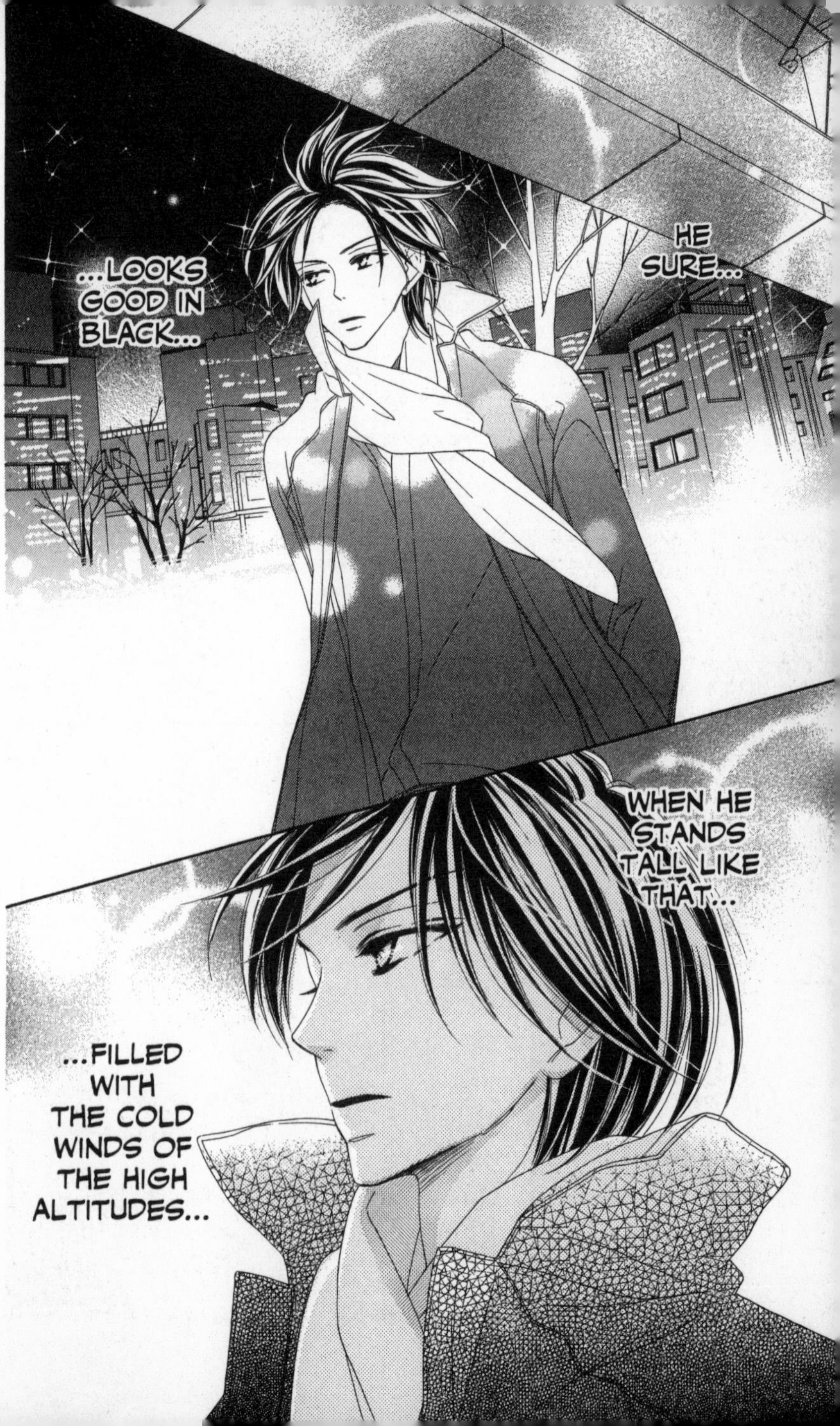
HE SURE...
...LOOKS GOOD IN BLACK...
WHEN HE STANDS TALL LIKE THAT...
...FILLED WITH THE COLD WINDS OF THE HIGH ALTITUDES...

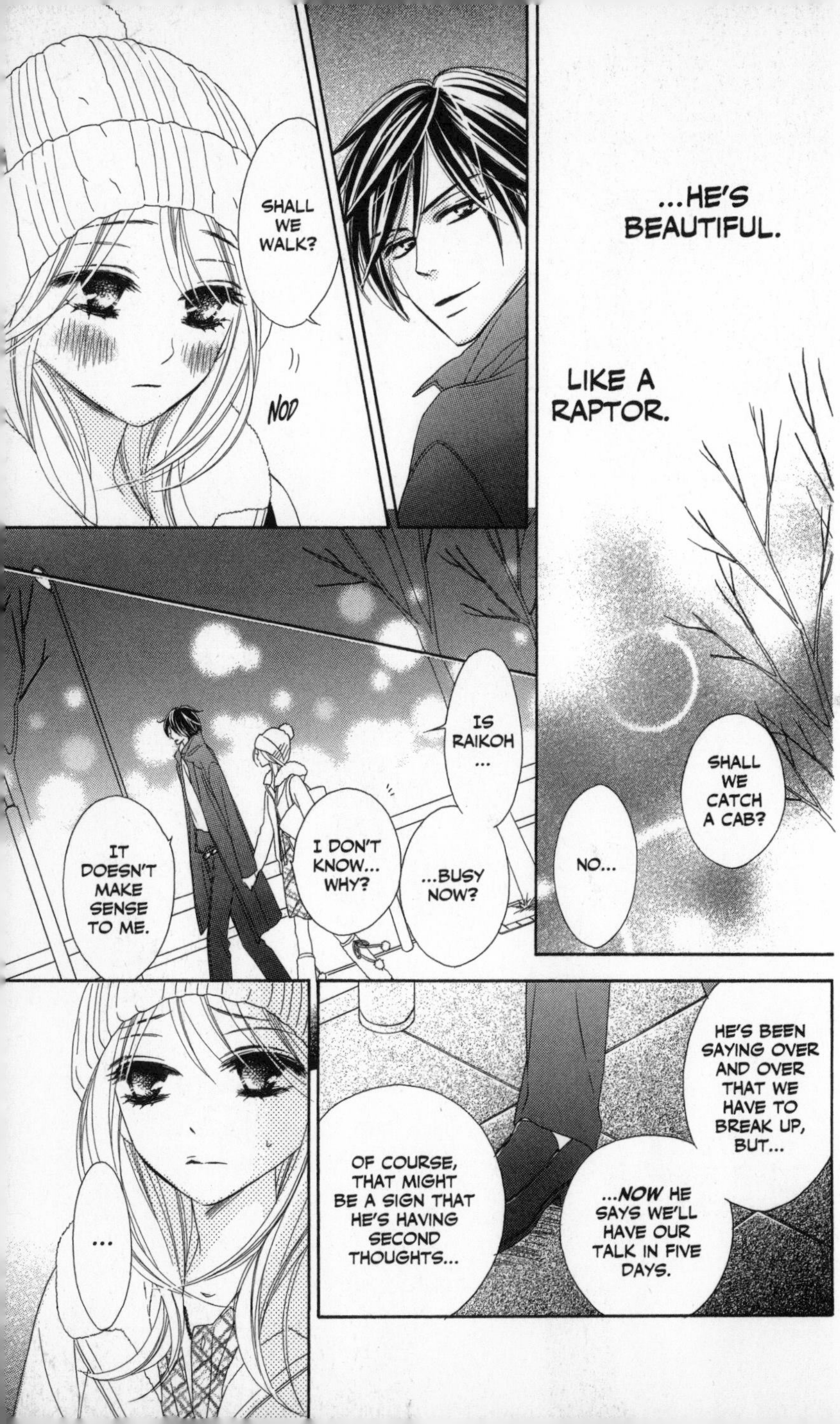

...HE'S BEAUTIFUL.
LIKE A RAPTOR.
SHALL WE CATCH A CAB?
NO...
SHALL WE WALK?
NOD
IS RAIKOH ...
...BUSY NOW?
I DON'T KNOW... WHY?
IT DOESN'T MAKE SENSE TO ME.
HE'S BEEN SAYING OVER AND OVER THAT WE HAVE TO BREAK UP, BUT...
...NOW HE SAYS WE'LL HAVE OUR TALK IN FIVE DAYS.
OF COURSE, THAT MIGHT BE A SIGN THAT HE'S HAVING SECOND THOUGHTS...
...

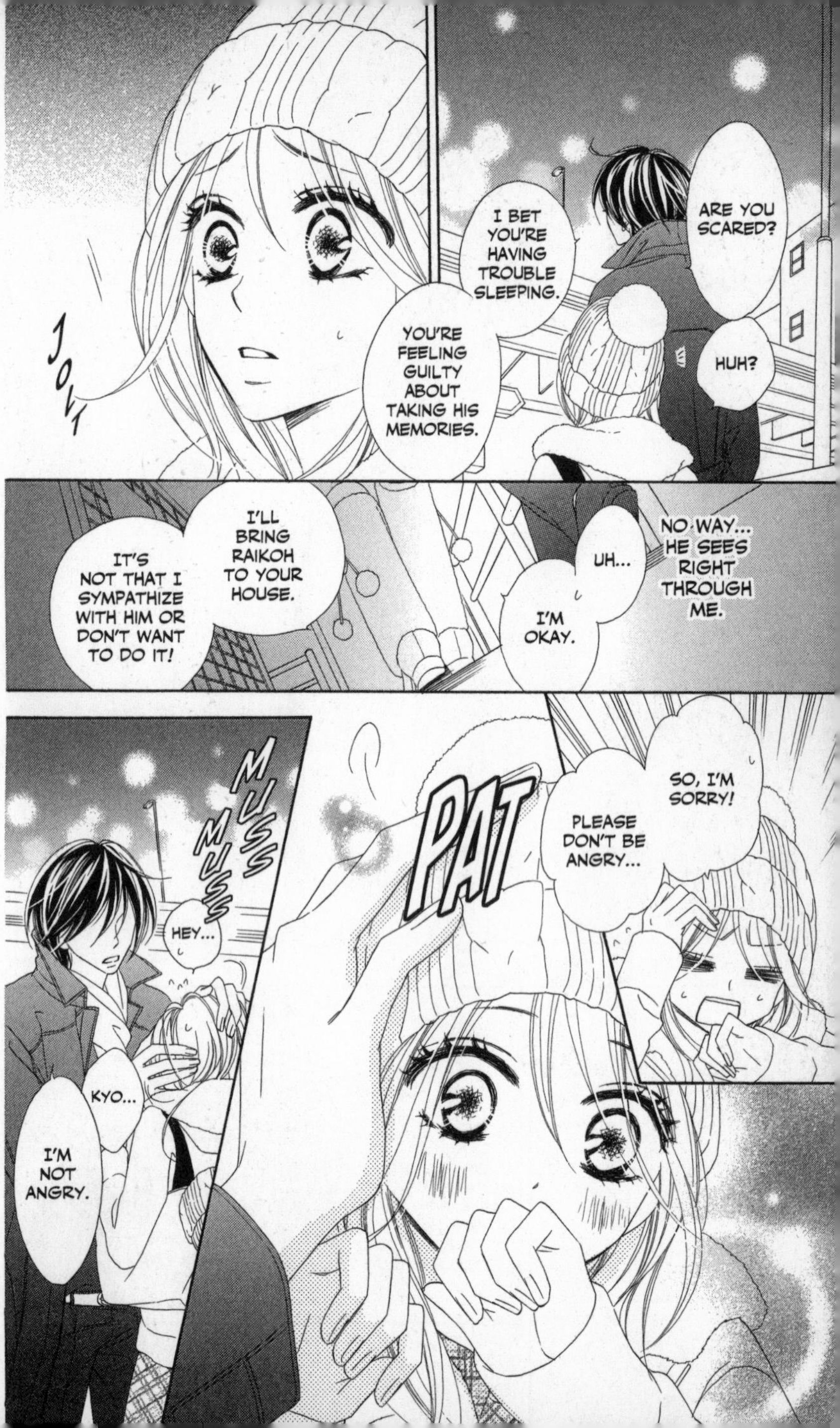
ARE YOU SCARED?
HUH?
I BET YOU'RE HAVING TROUBLE SLEEPING.
YOU'RE FEELING GUILTY ABOUT TAKING HIS MEMORIES.
JOLT
NO WAY... HE SEES RIGHT THROUGH ME.
UH...
I'M OKAY.
I'LL BRING RAIKOH TO YOUR HOUSE.
IT'S NOT THAT I SYMPATHIZE WITH HIM OR DON'T WANT TO DO IT!
SO, I'M SORRY!
PLEASE DON'T BE ANGRY...
PAT
MUSS MUSS
HEY...
KYO...
I'M NOT ANGRY.

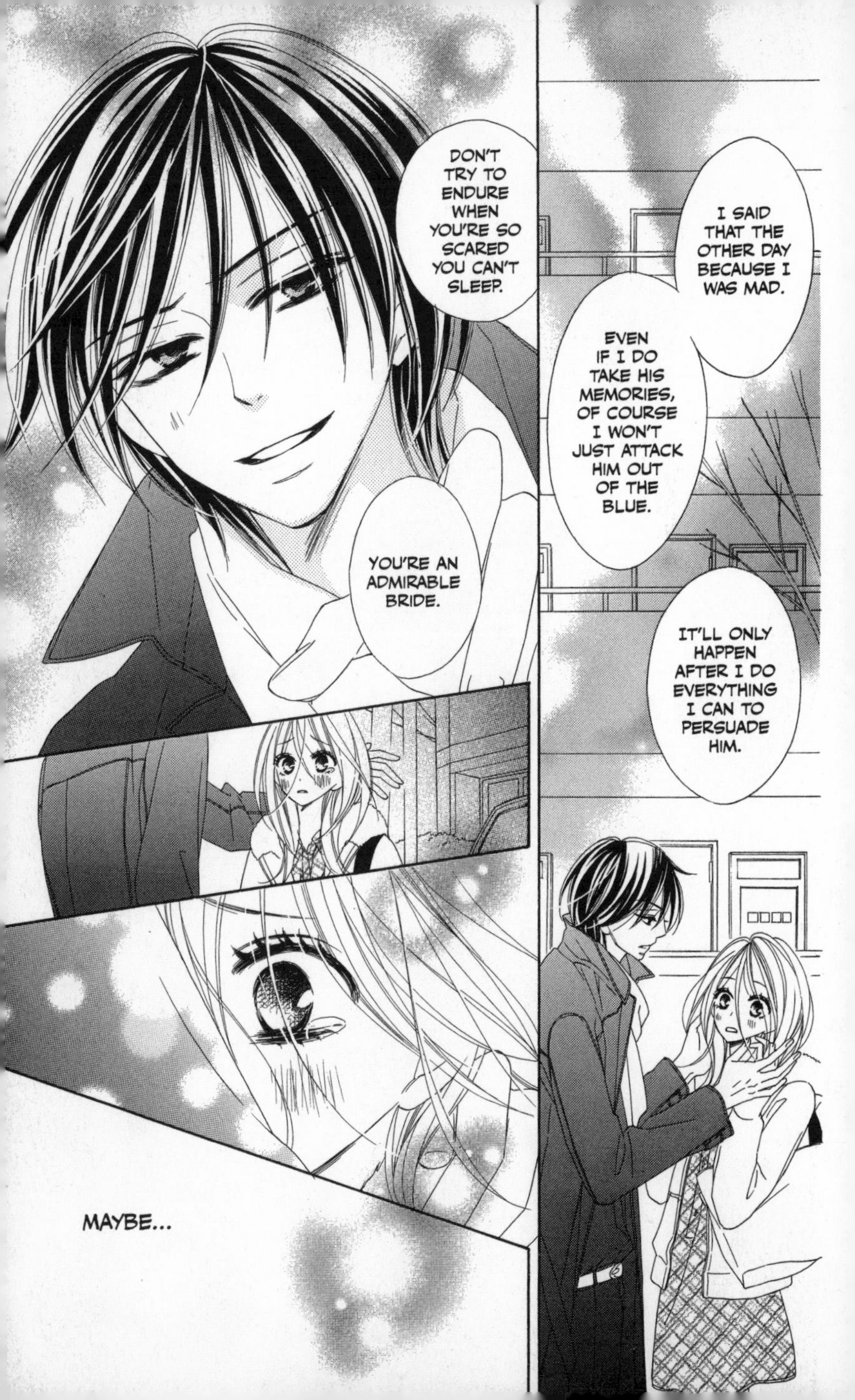
I SAID THAT THE OTHER DAY BECAUSE I WAS MAD.
EVEN IF I DO TAKE HIS MEMORIES, OF COURSE I WON'T JUST ATTACK HIM OUT OF THE BLUE.
IT'LL ONLY HAPPEN AFTER I DO EVERYTHING I CAN TO PERSUADE HIM.
DON'T TRY TO ENDURE WHEN YOU'RE SO SCARED YOU CAN'T SLEEP.
YOU'RE AN ADMIRABLE BRIDE.
MAYBE...

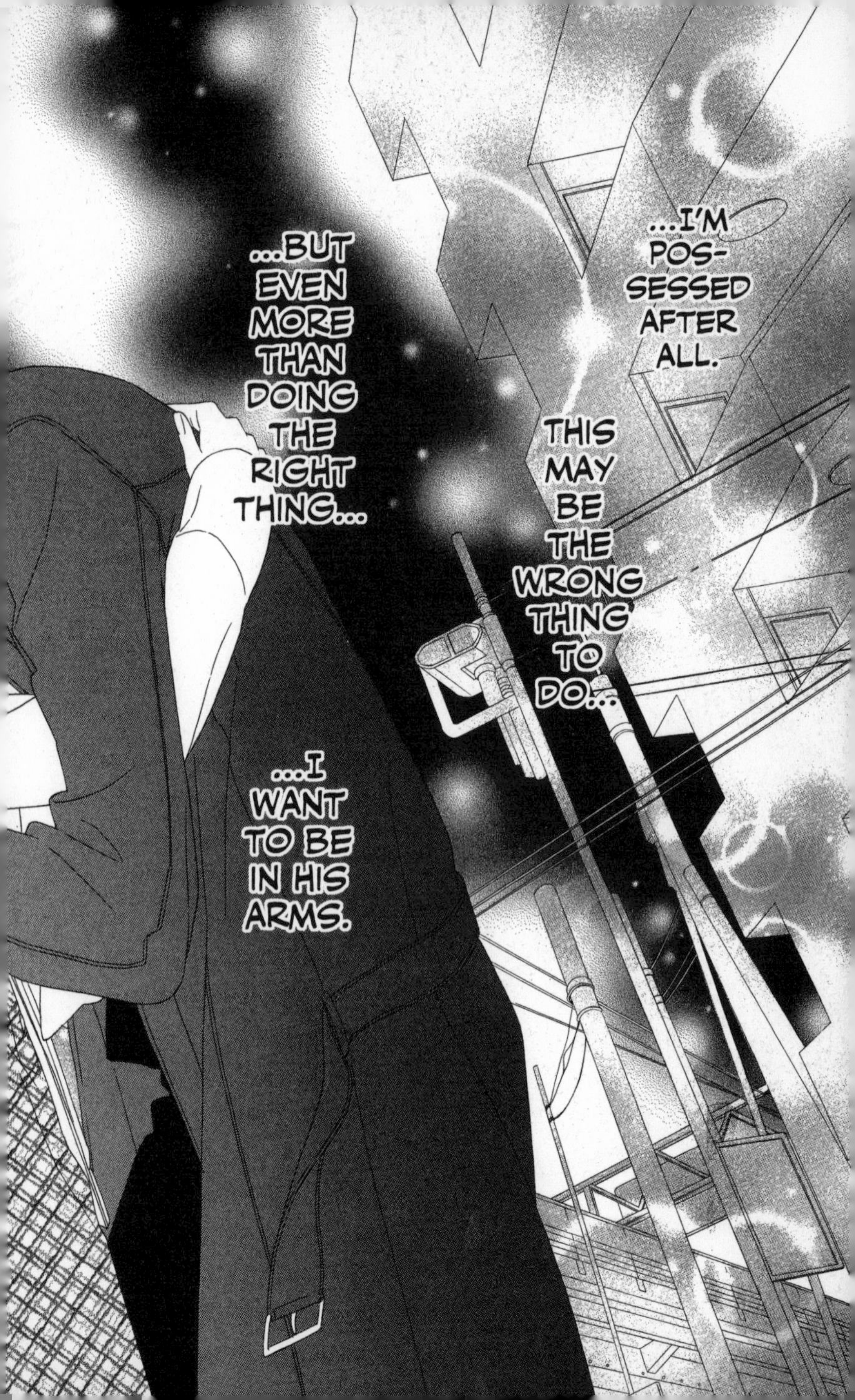
...I'M POS-SESSED AFTER ALL.
THIS MAY BE THE WRONG THING TO DO...
...BUT EVEN MORE THAN DOING THE RIGHT THING...
...I WANT TO BE IN HIS ARMS.

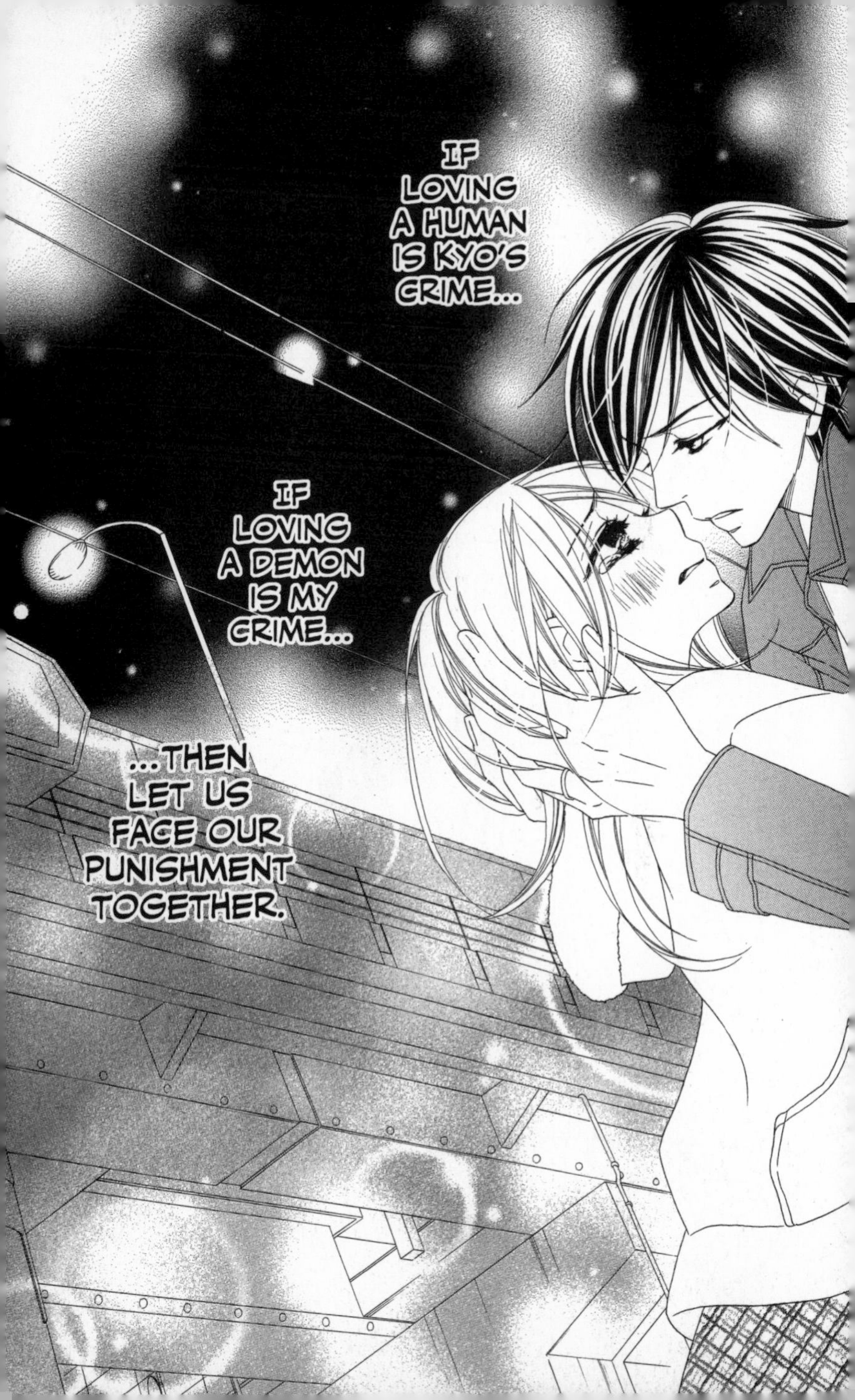
IF LOVING A HUMAN IS KYO'S CRIME...
IF LOVING A DEMON IS MY CRIME...
...THEN LET US FACE OUR PUNISHMENT TOGETHER.

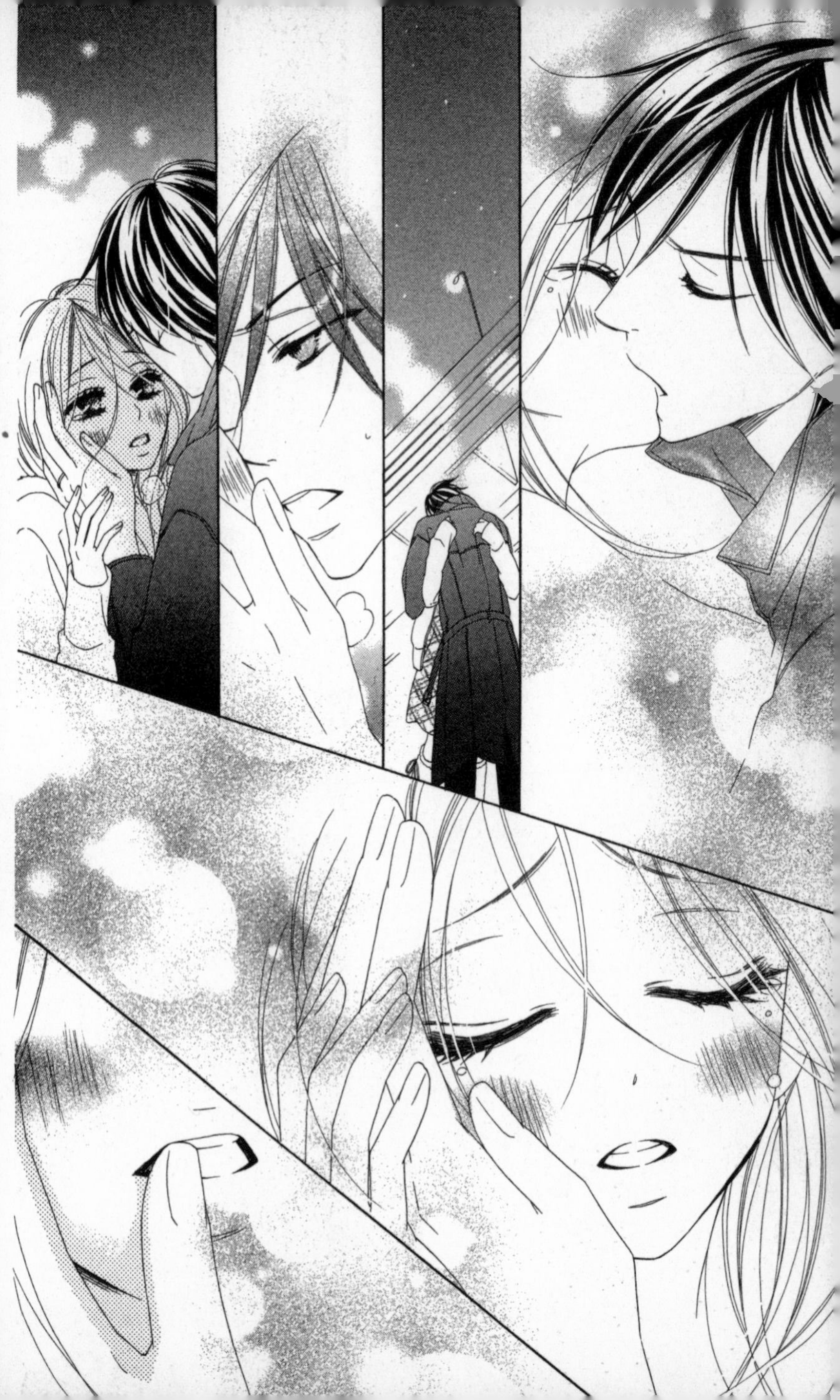

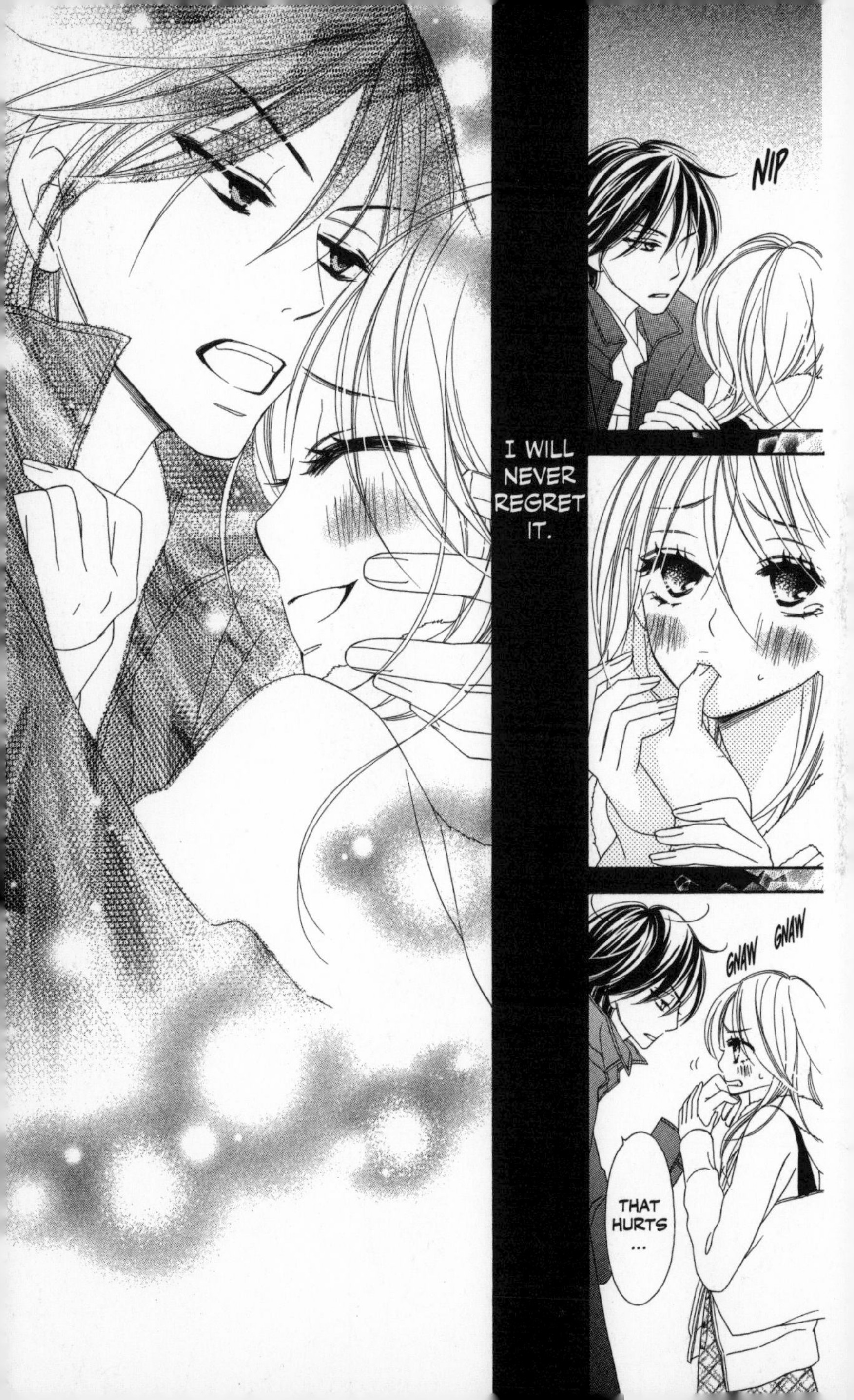
NIP
GNAW GNAW
THAT HURTS ...
I WILL NEVER REGRET IT.

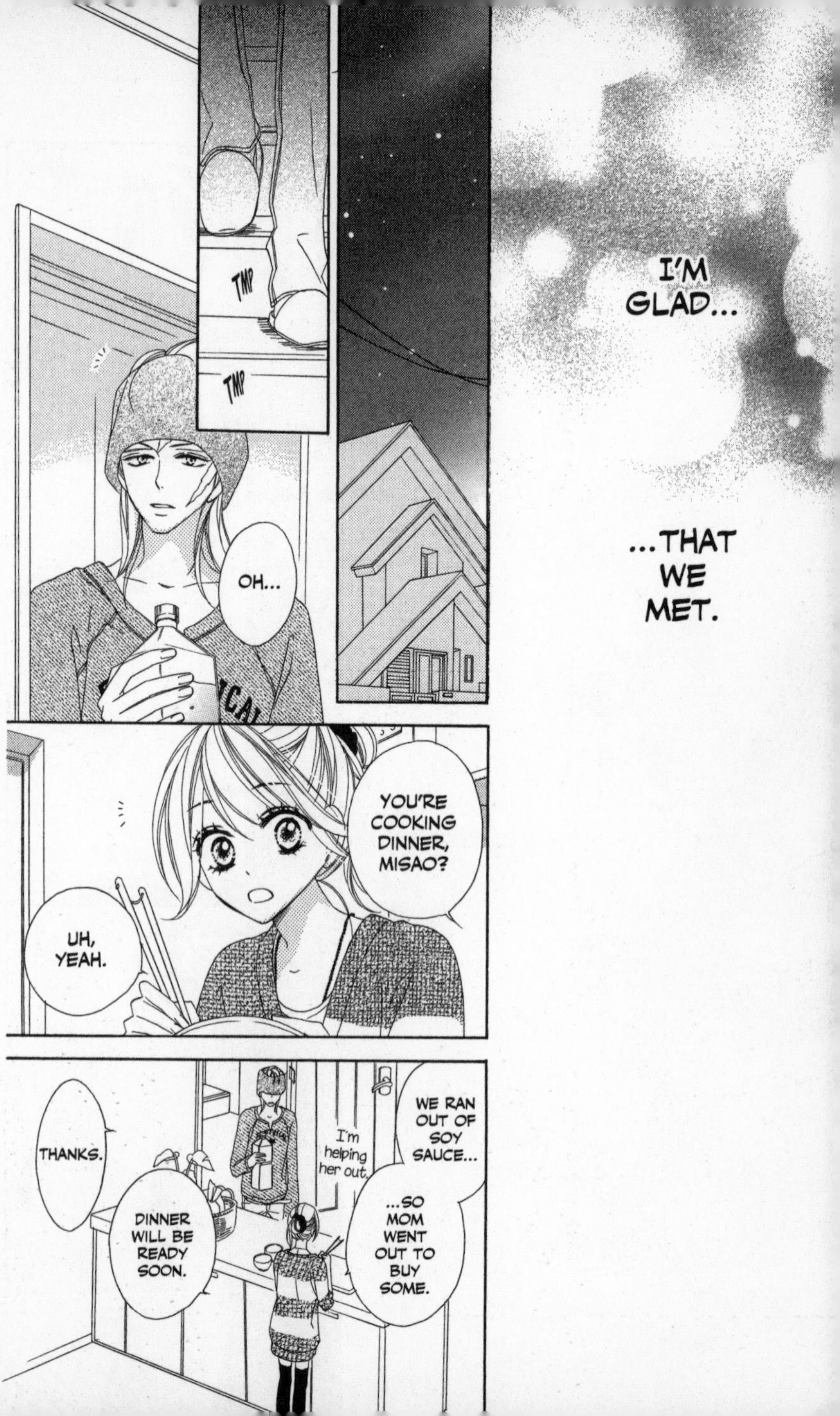
I'M GLAD...
...THAT WE MET.
TMP
TMP
OH...
YOU'RE COOKING DINNER, MISAO?
UH, YEAH.
WE RAN OUT OF SOY SAUCE...
...SO MOM WENT OUT TO BUY SOME.
I'm helping her out.
DINNER WILL BE READY SOON.
THANKS.

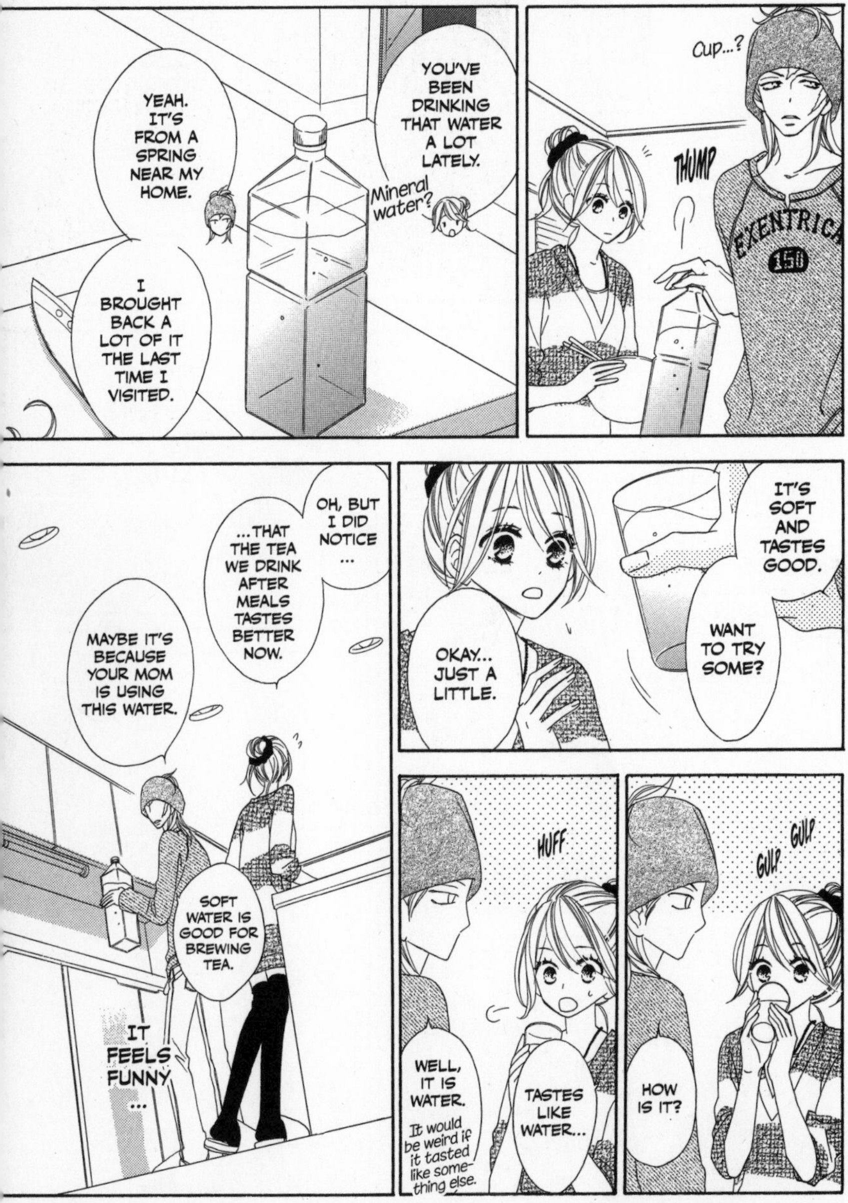
Cup...?
THUMP
YOU'VE BEEN DRINKING THAT WATER A LOT LATELY.
Mineral water?
YEAH. IT'S FROM A SPRING NEAR MY HOME.
I BROUGHT BACK A LOT OF IT THE LAST TIME I VISITED.
IT'S SOFT AND TASTES GOOD.
WANT TO TRY SOME?
OKAY... JUST A LITTLE.
GULP GULP
HOW IS IT?
HUFF
TASTES LIKE WATER...
WELL, IT IS WATER.
It would be weird if it tasted like something else.
OH, BUT I DID NOTICE...
...THAT THE TEA WE DRINK AFTER MEALS TASTES BETTER NOW.
MAYBE IT'S BECAUSE YOUR MOM IS USING THIS WATER.
SOFT WATER IS GOOD FOR BREWING TEA.
IT FEELS FUNNY...

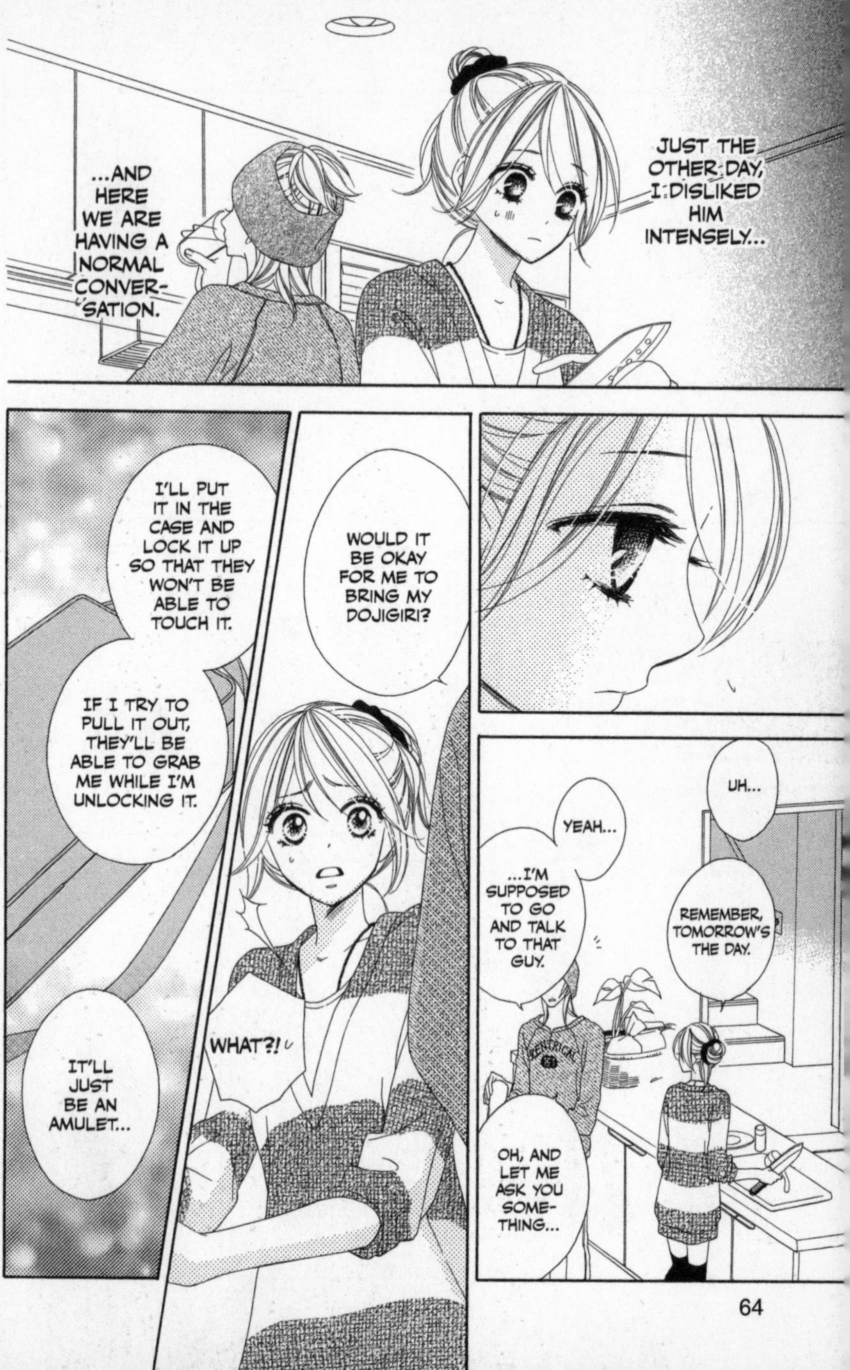
JUST THE OTHER DAY, I DISLIKED HIM INTENSELY...
...AND HERE WE ARE HAVING A NORMAL CONVER-SATION.
UH...
REMEMBER, TOMORROW'S THE DAY.
YEAH...
...I'M SUPPOSED TO GO AND TALK TO THAT GUY.
OH, AND LET ME ASK YOU SOME-THING...
WOULD IT BE OKAY FOR ME TO BRING MY DOJIGIRI?
WHAT?!
I'LL PUT IT IN THE CASE AND LOCK IT UP SO THAT THEY WON'T BE ABLE TO TOUCH IT.
IF I TRY TO PULL IT OUT, THEY'LL BE ABLE TO GRAB ME WHILE I'M UNLOCKING IT.
IT'LL JUST BE AN AMULET...

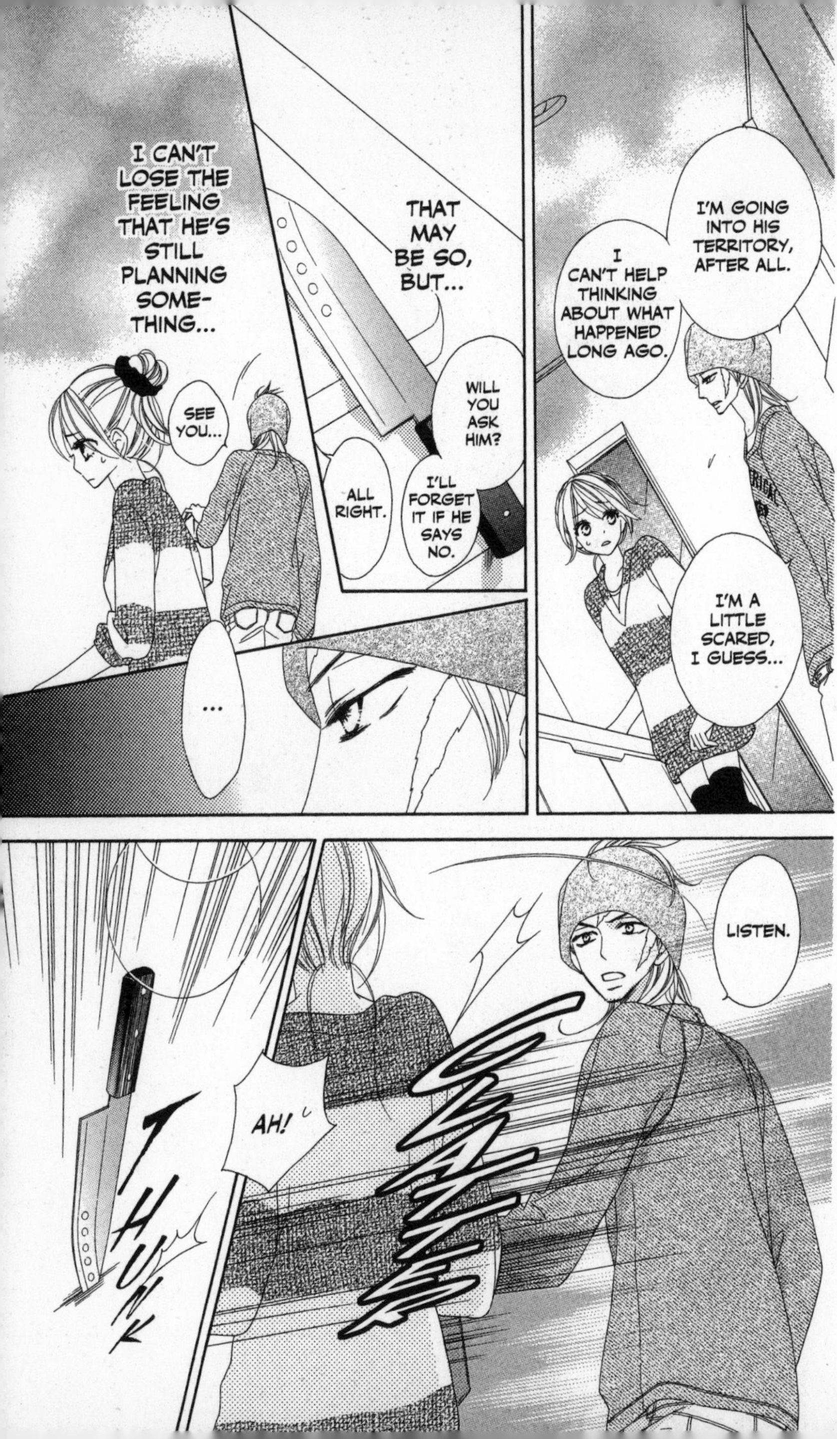
I'M GOING INTO HIS TERRITORY, AFTER ALL.
I CAN'T HELP THINKING ABOUT WHAT HAPPENED LONG AGO.
I'M A LITTLE SCARED, I GUESS...
THAT MAY BE SO, BUT...
WILL YOU ASK HIM?
I'LL FORGET IT IF HE SAYS NO.
ALL RIGHT.
I CAN'T LOSE THE FEELING THAT HE'S STILL PLANNING SOME-THING...
SEE YOU...
...
LISTEN.
AH!
THUNK

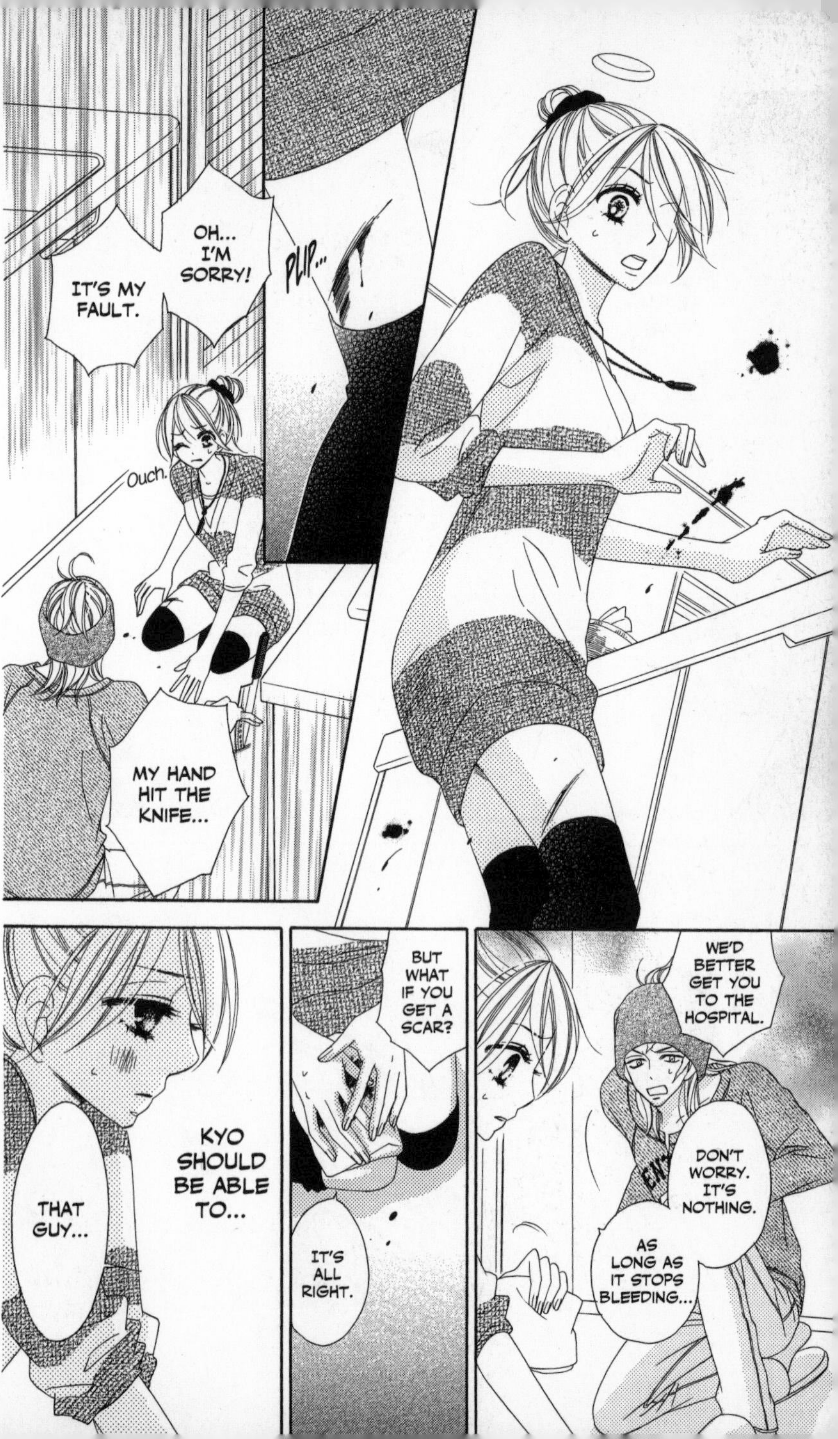
PLIP...
OH... I'M SORRY!
IT'S MY FAULT.
Ouch.
MY HAND HIT THE KNIFE...
WE'D BETTER GET YOU TO THE HOSPITAL.
DON'T WORRY. IT'S NOTHING.
AS LONG AS IT STOPS BLEEDING...
BUT WHAT IF YOU GET A SCAR?
IT'S ALL RIGHT.
KYO SHOULD BE ABLE TO...
THAT GUY...

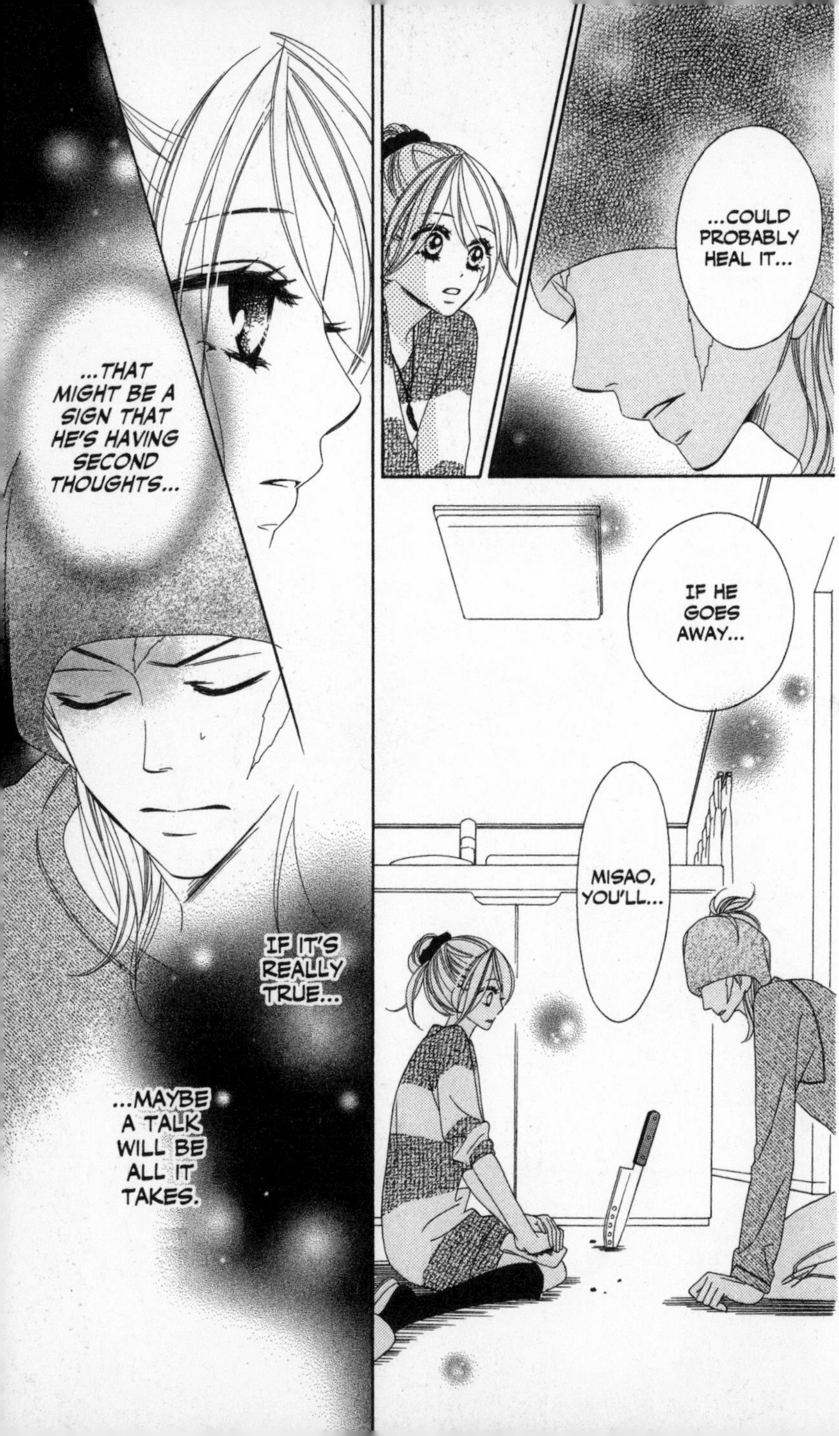
...COULD PROBABLY HEAL IT...
IF HE GOES AWAY...
MISAO, YOU'LL...
...THAT MIGHT BE A SIGN THAT HE'S HAVING SECOND THOUGHTS...
IF IT'S REALLY TRUE...
...MAYBE A TALK WILL BE ALL IT TAKES.

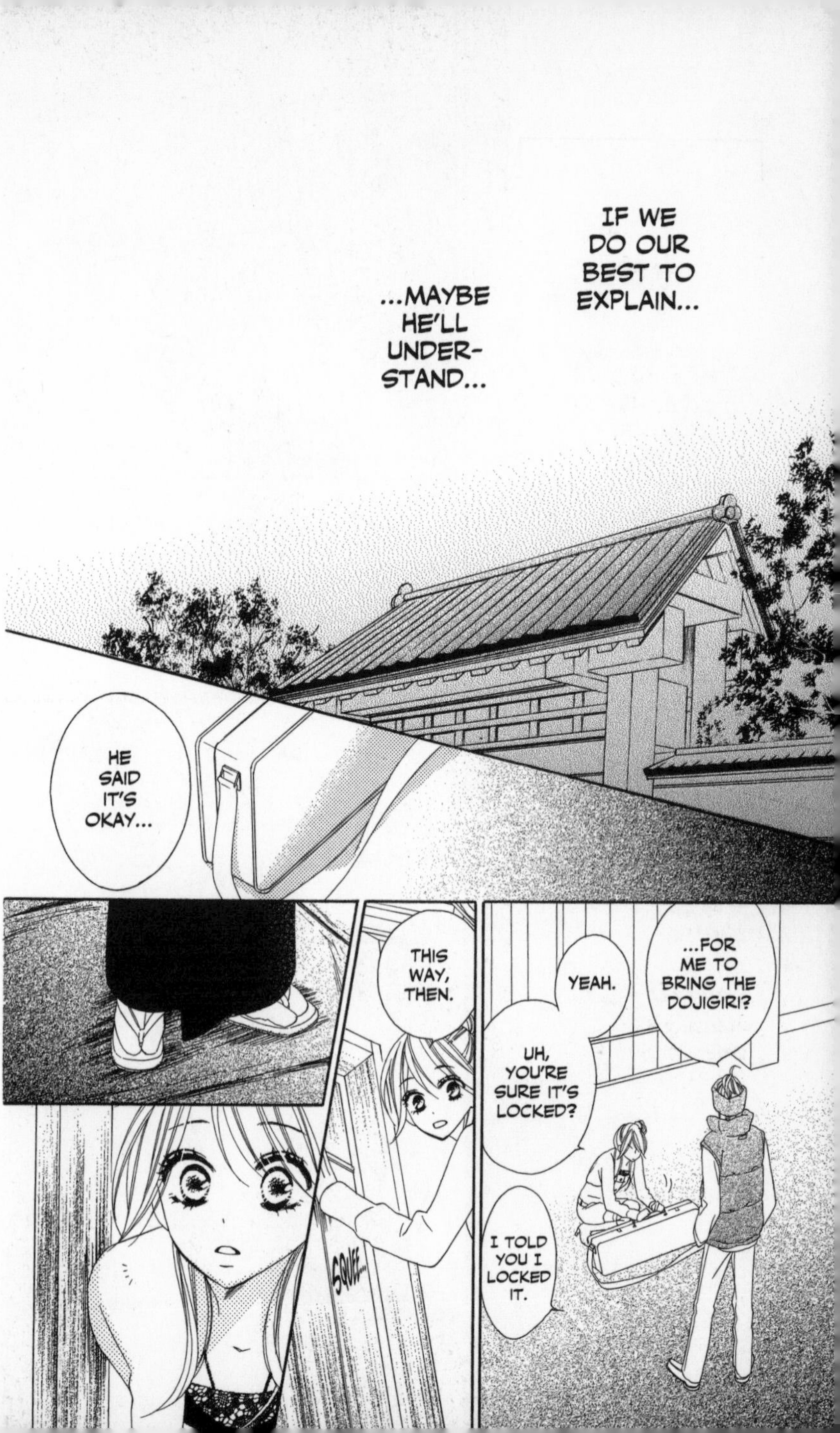
IF WE DO OUR BEST TO EXPLAIN...
...MAYBE HE'LL UNDER-STAND...
HE SAID IT'S OKAY...
...FOR ME TO BRING THE DOJIGIRI?
YEAH.
UH, YOU'RE SURE IT'S LOCKED?
I TOLD YOU I LOCKED IT.
THIS WAY, THEN.
SQUEE...

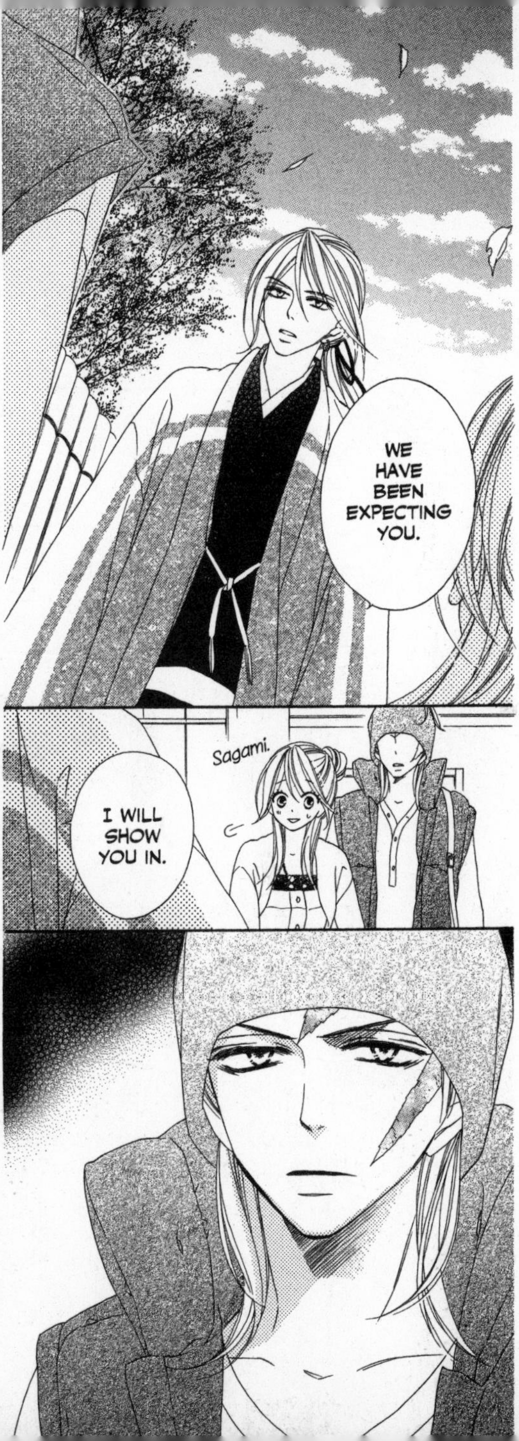
WE HAVE BEEN EXPECTING YOU.
Sagami.
I WILL SHOW YOU IN.

I'm sometimes told that there is no address in my books where you can send your letters to me, so here it is:

Kanoko Sakurakoji
c/o Shojo Beat
P.O. Box 77010
San Francisco,
CA 94107

You can also send me email via the Shojo Beat website: http://shojobeat.com or my own website: http://sakurakoujien.lolipop.jp

Your heartwarming messages have been nourishment for me...! ✧

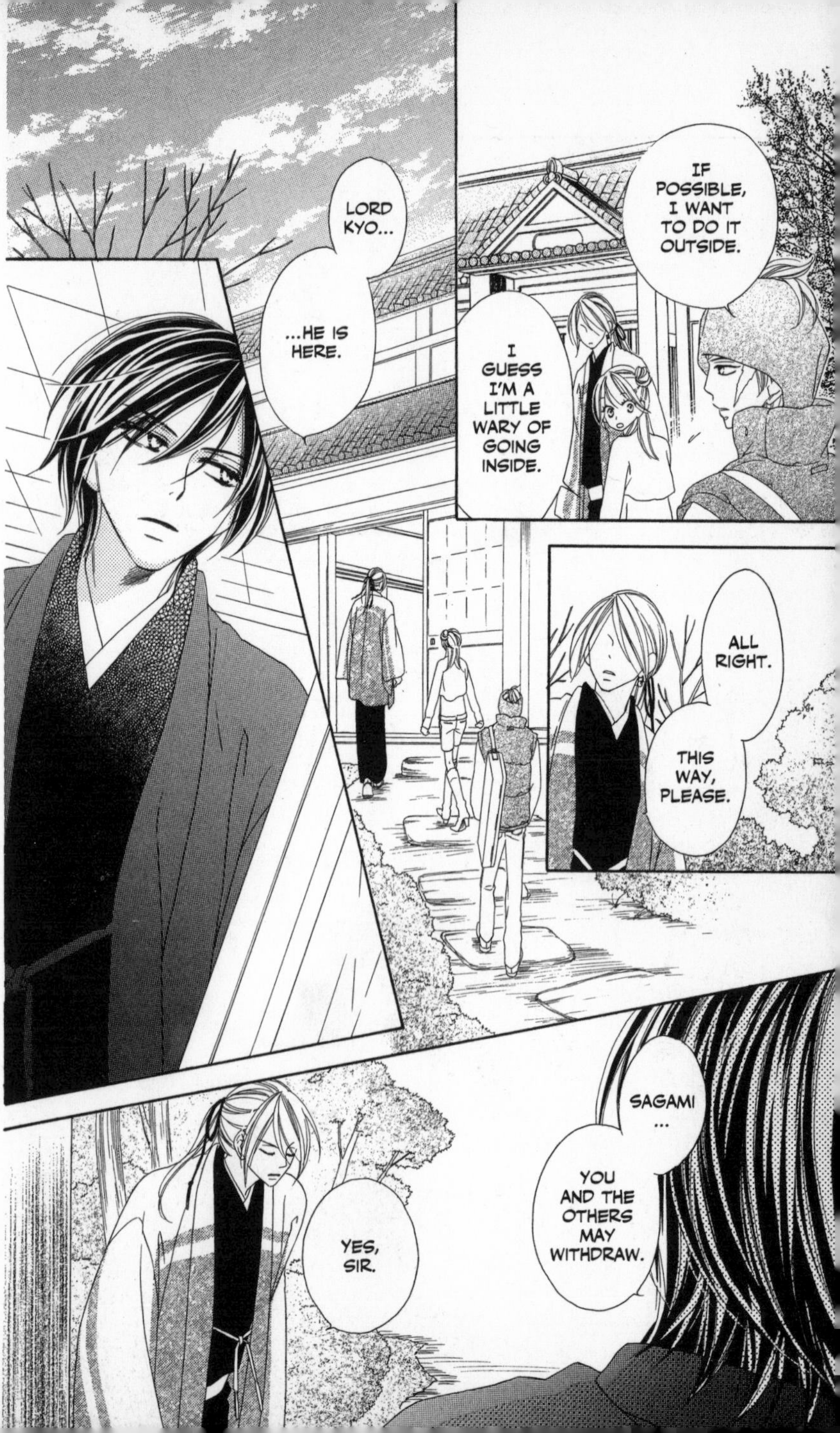
IF POSSIBLE, I WANT TO DO IT OUTSIDE.
I GUESS I'M A LITTLE WARY OF GOING INSIDE.
ALL RIGHT.
THIS WAY, PLEASE.
LORD KYO...
...HE IS HERE.
SAGAMI ...
YOU AND THE OTHERS MAY WITHDRAW.
YES, SIR.

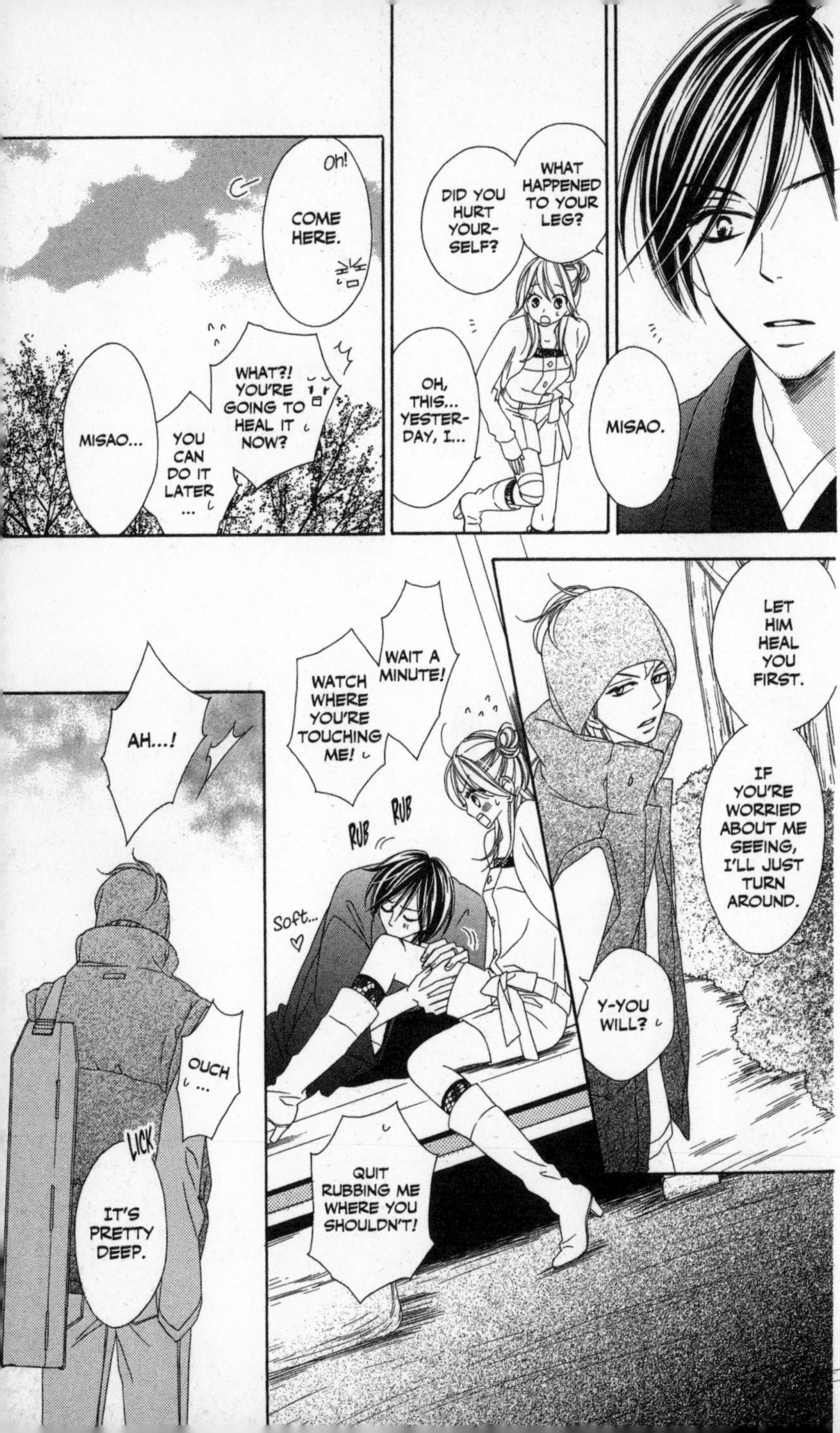
MISAO.
WHAT HAPPENED TO YOUR LEG?
DID YOU HURT YOURSELF?
OH, THIS... YESTERDAY, I...
Oh!
COME HERE.
WHAT?! YOU'RE GOING TO HEAL IT NOW?
YOU CAN DO IT LATER...
MISAO...
LET HIM HEAL YOU FIRST.
IF YOU'RE WORRIED ABOUT ME SEEING, I'LL JUST TURN AROUND.
Y-YOU WILL?
WAIT A MINUTE!
WATCH WHERE YOU'RE TOUCHING ME!
RUB
RUB
Soft...
QUIT RUBBING ME WHERE YOU SHOULDN'T!
AH...!
OUCH...
LICK
IT'S PRETTY DEEP.

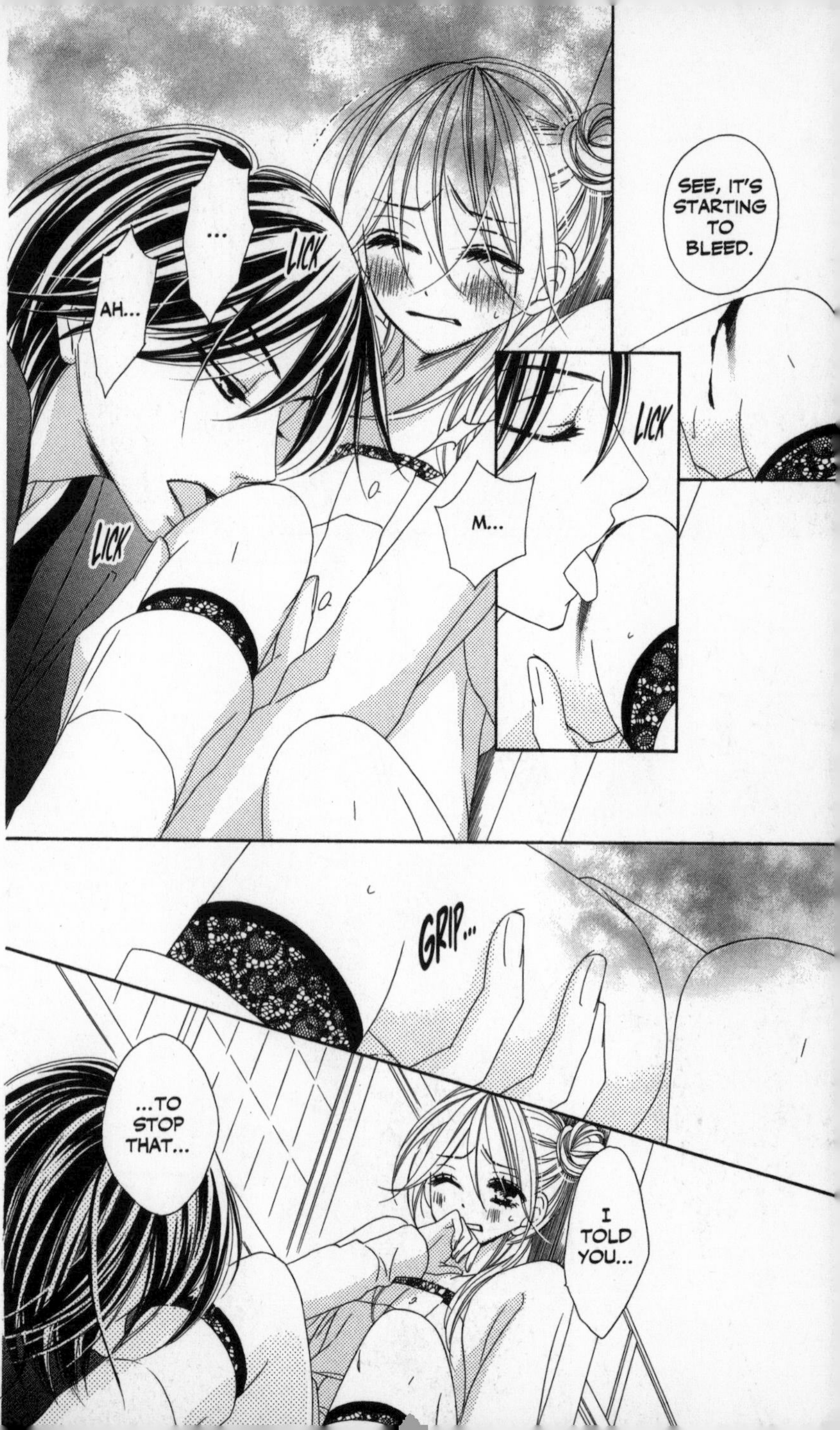
SEE, IT'S STARTING TO BLEED.
LICK
M...
...
LICK
AH...
LICK
GRIP...
I TOLD YOU...
...TO STOP THAT...

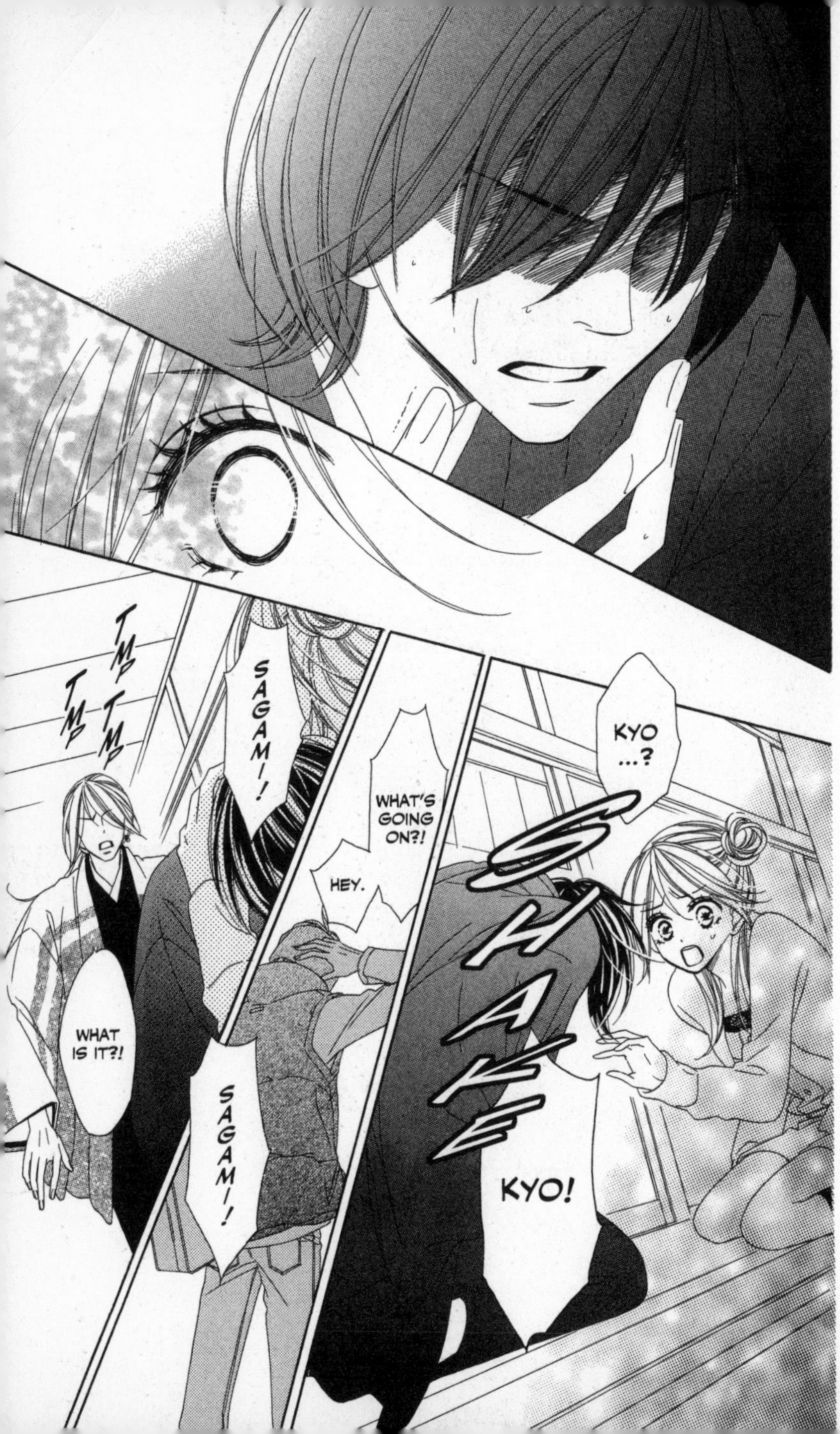
KYO ...?
SHAKE
KYO!
WHAT'S GOING ON?!
HEY.
SAGAMI!
TMP TMP TMP
WHAT IS IT?!
SAGAMI!

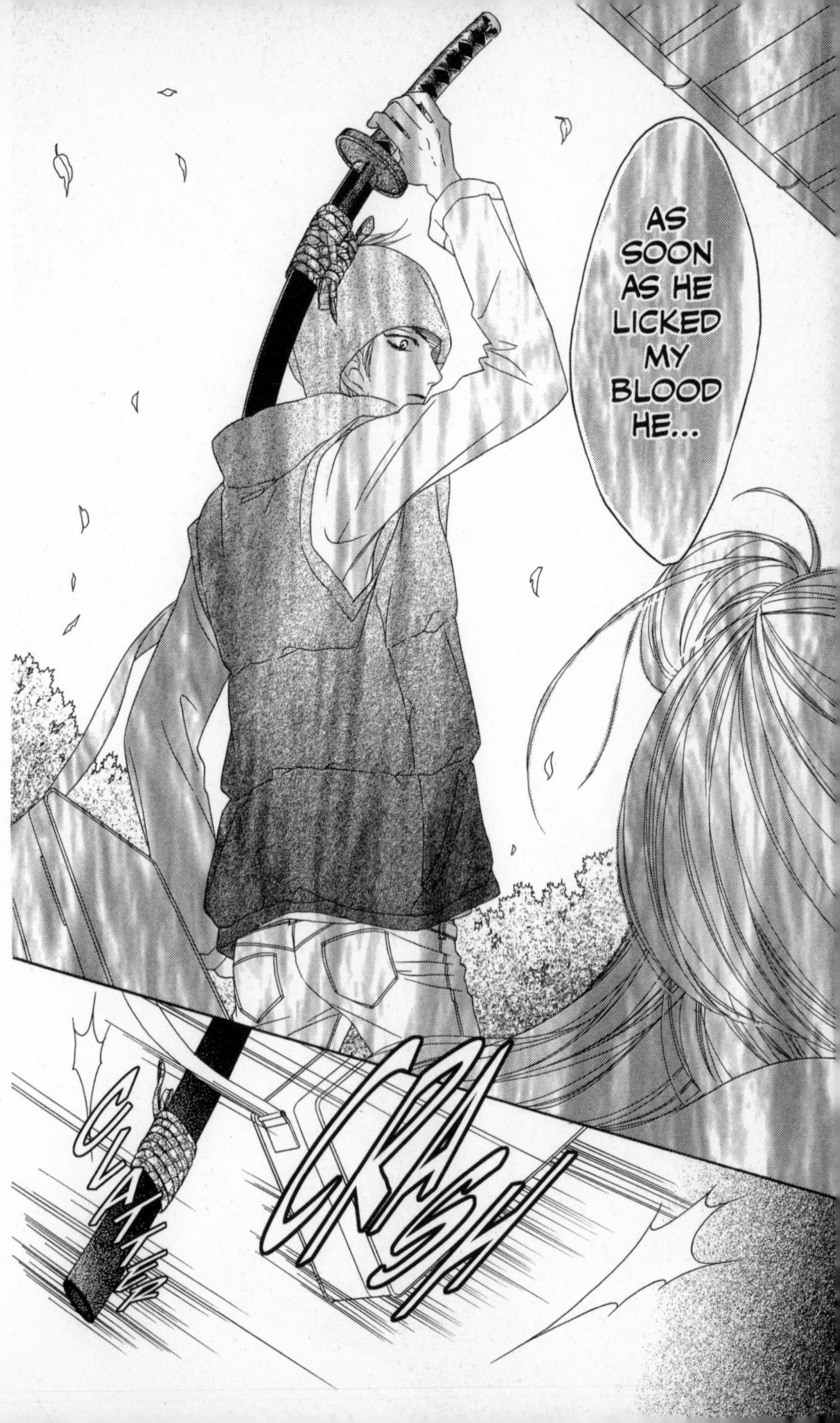
AS SOON AS HE LICKED MY BLOOD HE...
CRASH

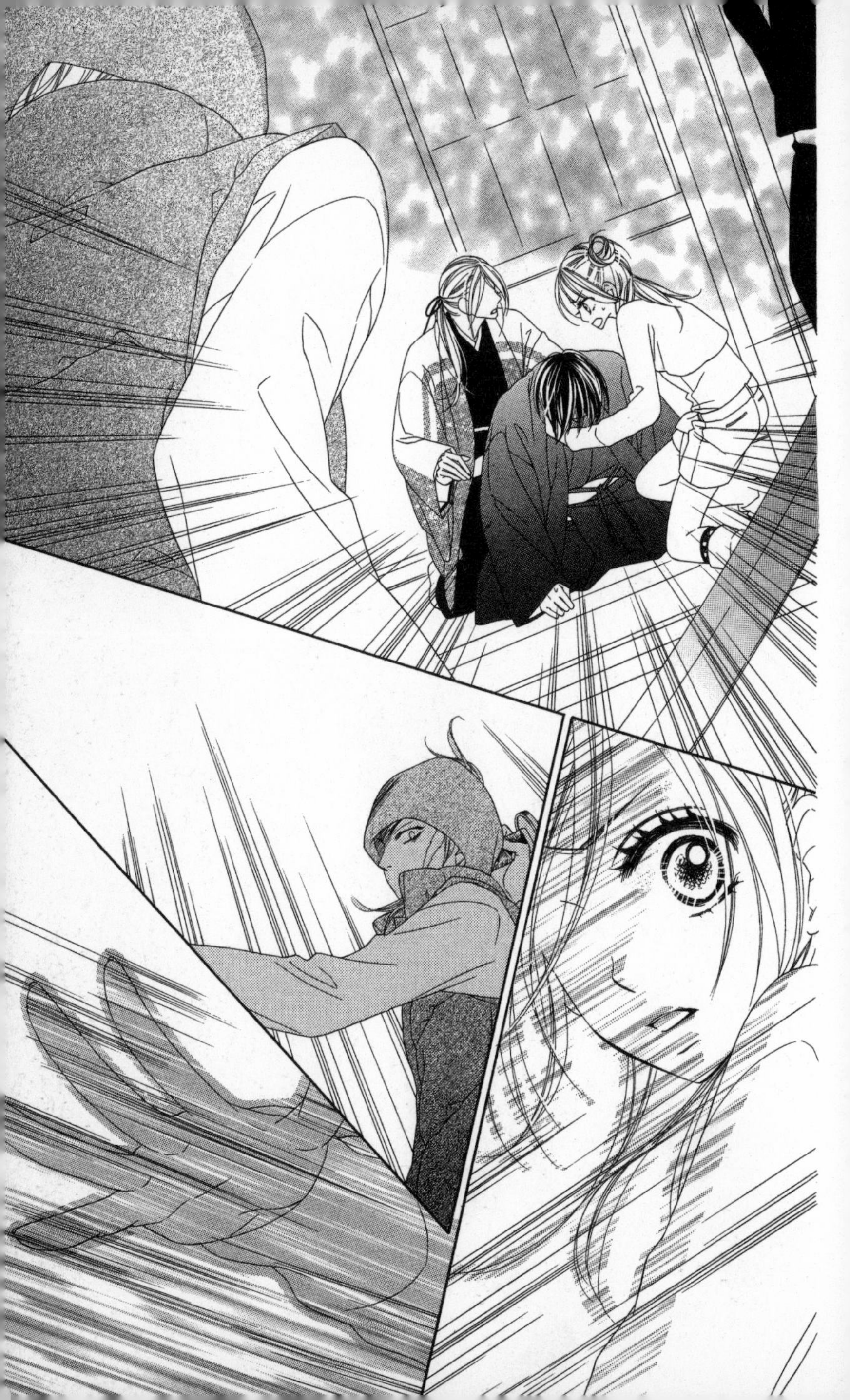

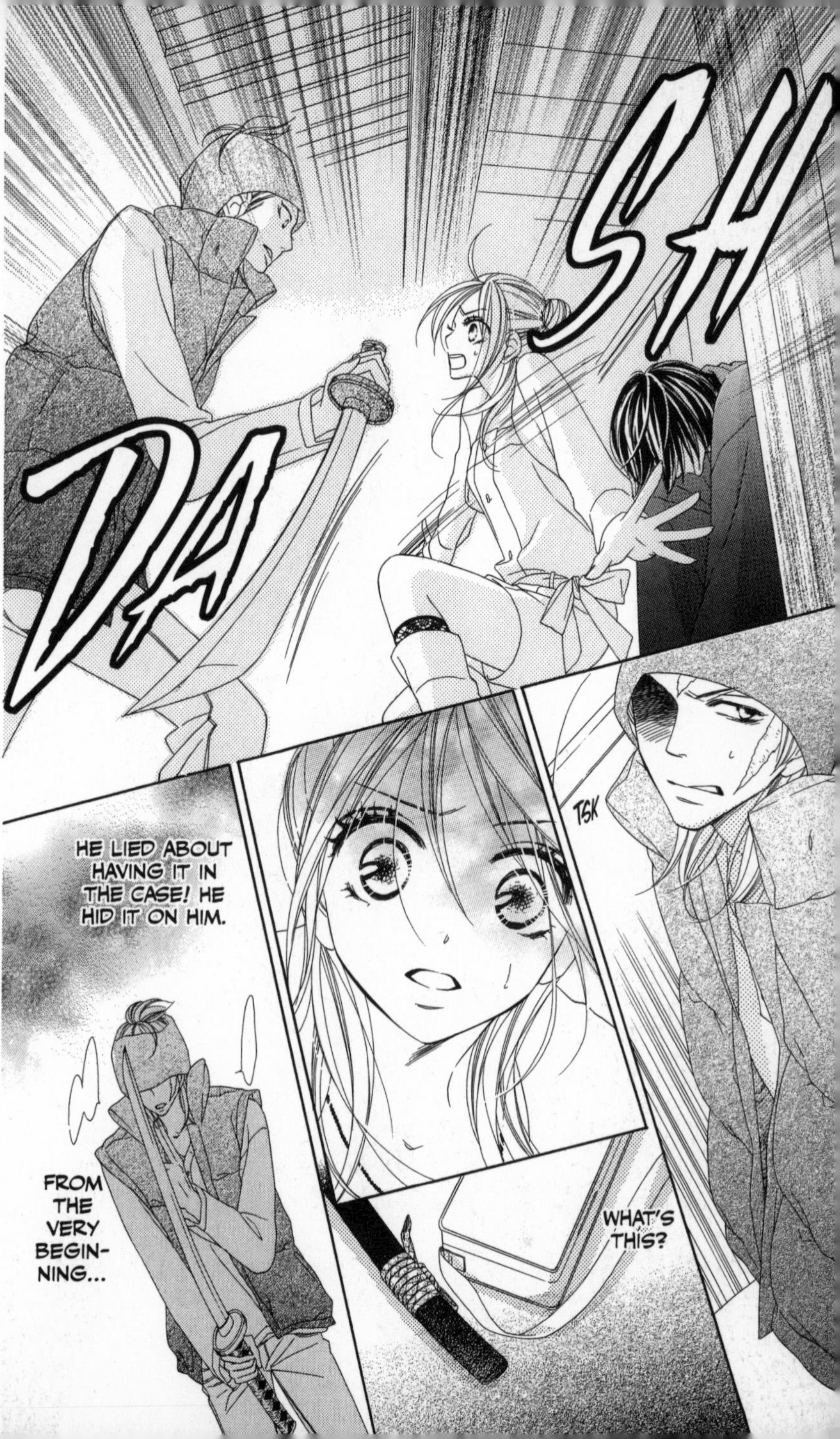
DA SH
TSK
WHAT'S THIS?
HE LIED ABOUT HAVING IT IN THE CASE! HE HID IT ON HIM.
FROM THE VERY BEGIN-NING...

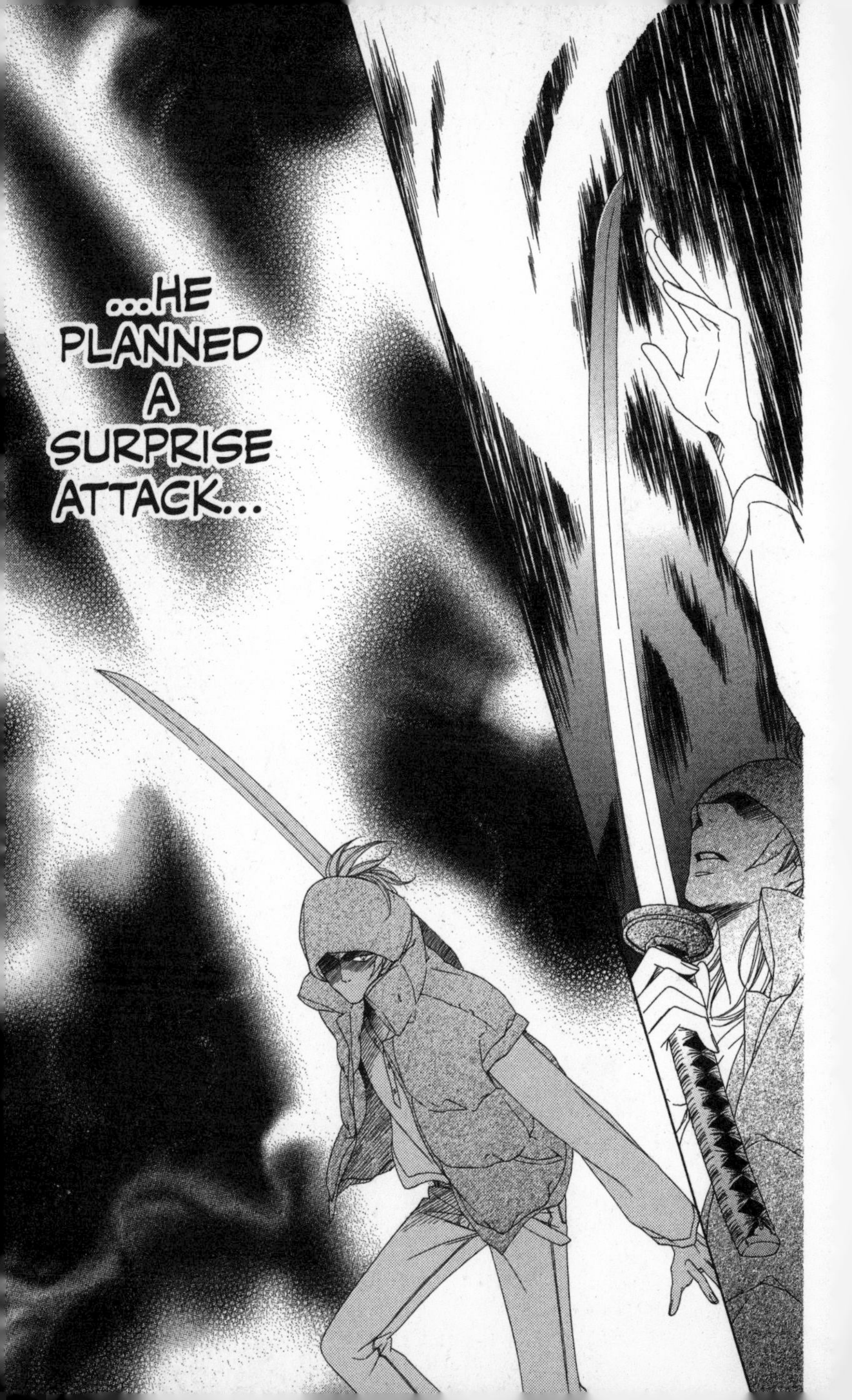
...HE PLANNED A SURPRISE ATTACK...

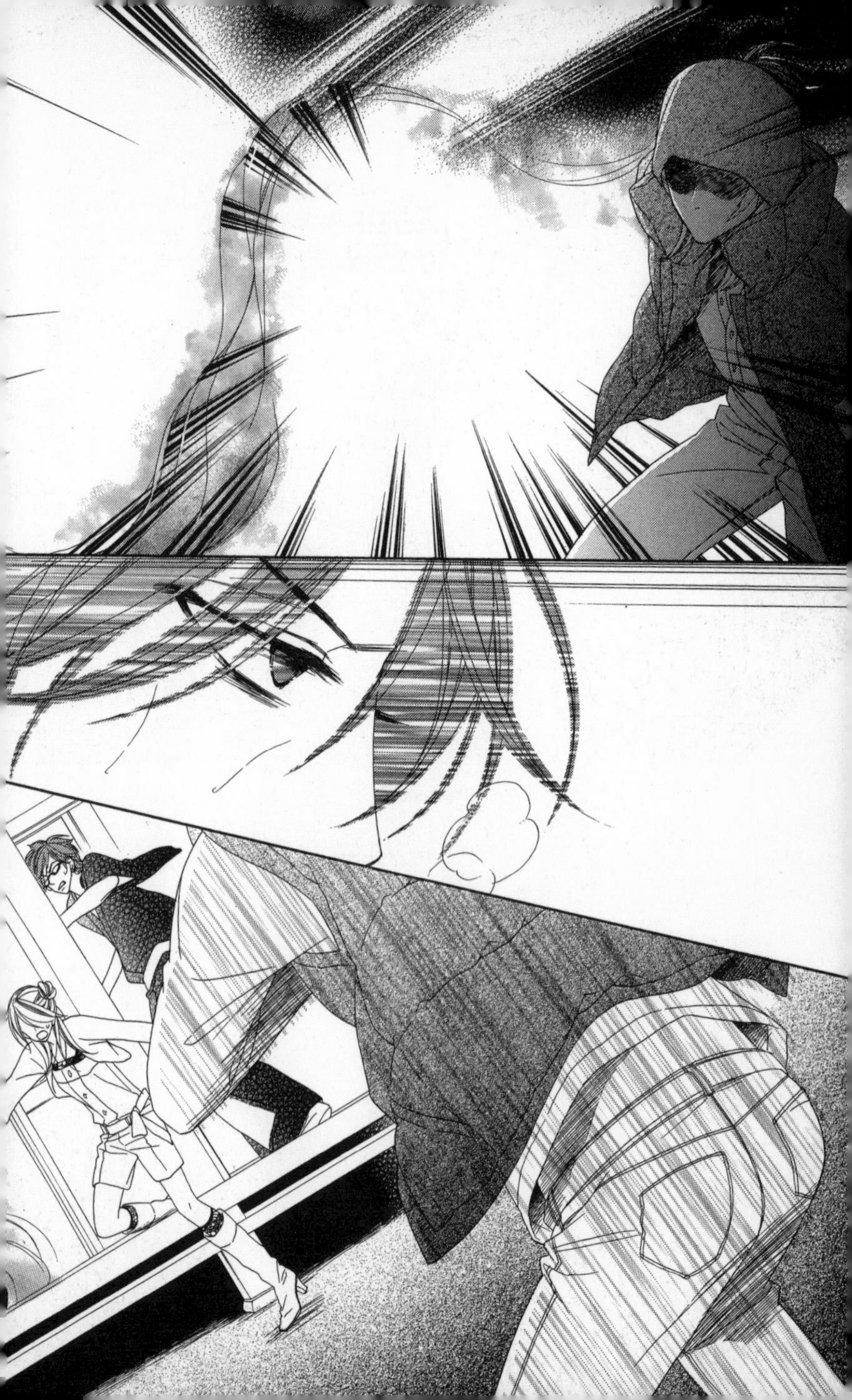

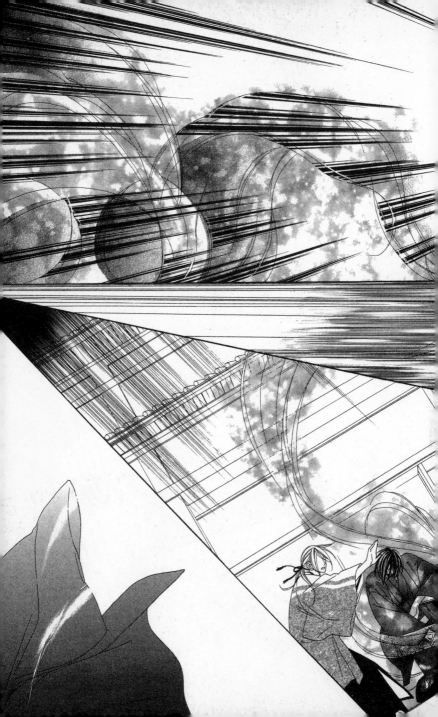

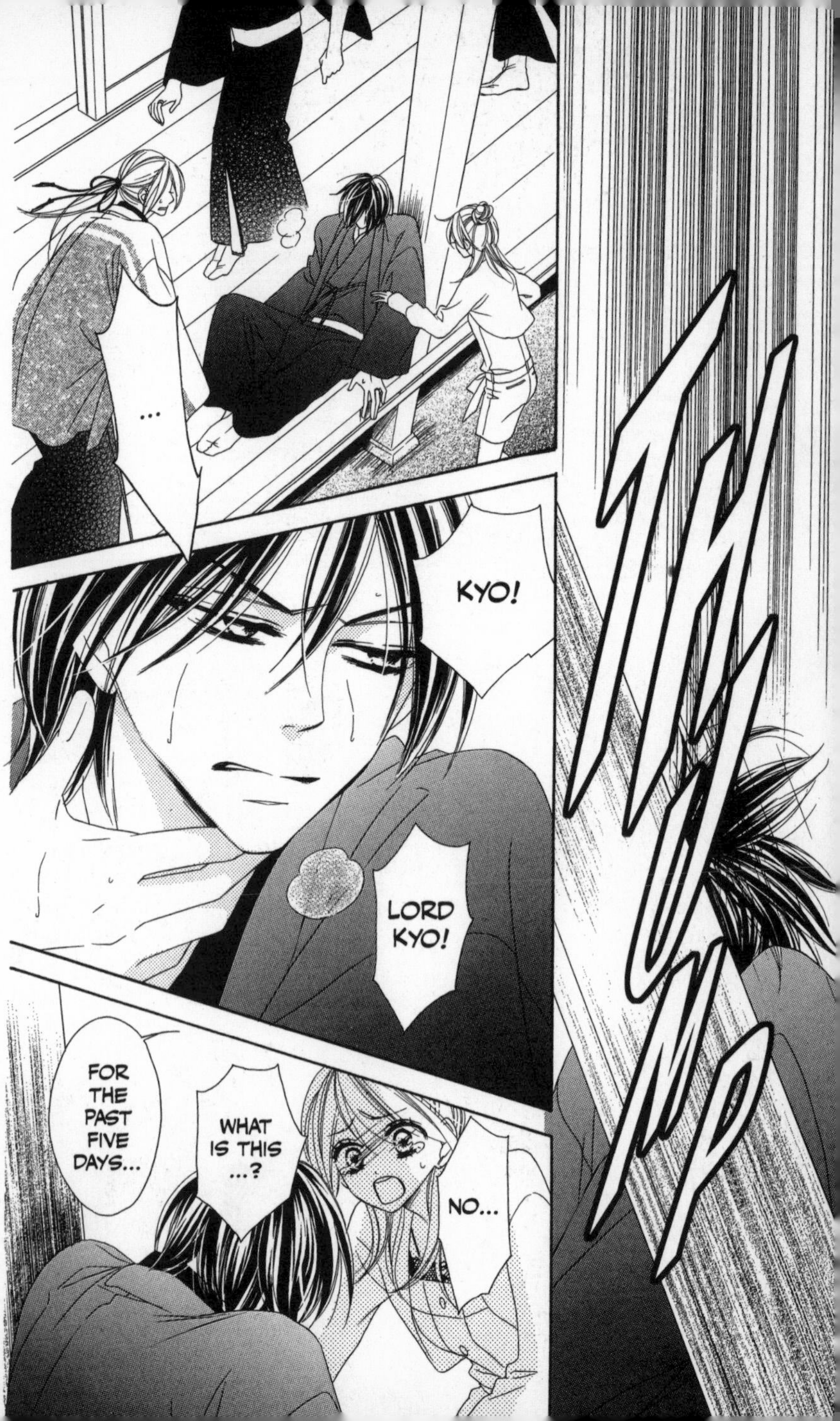
...
KYO!
LORD KYO!
NO...
WHAT IS THIS ...?
FOR THE PAST FIVE DAYS...

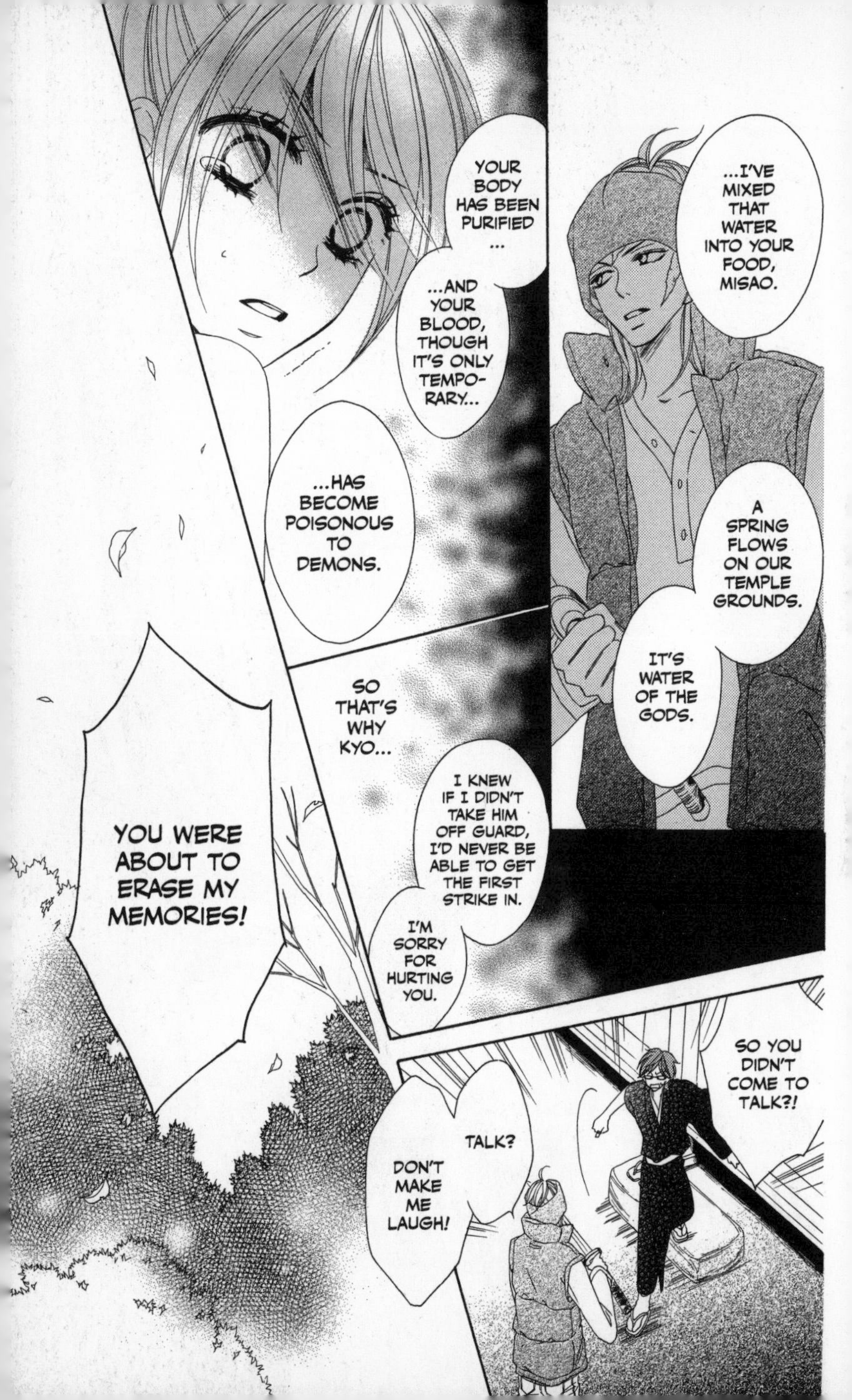
...I'VE MIXED THAT WATER INTO YOUR FOOD, MISAO.
A SPRING FLOWS ON OUR TEMPLE GROUNDS.
IT'S WATER OF THE GODS.
YOUR BODY HAS BEEN PURIFIED ...
...AND YOUR BLOOD, THOUGH IT'S ONLY TEMPO-RARY...
...HAS BECOME POISONOUS TO DEMONS.
SO THAT'S WHY KYO...
I KNEW IF I DIDN'T TAKE HIM OFF GUARD, I'D NEVER BE ABLE TO GET THE FIRST STRIKE IN.
I'M SORRY FOR HURTING YOU.
YOU WERE ABOUT TO ERASE MY MEMORIES!
SO YOU DIDN'T COME TO TALK?!
TALK?
DON'T MAKE ME LAUGH!

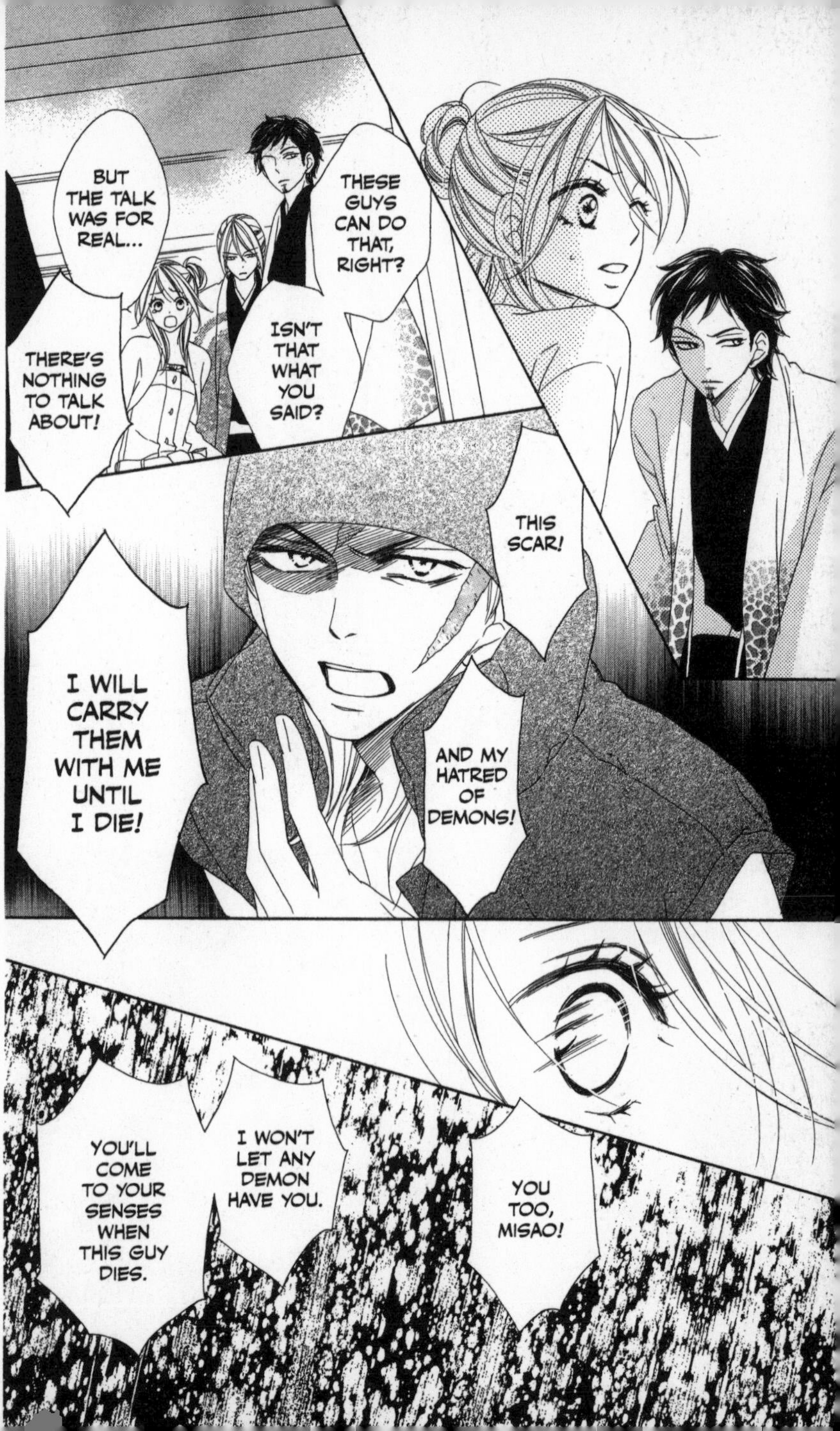
THESE GUYS CAN DO THAT, RIGHT?
ISN'T THAT WHAT YOU SAID?
BUT THE TALK WAS FOR REAL...
THERE'S NOTHING TO TALK ABOUT!
THIS SCAR!
AND MY HATRED OF DEMONS!
I WILL CARRY THEM WITH ME UNTIL I DIE!
YOU TOO, MISAO!
I WON'T LET ANY DEMON HAVE YOU.
YOU'LL COME TO YOUR SENSES WHEN THIS GUY DIES.

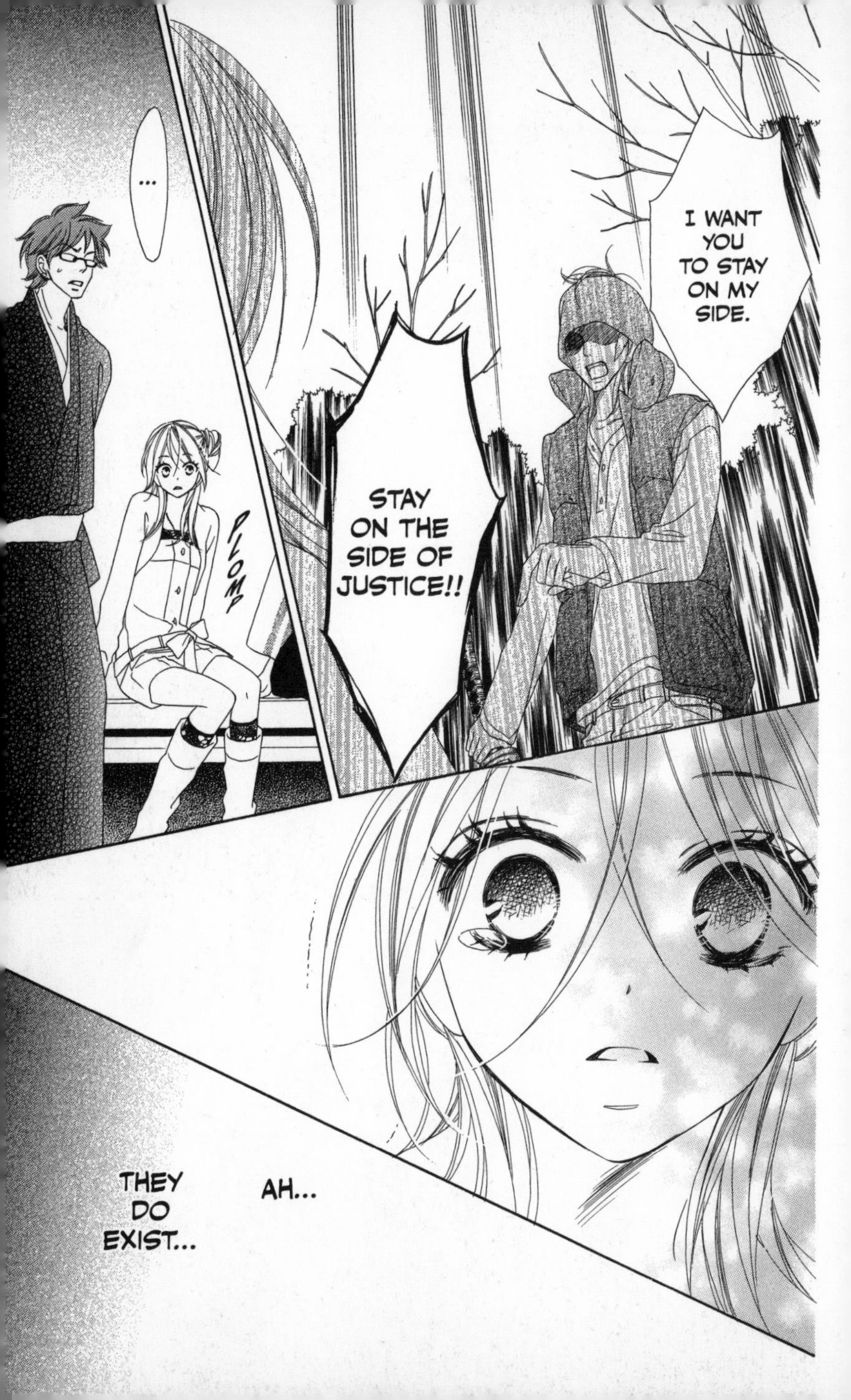
I WANT YOU TO STAY ON MY SIDE.
STAY ON THE SIDE OF JUSTICE!!
...
PLOMP
AH...
THEY DO EXIST...

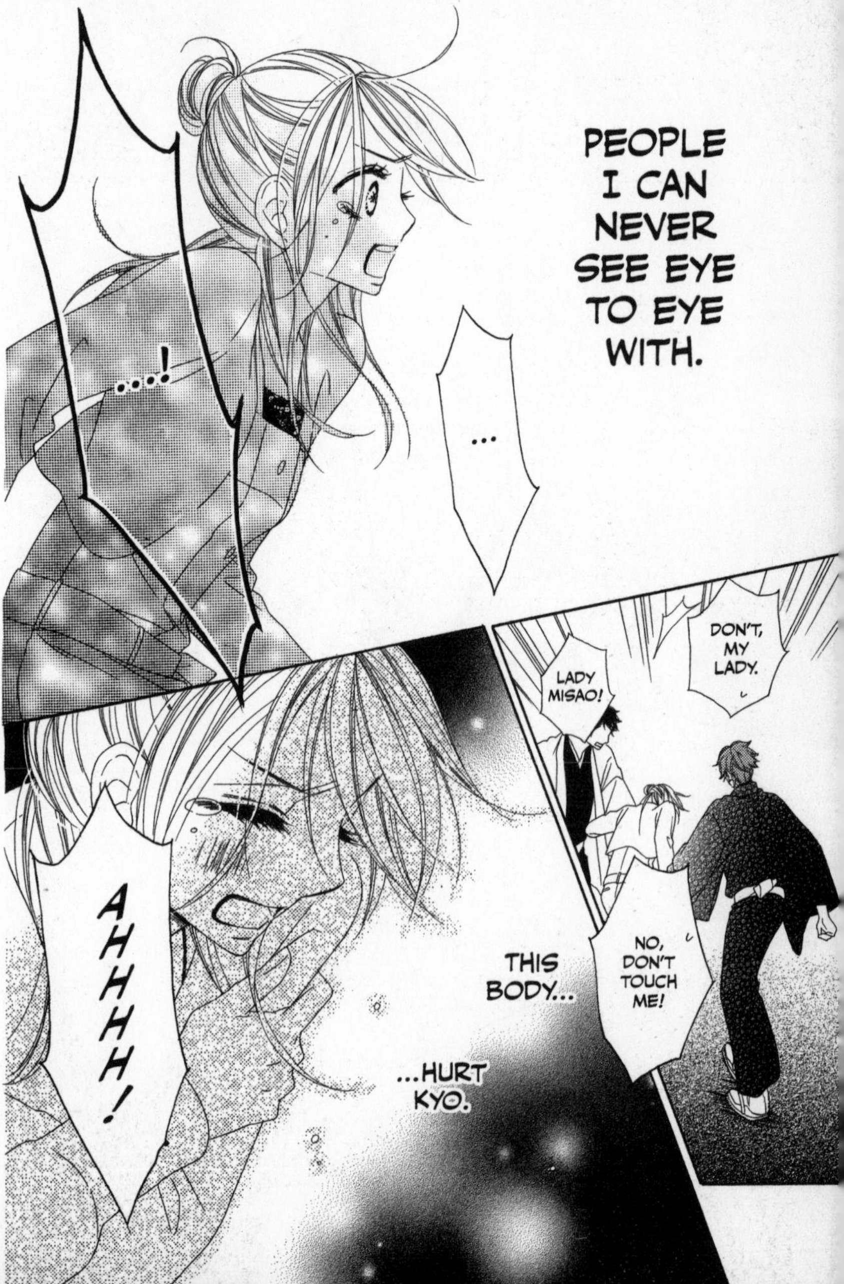
PEOPLE I CAN NEVER SEE EYE TO EYE WITH.
...
...!
DON'T, MY LADY.
LADY MISAO!
NO, DON'T TOUCH ME!
THIS BODY...
...HURT KYO.
AHHHHH!

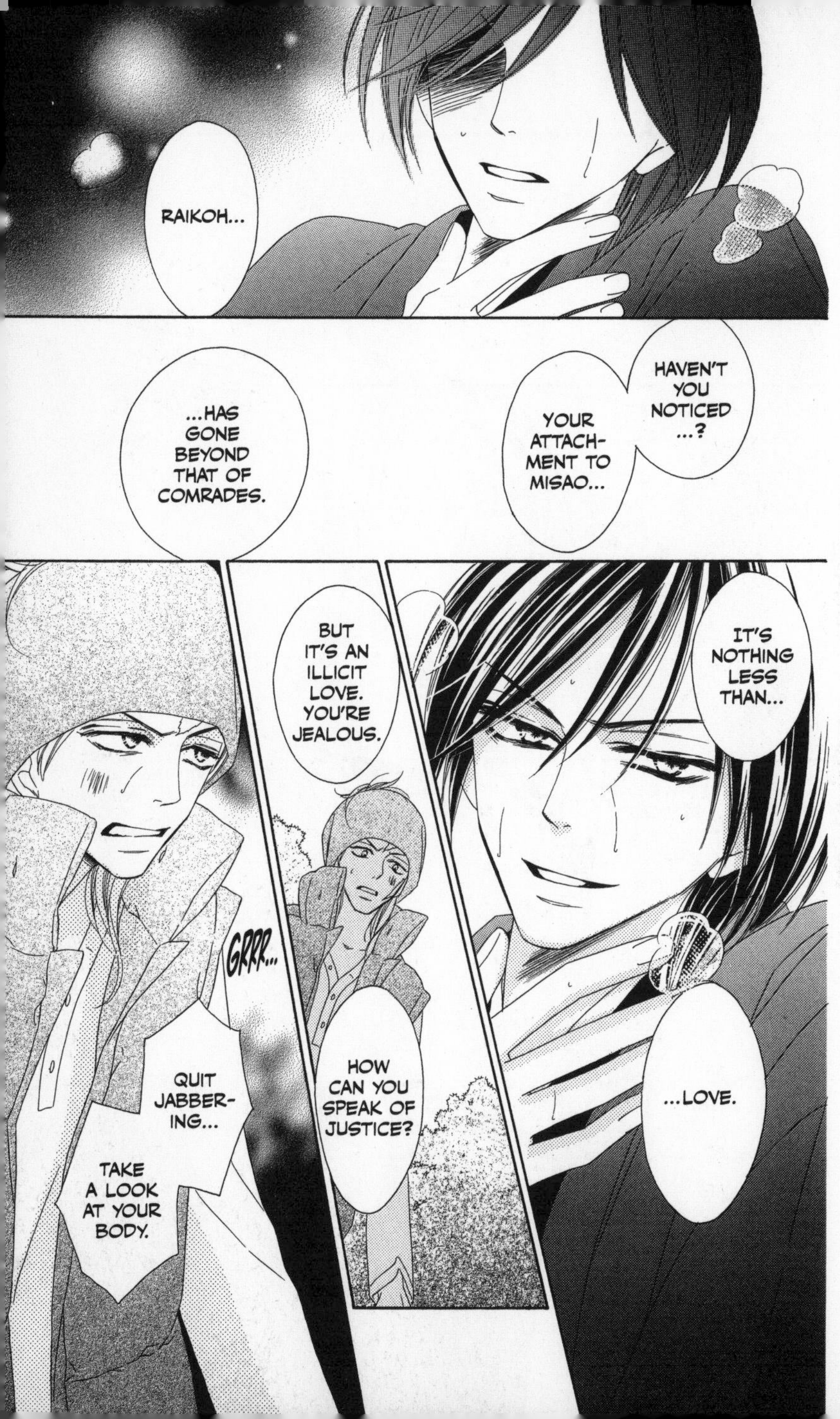
RAIKOH...
HAVEN'T YOU NOTICED...?
YOUR ATTACHMENT TO MISAO...
...HAS GONE BEYOND THAT OF COMRADES.
IT'S NOTHING LESS THAN...
...LOVE.
BUT IT'S AN ILLICIT LOVE. YOU'RE JEALOUS.
HOW CAN YOU SPEAK OF JUSTICE?
GRRR...
QUIT JABBERING...
TAKE A LOOK AT YOUR BODY.

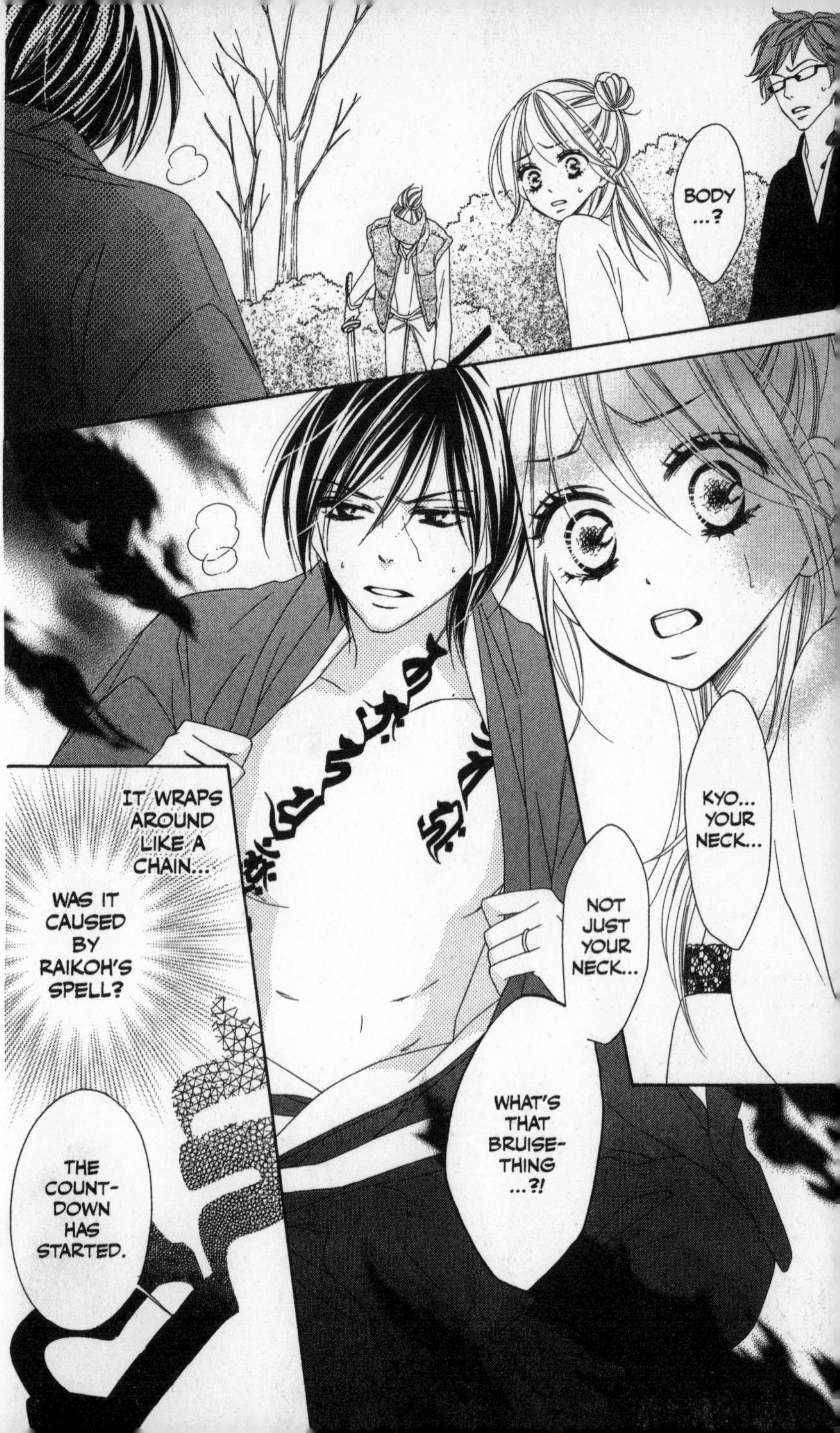
BODY ...?
KYO... YOUR NECK...
NOT JUST YOUR NECK...
WHAT'S THAT BRUISE-THING ...?!
IT WRAPS AROUND LIKE A CHAIN...
WAS IT CAUSED BY RAIKOH'S SPELL?
THE COUNT-DOWN HAS STARTED.

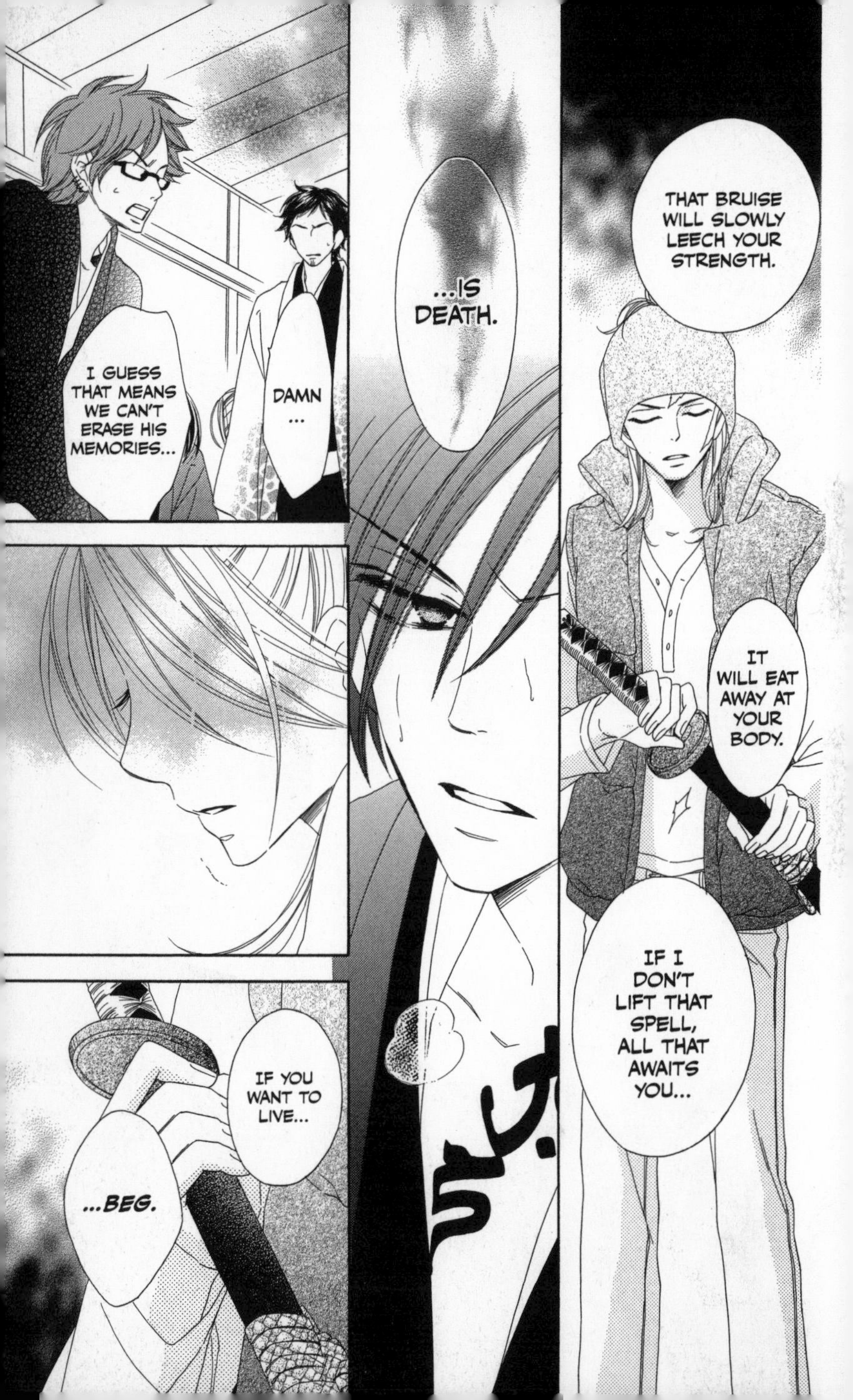
THAT BRUISE WILL SLOWLY LEECH YOUR STRENGTH.
IT WILL EAT AWAY AT YOUR BODY.
IF I DON'T LIFT THAT SPELL, ALL THAT AWAITS YOU...
...IS DEATH.
DAMN ...
I GUESS THAT MEANS WE CAN'T ERASE HIS MEMORIES...
IF YOU WANT TO LIVE...
...BEG.

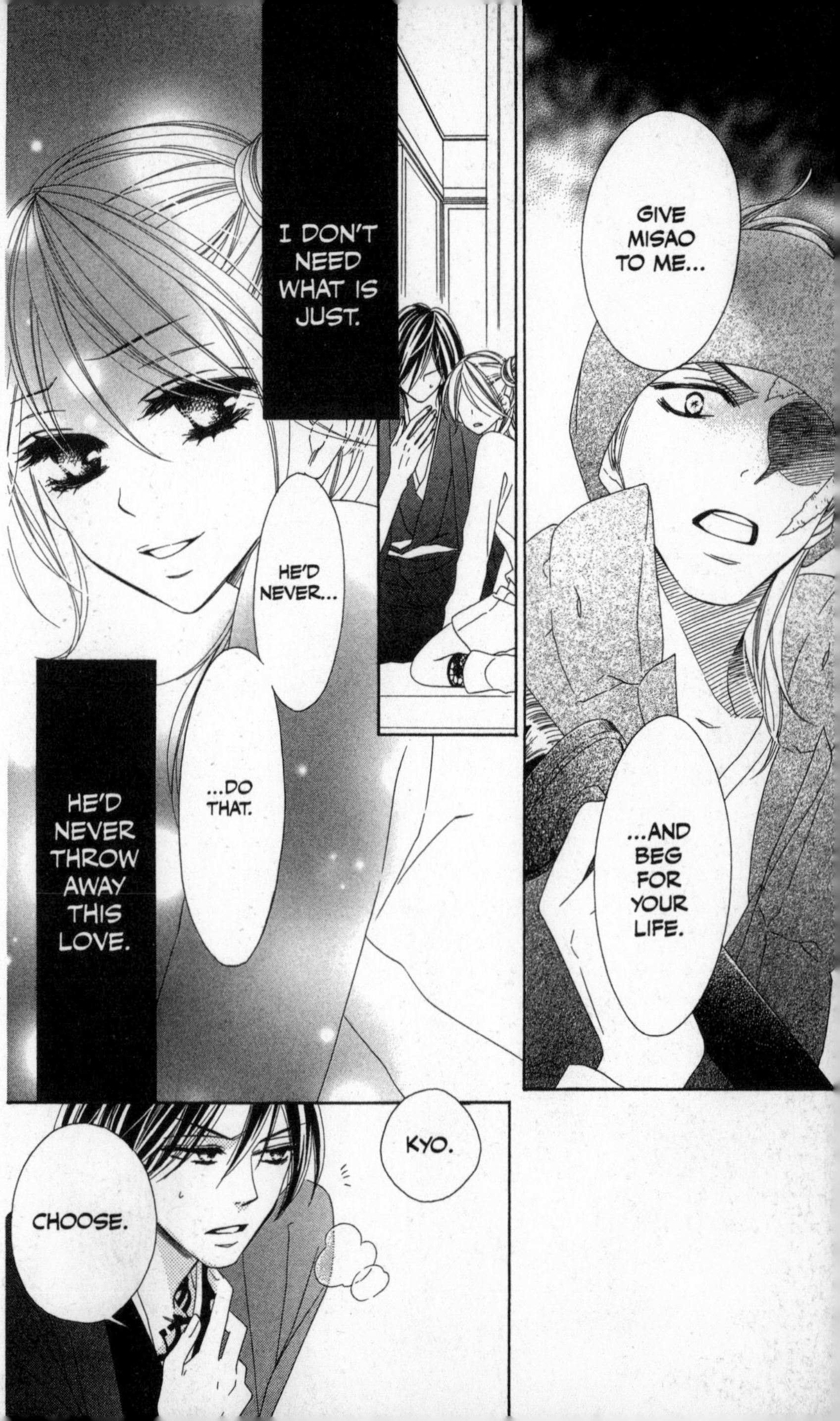
GIVE MISAO TO ME...
...AND BEG FOR YOUR LIFE.
I DON'T NEED WHAT IS JUST.
HE'D NEVER...
...DO THAT.
HE'D NEVER THROW AWAY THIS LOVE.
KYO.
CHOOSE.

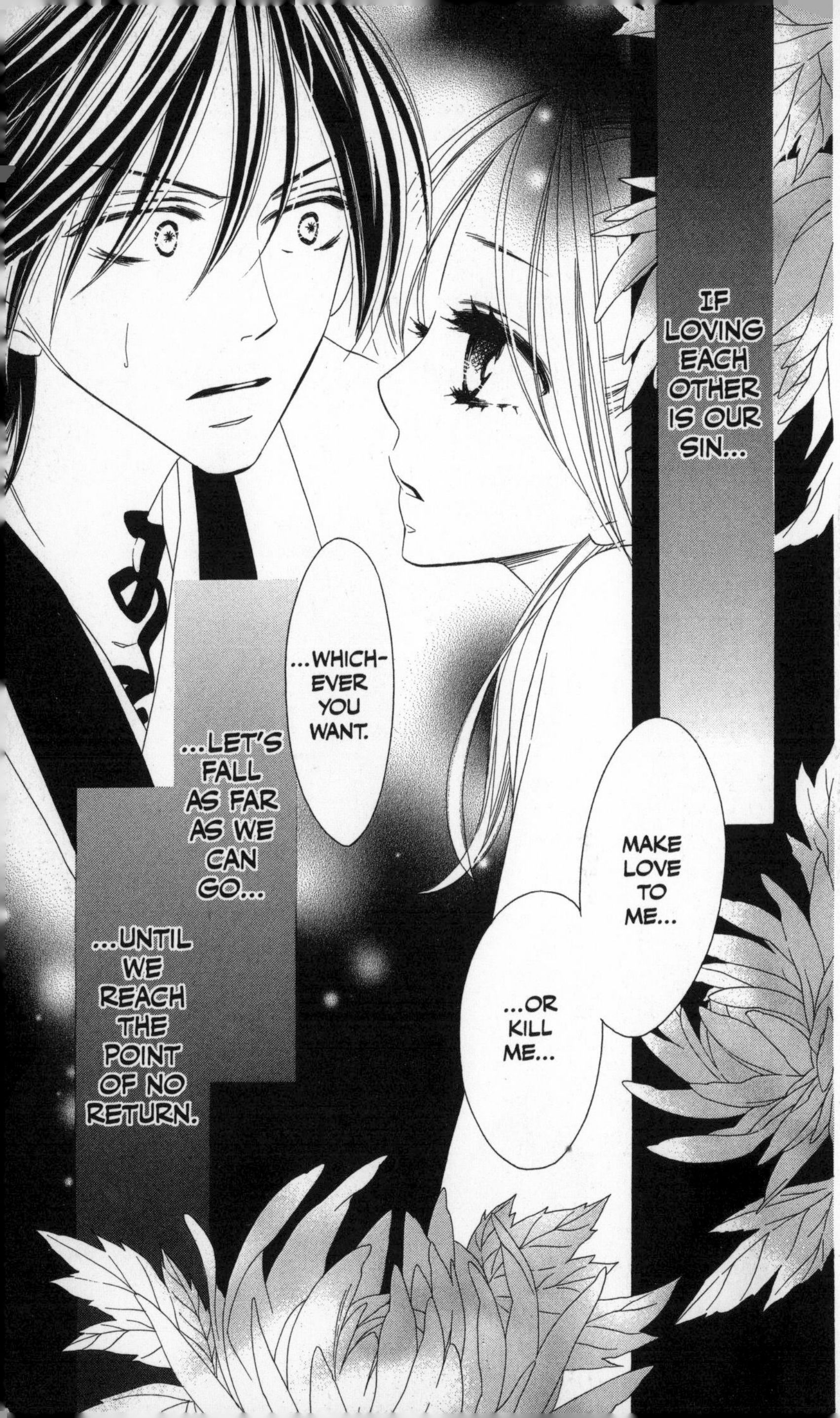
IF LOVING EACH OTHER IS OUR SIN...
MAKE LOVE TO ME...
...OR KILL ME...
...WHICH-EVER YOU WANT.
...LET'S FALL AS FAR AS WE CAN GO...
...UNTIL WE REACH THE POINT OF NO RETURN.

Illustration Request Extra

"Hoki in Uniform"

I did draw him in a school uniform before.

Whatever happened to the plan to make him Misao's classmate?

His name will appear in the next volume.

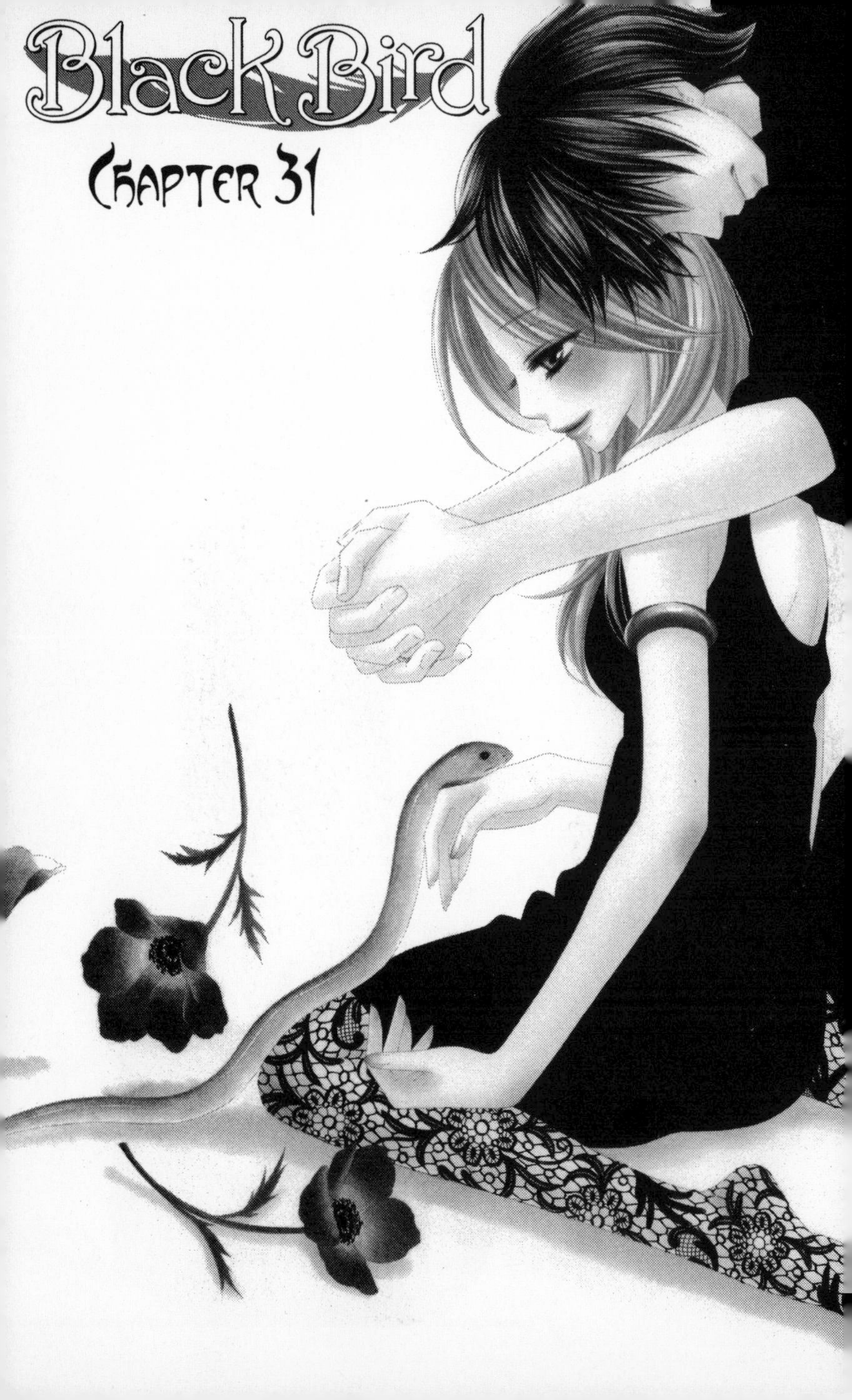
Black Bird
Chapter 31

MAKE
LOVE
TO ME,
OR KILL
ME...

...WHICH-
EVER
YOU
WANT.

Snake and anemone.

I like snakes. They're pretty. ♥

This snake is highly poisonous.
I drew it based on the story.

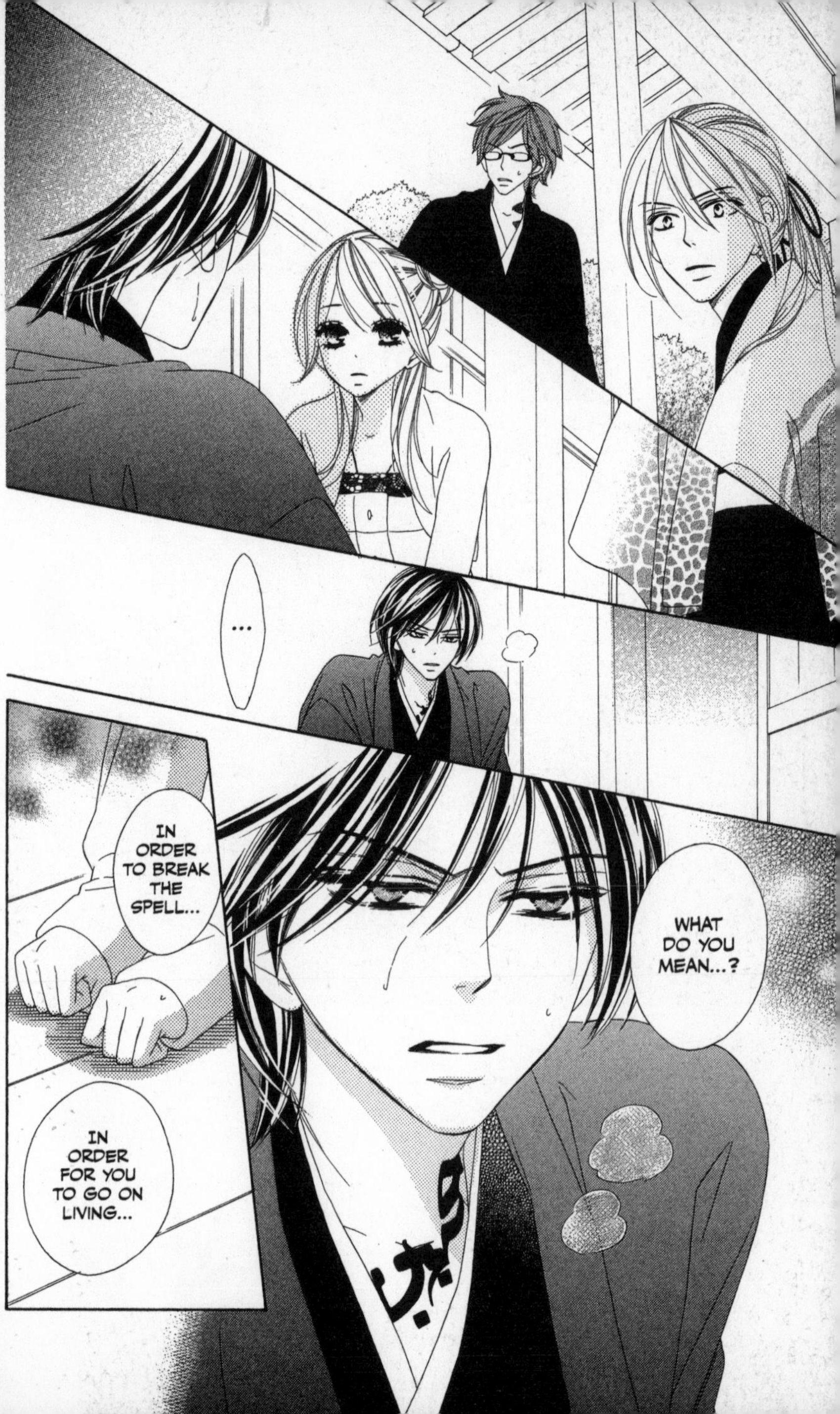
...
WHAT DO YOU MEAN...?
IN ORDER TO BREAK THE SPELL...
IN ORDER FOR YOU TO GO ON LIVING...

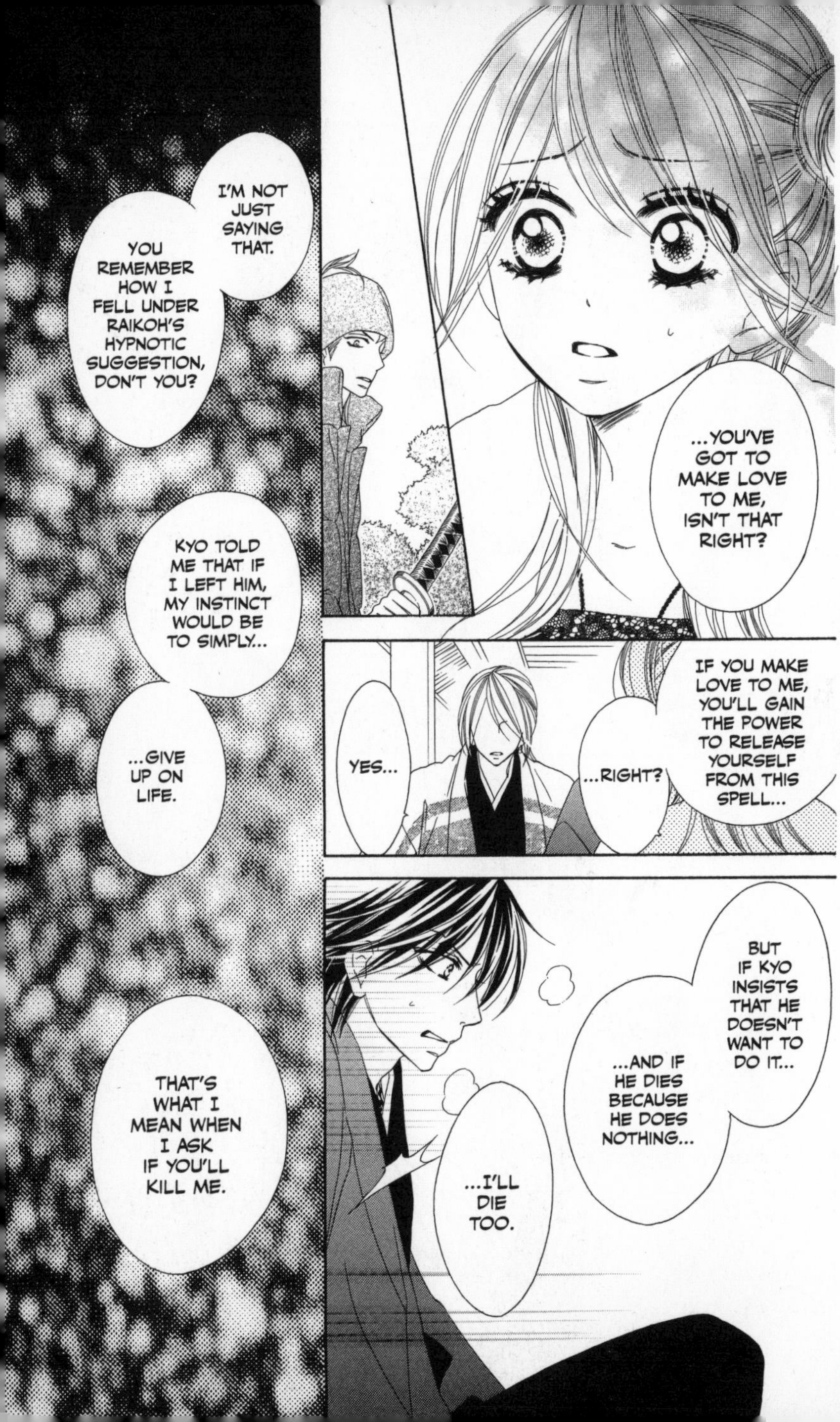
...YOU'VE GOT TO MAKE LOVE TO ME, ISN'T THAT RIGHT?
IF YOU MAKE LOVE TO ME, YOU'LL GAIN THE POWER TO RELEASE YOURSELF FROM THIS SPELL...
...RIGHT?
YES...
BUT IF KYO INSISTS THAT HE DOESN'T WANT TO DO IT...
...AND IF HE DIES BECAUSE HE DOES NOTHING...
...I'LL DIE TOO.
I'M NOT JUST SAYING THAT.
YOU REMEMBER HOW I FELL UNDER RAIKOH'S HYPNOTIC SUGGESTION, DON'T YOU?
KYO TOLD ME THAT IF I LEFT HIM, MY INSTINCT WOULD BE TO SIMPLY...
...GIVE UP ON LIFE.
THAT'S WHAT I MEAN WHEN I ASK IF YOU'LL KILL ME.

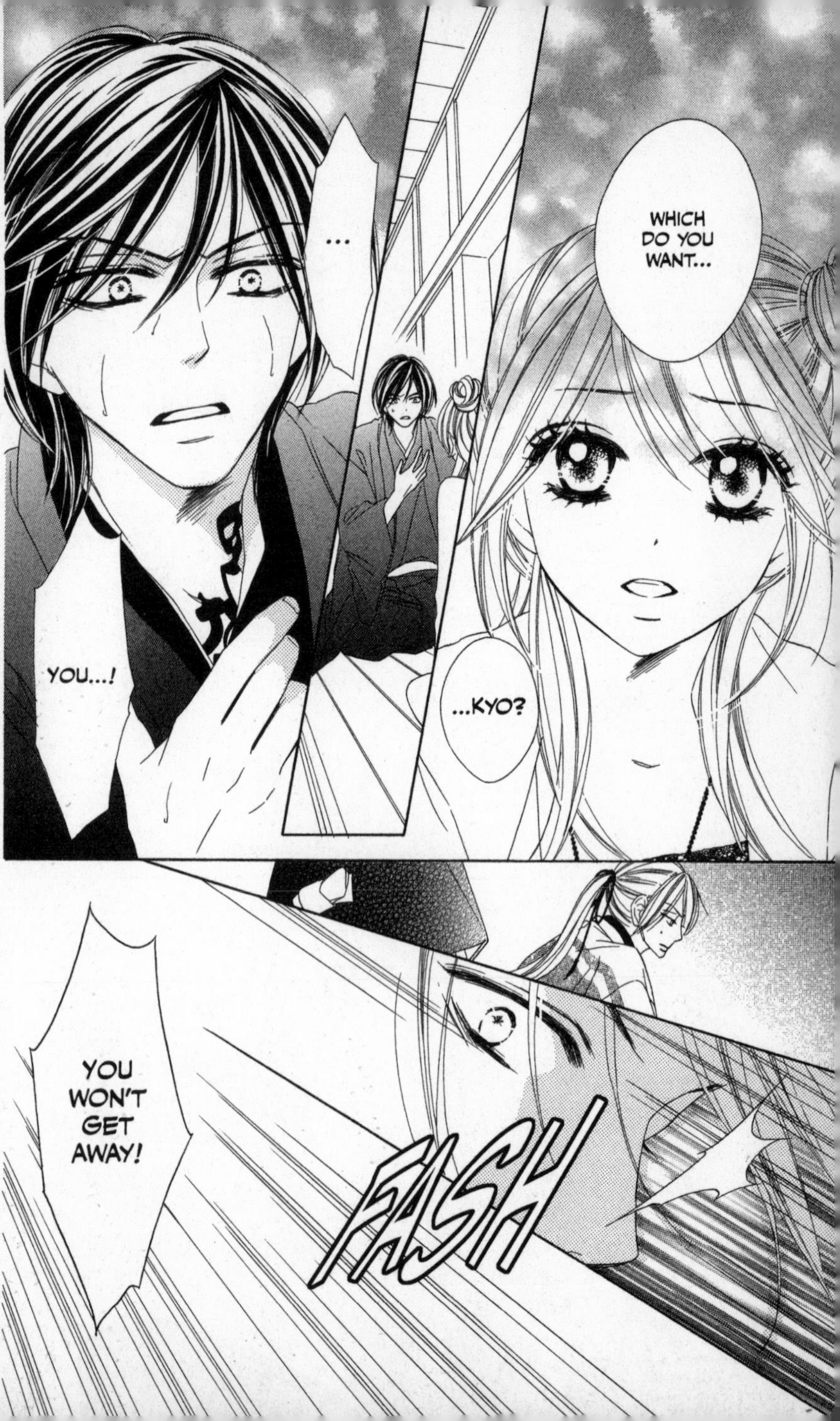
WHICH DO YOU WANT...
...KYO?
...
YOU...!
YOU WON'T GET AWAY!
FASH

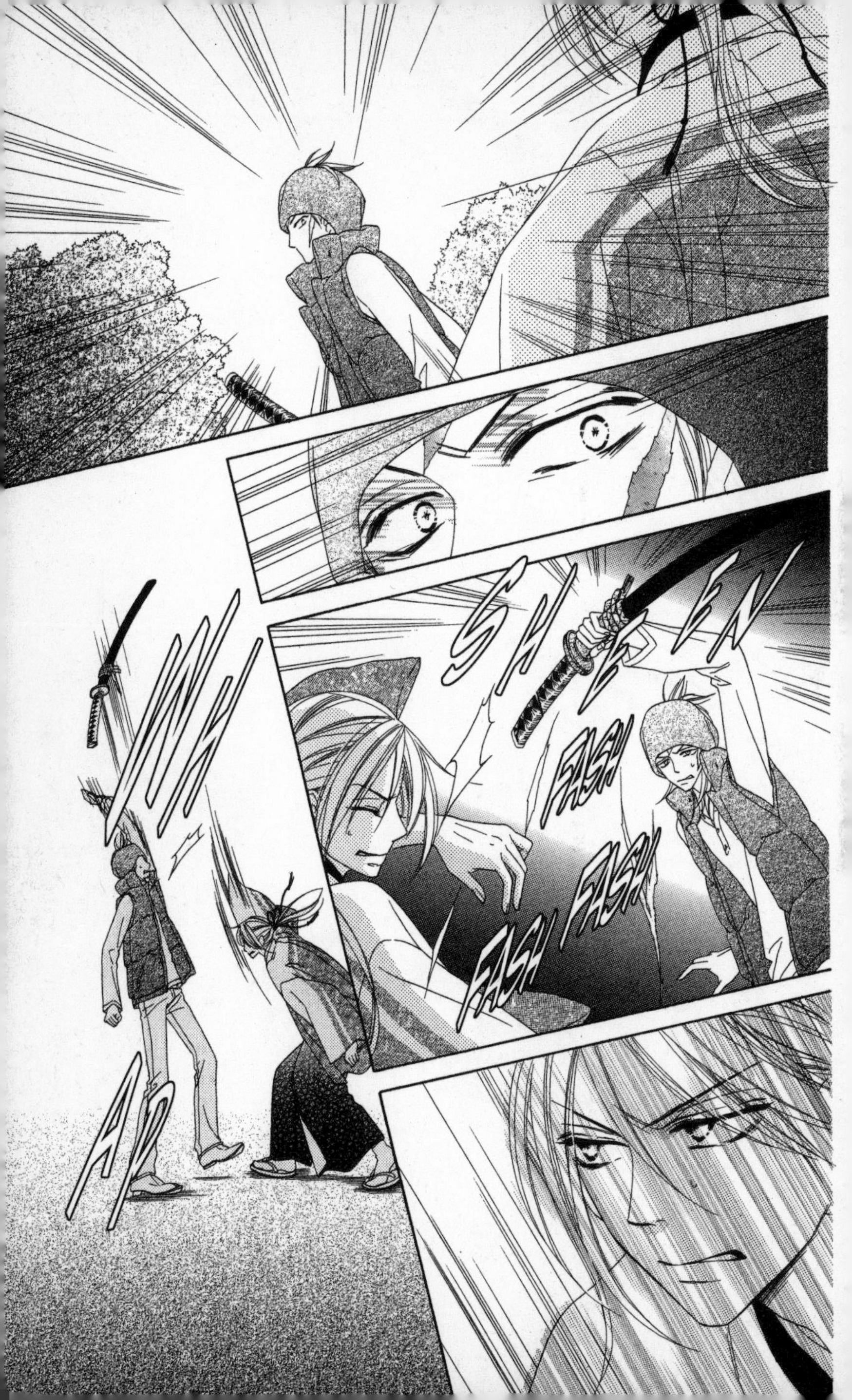
SHEEN
FASH
FASH
FASH

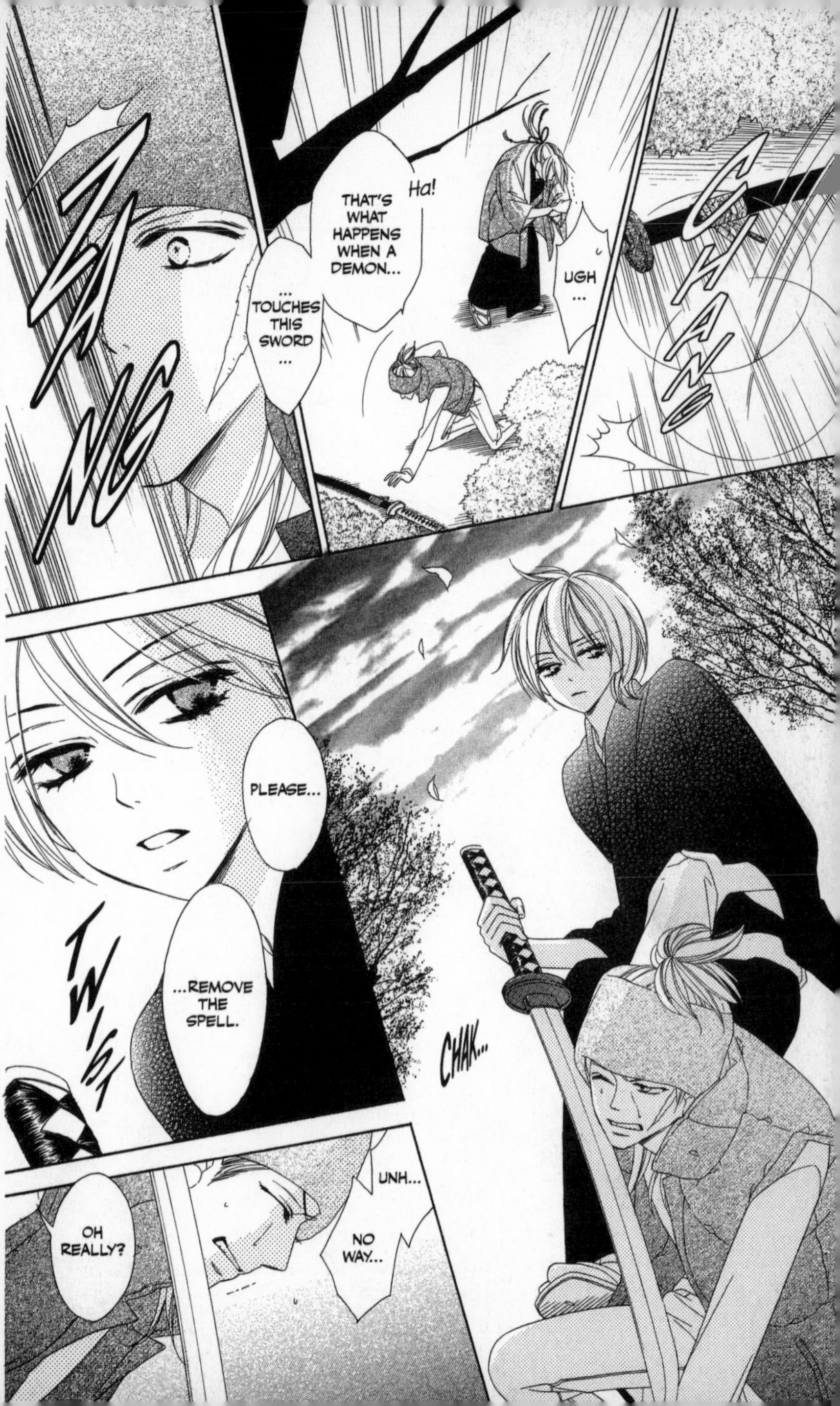
CHANG
Ha!
UGH ...
THAT'S WHAT HAPPENS WHEN A DEMON...
... TOUCHES THIS SWORD ...
ZANG
CHAK...
PLEASE...
...REMOVE THE SPELL.
TWIST
UNH...
NO WAY...
OH REALLY?

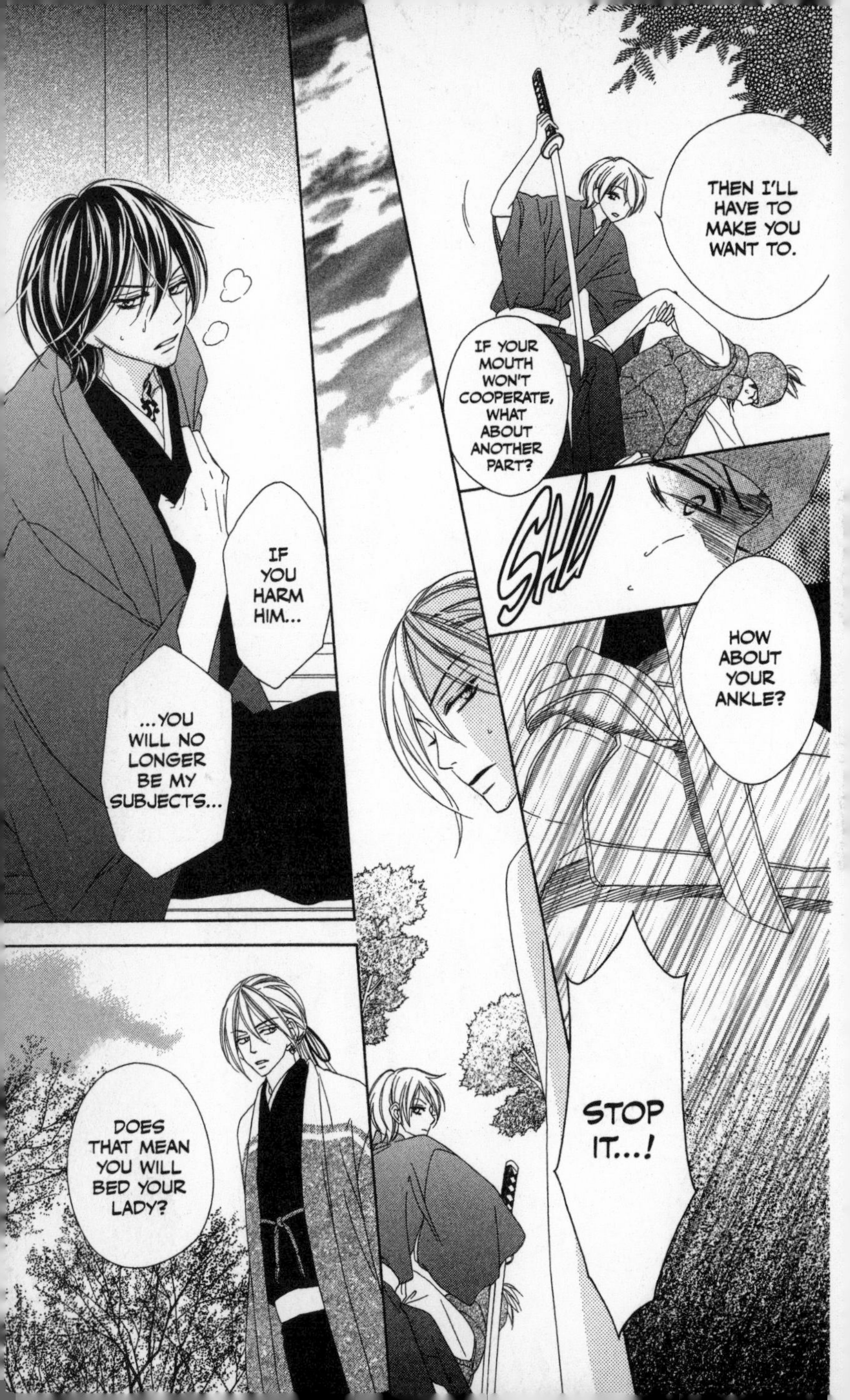

THEN I'LL HAVE TO MAKE YOU WANT TO.
IF YOUR MOUTH WON'T COOPERATE, WHAT ABOUT ANOTHER PART?
SHU
HOW ABOUT YOUR ANKLE?
STOP IT...!
IF YOU HARM HIM...
...YOU WILL NO LONGER BE MY SUBJECTS...
DOES THAT MEAN YOU WILL BED YOUR LADY?

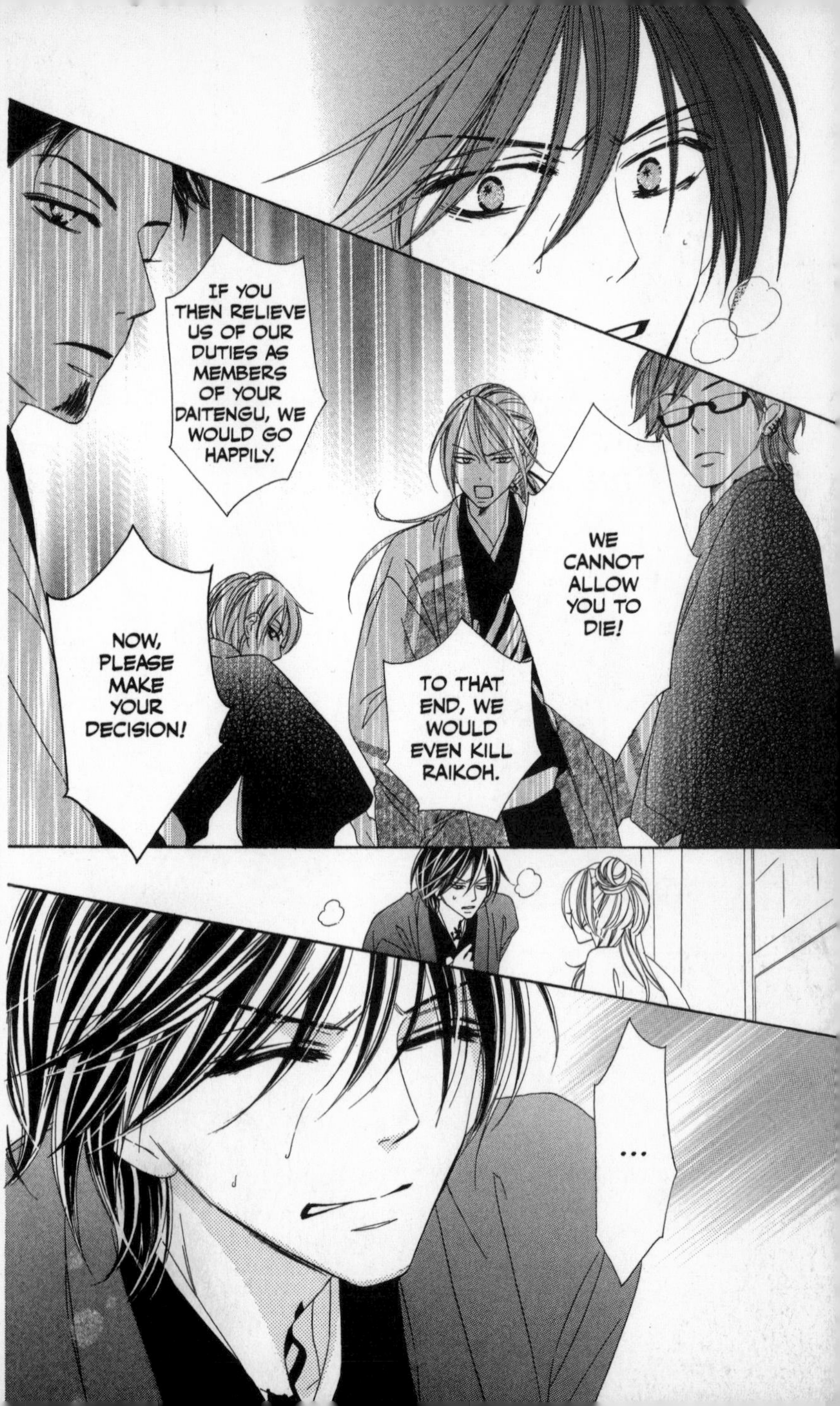
WE CANNOT ALLOW YOU TO DIE!
TO THAT END, WE WOULD EVEN KILL RAIKOH.
IF YOU THEN RELIEVE US OF OUR DUTIES AS MEMBERS OF YOUR DAITENGU, WE WOULD GO HAPPILY.
NOW, PLEASE MAKE YOUR DECISION!
...

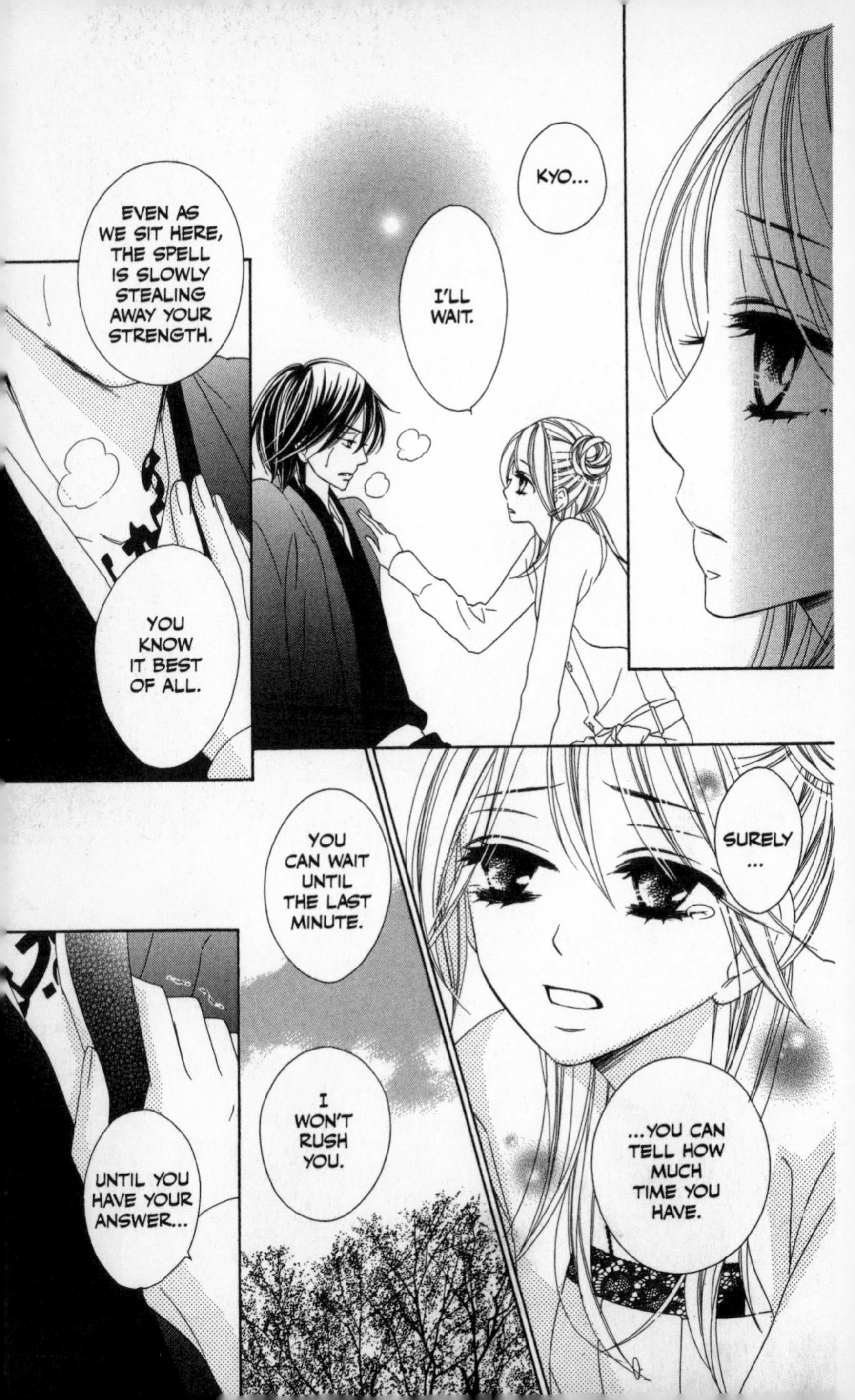
KYO...
I'LL WAIT.
EVEN AS WE SIT HERE, THE SPELL IS SLOWLY STEALING AWAY YOUR STRENGTH.
YOU KNOW IT BEST OF ALL.
SURELY ...
...YOU CAN TELL HOW MUCH TIME YOU HAVE.
YOU CAN WAIT UNTIL THE LAST MINUTE.
I WON'T RUSH YOU.
UNTIL YOU HAVE YOUR ANSWER...

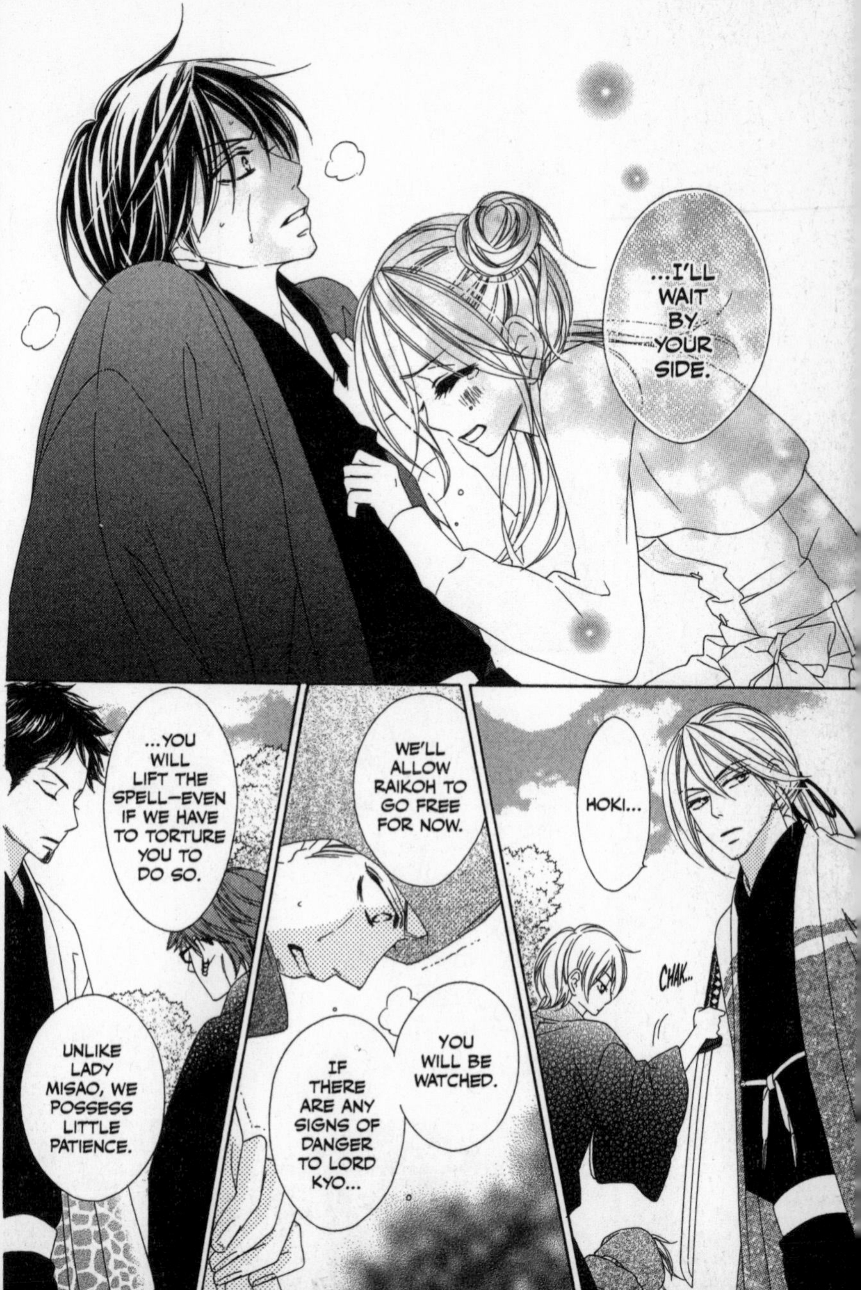
...I'LL WAIT BY YOUR SIDE.
HOKI...
CHAK...
WE'LL ALLOW RAIKOH TO GO FREE FOR NOW.
YOU WILL BE WATCHED.
IF THERE ARE ANY SIGNS OF DANGER TO LORD KYO...
...YOU WILL LIFT THE SPELL—EVEN IF WE HAVE TO TORTURE YOU TO DO SO.
UNLIKE LADY MISAO, WE POSSESS LITTLE PATIENCE.

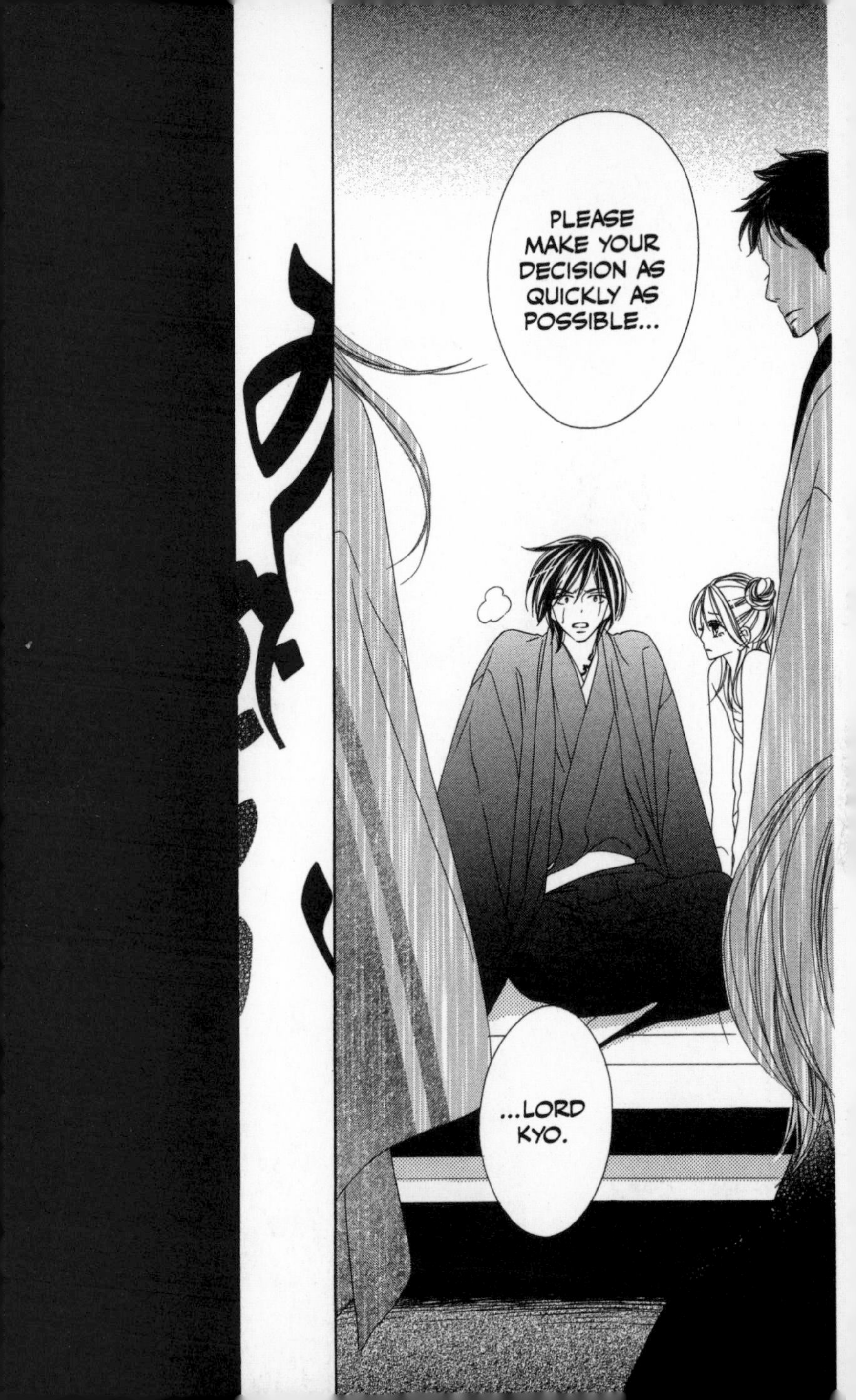
PLEASE MAKE YOUR DECISION AS QUICKLY AS POSSIBLE...
...LORD KYO.

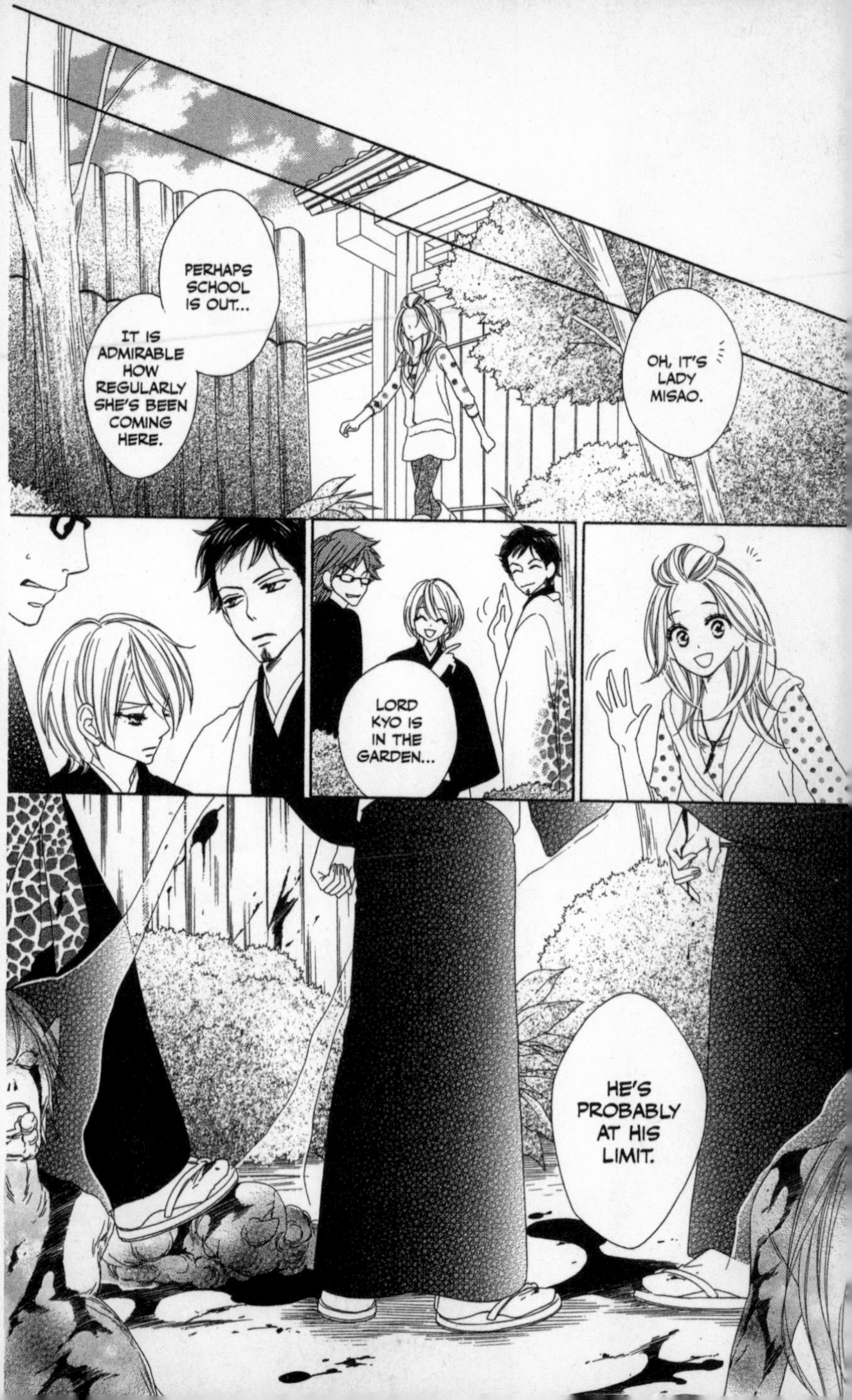
OH, IT'S LADY MISAO.
PERHAPS SCHOOL IS OUT...
IT IS ADMIRABLE HOW REGULARLY SHE'S BEEN COMING HERE.
LORD KYO IS IN THE GARDEN...
HE'S PROBABLY AT HIS LIMIT.

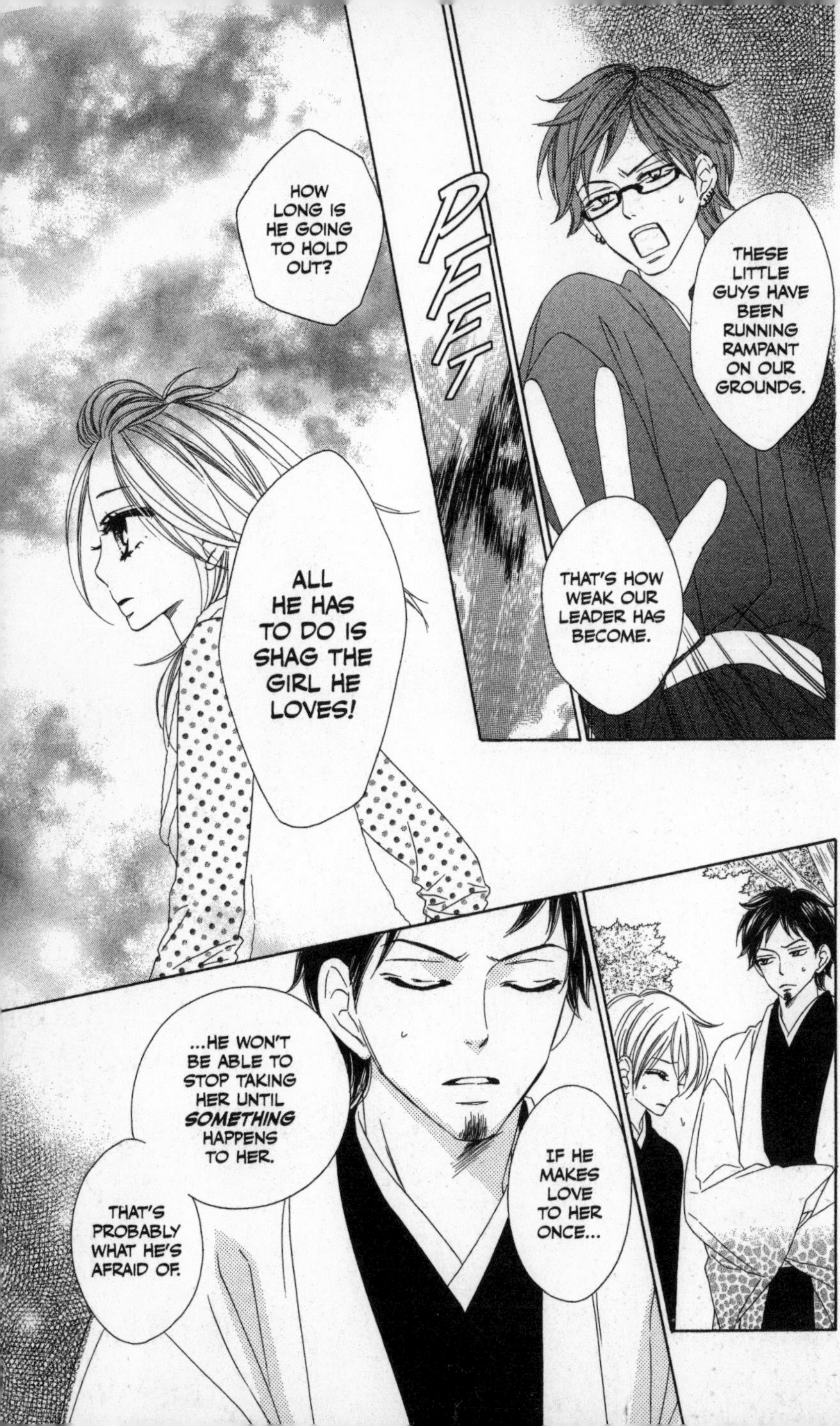

THESE LITTLE GUYS HAVE BEEN RUNNING RAMPANT ON OUR GROUNDS.
THAT'S HOW WEAK OUR LEADER HAS BECOME.
PFFT
HOW LONG IS HE GOING TO HOLD OUT?
ALL HE HAS TO DO IS SHAG THE GIRL HE LOVES!
IF HE MAKES LOVE TO HER ONCE...
...HE WON'T BE ABLE TO STOP TAKING HER UNTIL *SOMETHING* HAPPENS TO HER.
THAT'S PROBABLY WHAT HE'S AFRAID OF.

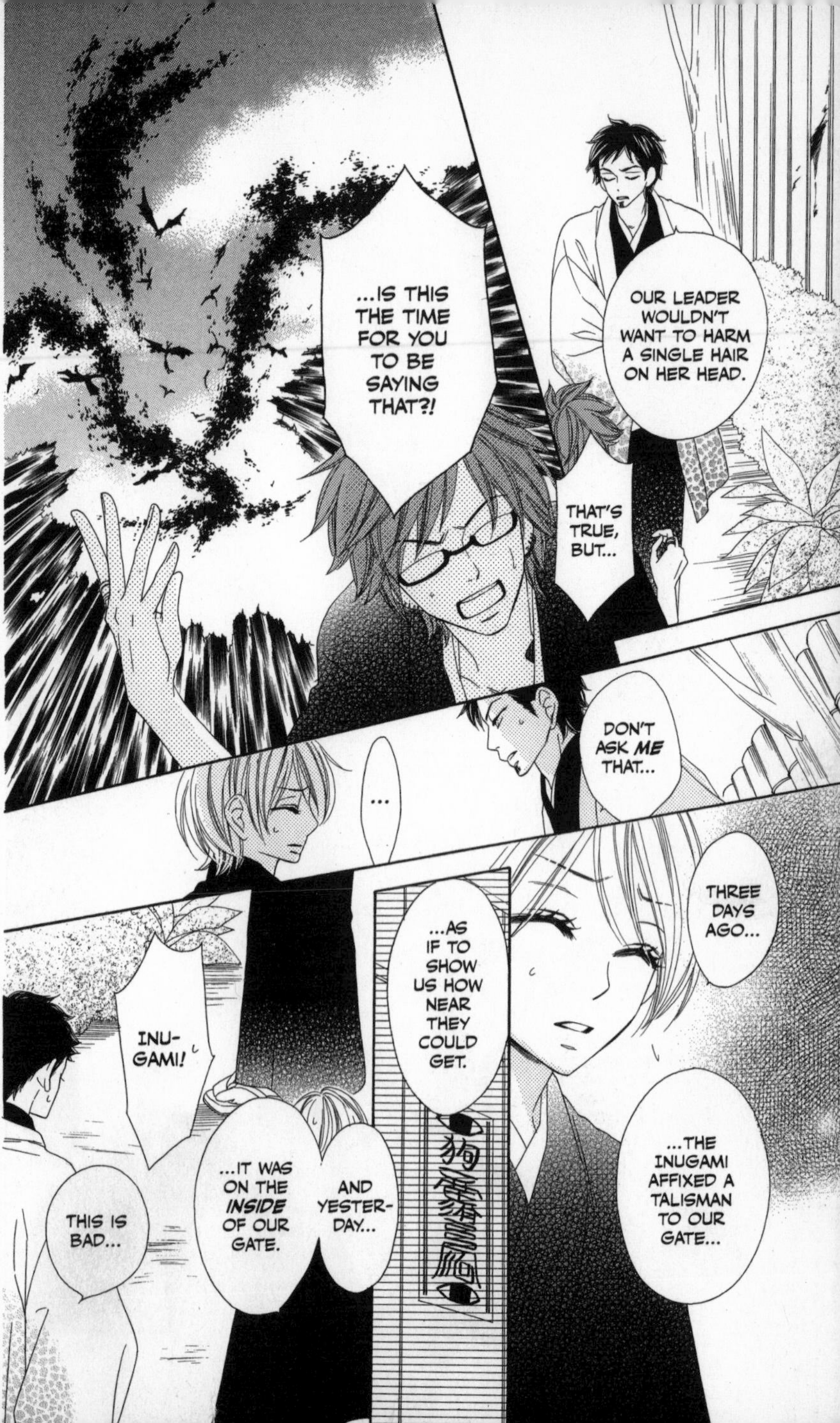
OUR LEADER WOULDN'T WANT TO HARM A SINGLE HAIR ON HER HEAD.
THAT'S TRUE, BUT...
...IS THIS THE TIME FOR YOU TO BE SAYING THAT?!
DON'T ASK *ME* THAT...
...
THREE DAYS AGO...
...THE INUGAMI AFFIXED A TALISMAN TO OUR GATE...
AND YESTERDAY...
...IT WAS ON THE *INSIDE* OF OUR GATE.
...AS IF TO SHOW US HOW NEAR THEY COULD GET.
INUGAMI!
THIS IS BAD...

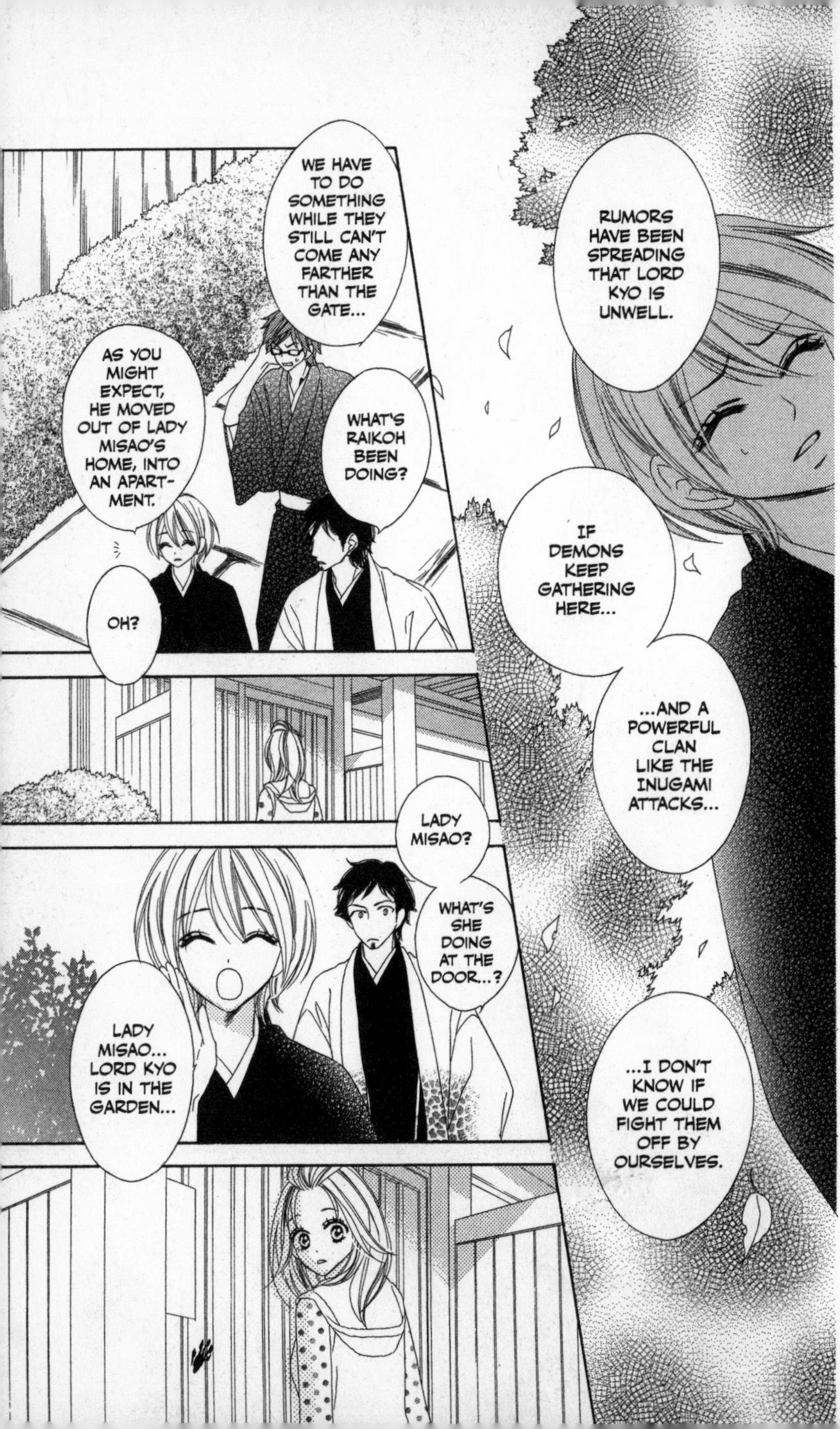
RUMORS HAVE BEEN SPREADING THAT LORD KYO IS UNWELL.
IF DEMONS KEEP GATHERING HERE...
...AND A POWERFUL CLAN LIKE THE INUGAMI ATTACKS...
...I DON'T KNOW IF WE COULD FIGHT THEM OFF BY OURSELVES.
WE HAVE TO DO SOMETHING WHILE THEY STILL CAN'T COME ANY FARTHER THAN THE GATE...
WHAT'S RAIKOH BEEN DOING?
AS YOU MIGHT EXPECT, HE MOVED OUT OF LADY MISAO'S HOME, INTO AN APART-MENT.
OH?
LADY MISAO?
WHAT'S SHE DOING AT THE DOOR...?
LADY MISAO... LORD KYO IS IN THE GARDEN...

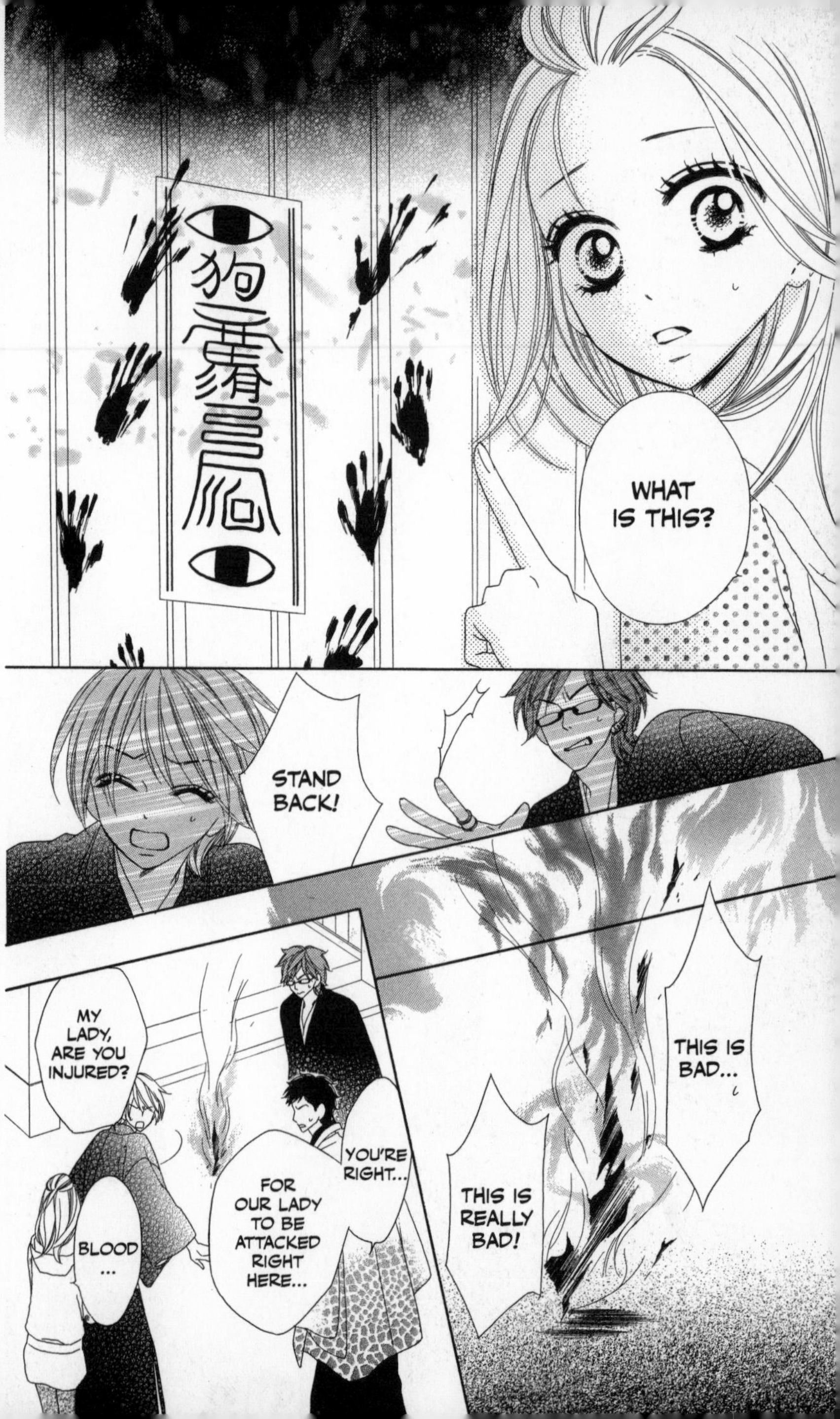
WHAT IS THIS?
STAND BACK!
THIS IS BAD...
THIS IS REALLY BAD!
MY LADY, ARE YOU INJURED?
BLOOD...
FOR OUR LADY TO BE ATTACKED RIGHT HERE...
YOU'RE RIGHT...

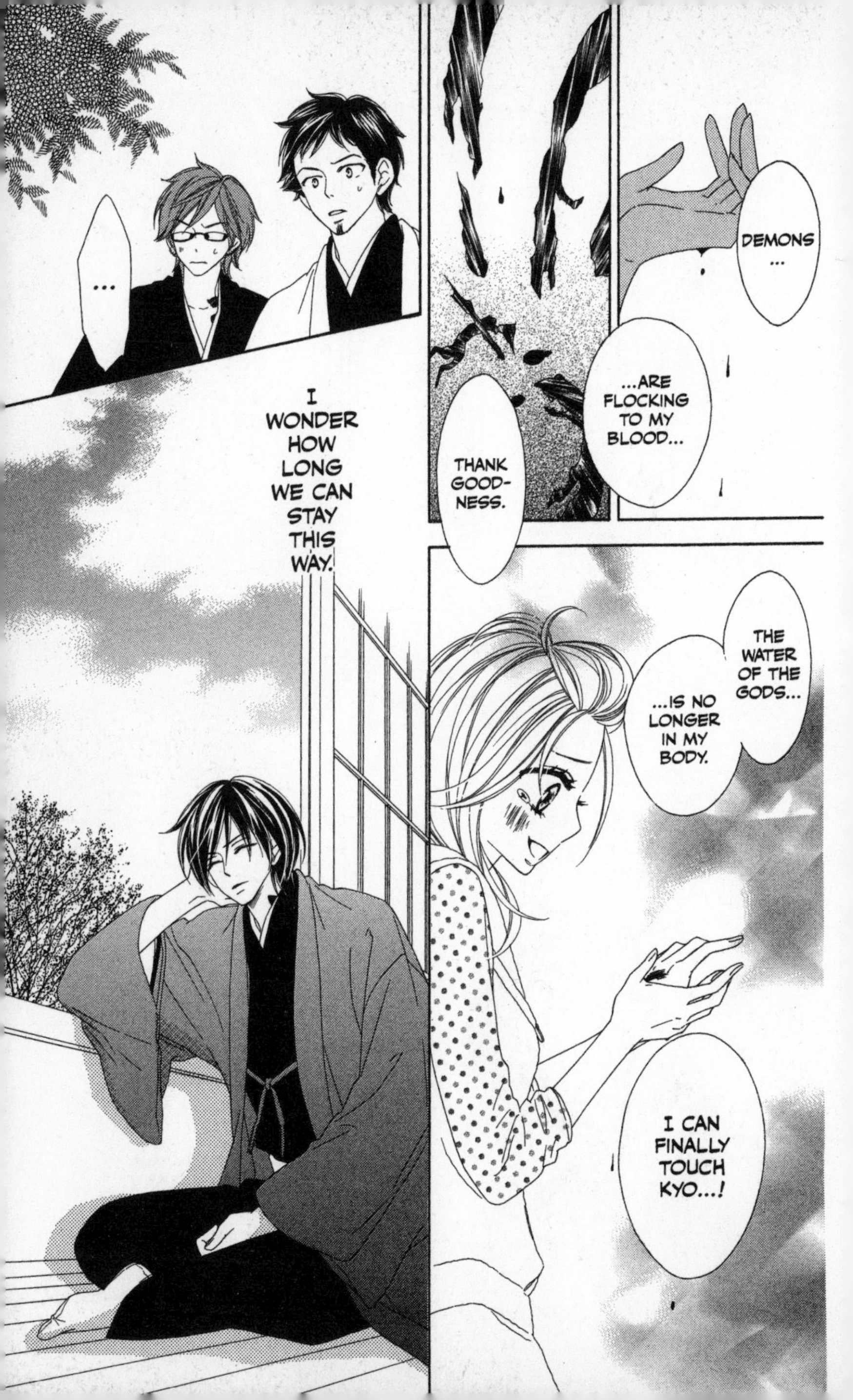
DEMONS...
...ARE FLOCKING TO MY BLOOD...
THANK GOODNESS.
...
THE WATER OF THE GODS...
...IS NO LONGER IN MY BODY.
I CAN FINALLY TOUCH KYO...!
I WONDER HOW LONG WE CAN STAY THIS WAY.

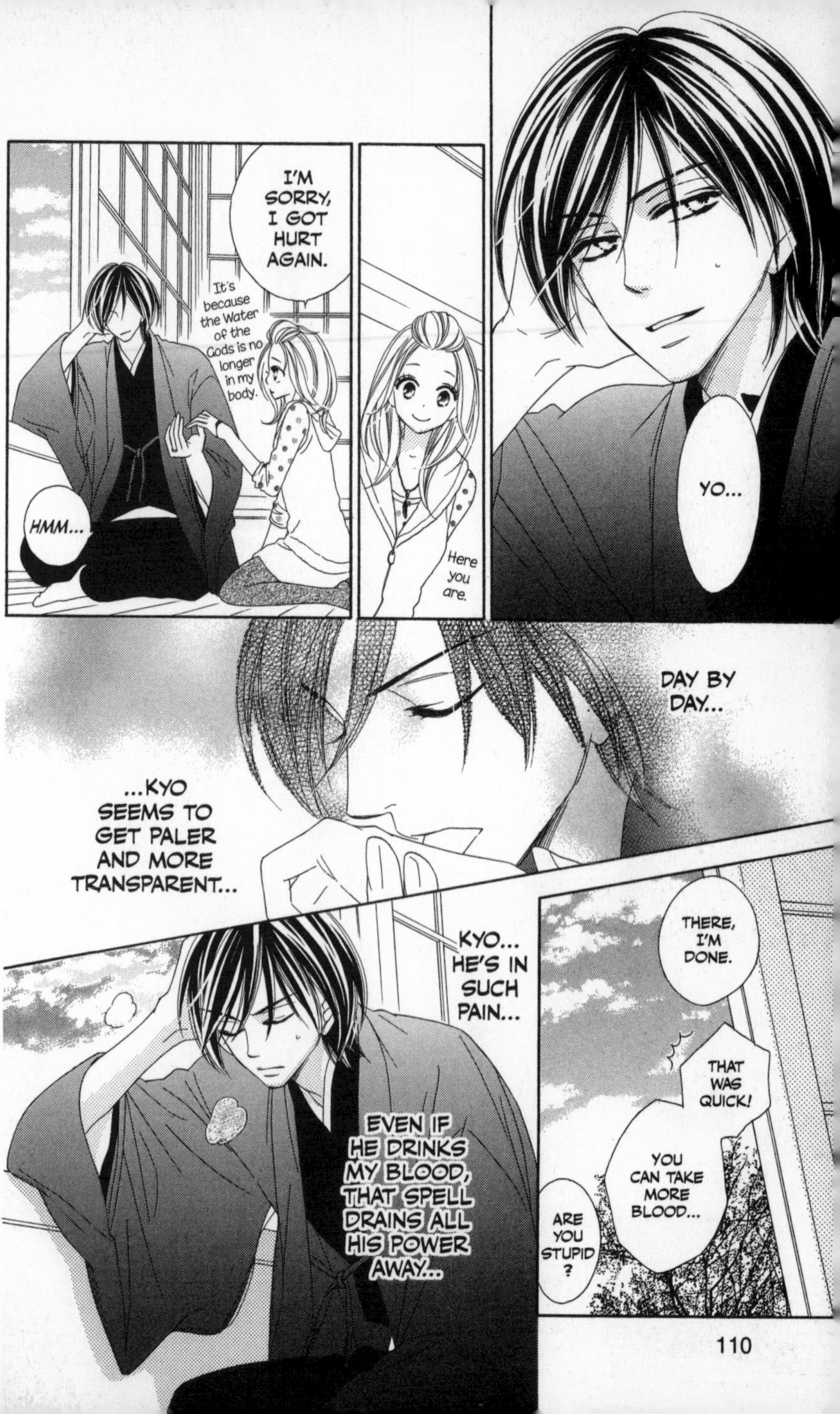
YO...
Here you are.
I'M SORRY, I GOT HURT AGAIN.
It's because the Water of the Gods is no longer in my body.
HMM...
DAY BY DAY...
...KYO SEEMS TO GET PALER AND MORE TRANSPARENT...
THERE, I'M DONE.
THAT WAS QUICK!
YOU CAN TAKE MORE BLOOD...
ARE YOU STUPID?
KYO... HE'S IN SUCH PAIN...
EVEN IF HE DRINKS MY BLOOD, THAT SPELL DRAINS ALL HIS POWER AWAY...

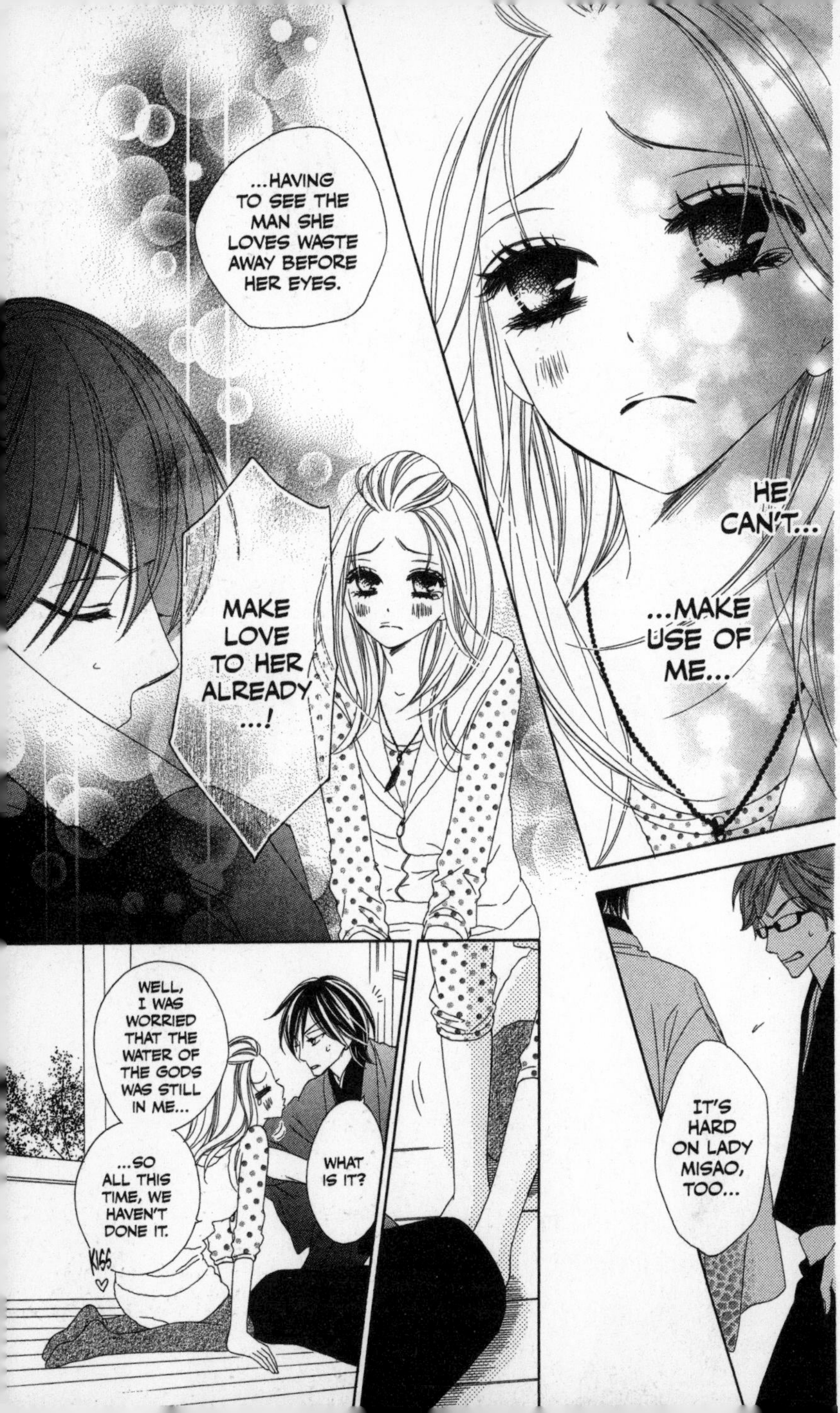
HE CAN'T...
...MAKE USE OF ME...
IT'S HARD ON LADY MISAO, TOO...
...HAVING TO SEE THE MAN SHE LOVES WASTE AWAY BEFORE HER EYES.
MAKE LOVE TO HER ALREADY ...!
KISS
WHAT IS IT?
WELL, I WAS WORRIED THAT THE WATER OF THE GODS WAS STILL IN ME...
...SO ALL THIS TIME, WE HAVEN'T DONE IT.

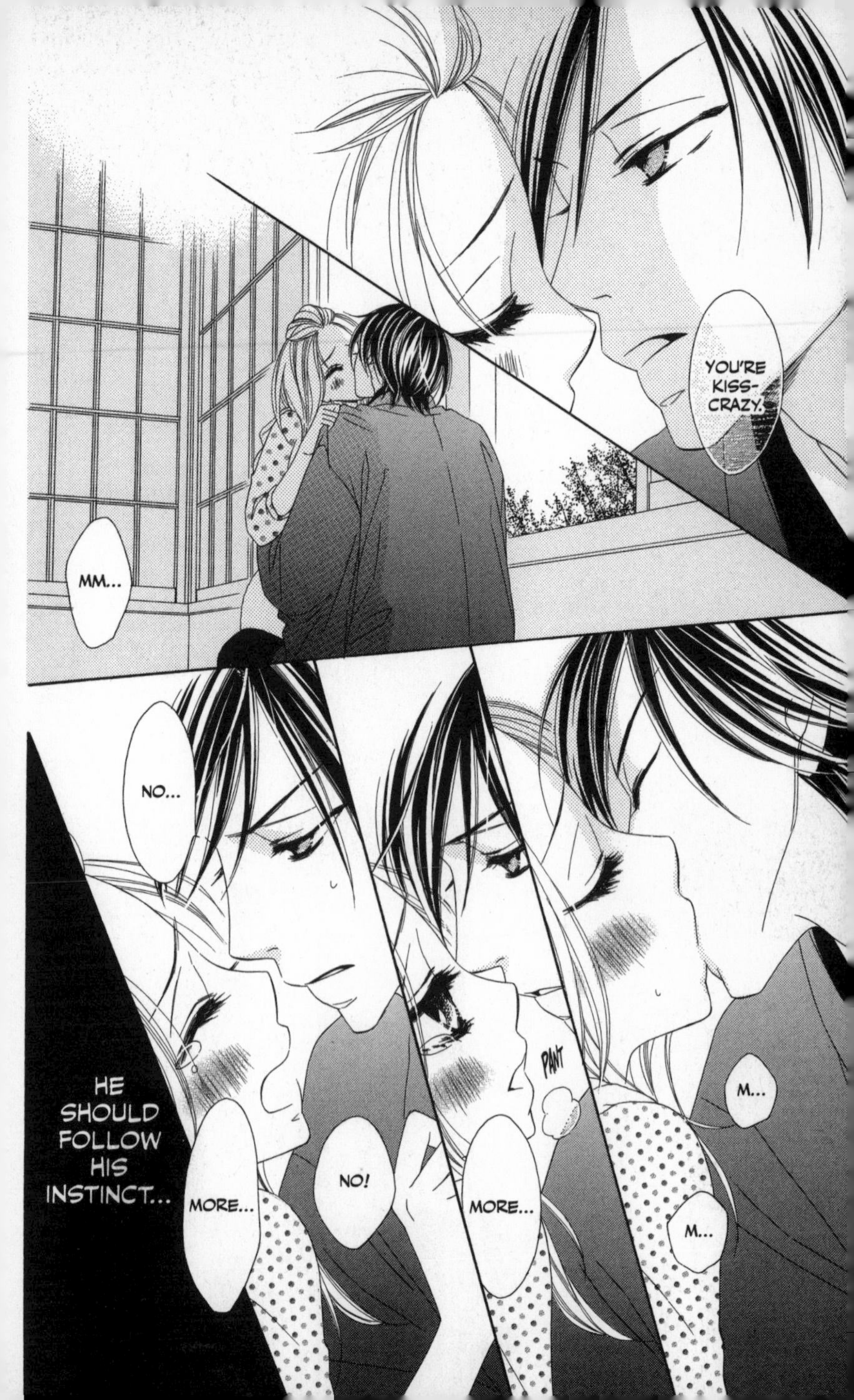
YOU'RE KISS-CRAZY.
MM...
M...
M...
PANT
MORE...
NO...
NO!
MORE...
HE SHOULD FOLLOW HIS INSTINCT...

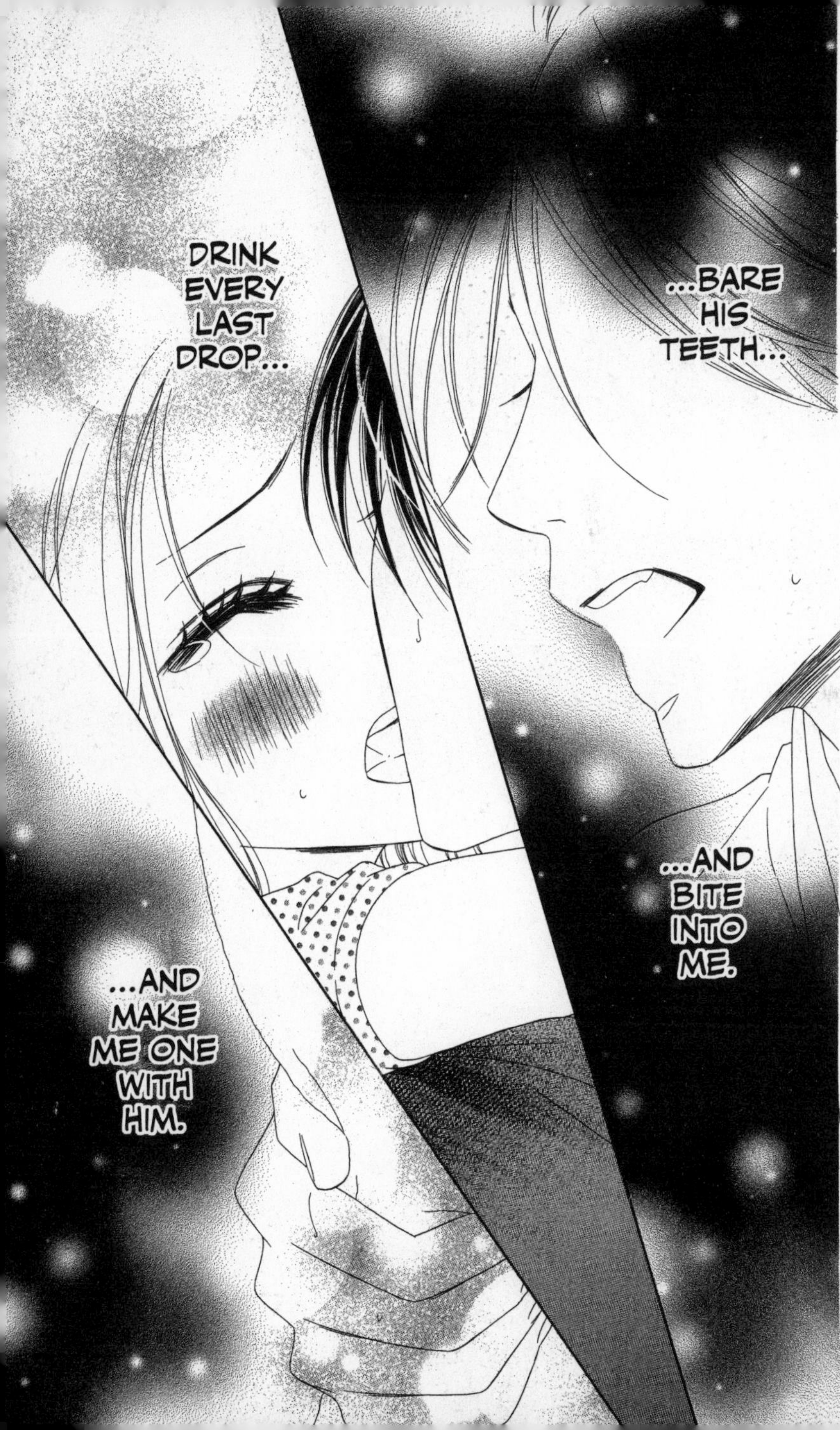
...BARE HIS TEETH...
...AND BITE INTO ME.
DRINK EVERY LAST DROP...
...AND MAKE ME ONE WITH HIM.

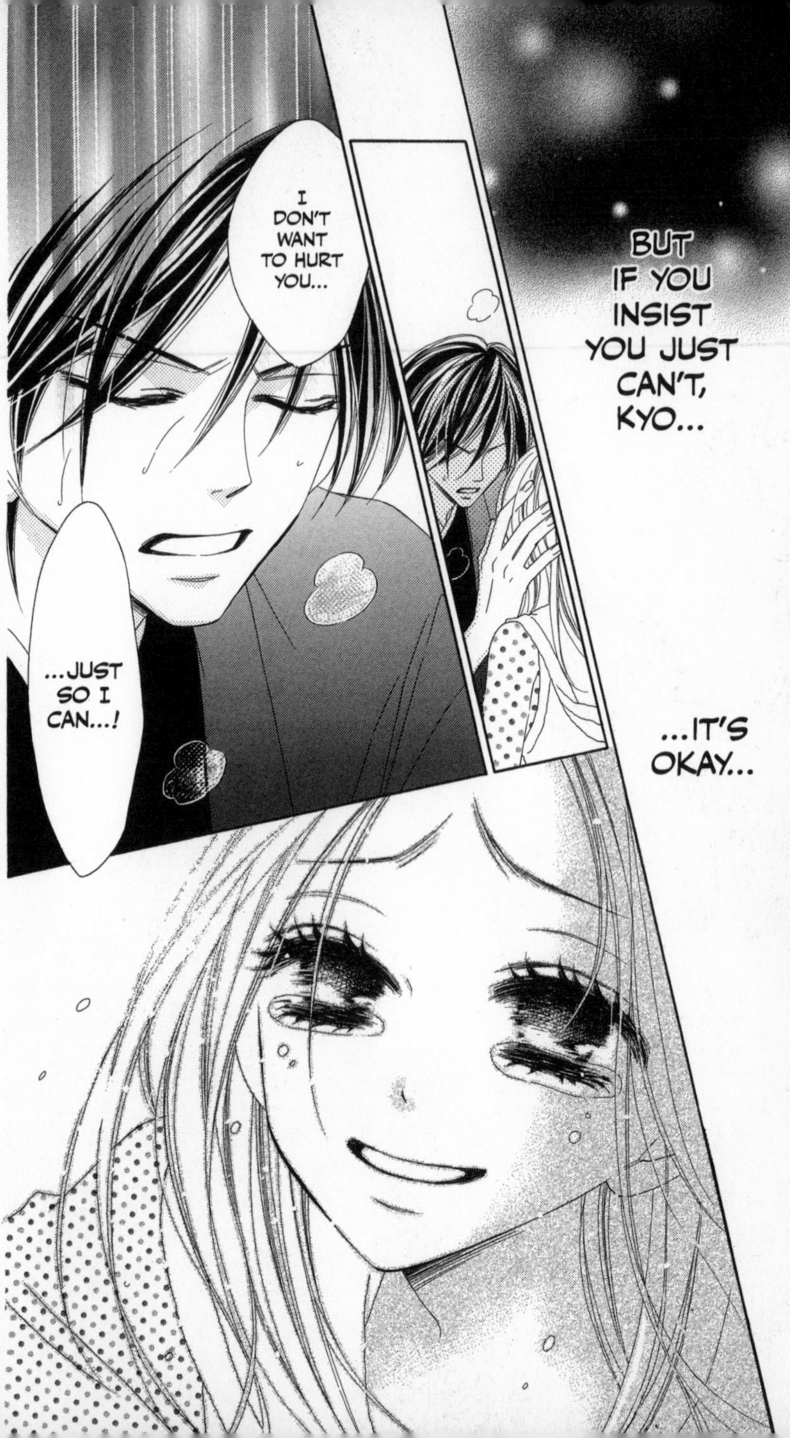
I DON'T WANT TO HURT YOU...
...JUST SO I CAN...!
BUT IF YOU INSIST YOU JUST CAN'T, KYO...
...IT'S OKAY...

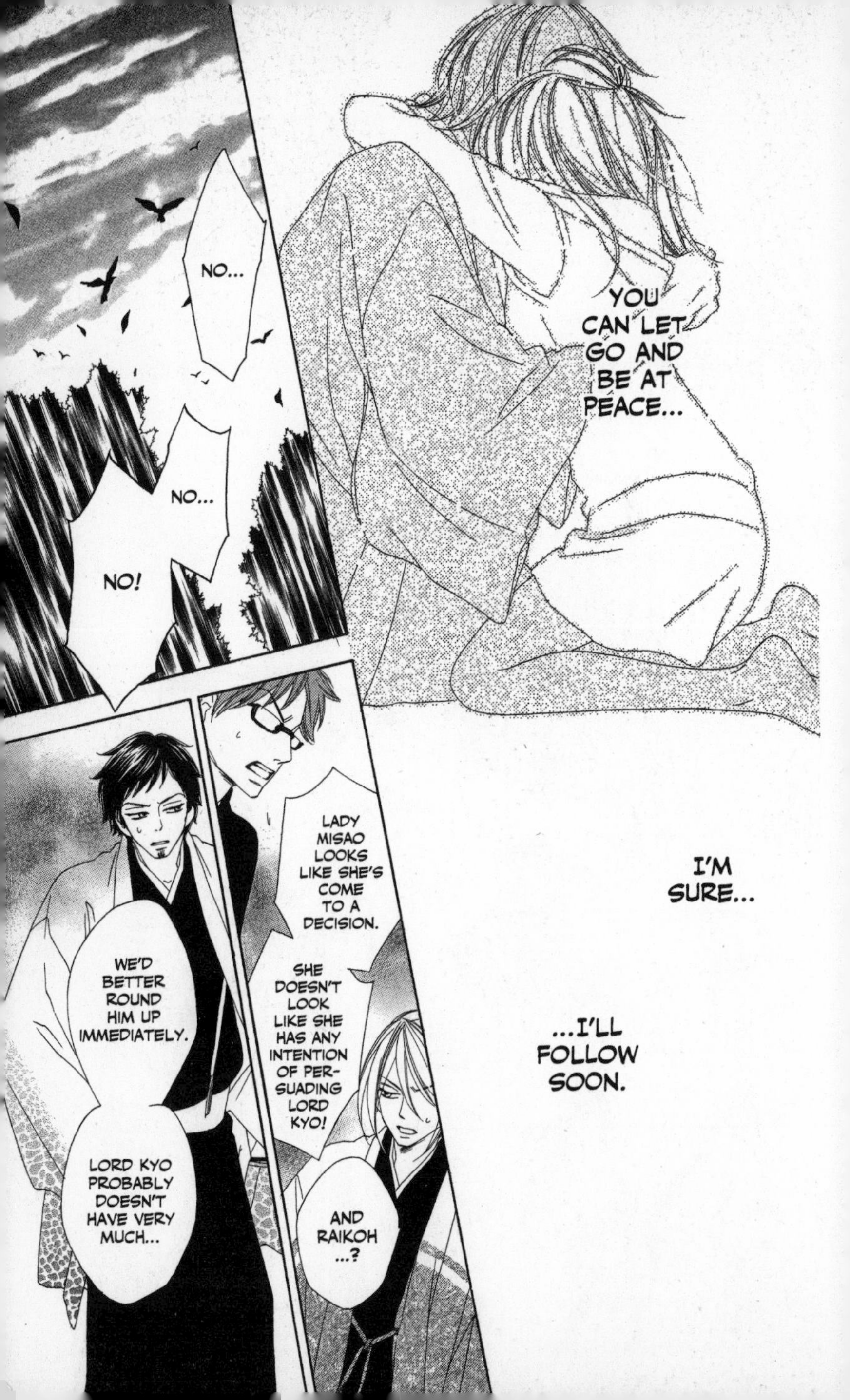
YOU CAN LET GO AND BE AT PEACE...
I'M SURE...
...I'LL FOLLOW SOON.
NO...
NO...
NO!
LADY MISAO LOOKS LIKE SHE'S COME TO A DECISION.
SHE DOESN'T LOOK LIKE SHE HAS ANY INTENTION OF PER-SUADING LORD KYO!
AND RAIKOH ...?
WE'D BETTER ROUND HIM UP IMMEDIATELY.
LORD KYO PROBABLY DOESN'T HAVE VERY MUCH...

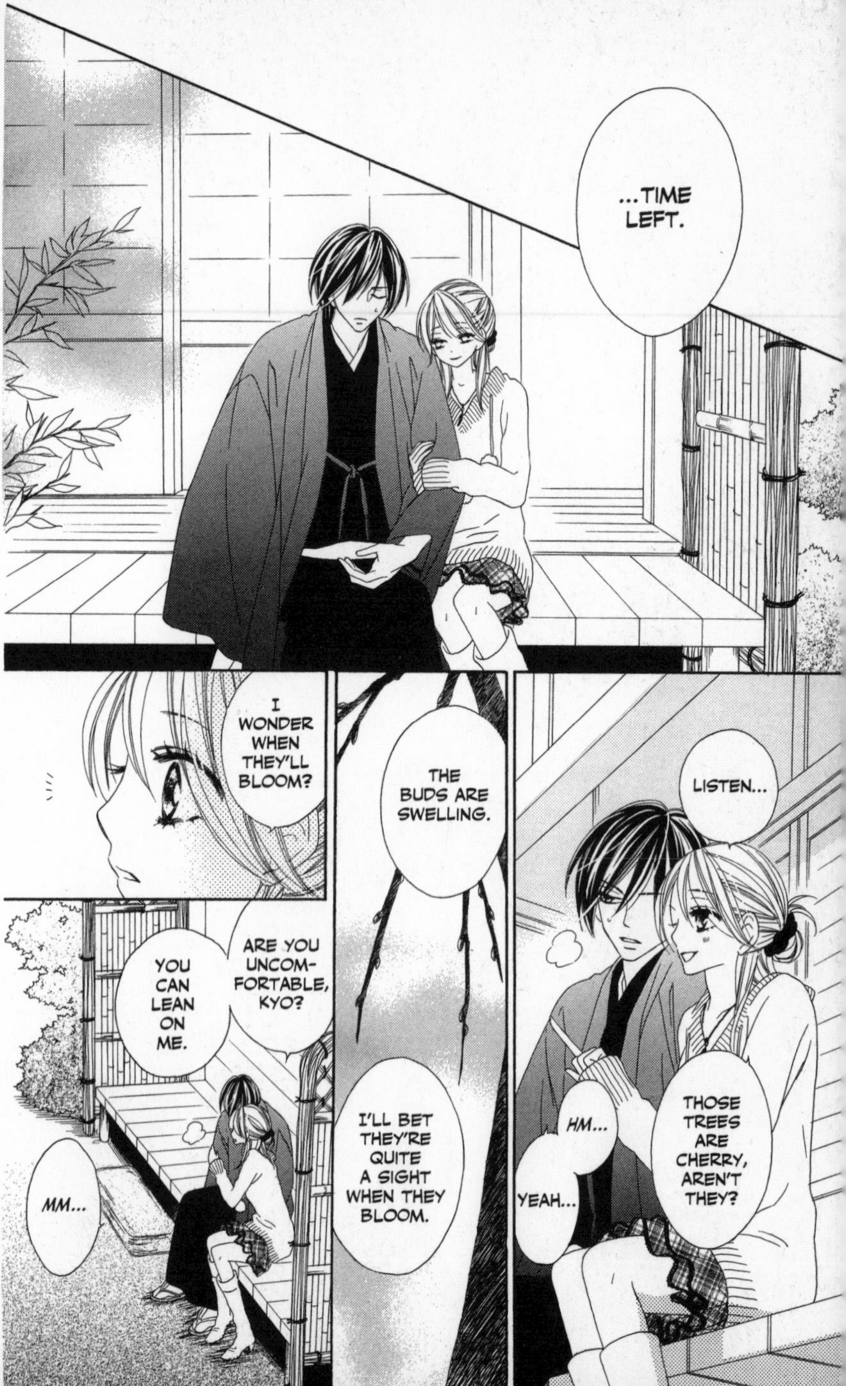
...TIME LEFT.
LISTEN...
THOSE TREES ARE CHERRY, AREN'T THEY?
HM...
YEAH...
THE BUDS ARE SWELLING.
I'LL BET THEY'RE QUITE A SIGHT WHEN THEY BLOOM.
I WONDER WHEN THEY'LL BLOOM?
ARE YOU UNCOMFORTABLE, KYO?
YOU CAN LEAN ON ME.
MM...

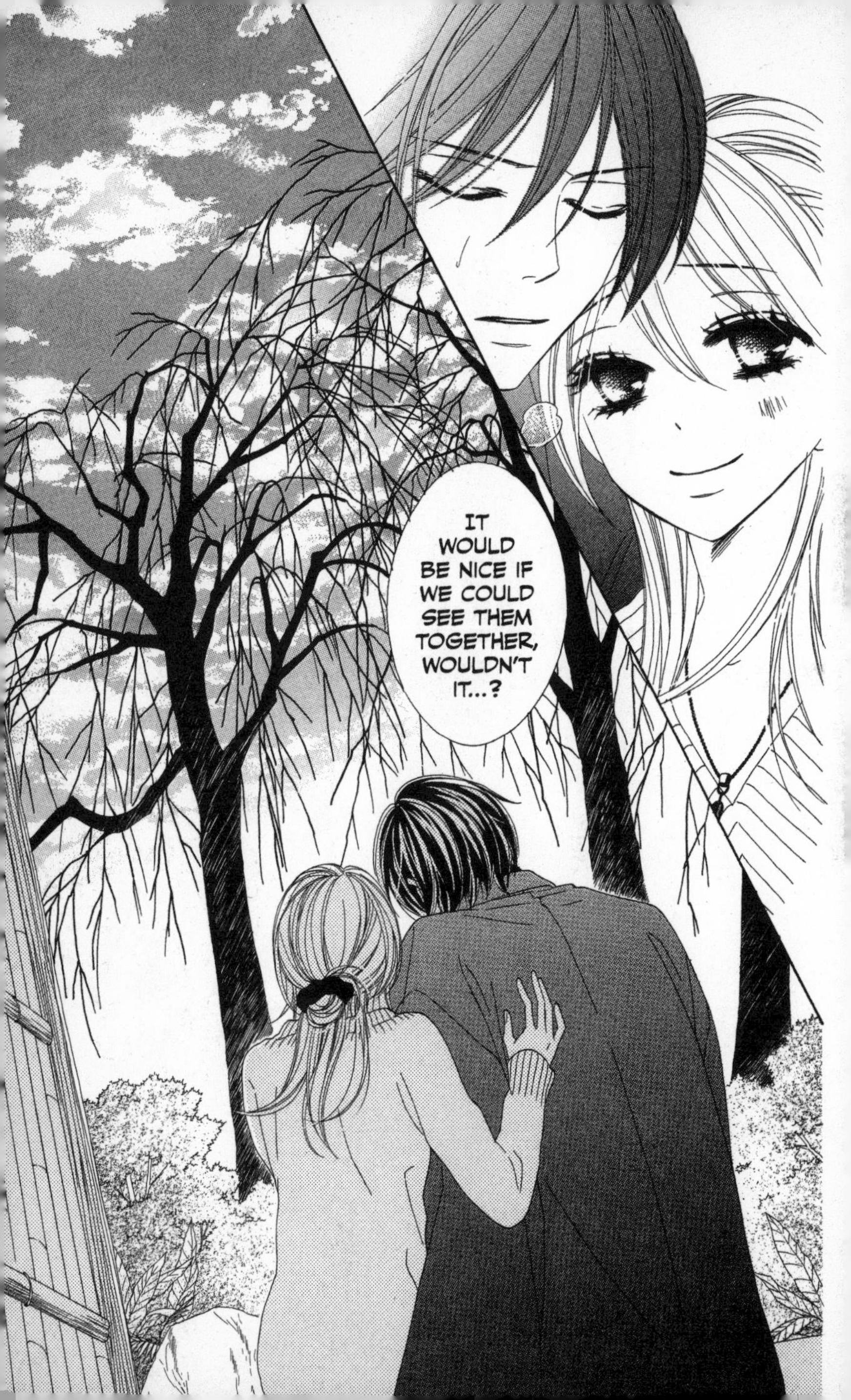
IT WOULD BE NICE IF WE COULD SEE THEM TOGETHER, WOULDN'T IT...?

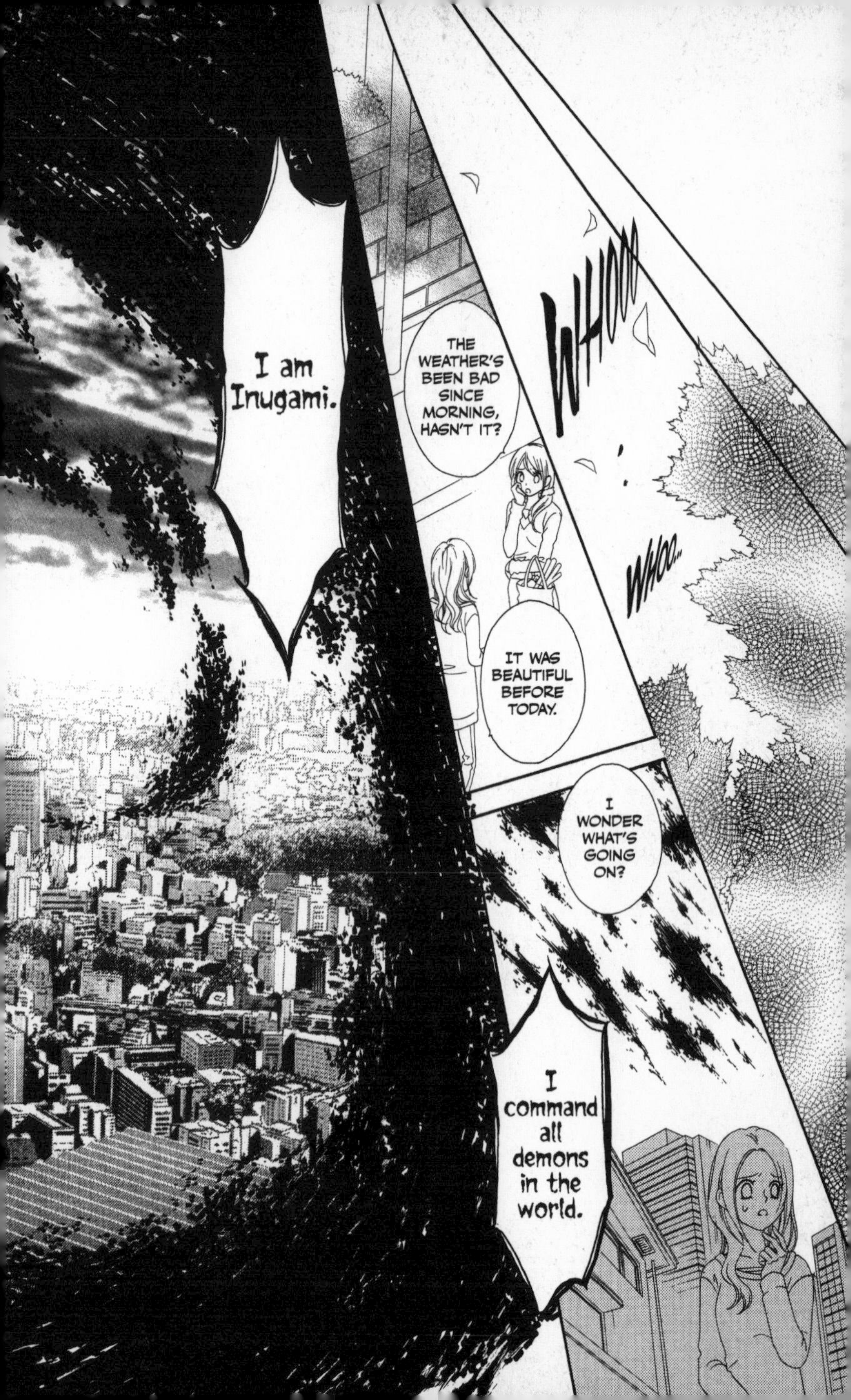
WHOOO
THE WEATHER'S BEEN BAD SINCE MORNING, HASN'T IT?
WHOO...
IT WAS BEAUTIFUL BEFORE TODAY.
I WONDER WHAT'S GOING ON?
I am Inugami.
I command all demons in the world.

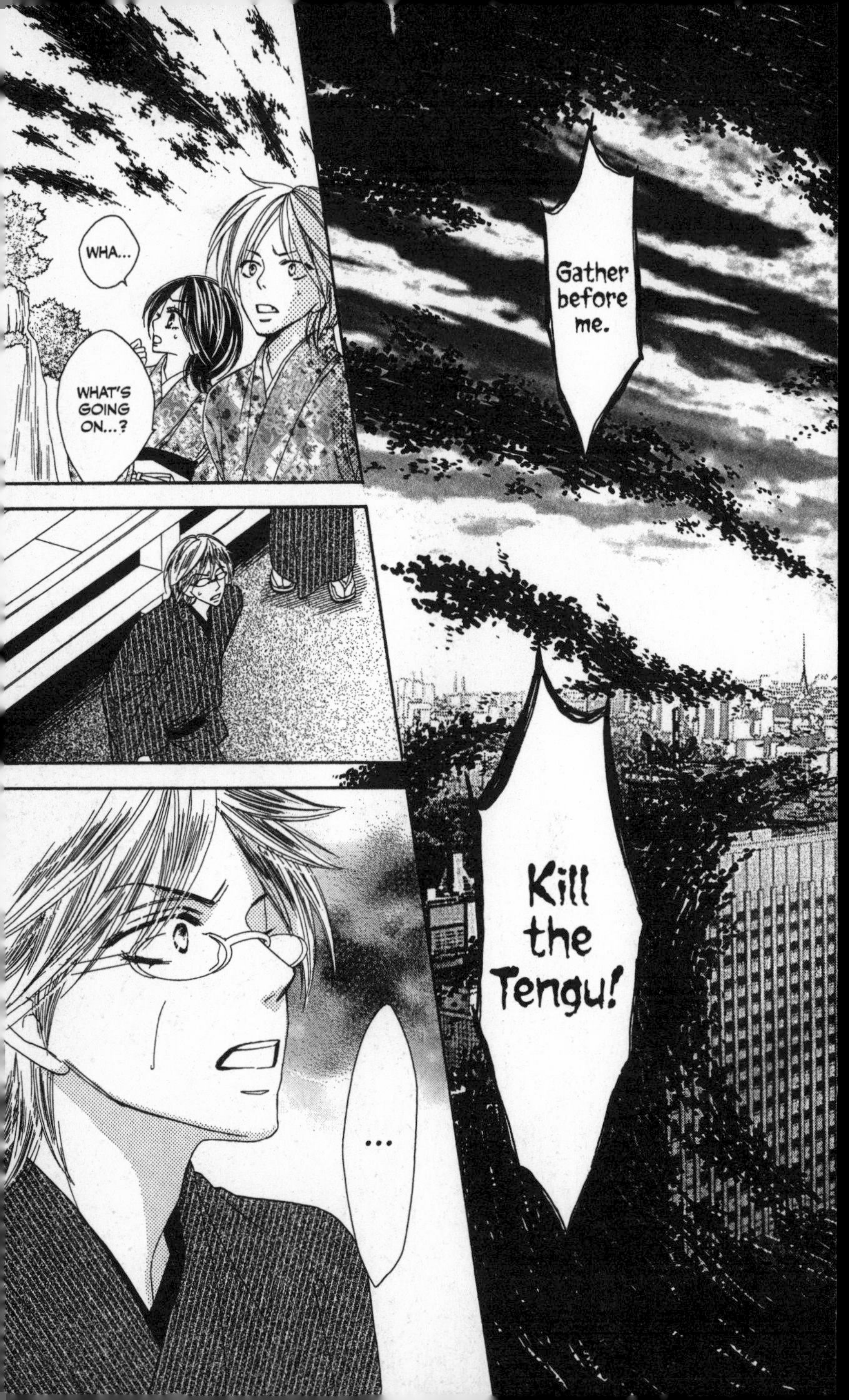
Gather before me.
Kill the Tengu!
WHA...
WHAT'S GOING ON...?
...

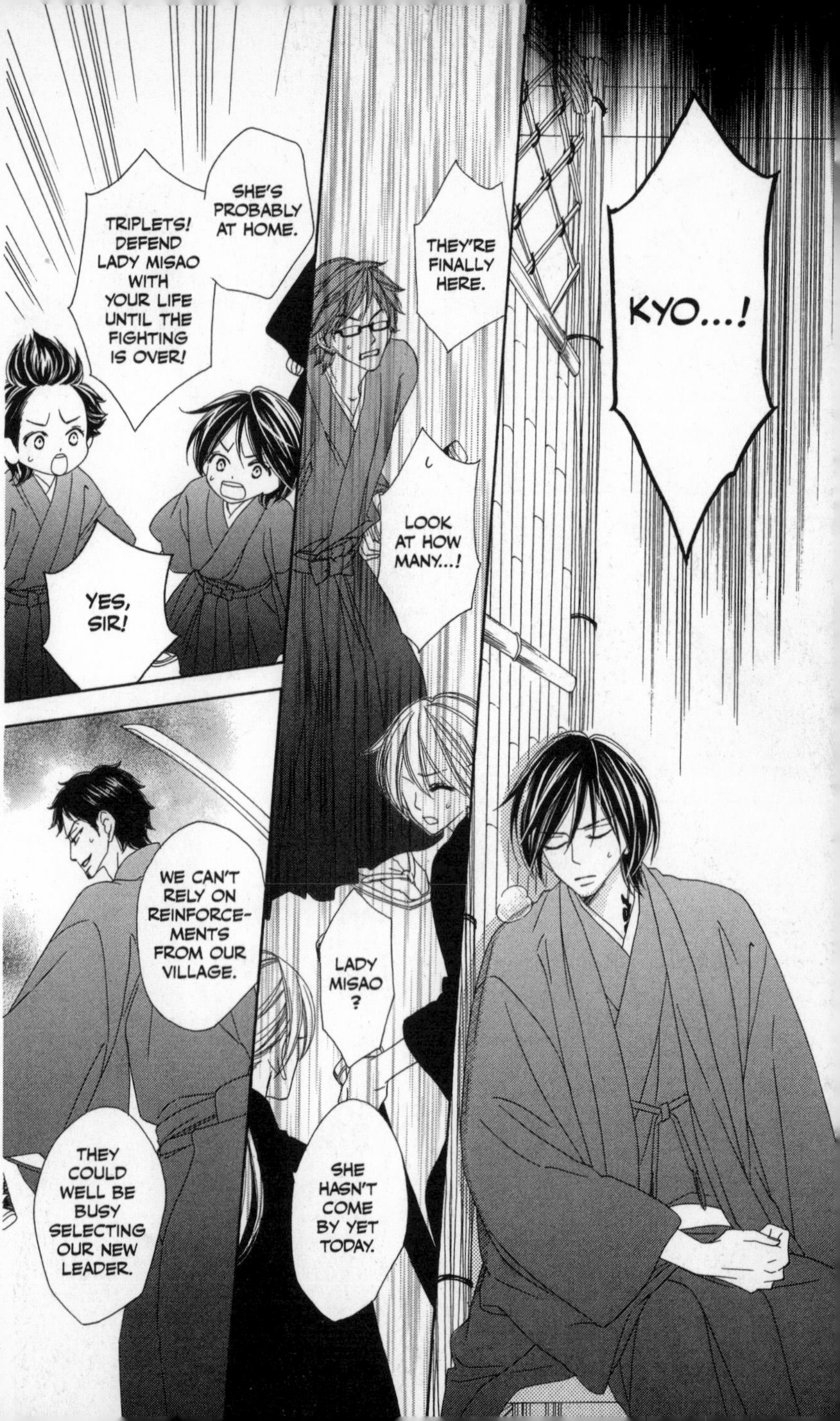
KYO...!
THEY'RE FINALLY HERE.
LOOK AT HOW MANY...!
LADY MISAO?
SHE HASN'T COME BY YET TODAY.
SHE'S PROBABLY AT HOME.
TRIPLETS! DEFEND LADY MISAO WITH YOUR LIFE UNTIL THE FIGHTING IS OVER!
YES, SIR!
WE CAN'T RELY ON REINFORCEMENTS FROM OUR VILLAGE.
THEY COULD WELL BE BUSY SELECTING OUR NEW LEADER.

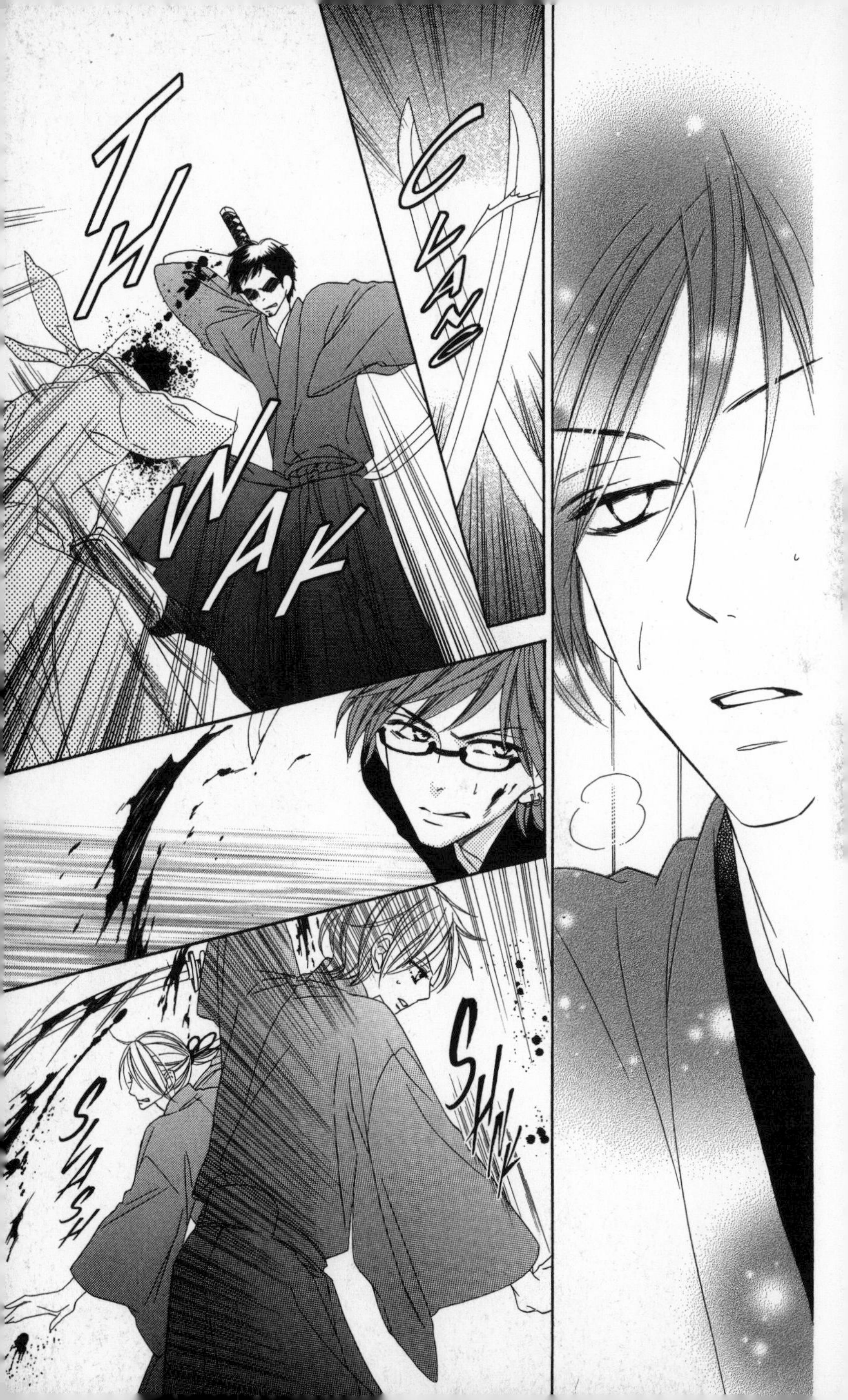
CLANG
THWAK
SHNK
SLASH

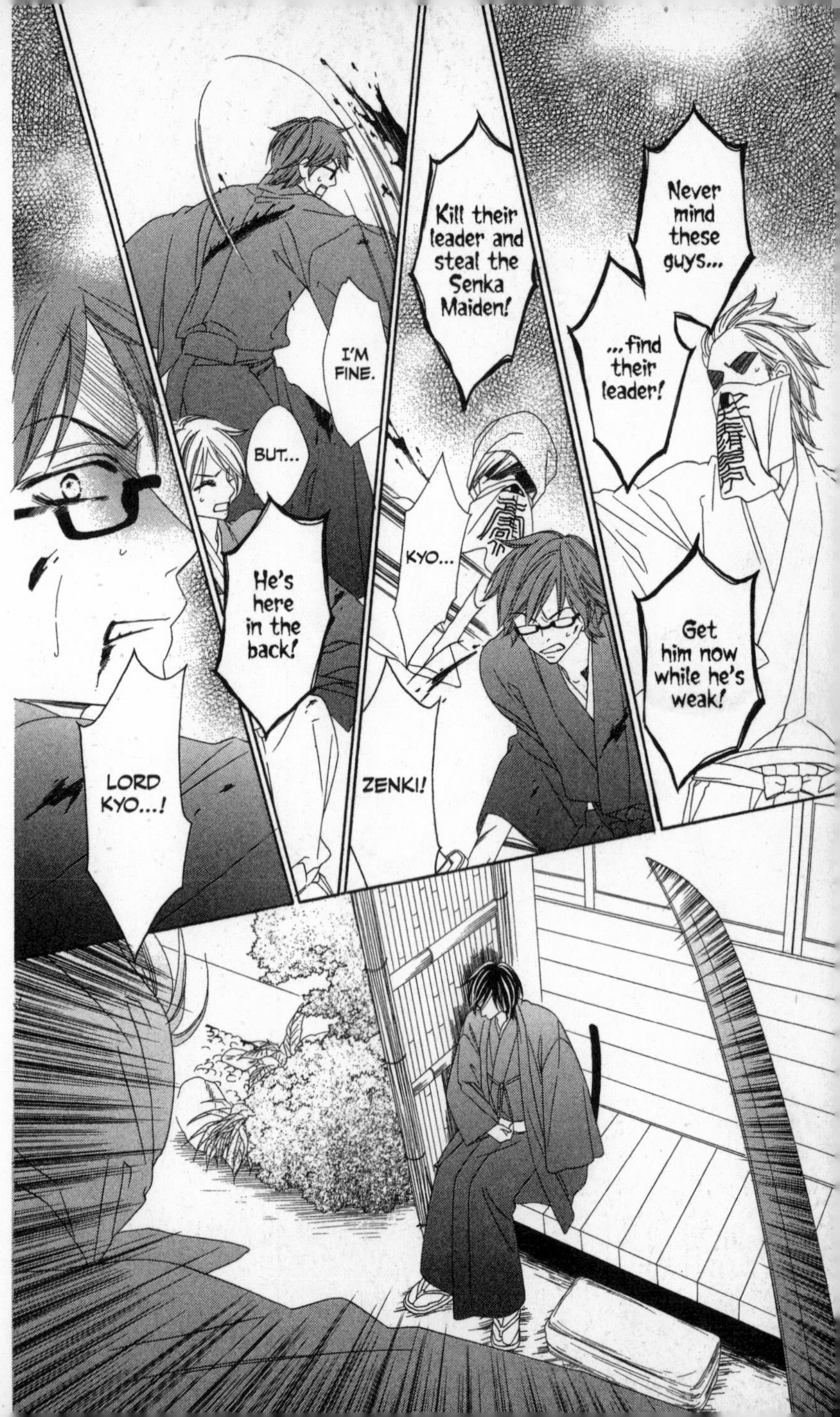
Never mind these guys...
...find their leader!
Get him now while he's weak!
Kill their leader and steal the Senka Maiden!
KYO...
ZENKI!
I'M FINE.
BUT...
He's here in the back!
LORD KYO...!

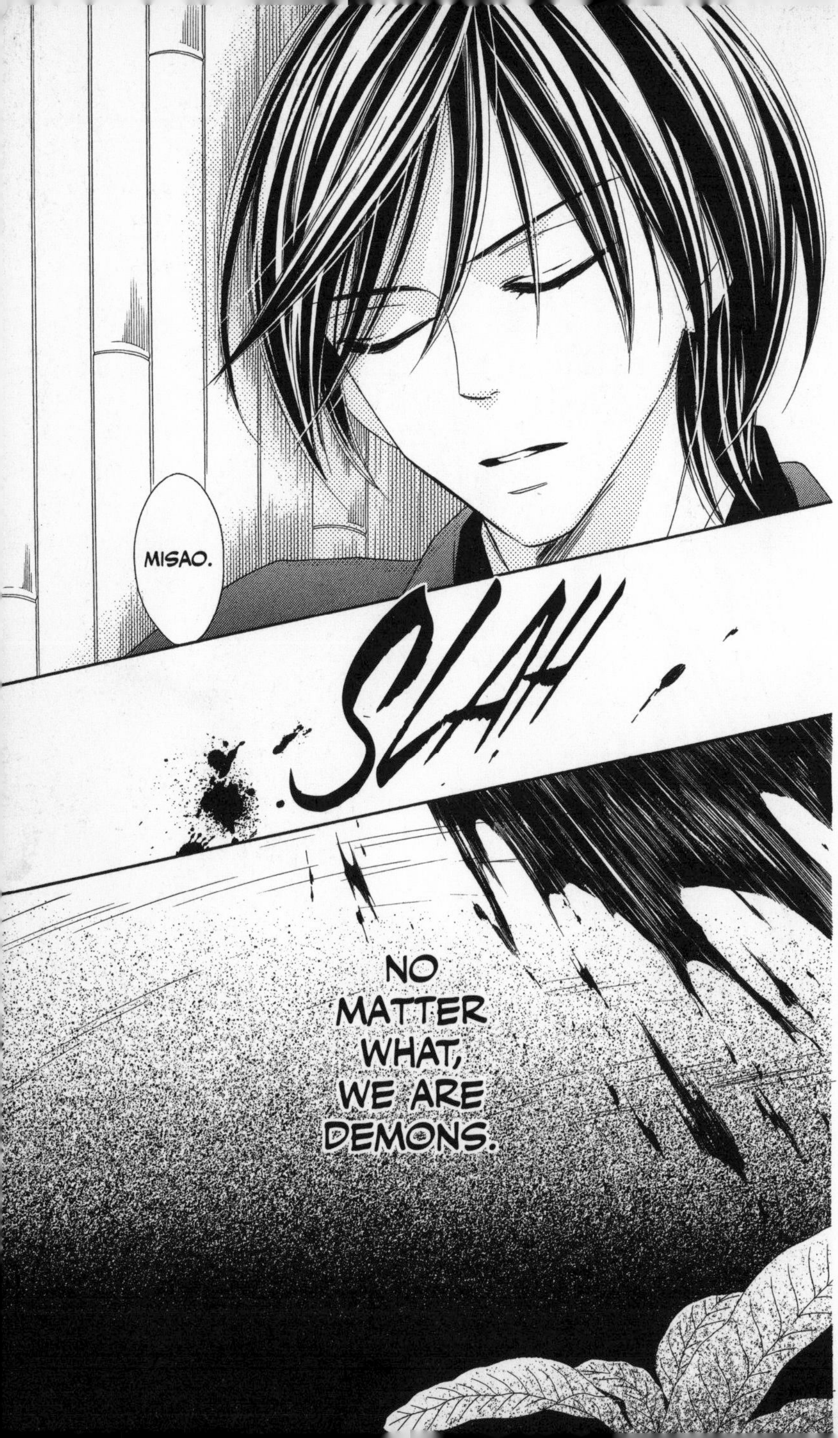
MISAO.
SLAH
NO MATTER WHAT, WE ARE DEMONS.

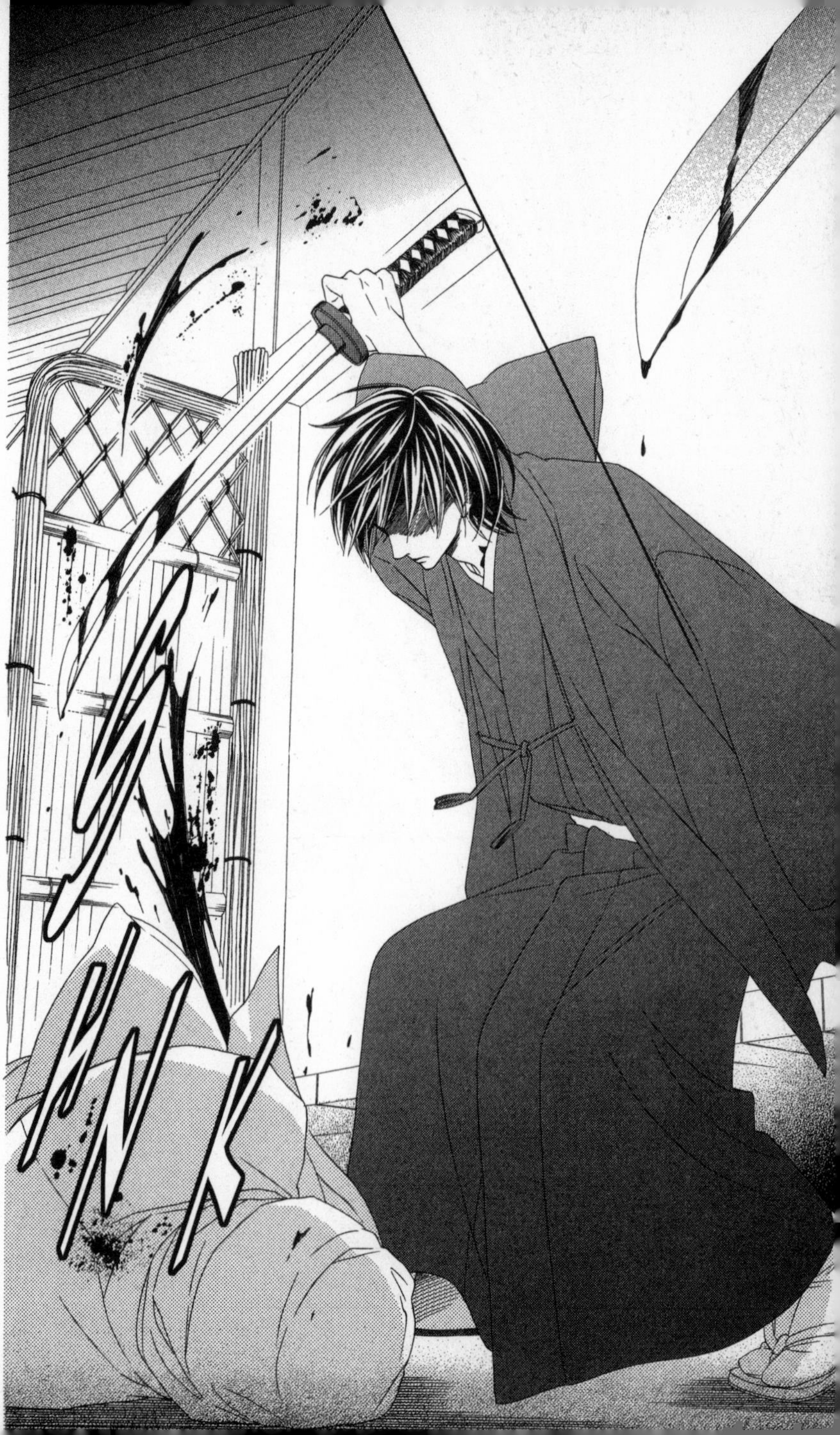
SHNK

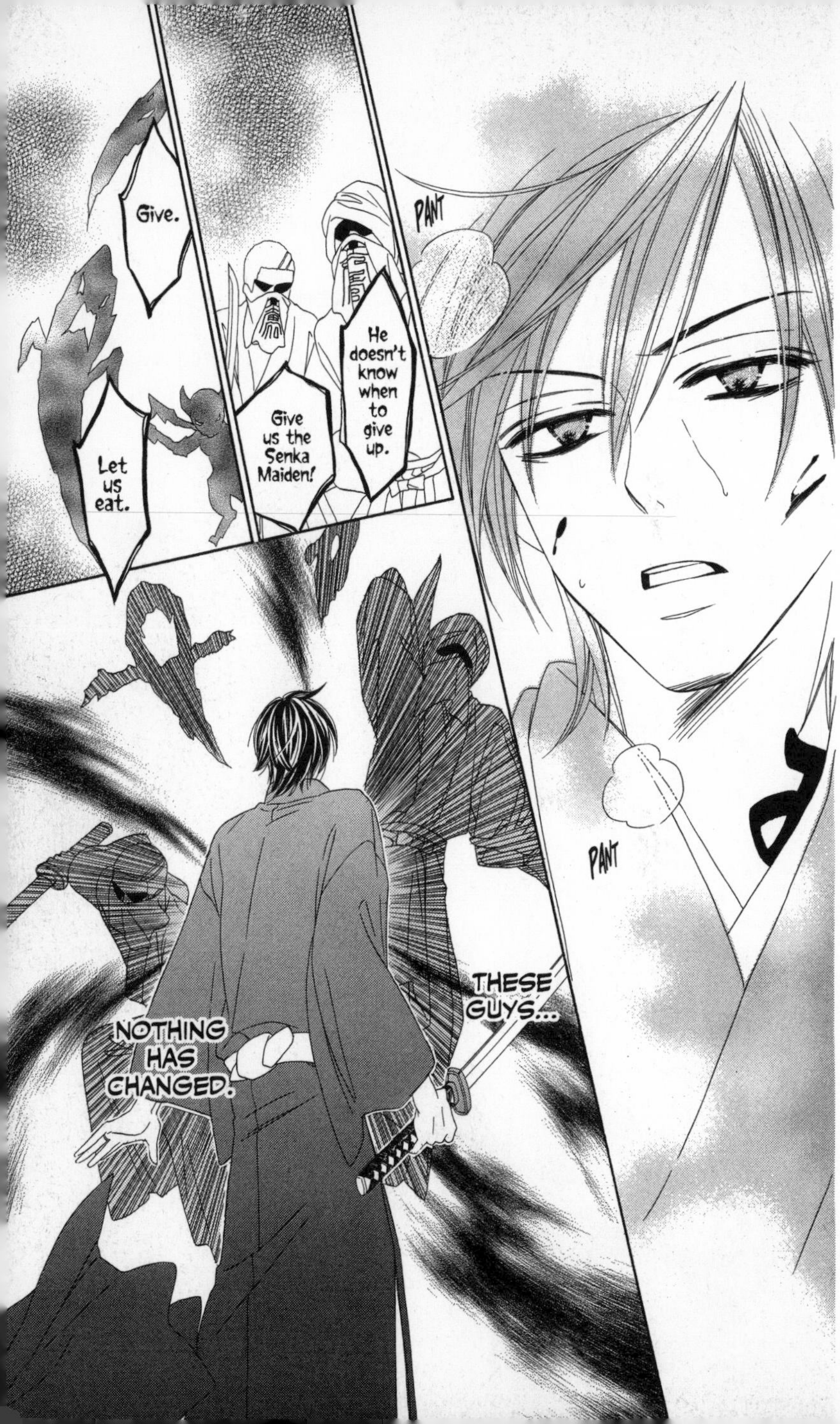
PANT
PANT
He doesn't know when to give up.
Give us the Senka Maiden!
Give.
Let us eat.
THESE GUYS...
NOTHING HAS CHANGED.

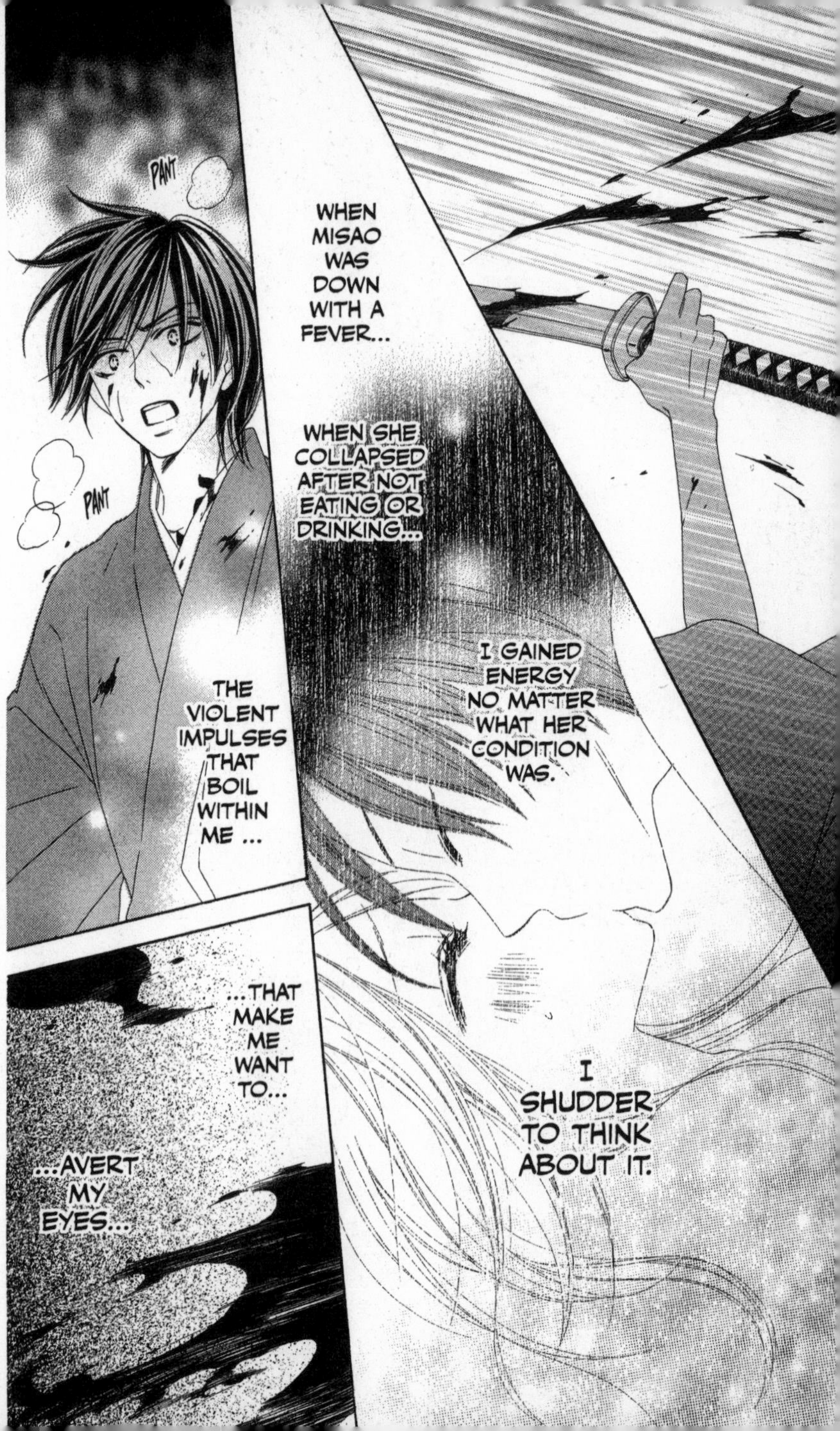
WHEN MISAO WAS DOWN WITH A FEVER...
WHEN SHE COLLAPSED AFTER NOT EATING OR DRINKING...
I GAINED ENERGY NO MATTER WHAT HER CONDITION WAS.
I SHUDDER TO THINK ABOUT IT.
PANT
PANT
THE VIOLENT IMPULSES THAT BOIL WITHIN ME ...
...THAT MAKE ME WANT TO...
...AVERT MY EYES...

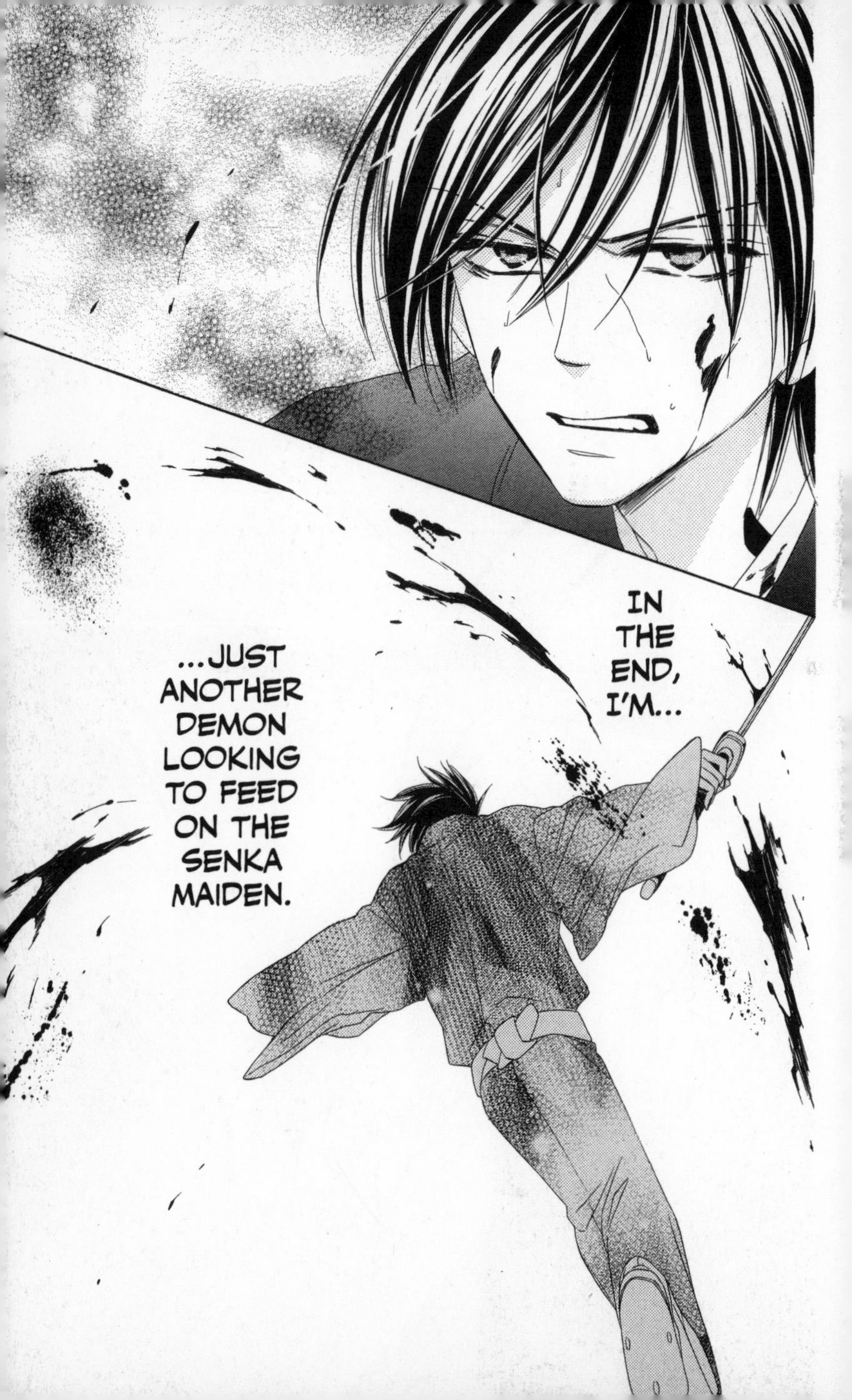
IN THE END, I'M...
...JUST ANOTHER DEMON LOOKING TO FEED ON THE SENKA MAIDEN.

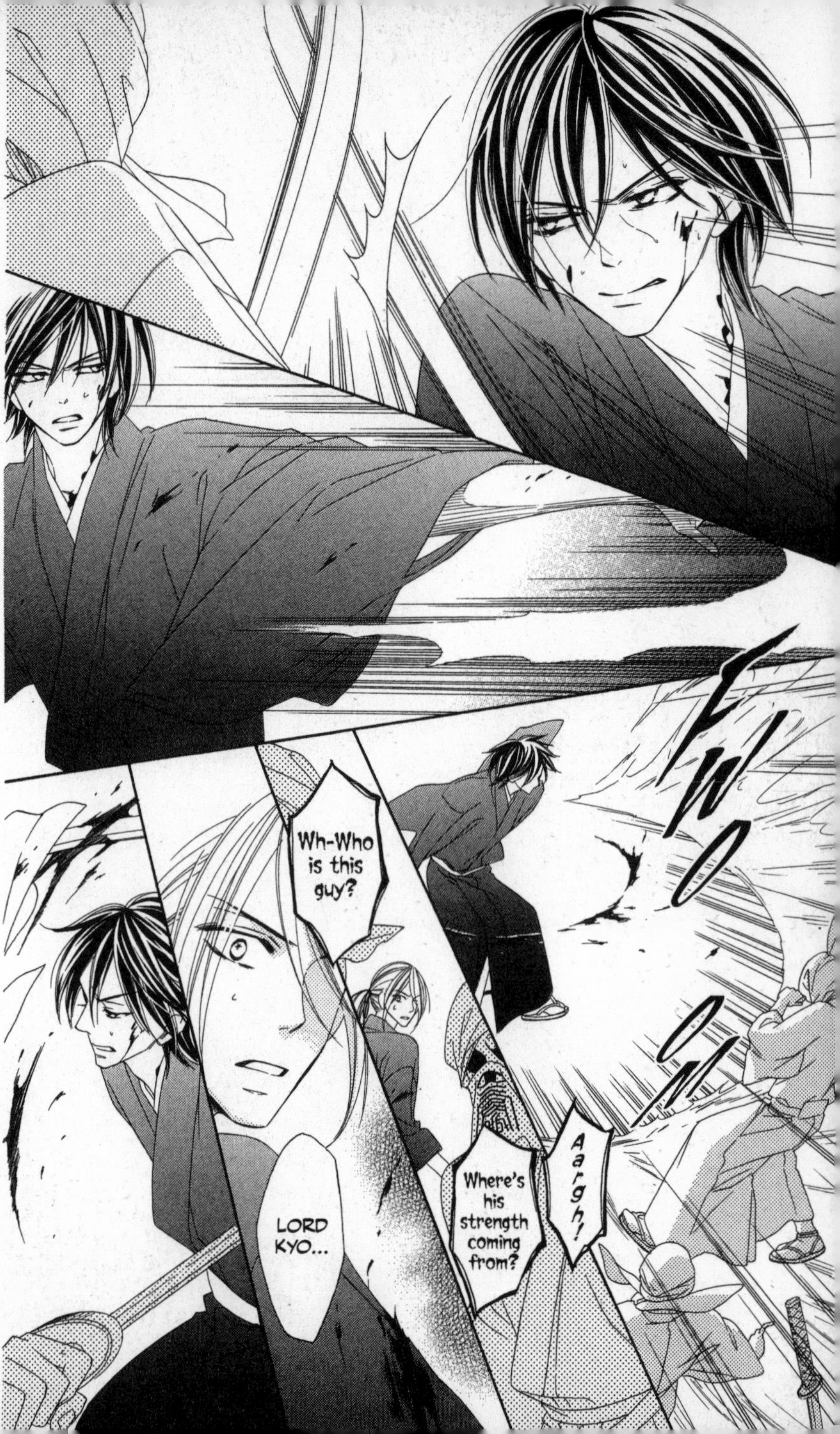
FWOOM
Aargh!
Where's his strength coming from?
Wh-Who is this guy?
LORD KYO...

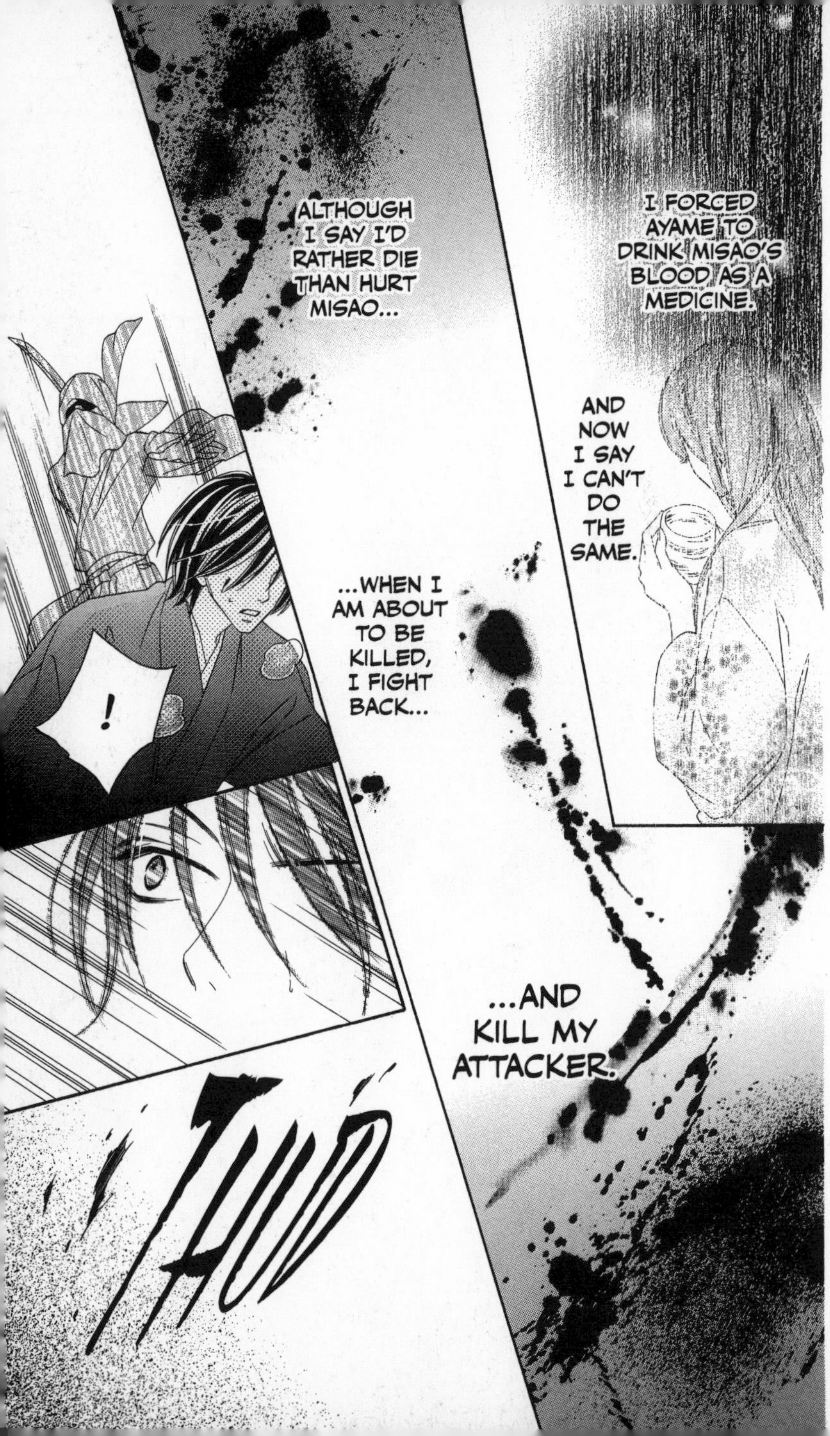
I FORCED AYAME TO DRINK MISAO'S BLOOD AS A MEDICINE.
AND NOW I SAY I CAN'T DO THE SAME.
ALTHOUGH I SAY I'D RATHER DIE THAN HURT MISAO...
...WHEN I AM ABOUT TO BE KILLED, I FIGHT BACK...
!
...AND KILL MY ATTACKER.
THUD

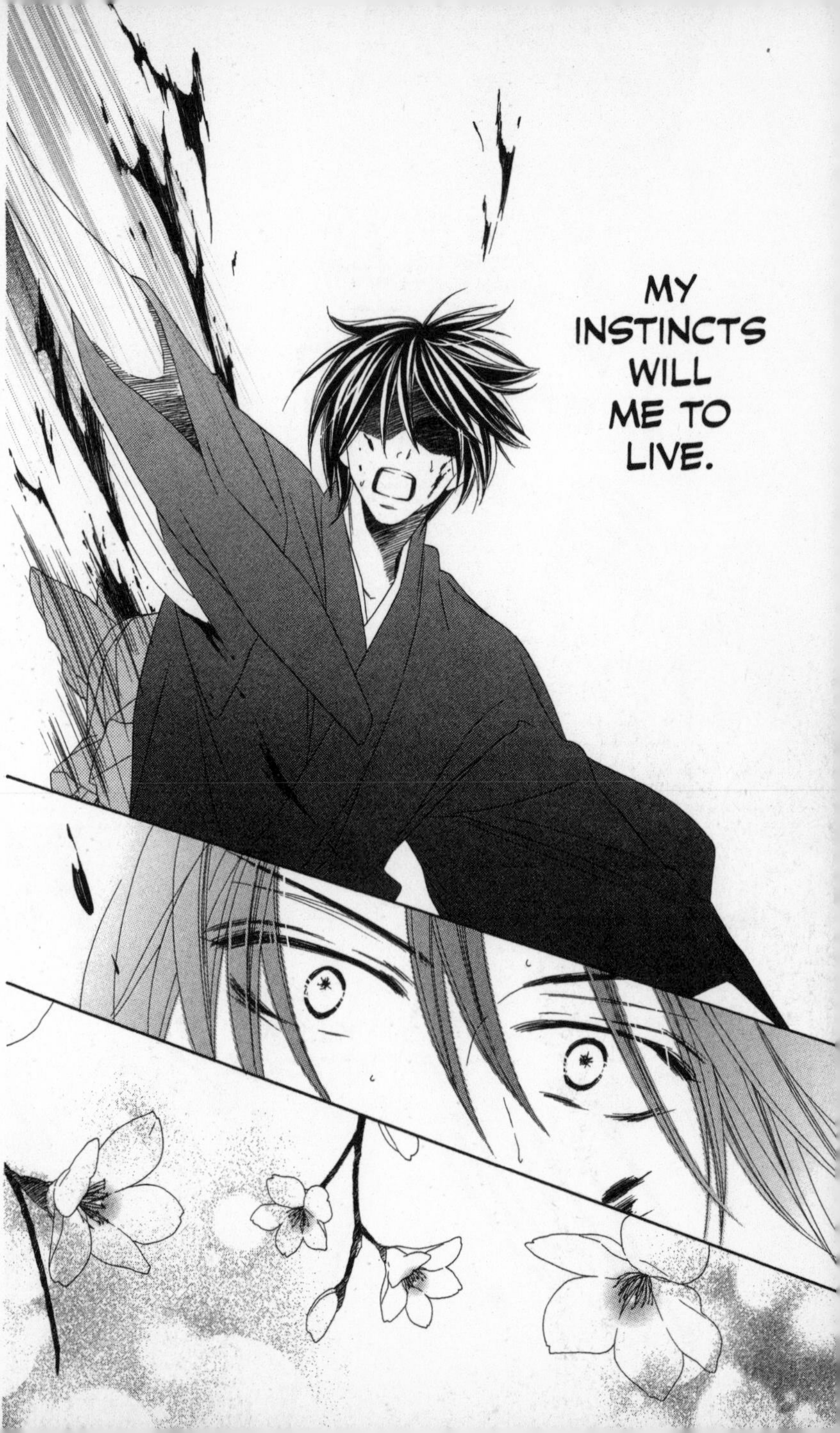
MY INSTINCTS WILL ME TO LIVE.

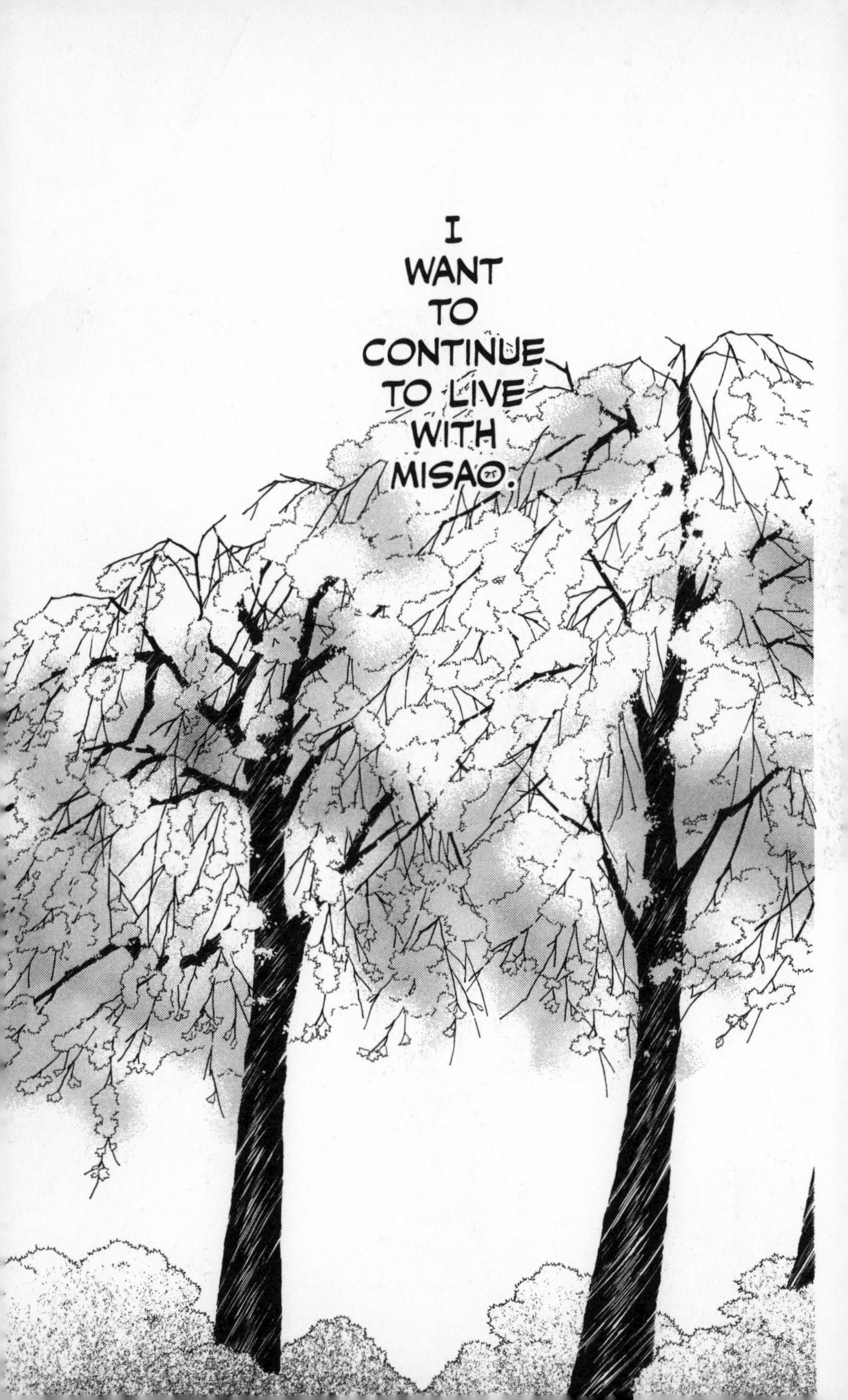
I WANT TO CONTINUE TO LIVE WITH MISAO.

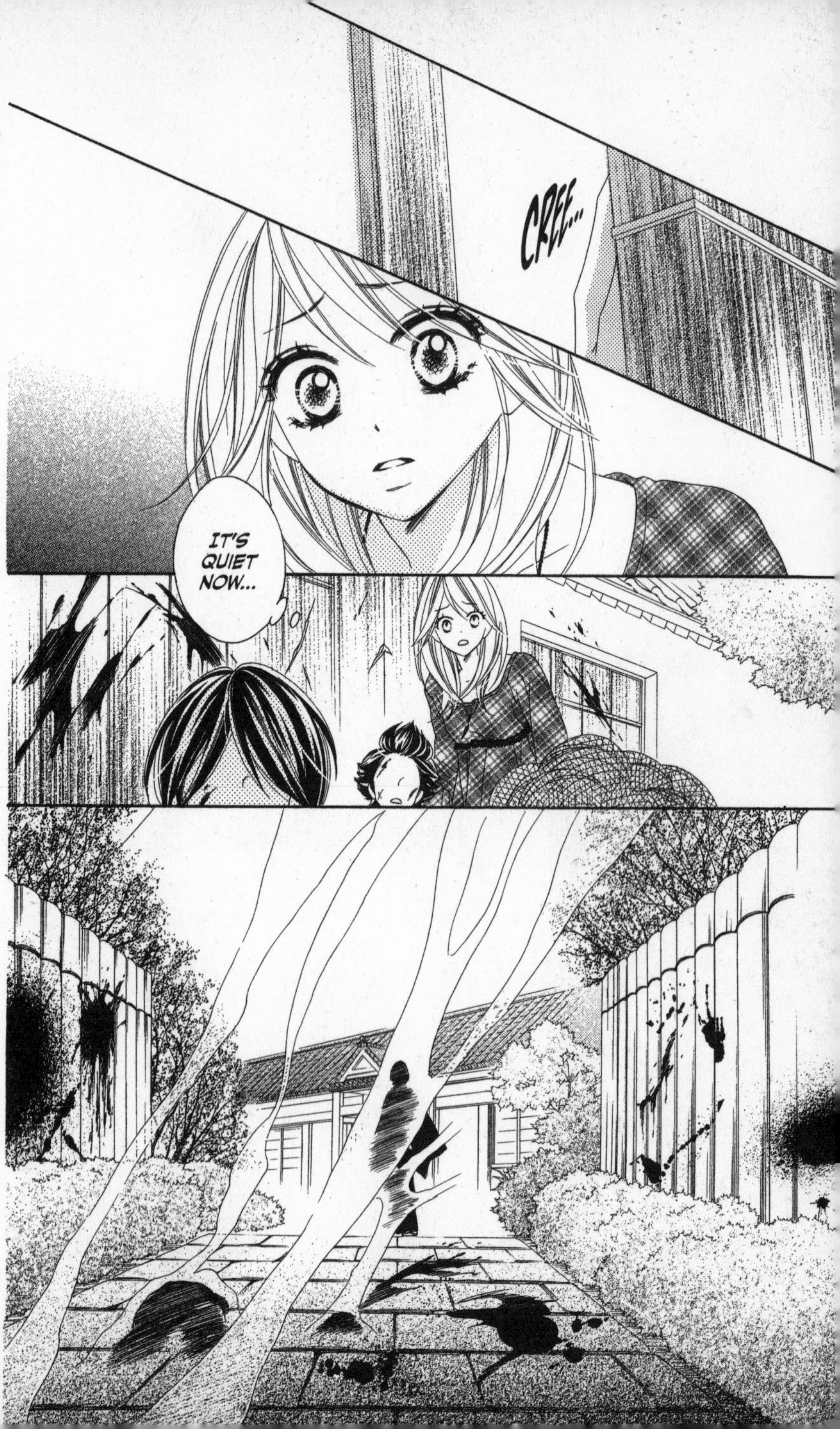
CREE...
IT'S QUIET NOW...

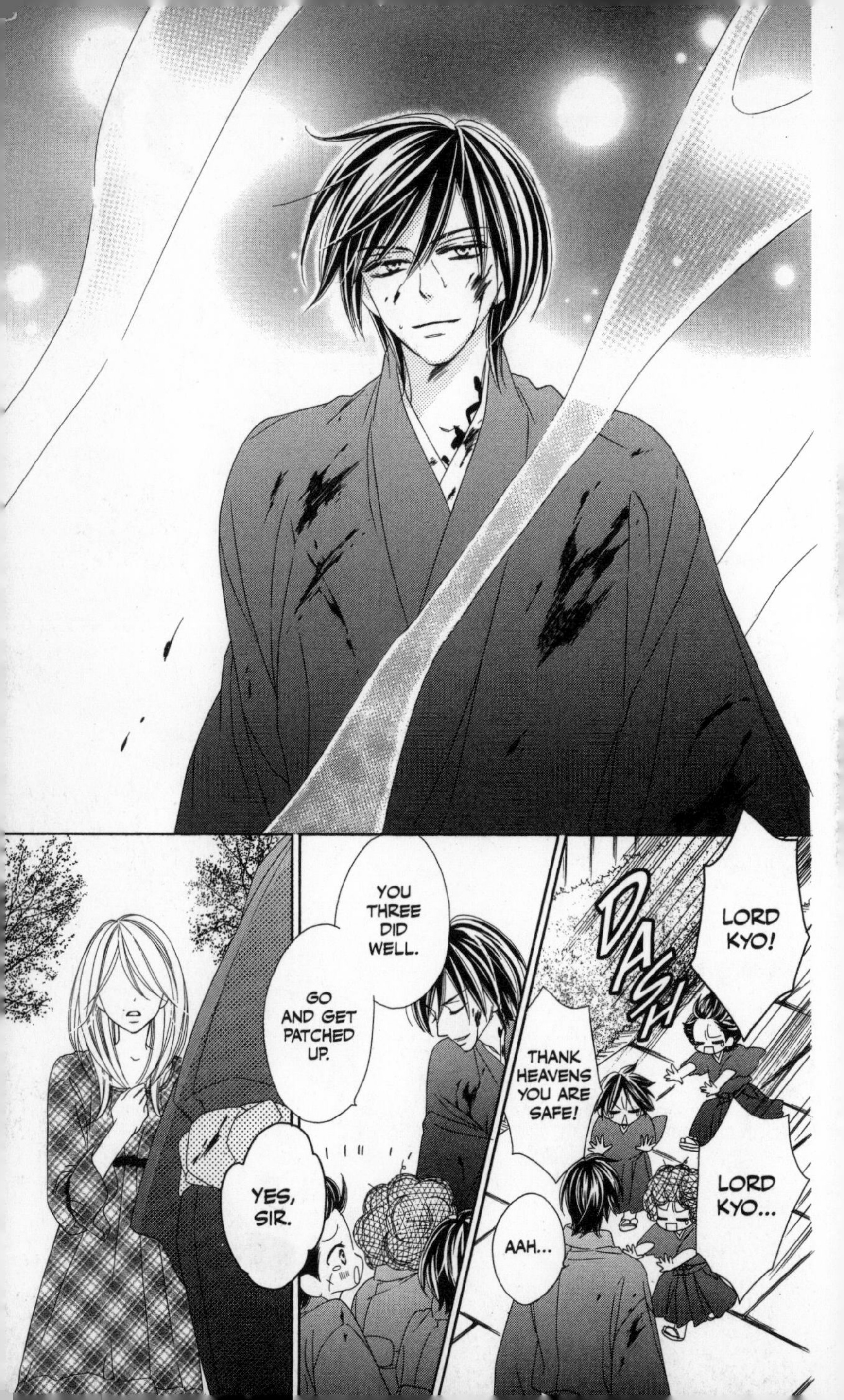
LORD KYO!
DASH
THANK HEAVENS YOU ARE SAFE!
LORD KYO...
AAH...
YOU THREE DID WELL.
GO AND GET PATCHED UP.
YES, SIR.

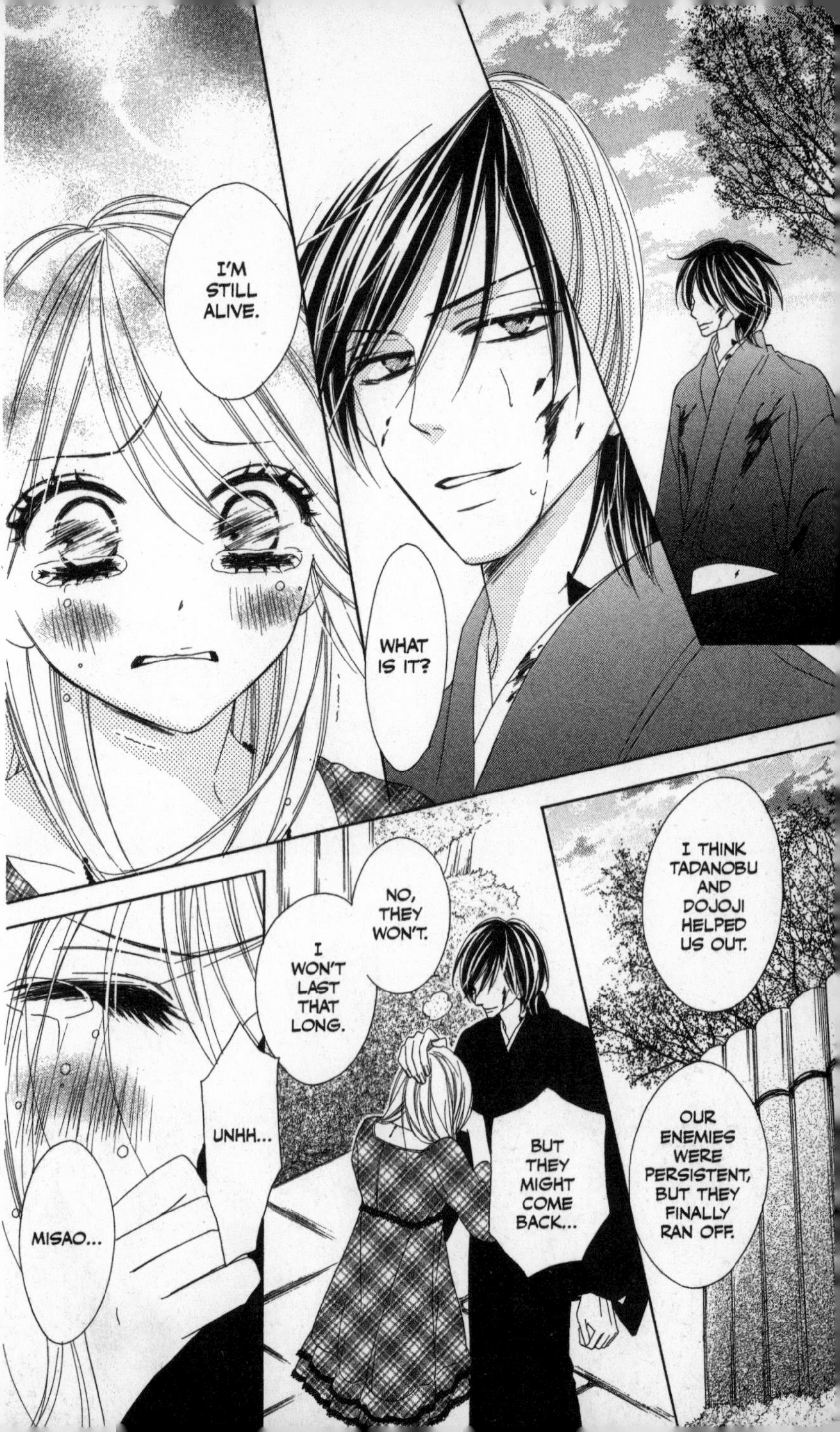
WHAT IS IT?
I'M STILL ALIVE.
I THINK TADANOBU AND DOJOJI HELPED US OUT.
OUR ENEMIES WERE PERSISTENT, BUT THEY FINALLY RAN OFF.
BUT THEY MIGHT COME BACK...
NO, THEY WON'T.
I WON'T LAST THAT LONG.
UNHH...
MISAO...

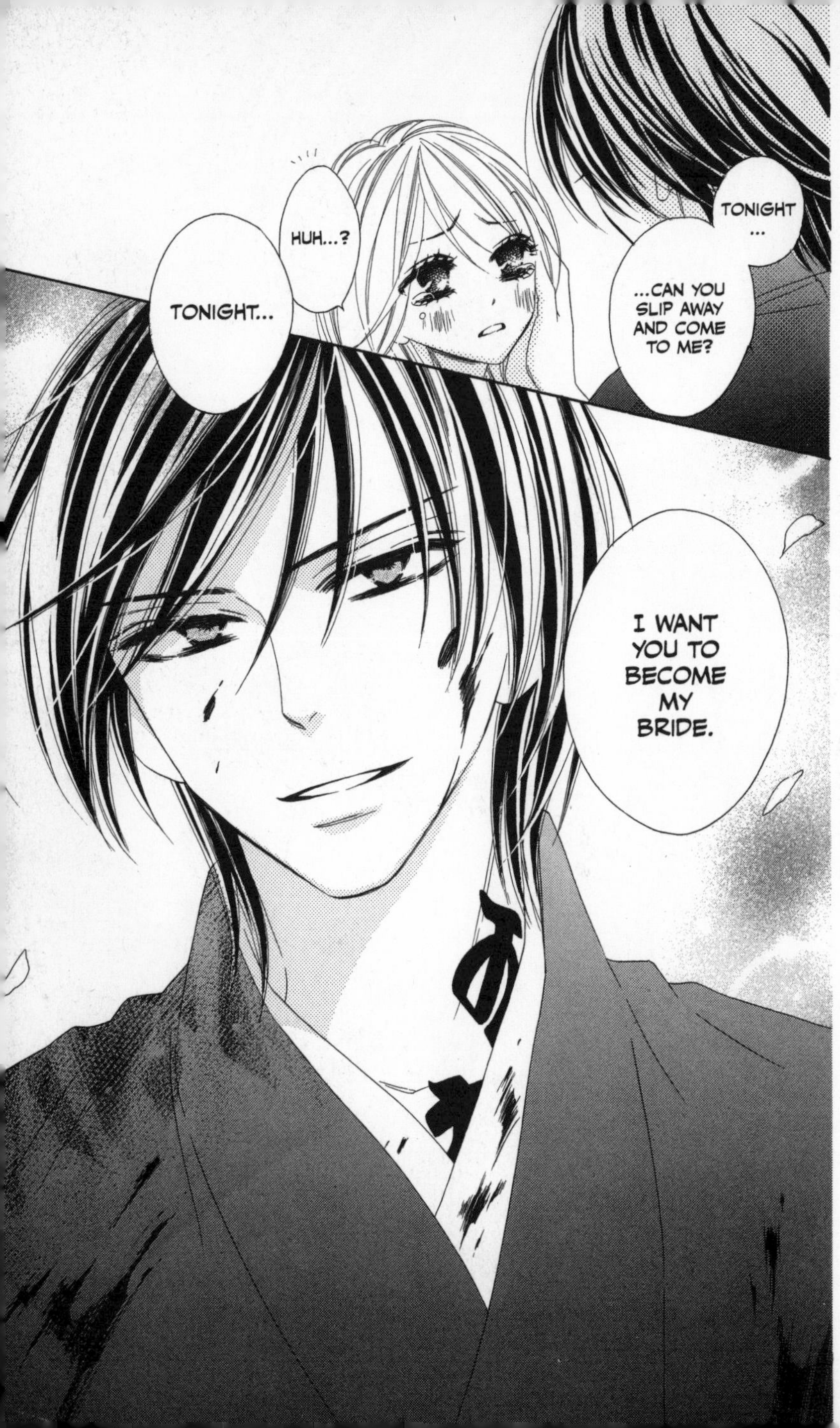
TONIGHT ...
...CAN YOU SLIP AWAY AND COME TO ME?
HUH...?
TONIGHT...
I WANT YOU TO BECOME MY BRIDE.

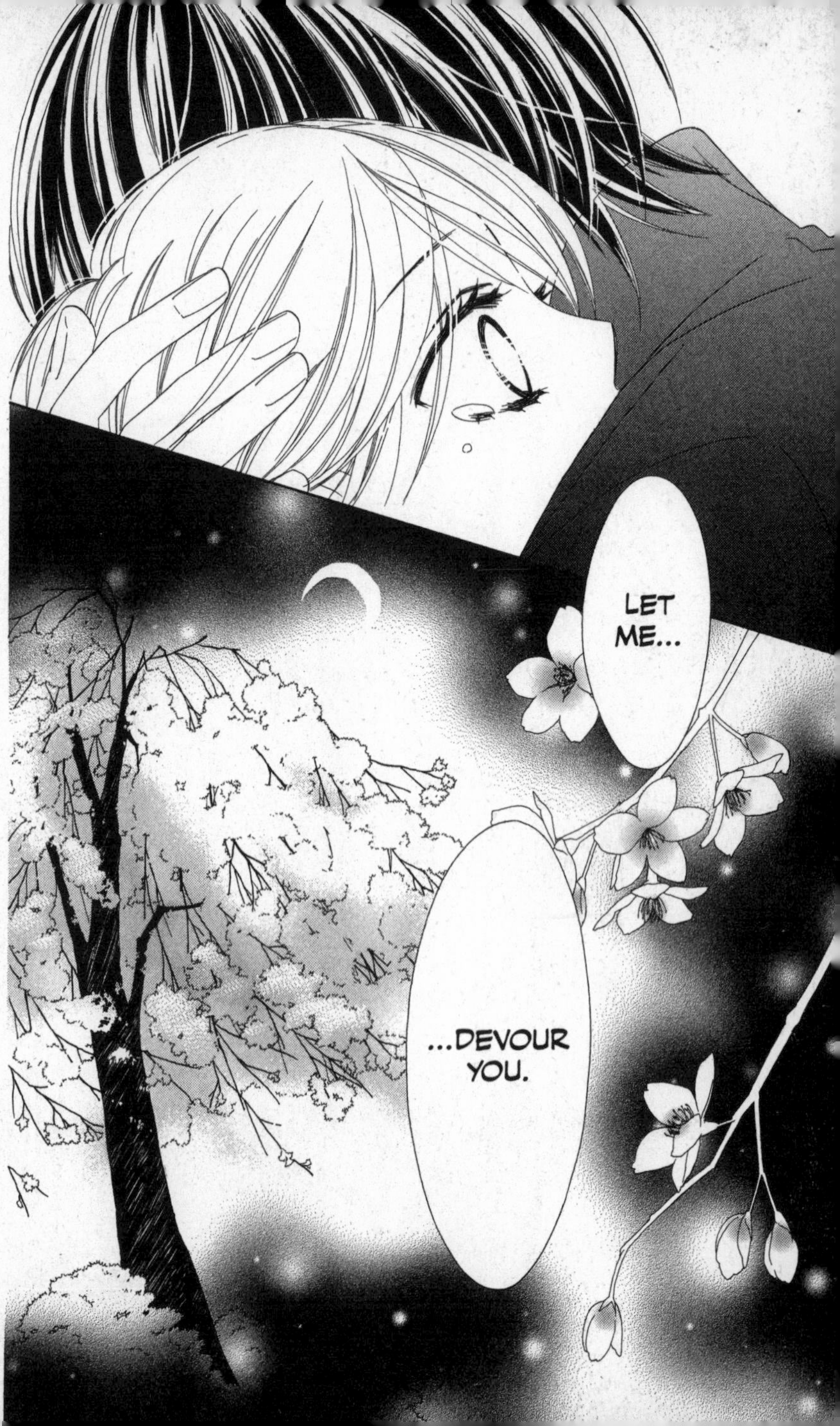
LET ME...
...DEVOUR YOU.

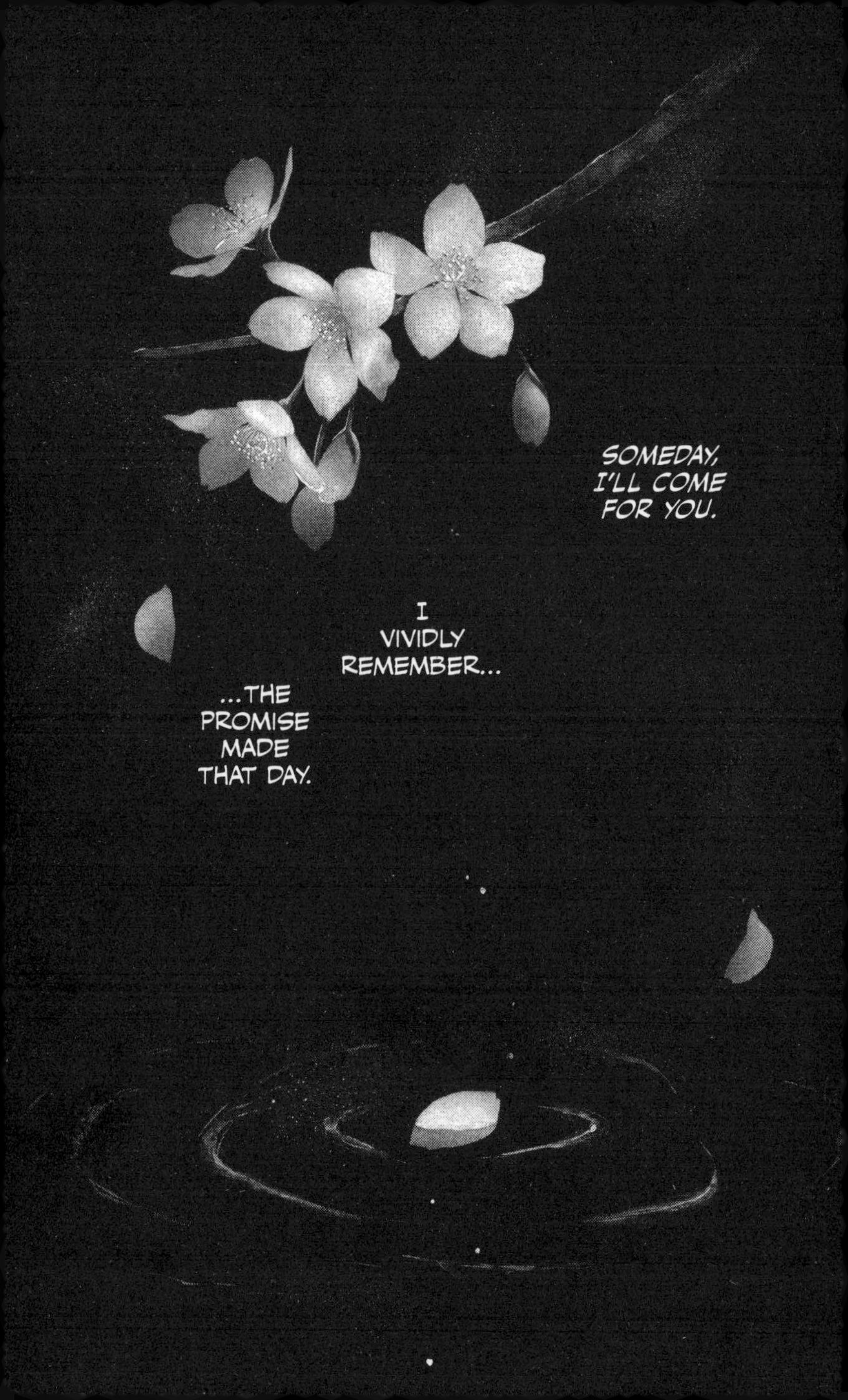
SOMEDAY, I'LL COME FOR YOU.
I VIVIDLY REMEMBER...
...THE PROMISE MADE THAT DAY.

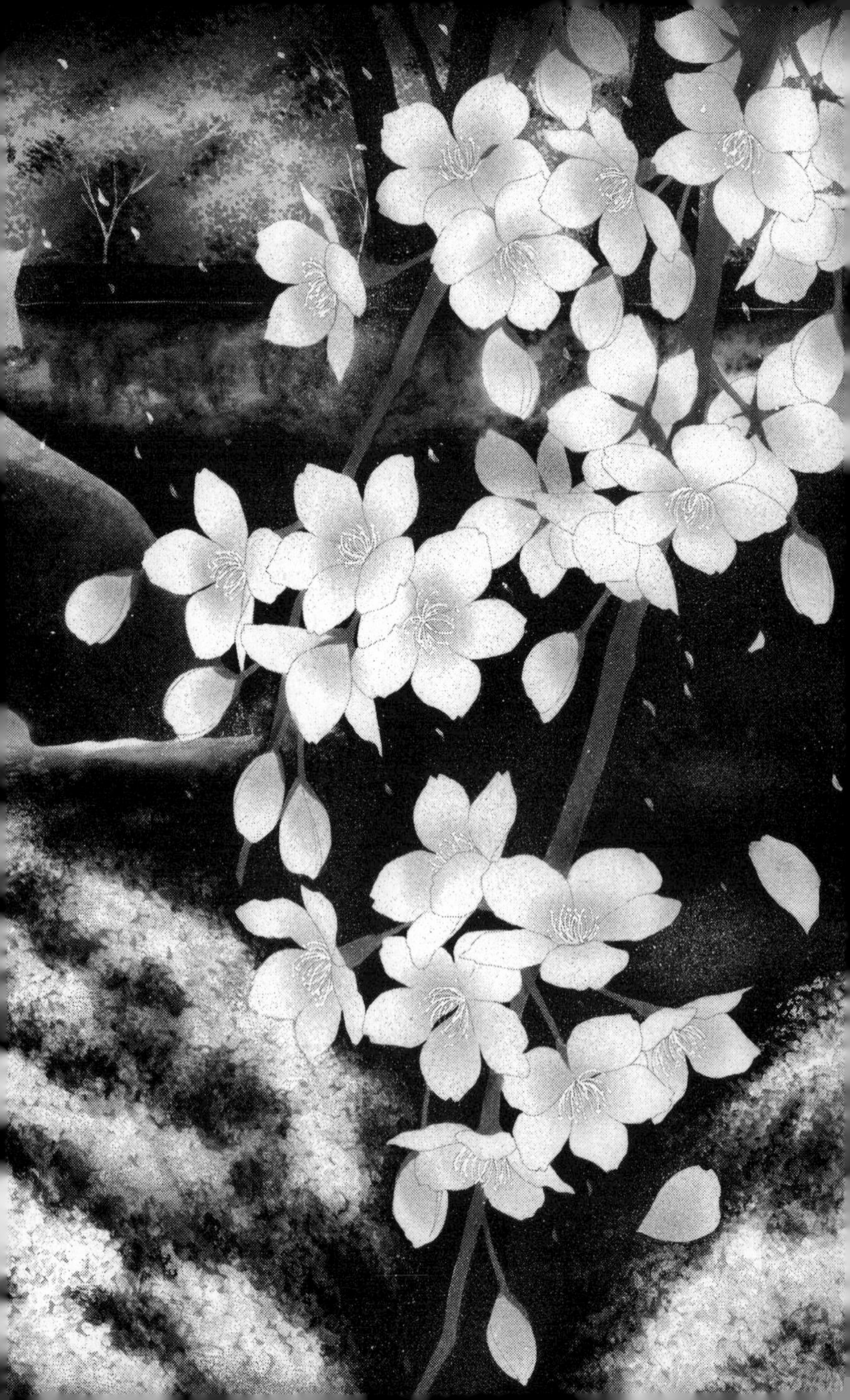

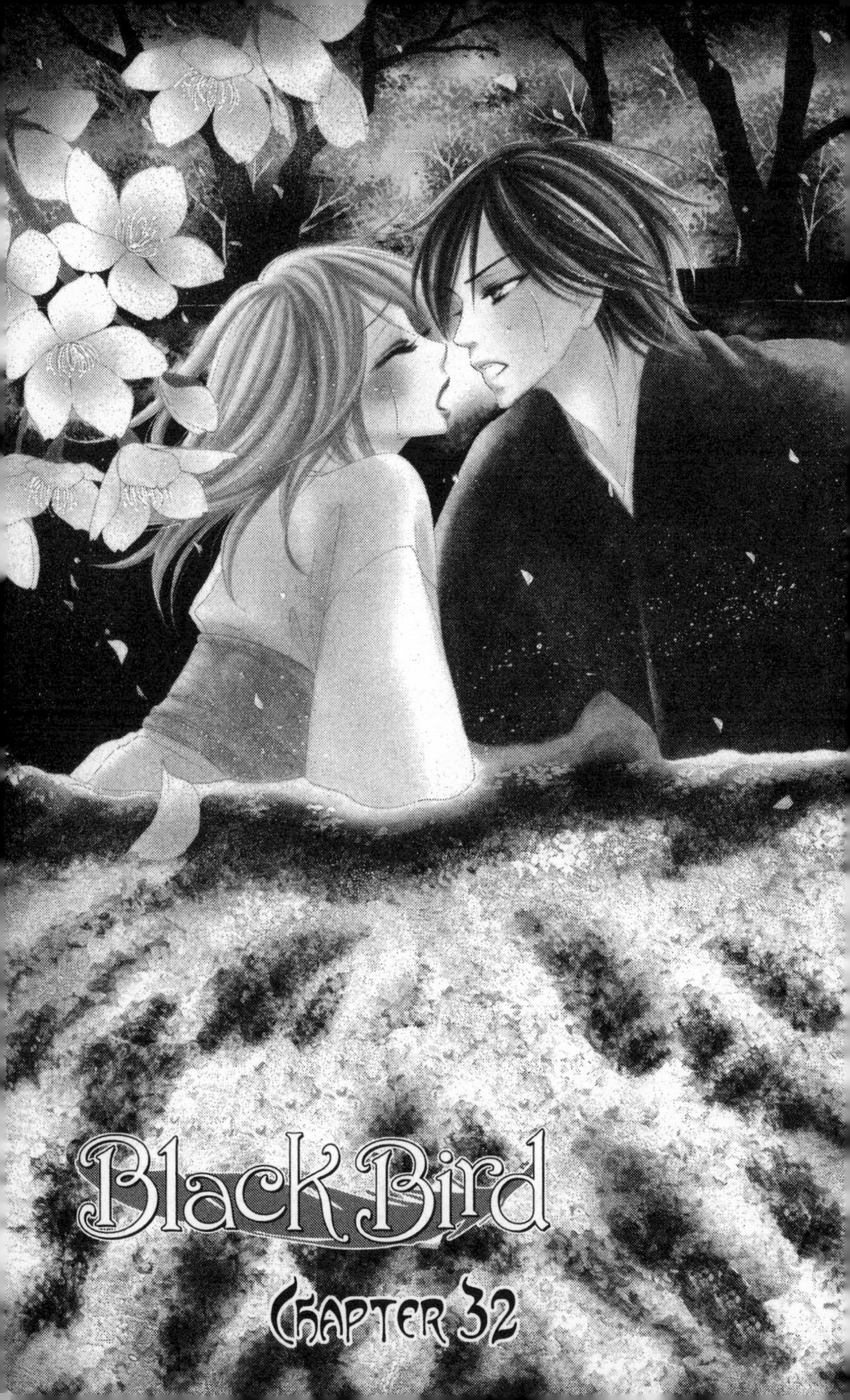
Black Bird
Chapter 32

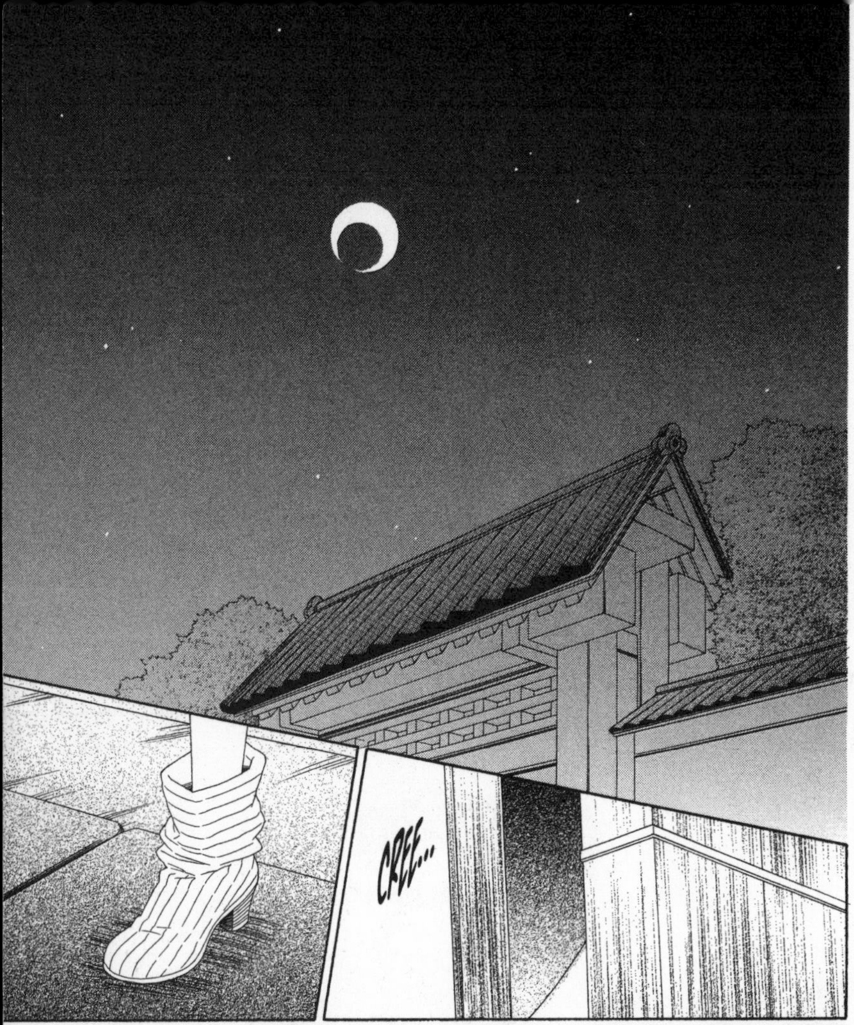
CREE...

Cherry Blossoms at Night

From the start, I knew I wanted to use this theme for the cover, so I drew this image.

Drawing cherry blossoms was difficult, as I knew it would be. But I'd still like to draw them again.

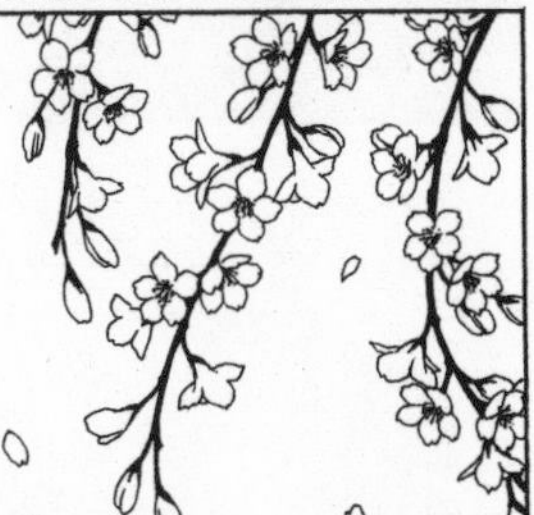

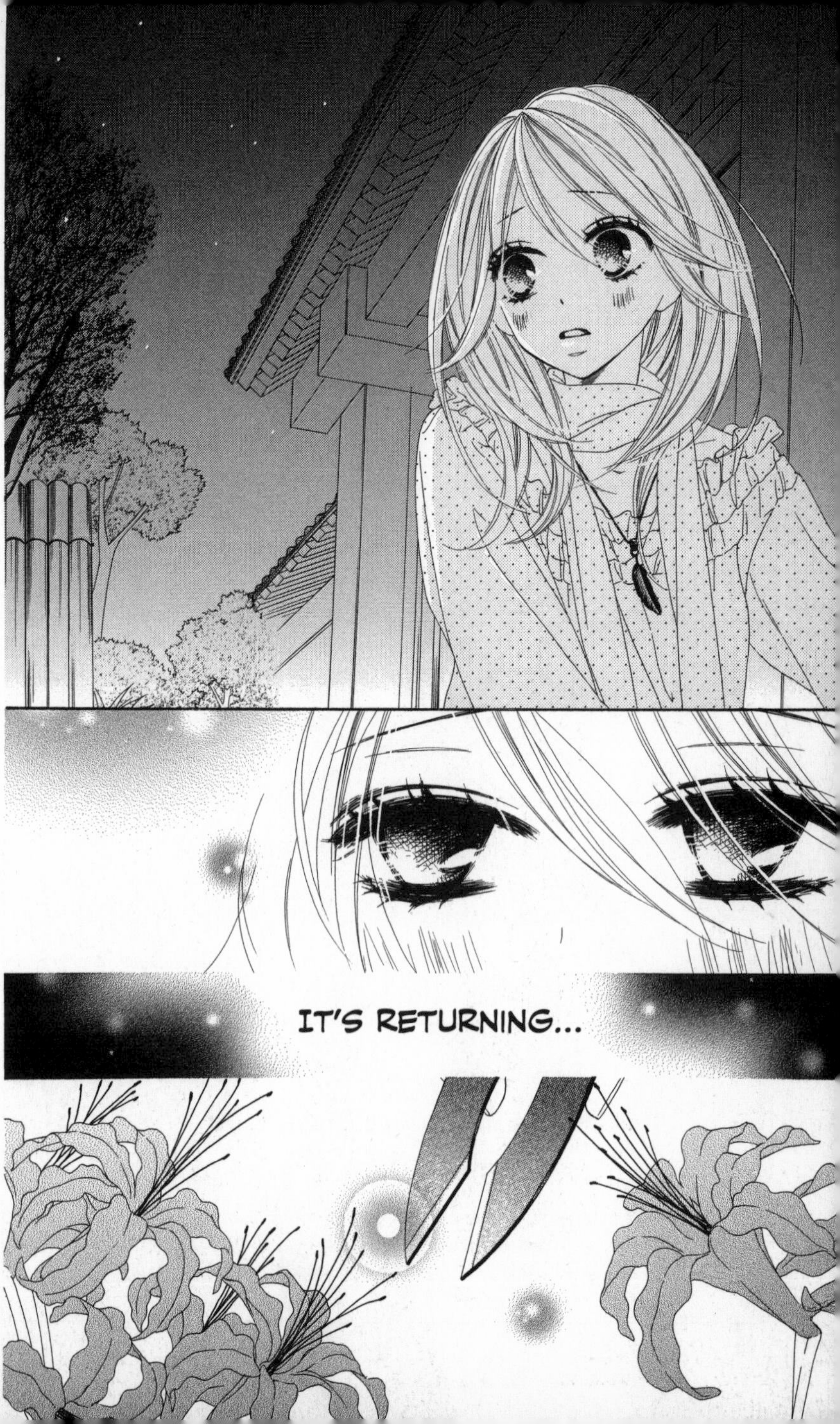
IT'S RETURNING...

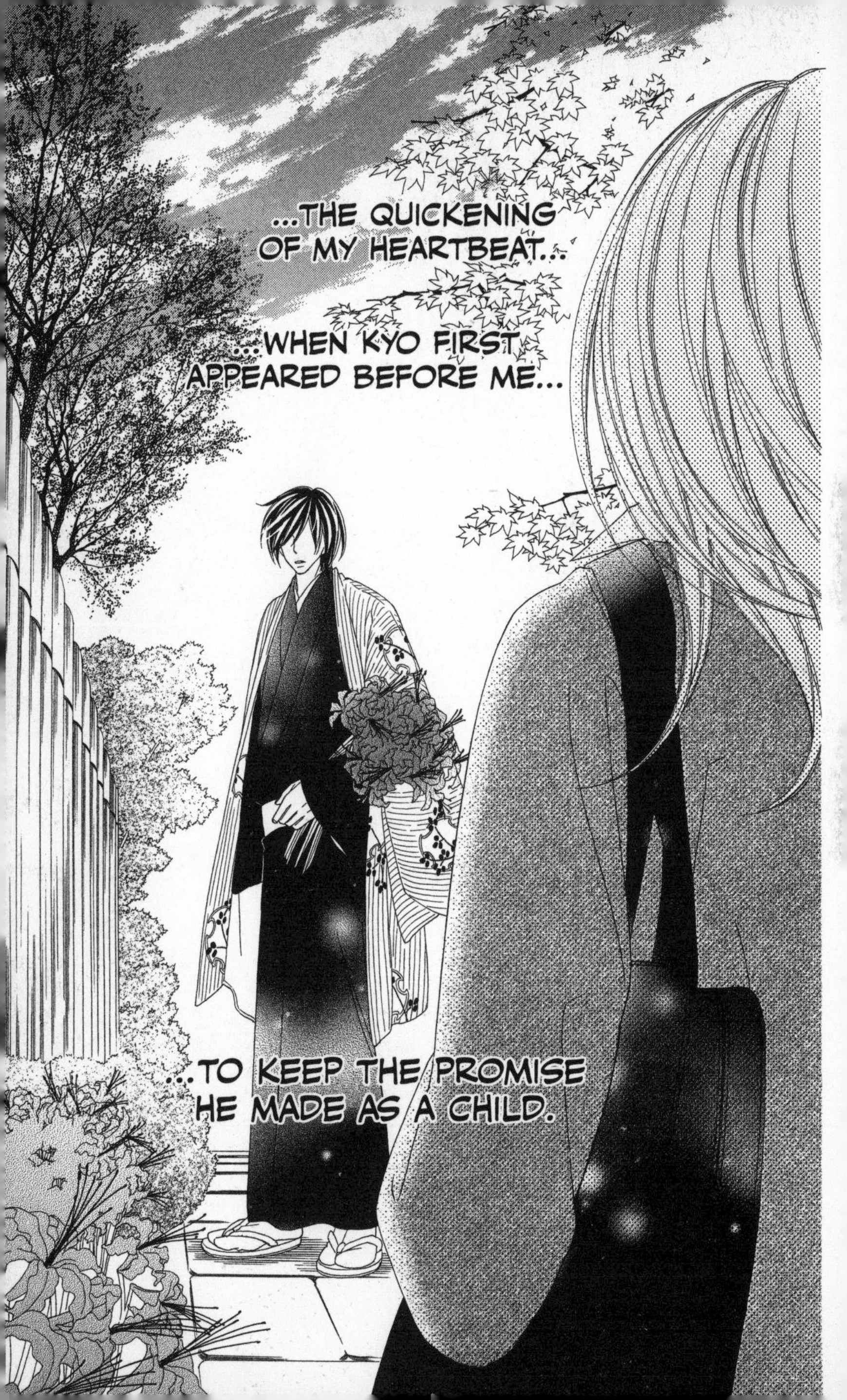
...THE QUICKENING OF MY HEARTBEAT...
...WHEN KYO FIRST APPEARED BEFORE ME...
...TO KEEP THE PROMISE HE MADE AS A CHILD.

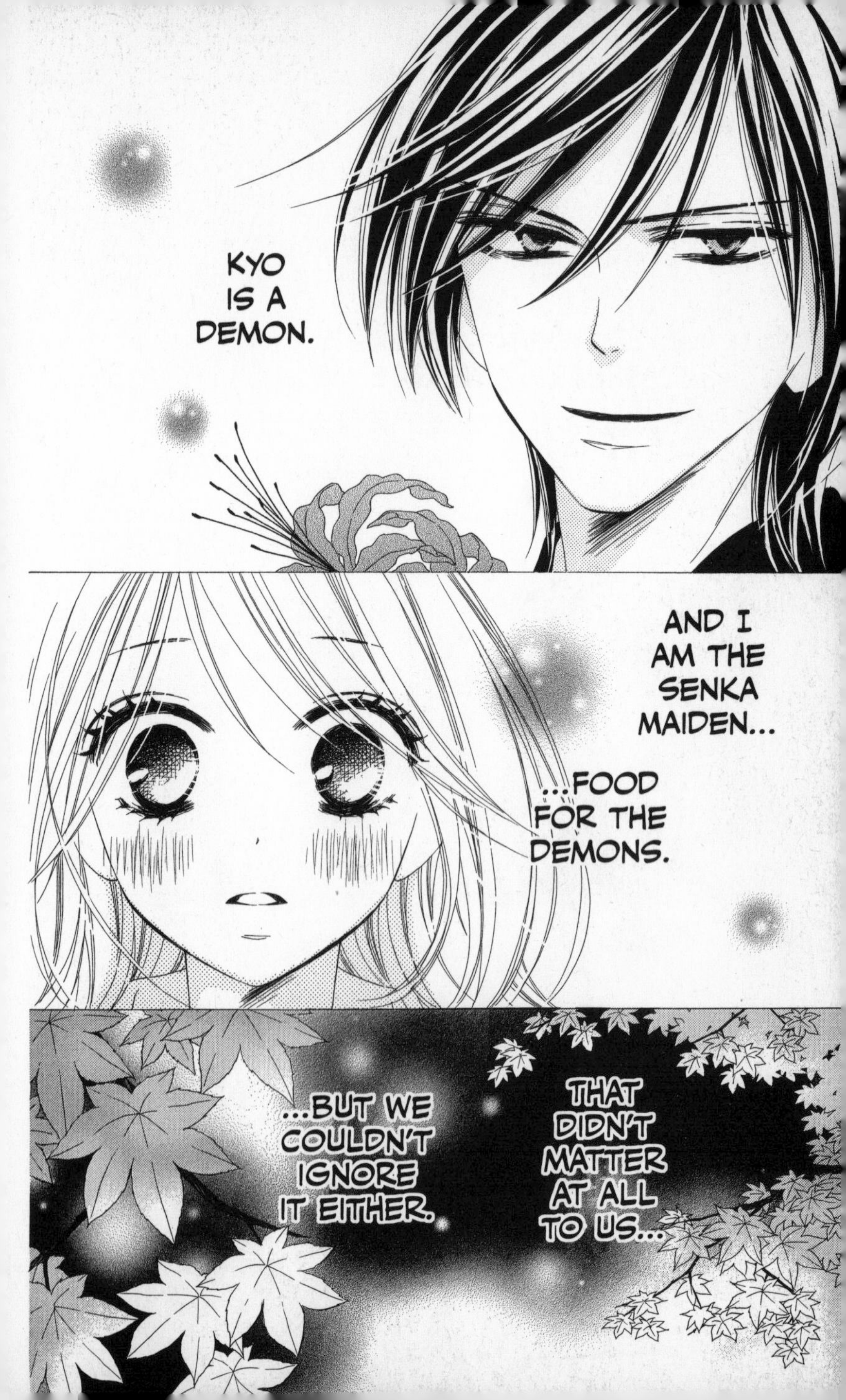
KYO IS A DEMON.
AND I AM THE SENKA MAIDEN...
...FOOD FOR THE DEMONS.
THAT DIDN'T MATTER AT ALL TO US...
...BUT WE COULDN'T IGNORE IT EITHER.

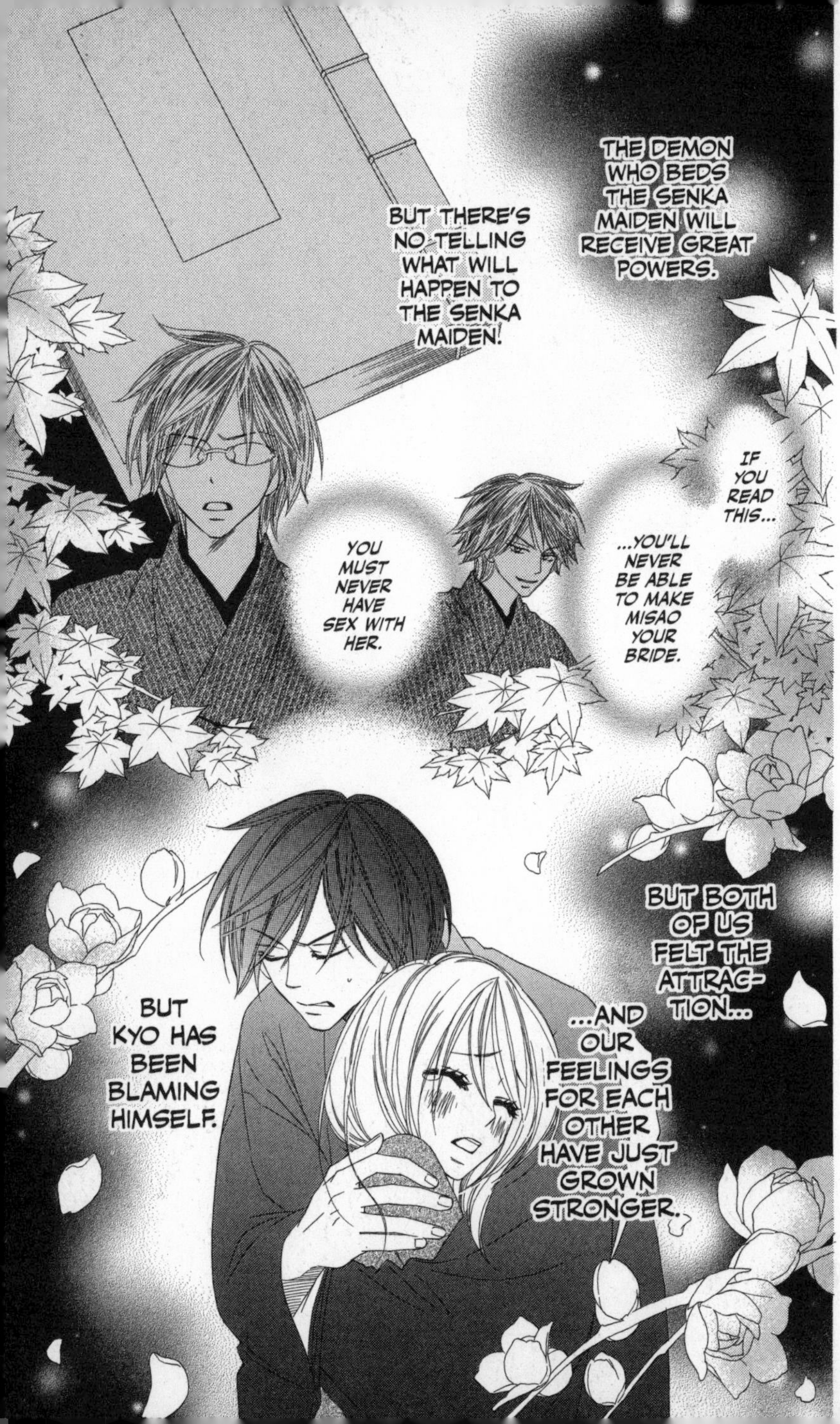
THE DEMON WHO BEDS THE SENKA MAIDEN WILL RECEIVE GREAT POWERS.
BUT THERE'S NO TELLING WHAT WILL HAPPEN TO THE SENKA MAIDEN!
IF YOU READ THIS...
...YOU'LL NEVER BE ABLE TO MAKE MISAO YOUR BRIDE.
YOU MUST NEVER HAVE SEX WITH HER.
BUT BOTH OF US FELT THE ATTRAC-TION...
...AND OUR FEELINGS FOR EACH OTHER HAVE JUST GROWN STRONGER.
BUT KYO HAS BEEN BLAMING HIMSELF.

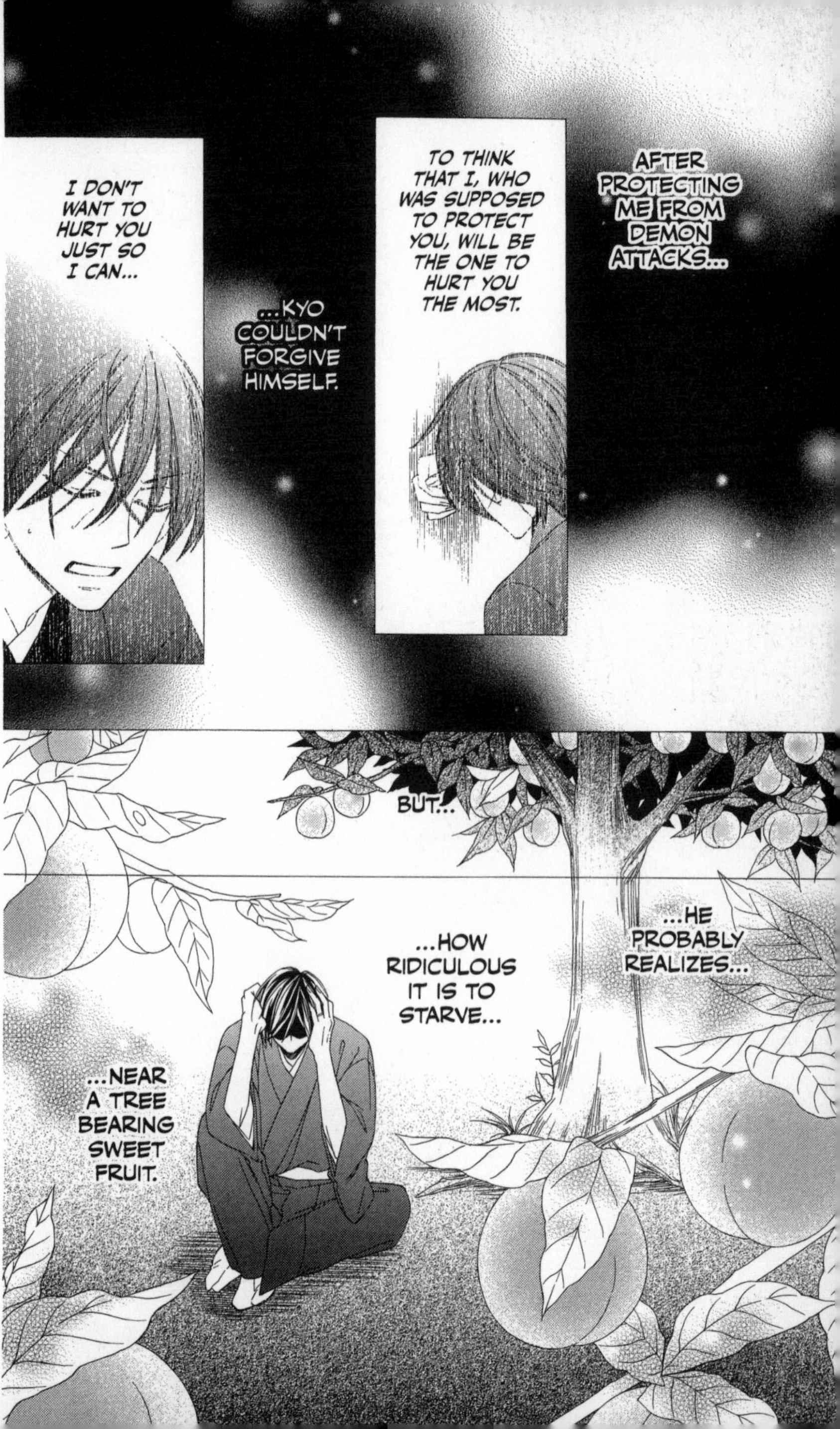
AFTER PROTECTING ME FROM DEMON ATTACKS...
TO THINK THAT I, WHO WAS SUPPOSED TO PROTECT YOU, WILL BE THE ONE TO HURT YOU THE MOST.
...KYO COULDN'T FORGIVE HIMSELF.
I DON'T WANT TO HURT YOU JUST SO I CAN...
BUT...
...HE PROBABLY REALIZES...
...HOW RIDICULOUS IT IS TO STARVE...
...NEAR A TREE BEARING SWEET FRUIT.

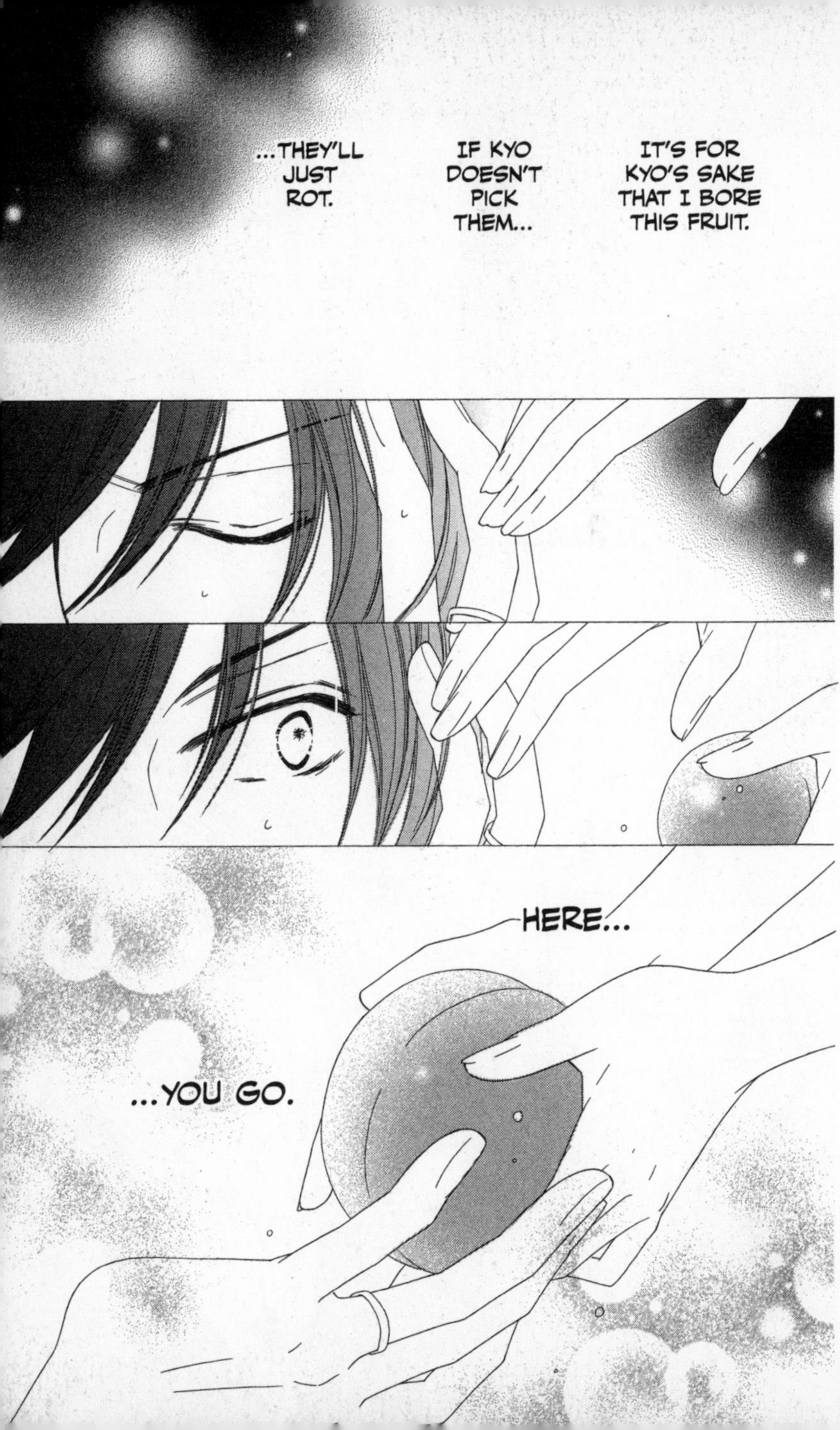
IT'S FOR KYO'S SAKE THAT I BORE THIS FRUIT.
IF KYO DOESN'T PICK THEM...
...THEY'LL JUST ROT.
HERE...
...YOU GO.

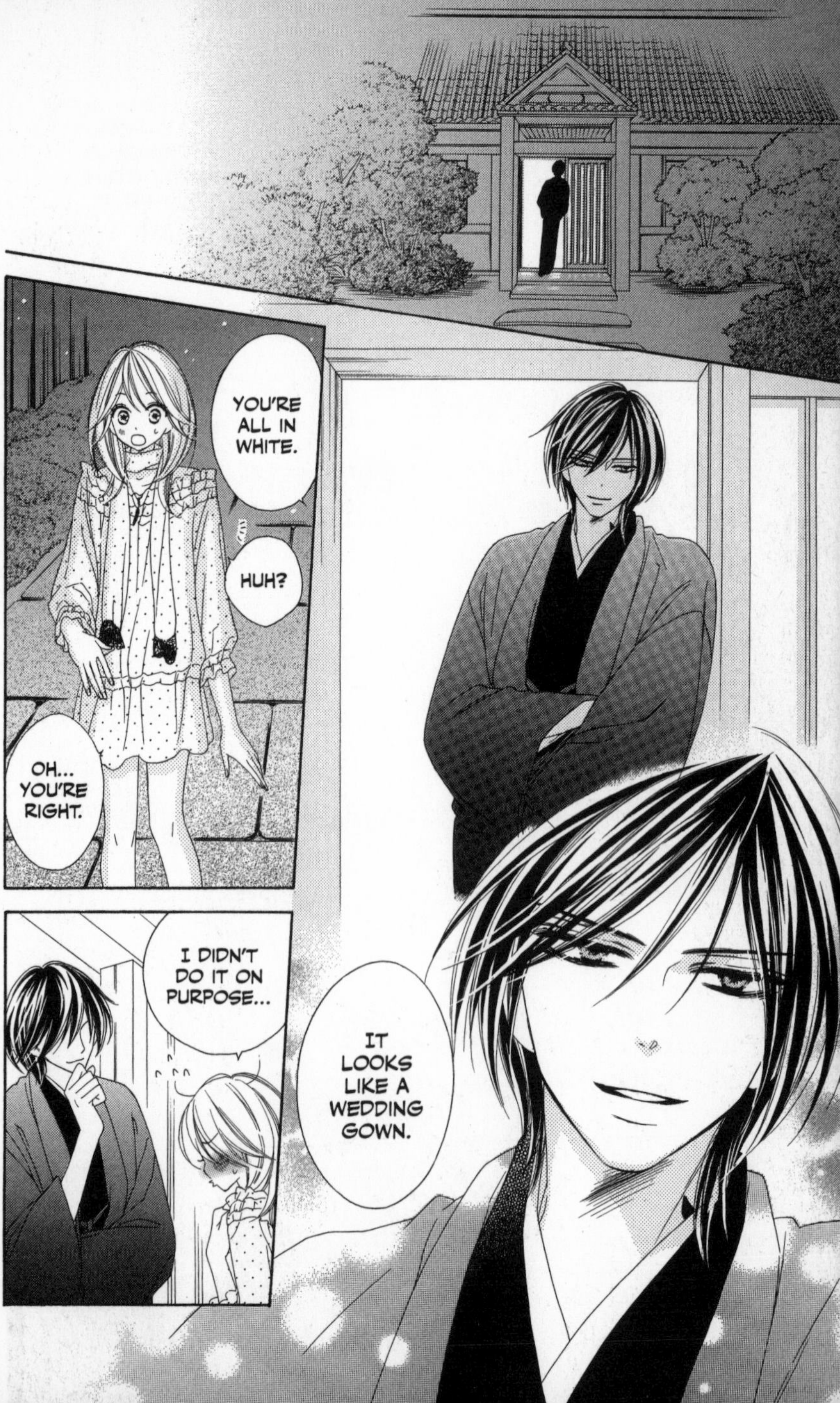
YOU'RE ALL IN WHITE.
HUH?
OH... YOU'RE RIGHT.
IT LOOKS LIKE A WEDDING GOWN.
I DIDN'T DO IT ON PURPOSE...

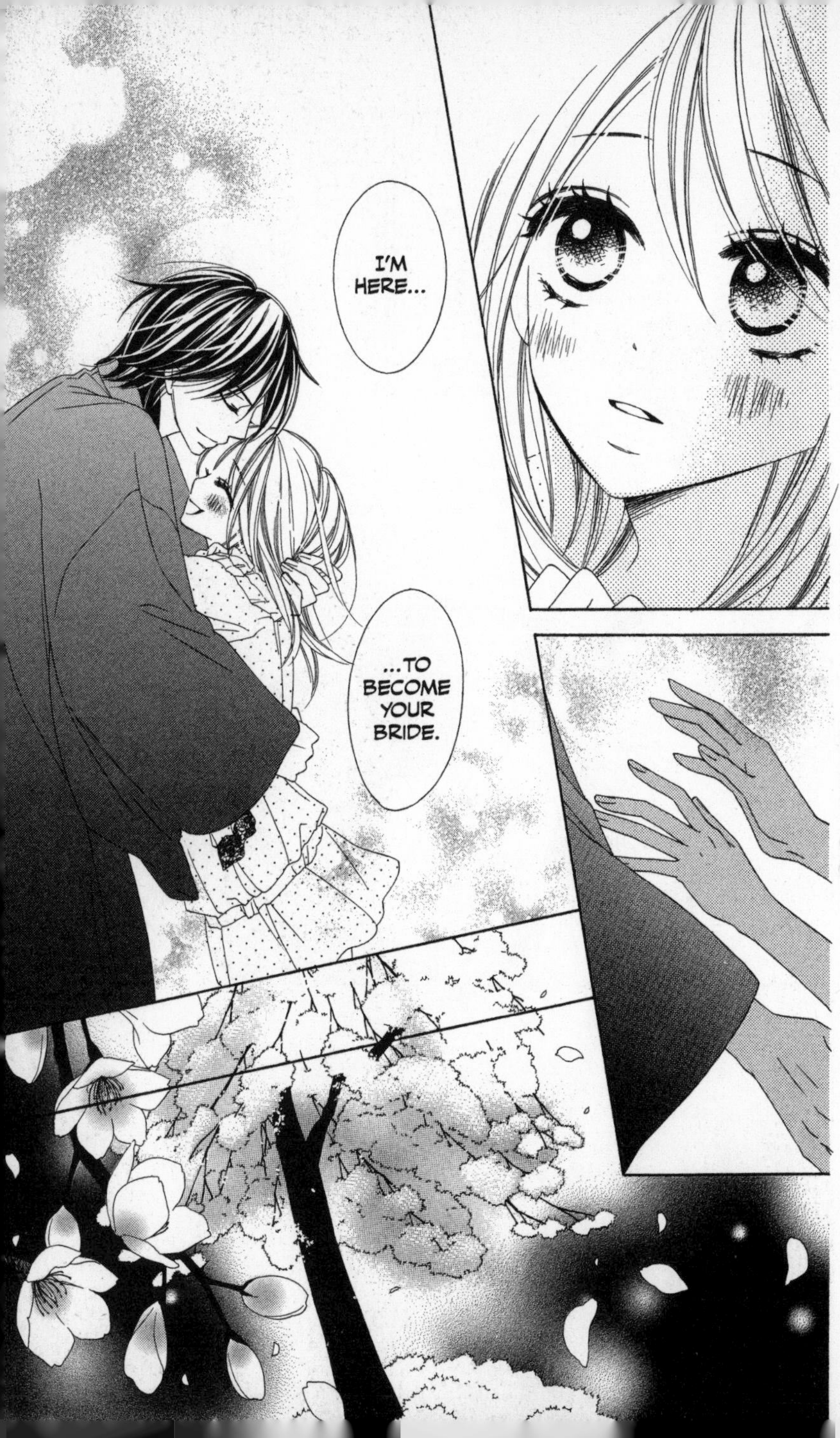
I'M HERE...
...TO BECOME YOUR BRIDE.

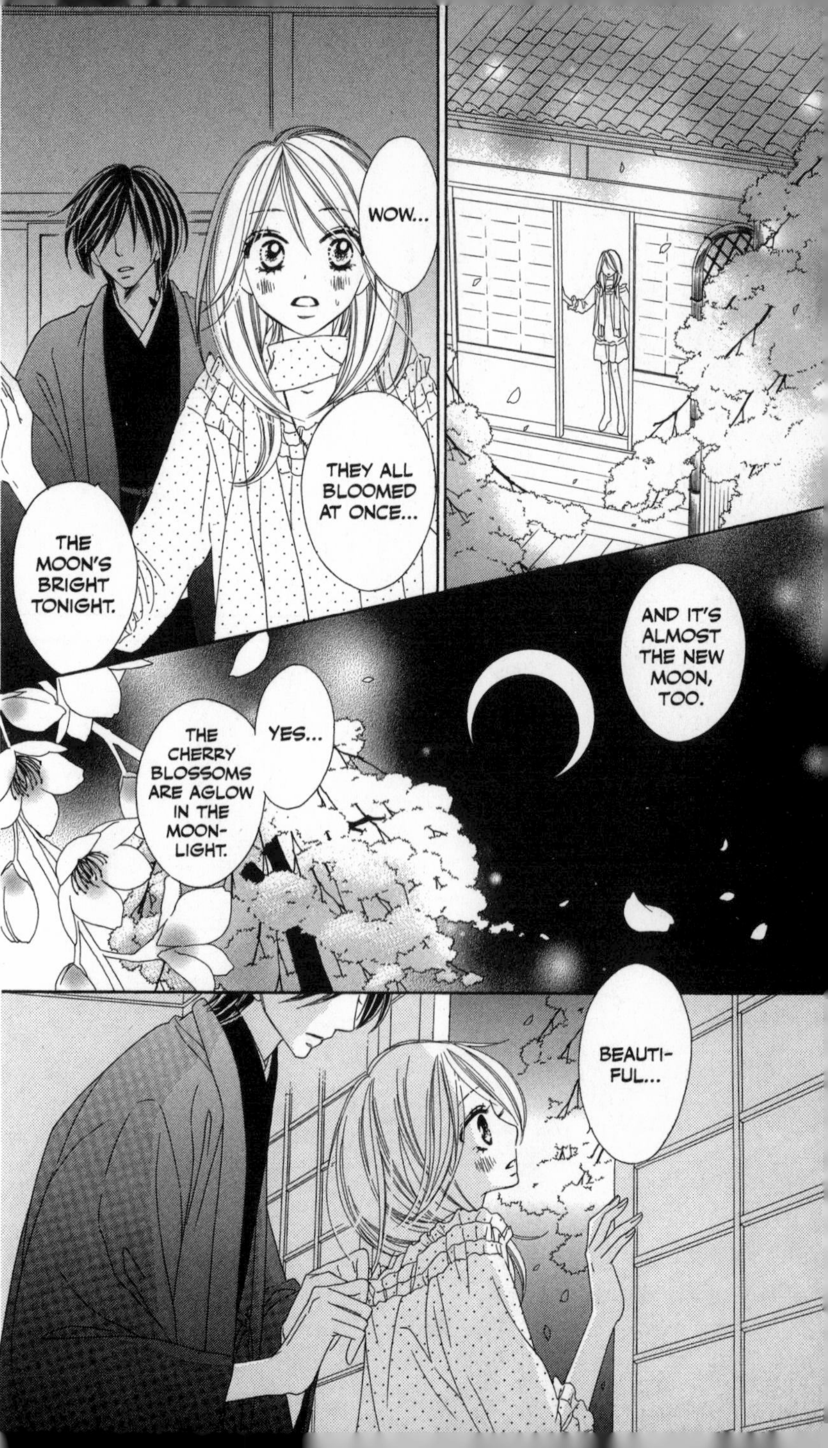
WOW...
THEY ALL BLOOMED AT ONCE...
THE MOON'S BRIGHT TONIGHT.
AND IT'S ALMOST THE NEW MOON, TOO.
YES...
THE CHERRY BLOSSOMS ARE AGLOW IN THE MOON-LIGHT.
BEAUTI-FUL...

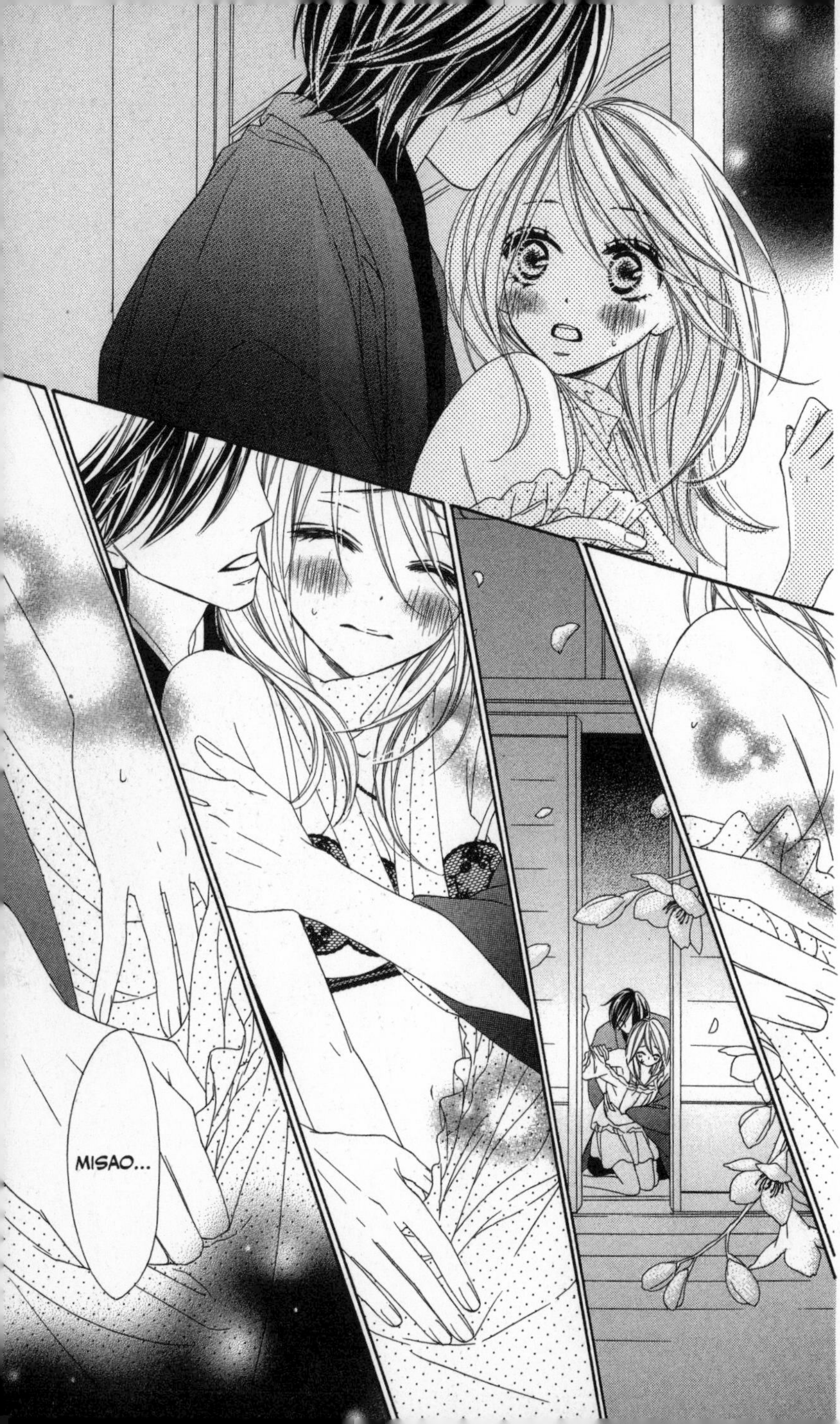
MISAO...

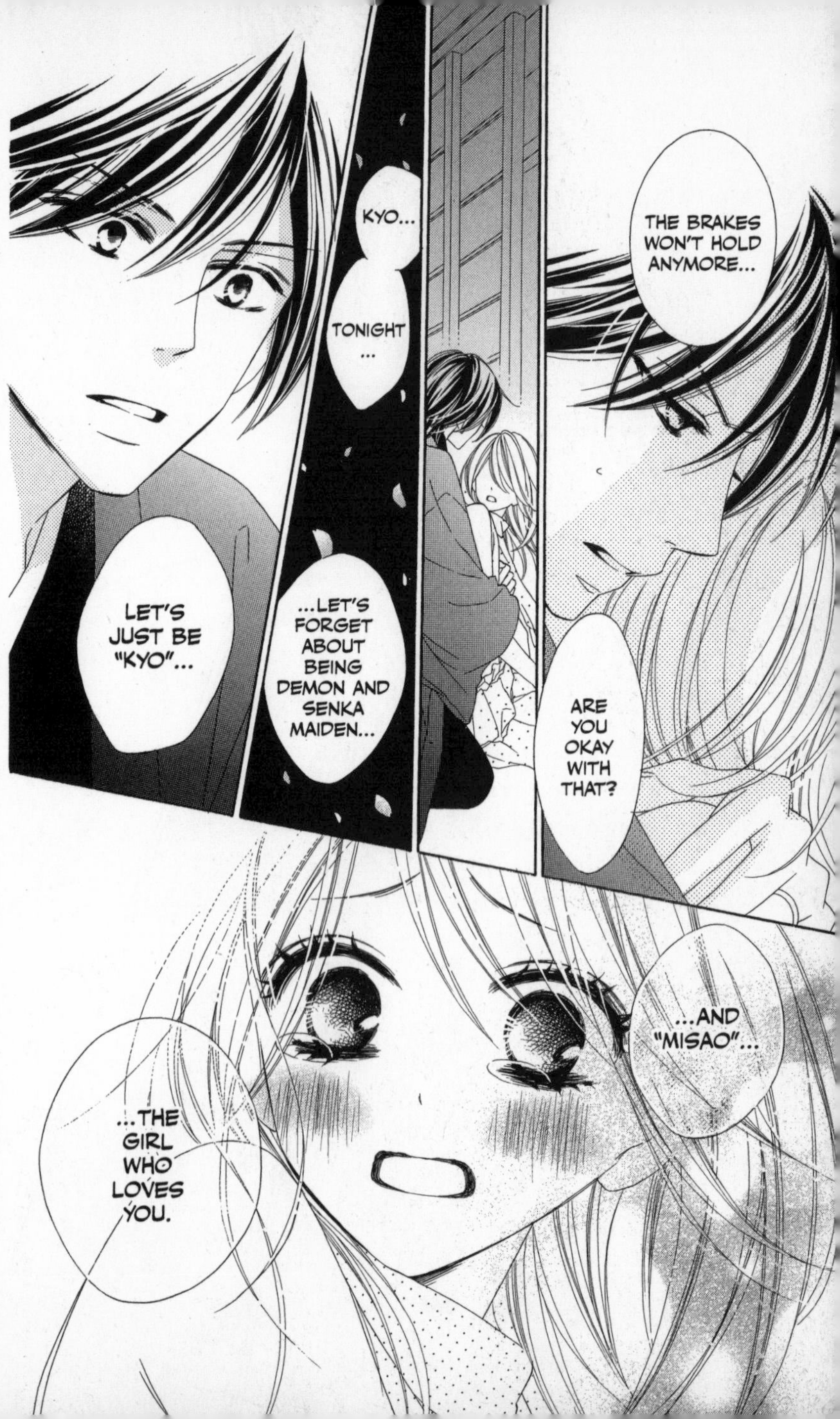
THE BRAKES WON'T HOLD ANYMORE...
ARE YOU OKAY WITH THAT?
KYO...
TONIGHT...
...LET'S FORGET ABOUT BEING DEMON AND SENKA MAIDEN...
LET'S JUST BE "KYO"...
...AND "MISAO"...
...THE GIRL WHO LOVES YOU.

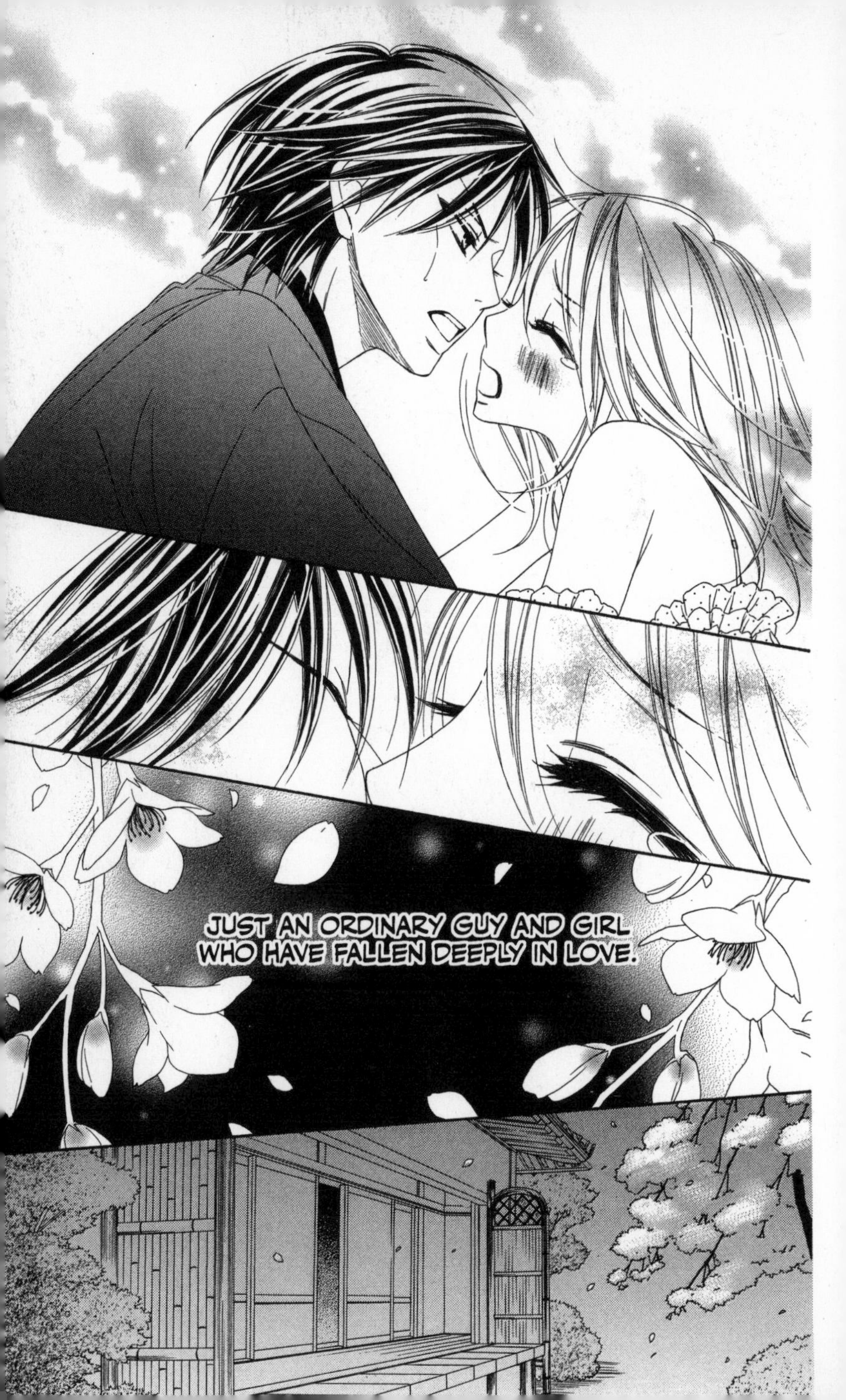
JUST AN ORDINARY GUY AND GIRL WHO HAVE FALLEN DEEPLY IN LOVE.

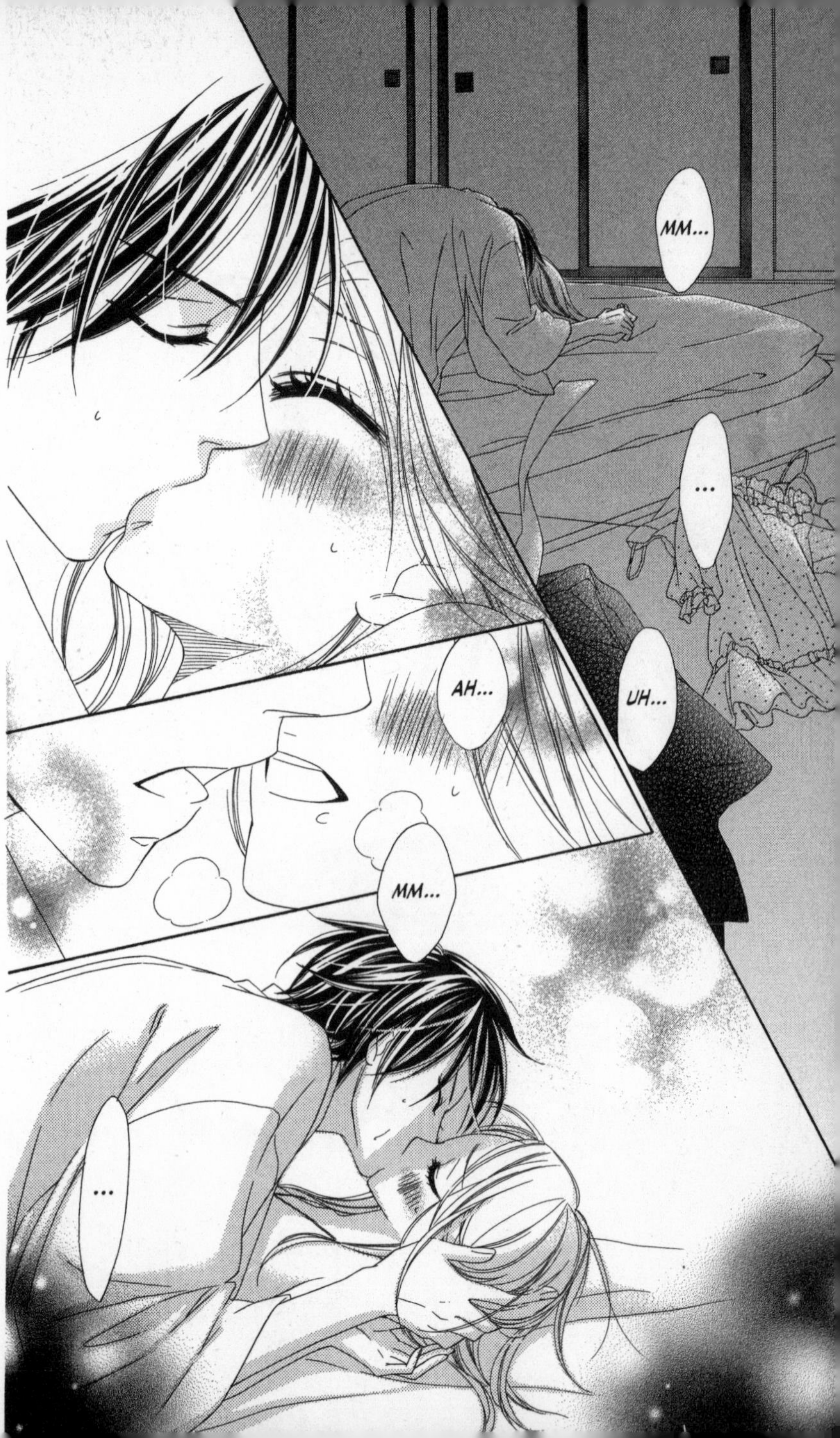
MM...
...
UH...
AH...
MM...
...

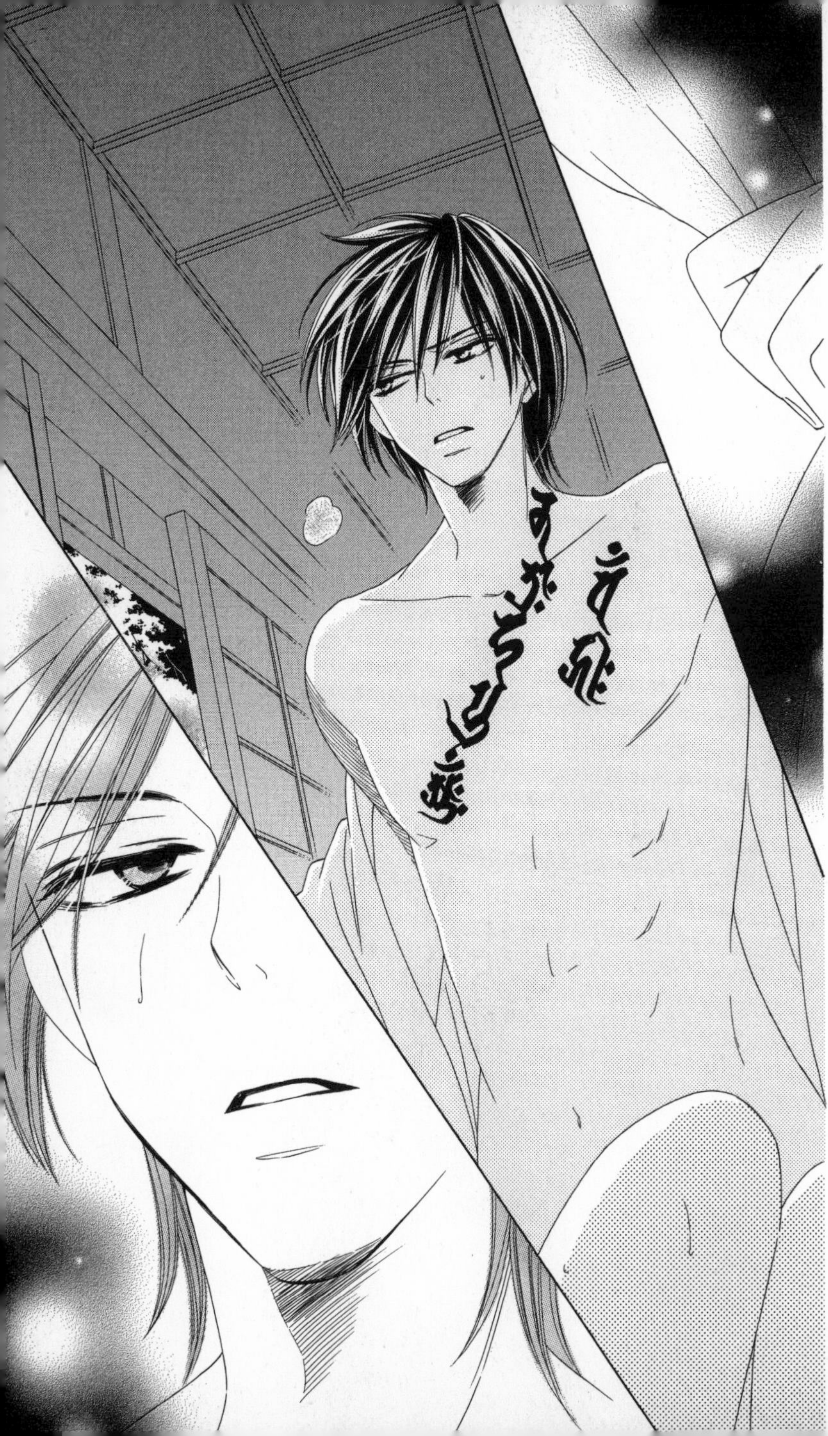

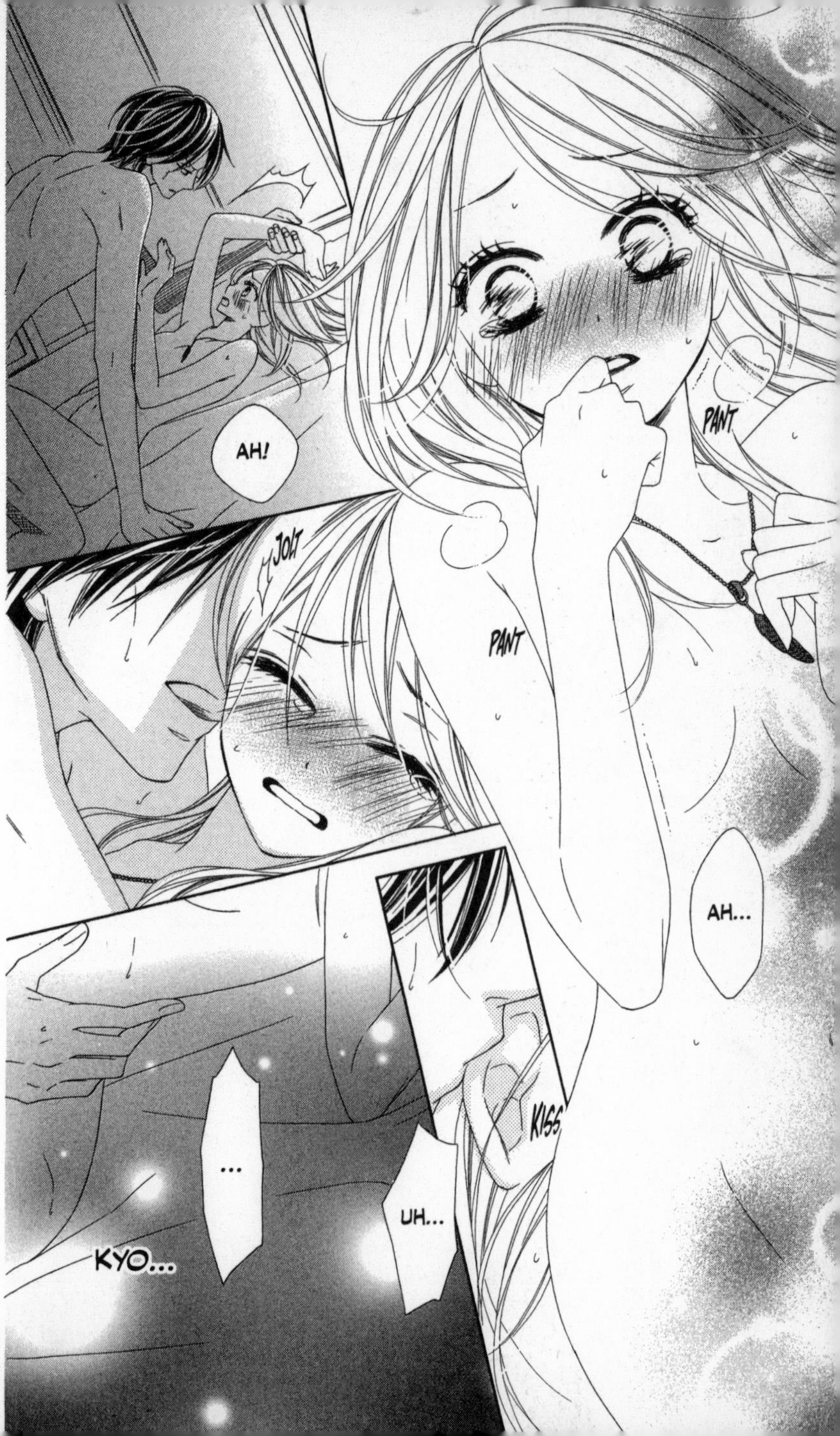
PANT
PANT
AH...
AH!
JOLT
KISS
UH...
...
KYO...

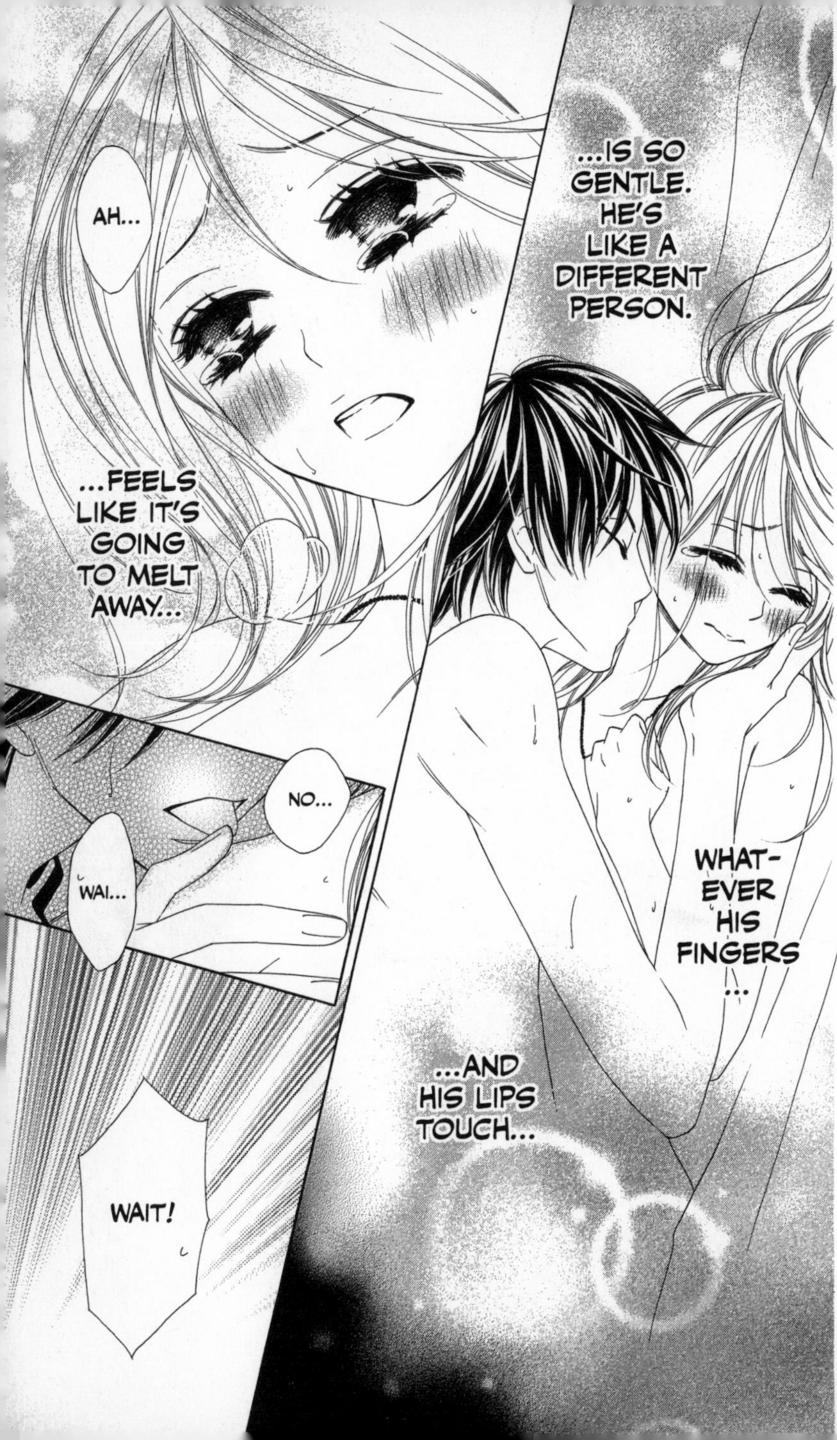
...IS SO GENTLE. HE'S LIKE A DIFFERENT PERSON.
WHAT-EVER HIS FINGERS...
...AND HIS LIPS TOUCH...
AH...
...FEELS LIKE IT'S GOING TO MELT AWAY...
NO...
WAI...
WAIT!

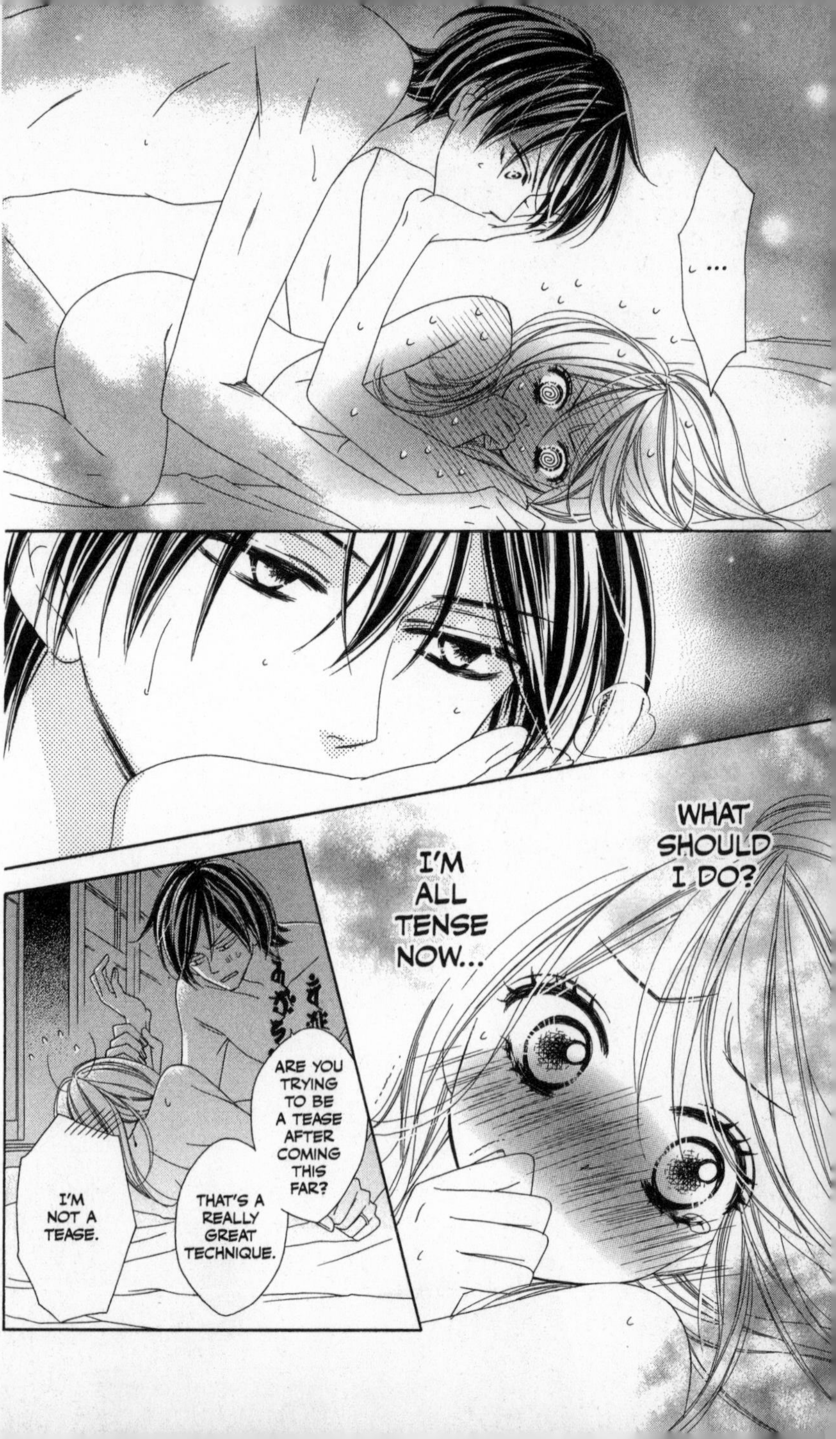
...
WHAT SHOULD I DO?
I'M ALL TENSE NOW...
ARE YOU TRYING TO BE A TEASE AFTER COMING THIS FAR?
THAT'S A REALLY GREAT TECHNIQUE.
I'M NOT A TEASE.

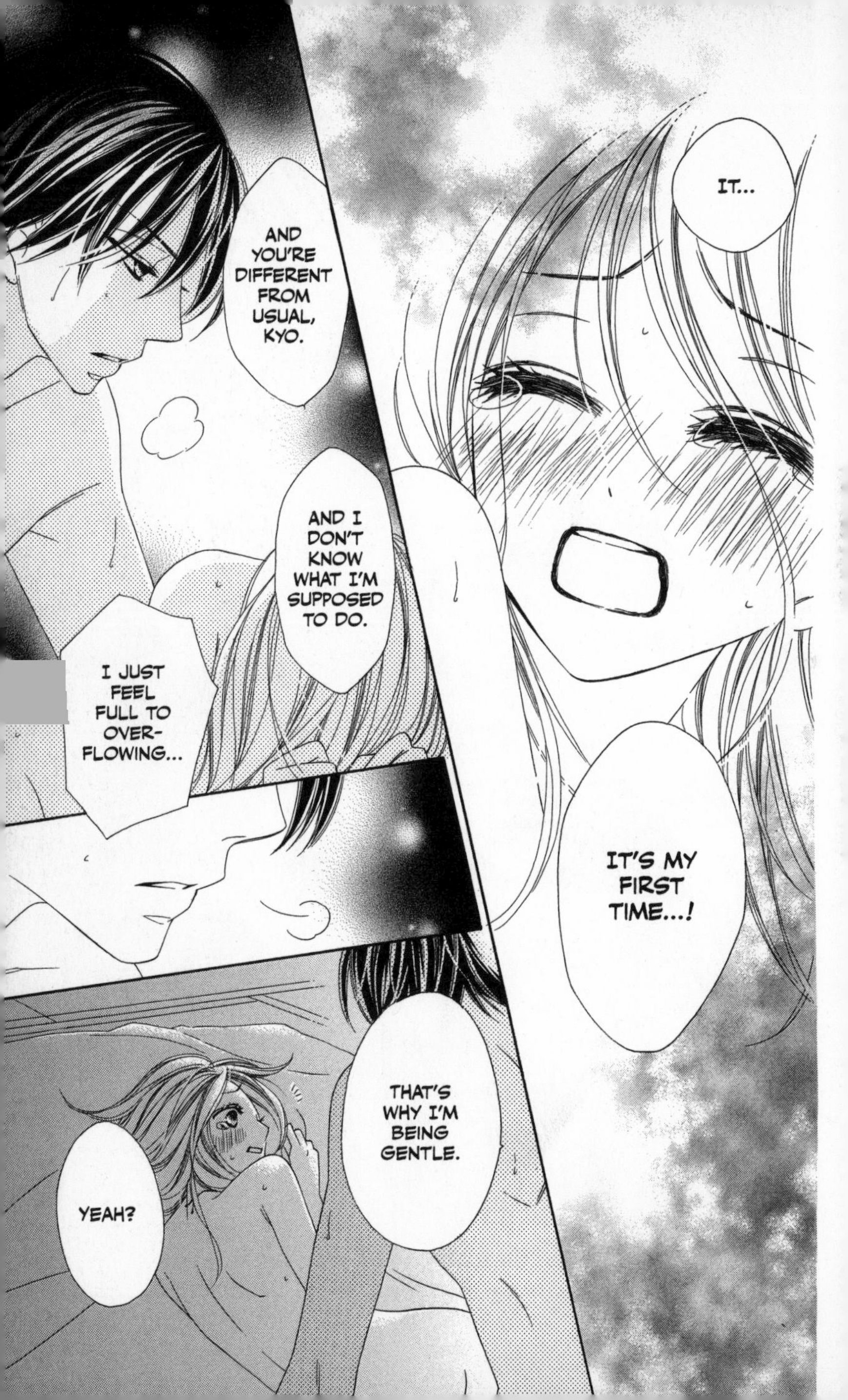
IT...
IT'S MY FIRST TIME...!
AND YOU'RE DIFFERENT FROM USUAL, KYO.
AND I DON'T KNOW WHAT I'M SUPPOSED TO DO.
I JUST FEEL FULL TO OVER-FLOWING...
THAT'S WHY I'M BEING GENTLE.
YEAH?

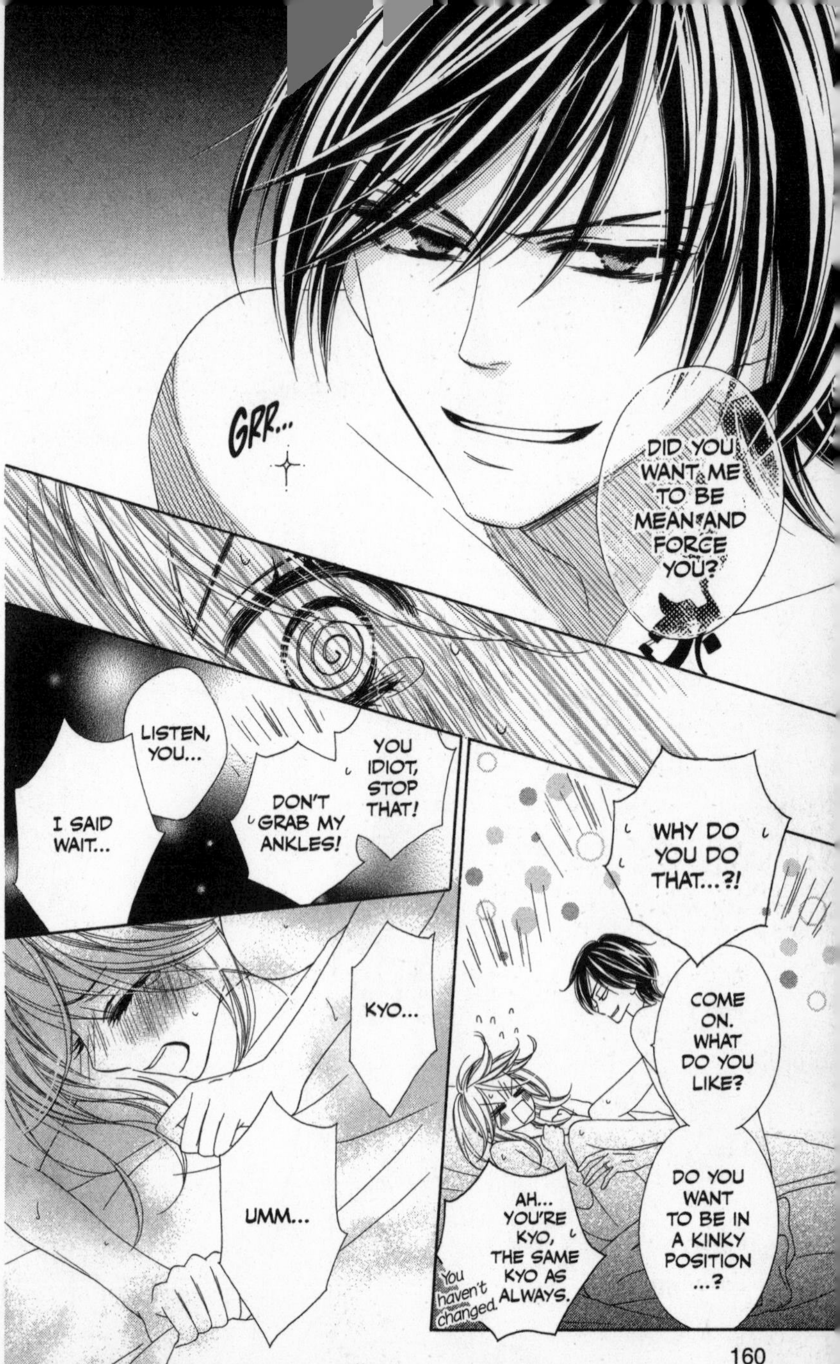
DID YOU WANT ME TO BE MEAN AND FORCE YOU?
GRR...
WHY DO YOU DO THAT...?!
COME ON. WHAT DO YOU LIKE?
DO YOU WANT TO BE IN A KINKY POSITION ...?
AH... YOU'RE KYO, THE SAME KYO AS ALWAYS.
You haven't changed.
YOU IDIOT, STOP THAT!
DON'T GRAB MY ANKLES!
LISTEN, YOU...
I SAID WAIT...
KYO...
UMM...

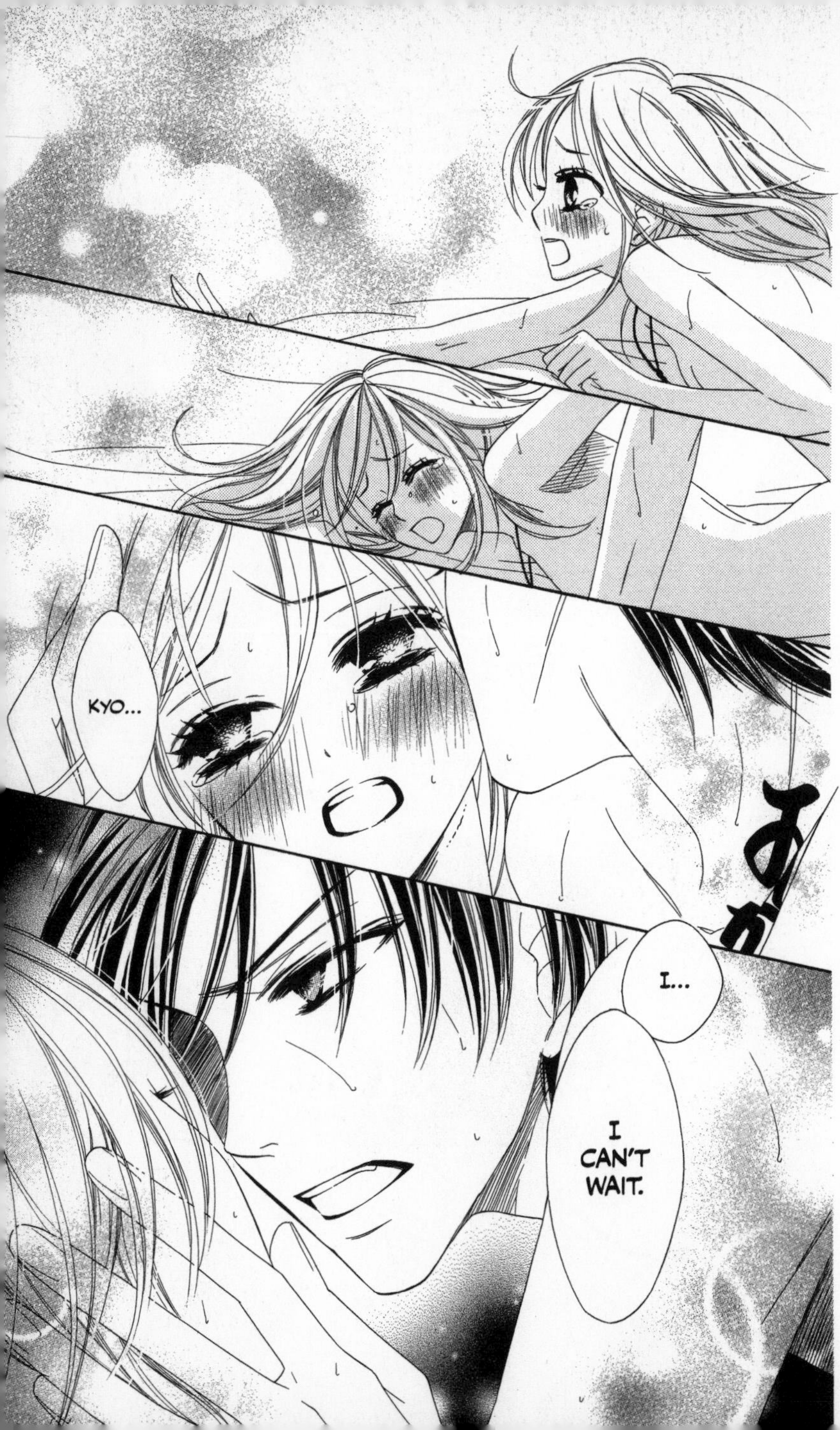
KYO...
I...
I CAN'T WAIT.

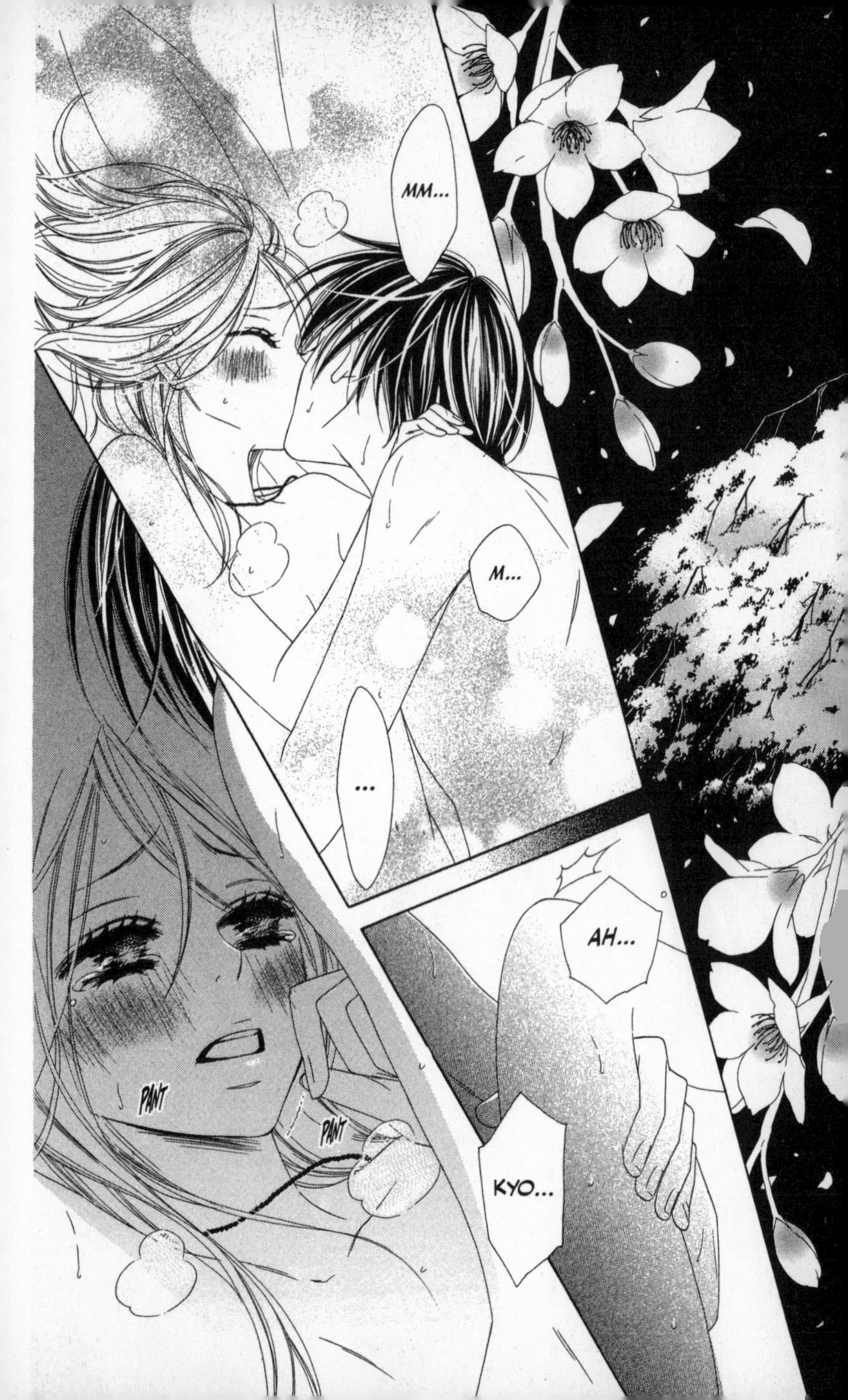

MM...
M...
...
AH...
KYO...
PANT
PANT

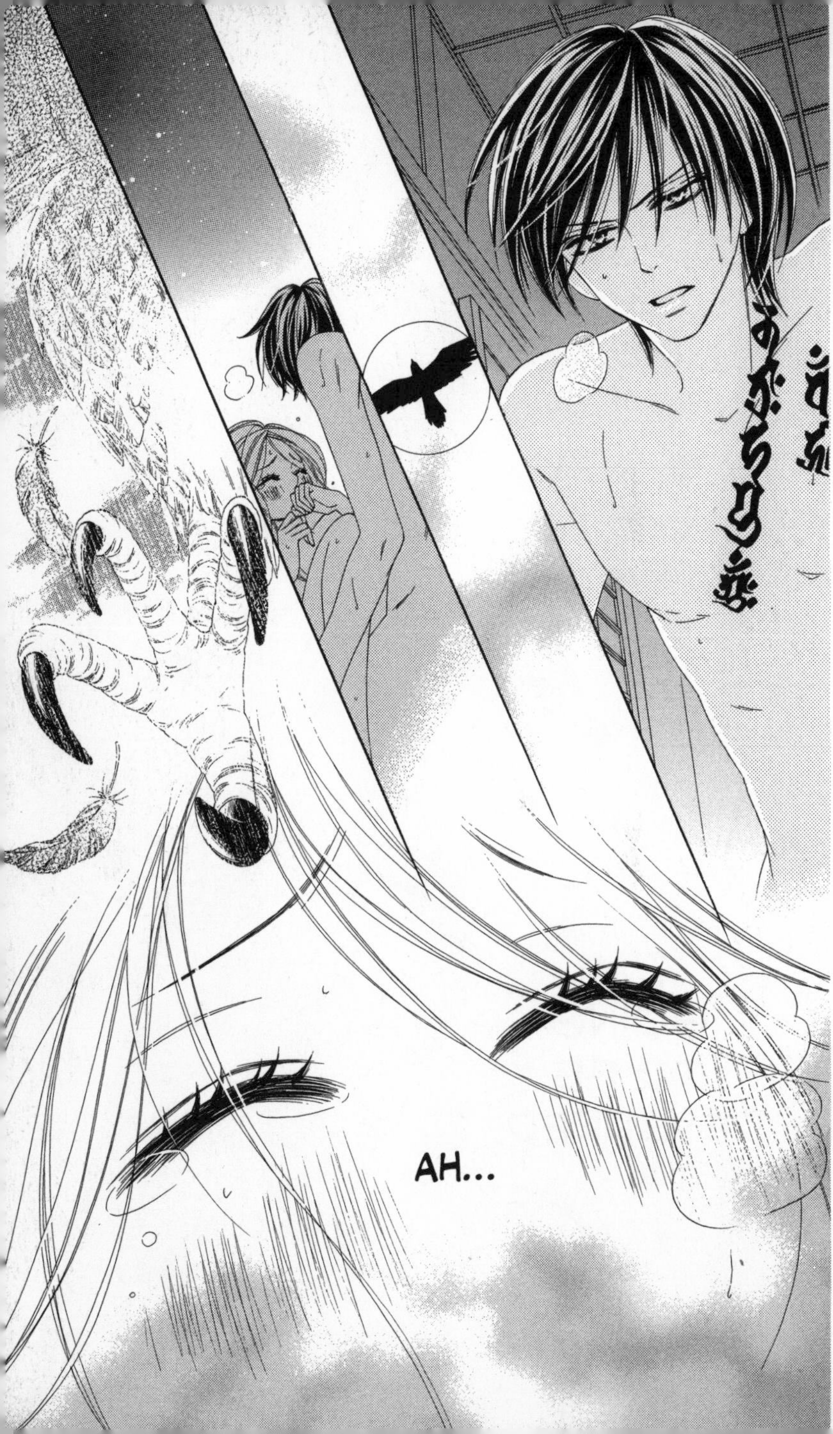
AH...

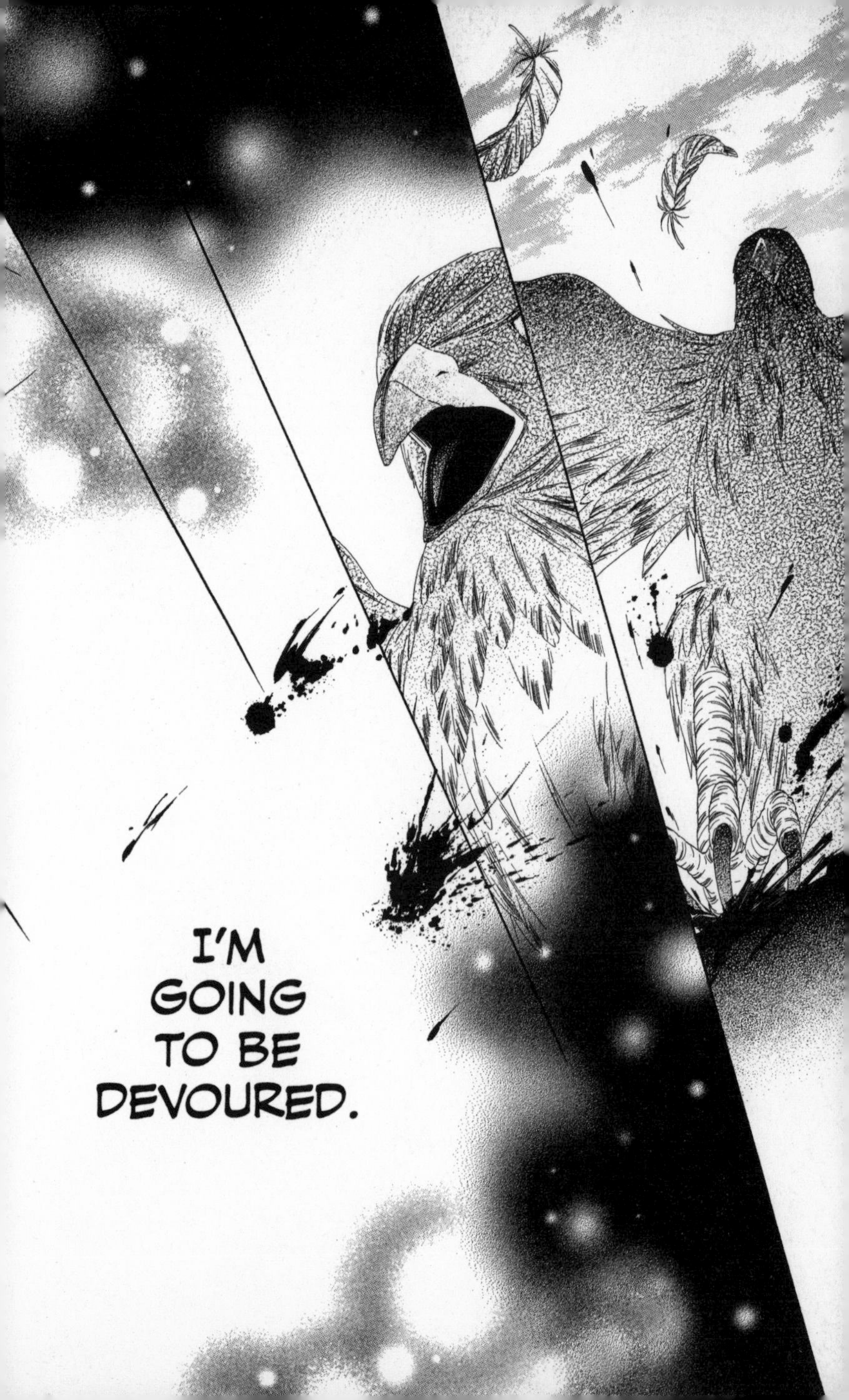
I'M GOING TO BE DEVOURED.

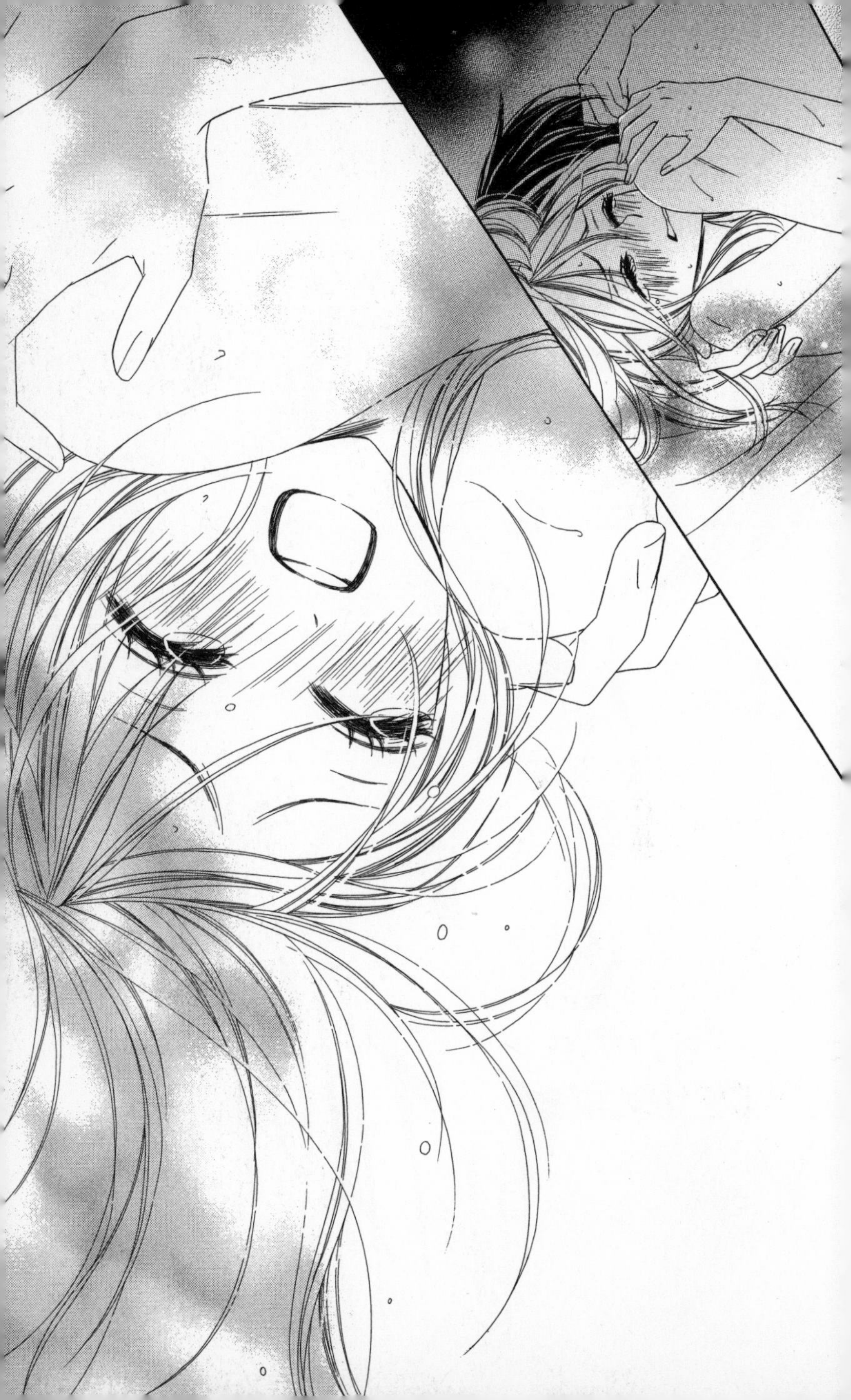

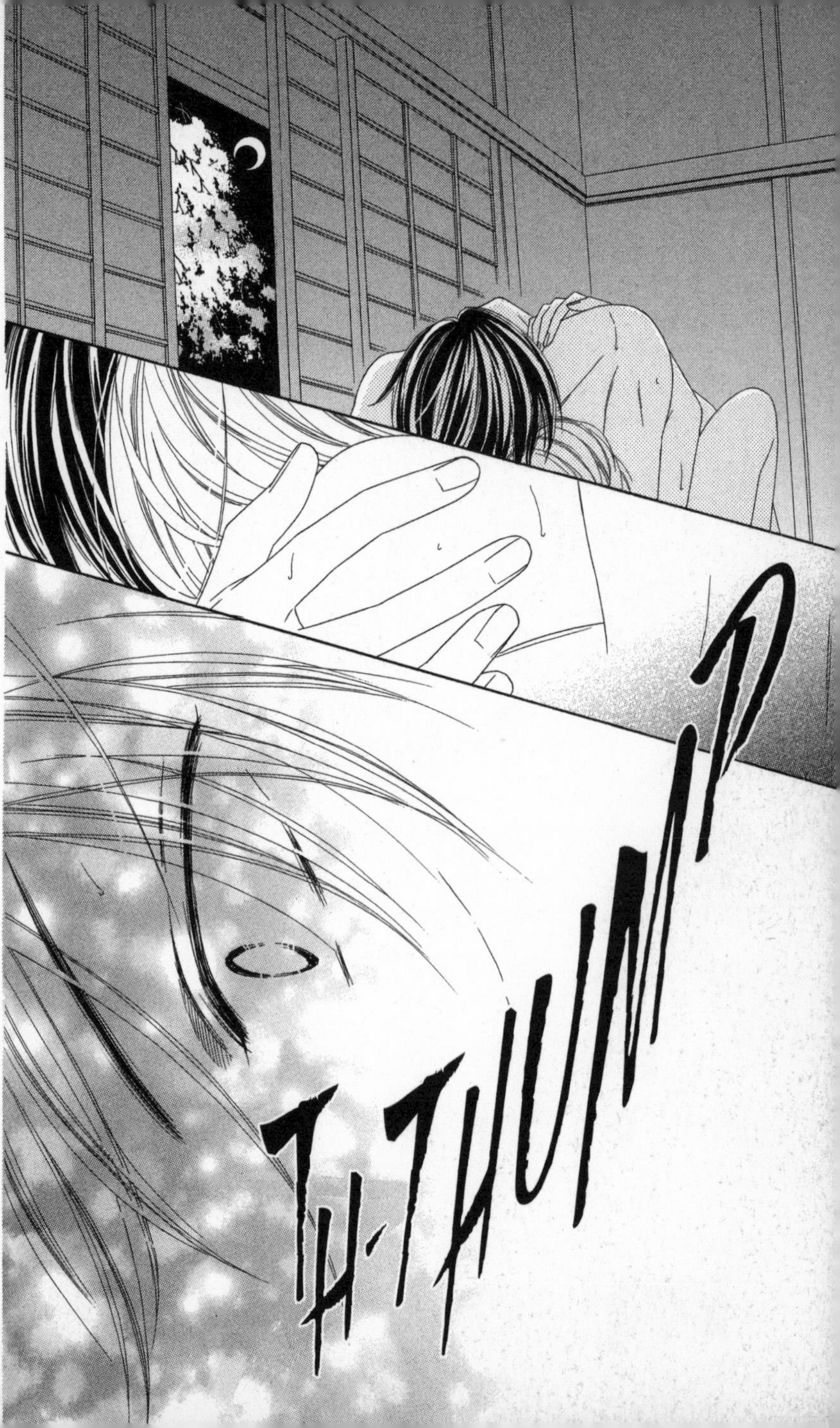

TH-THUMP

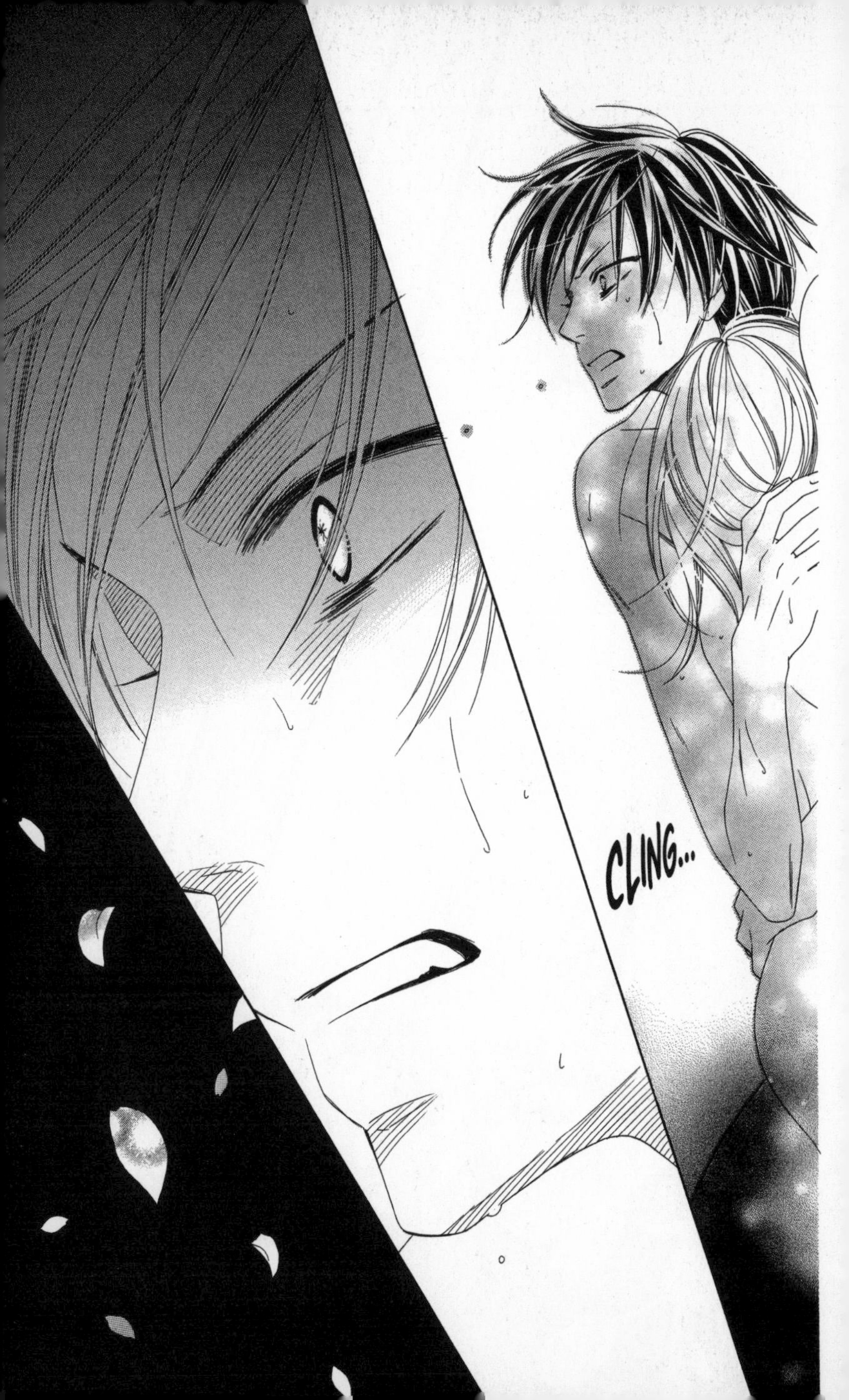
CLING...

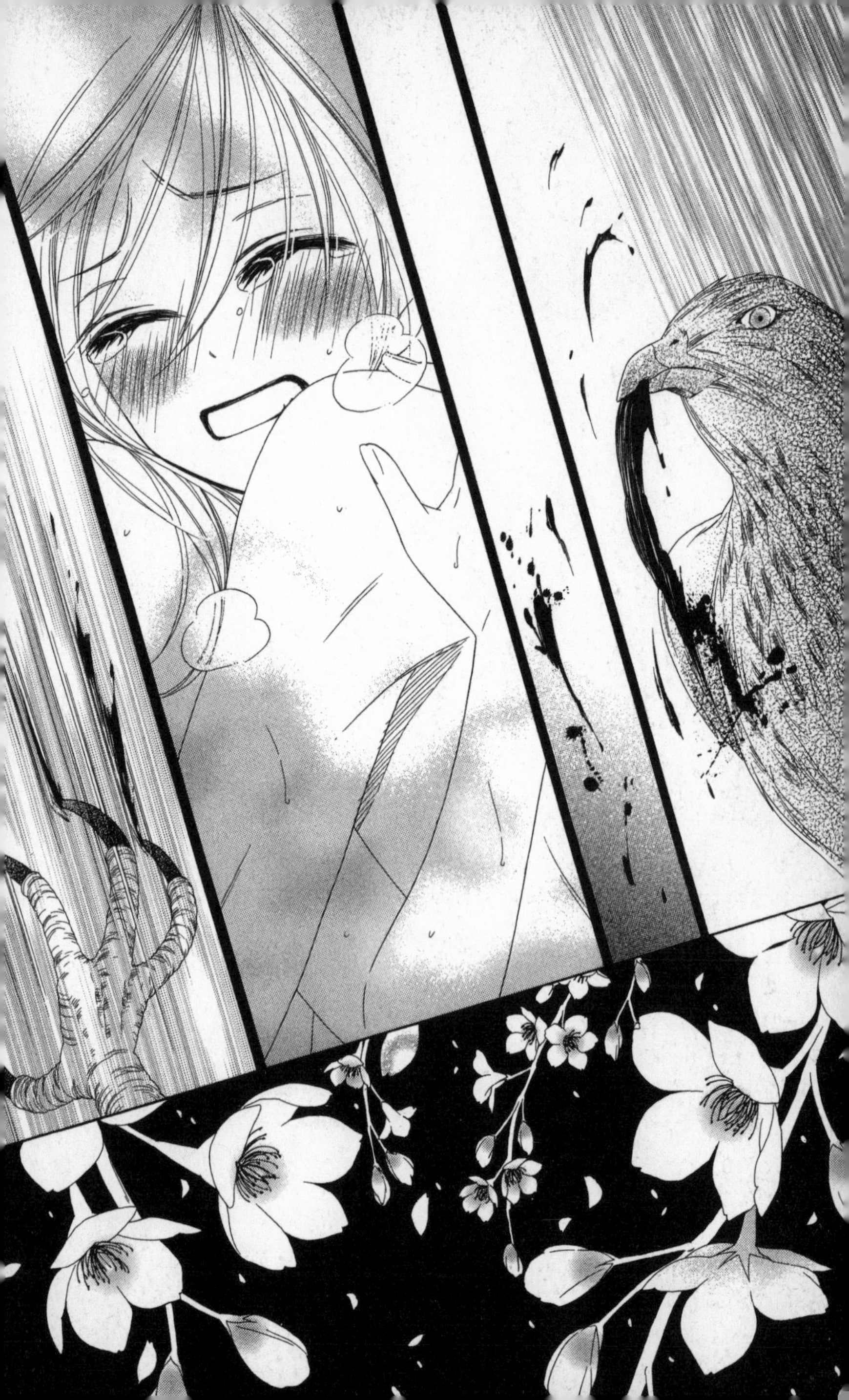

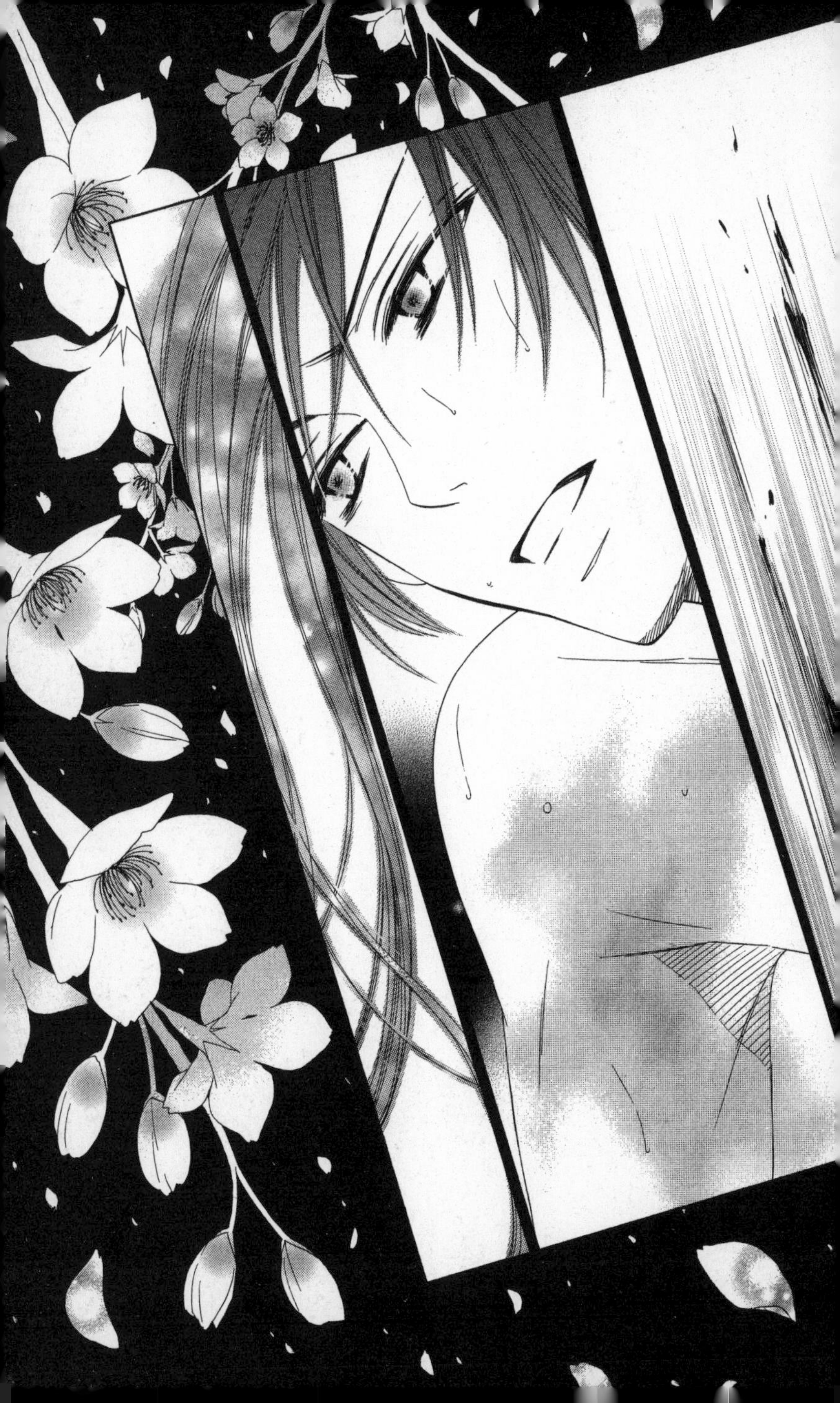

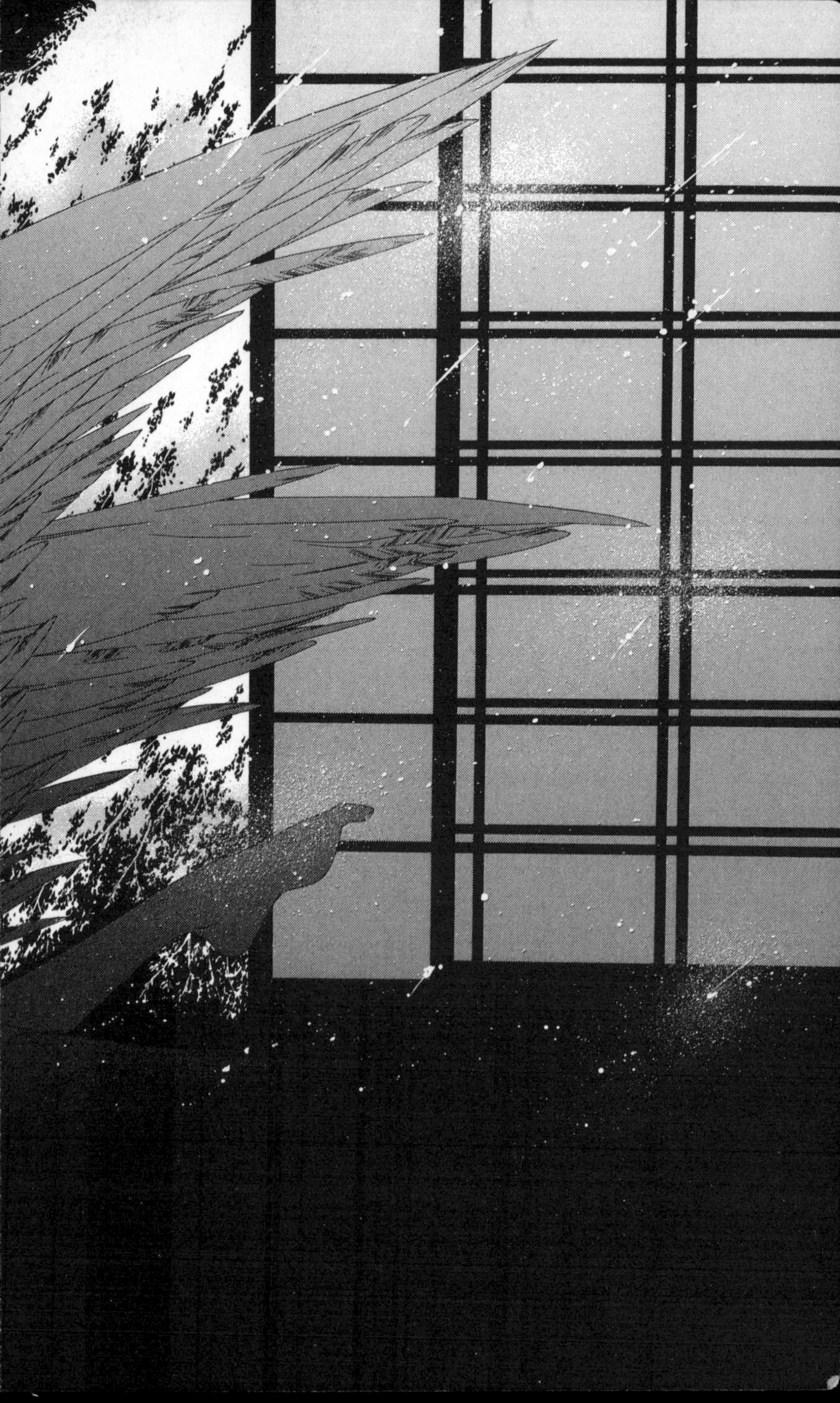

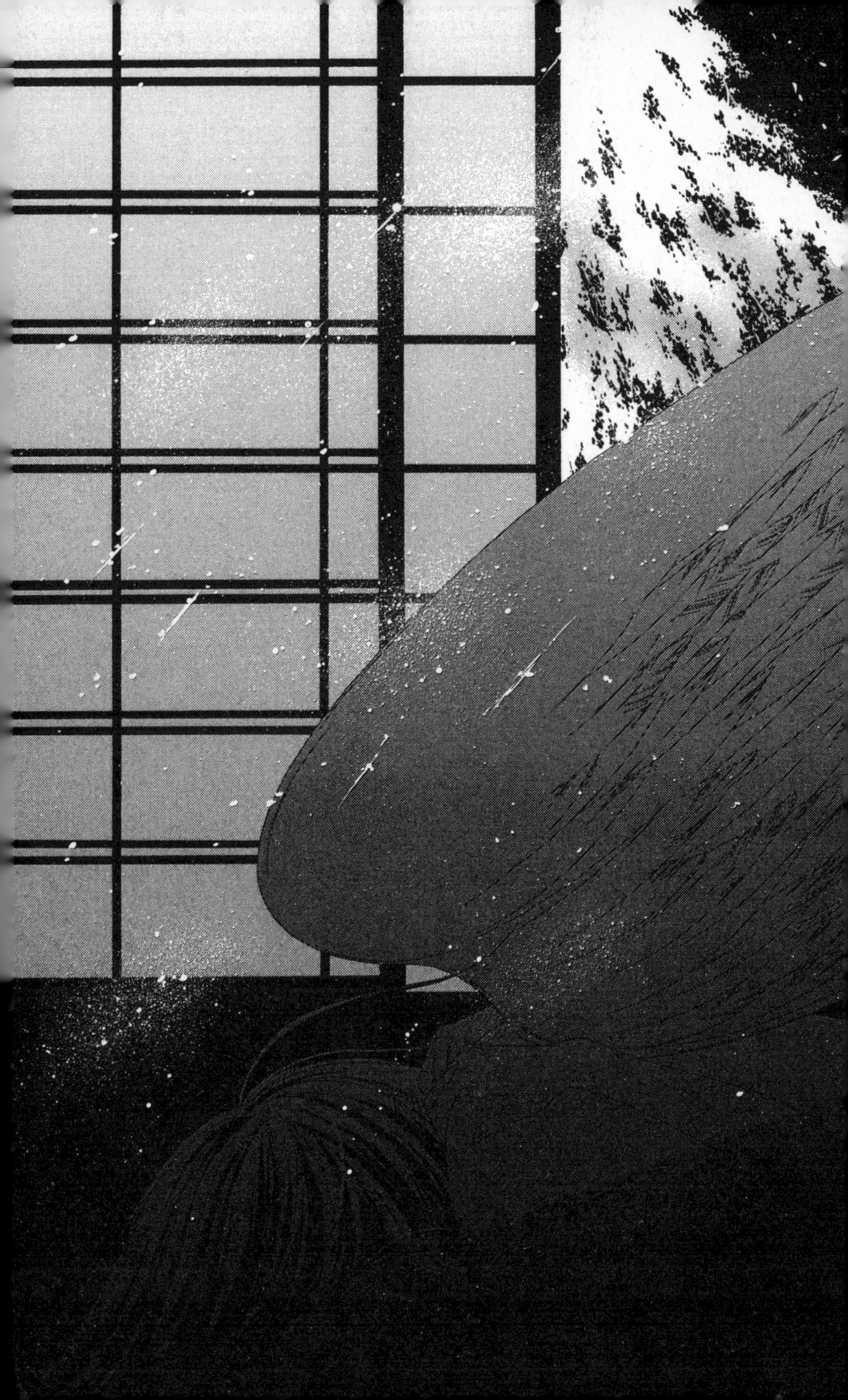

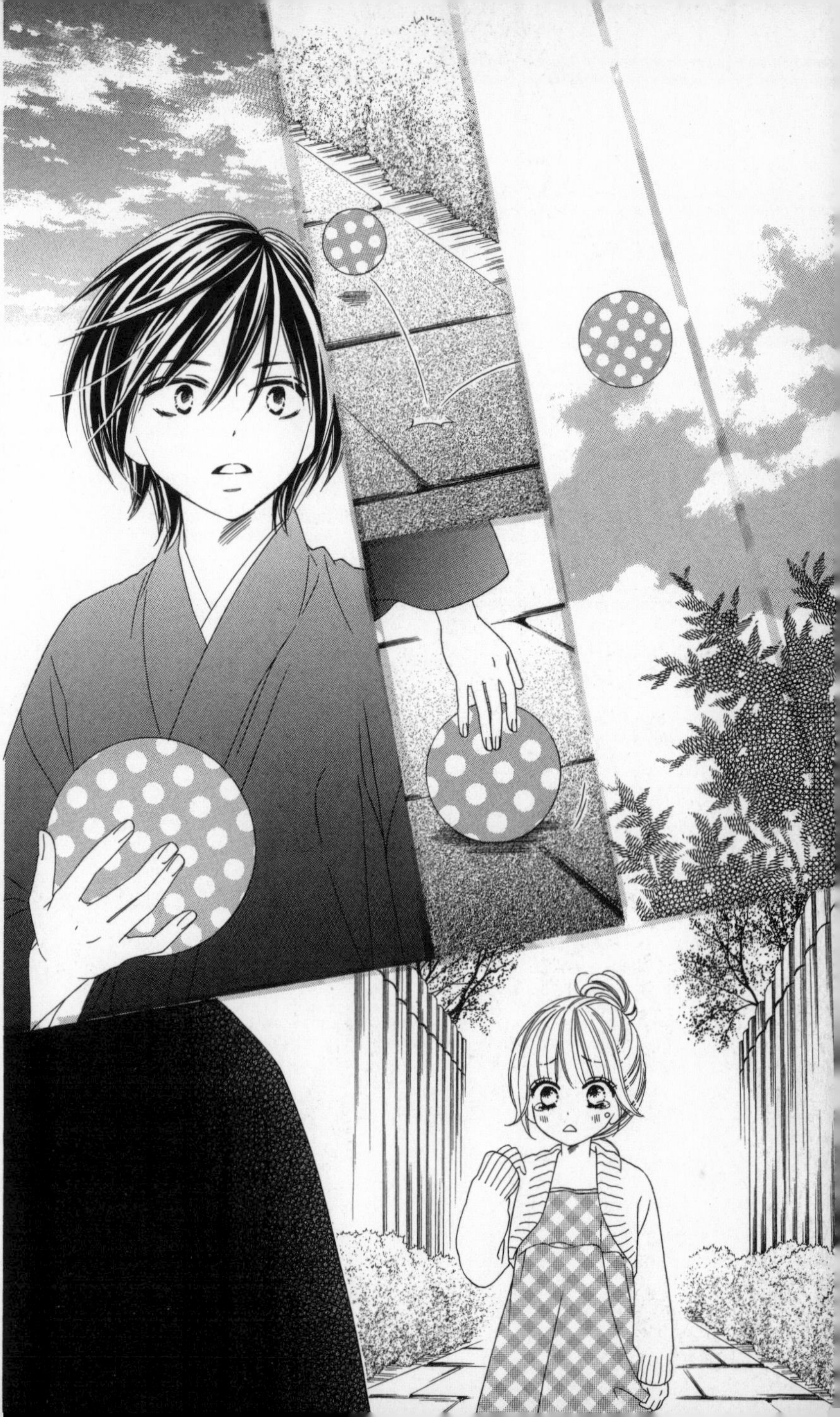

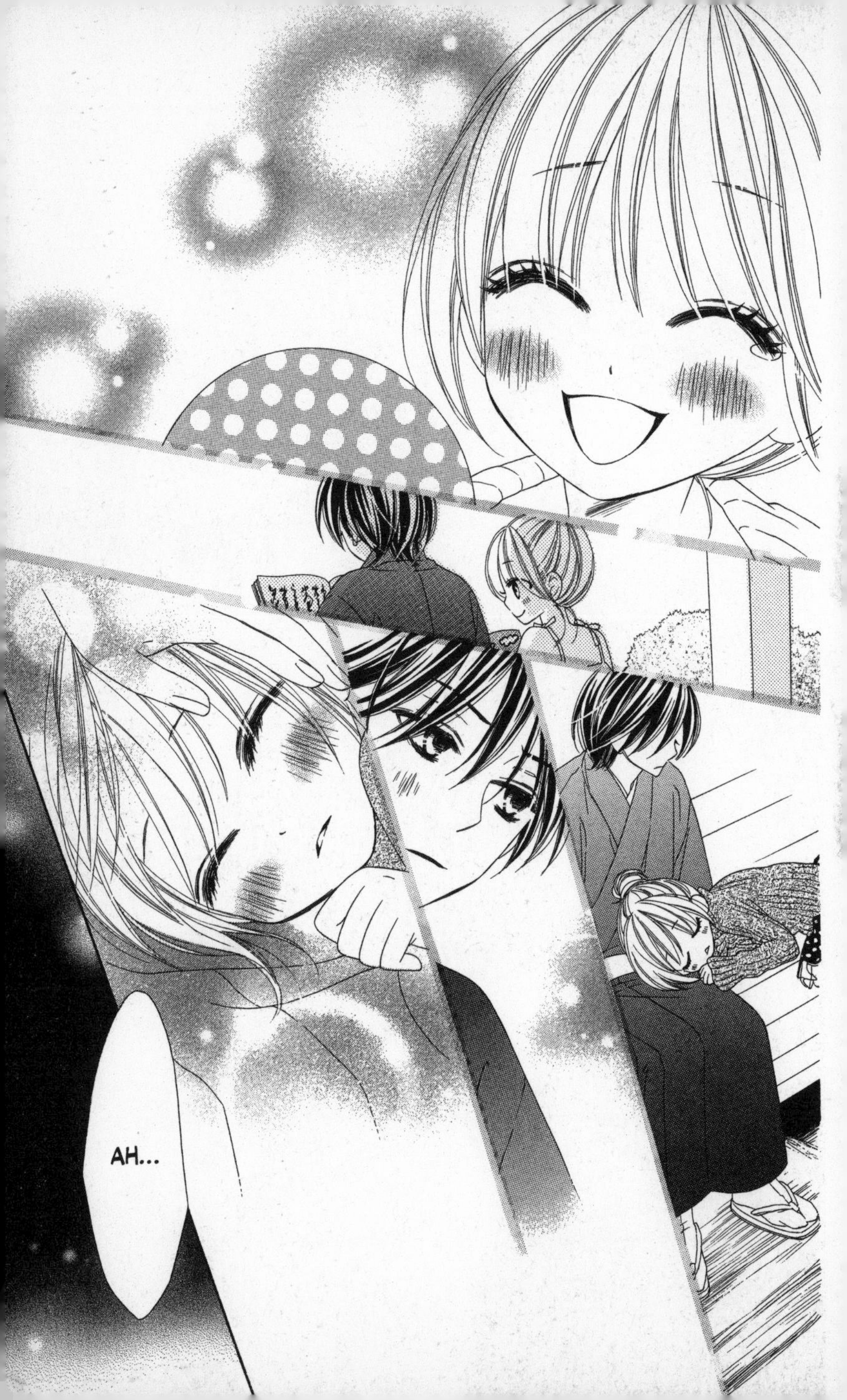
AH...

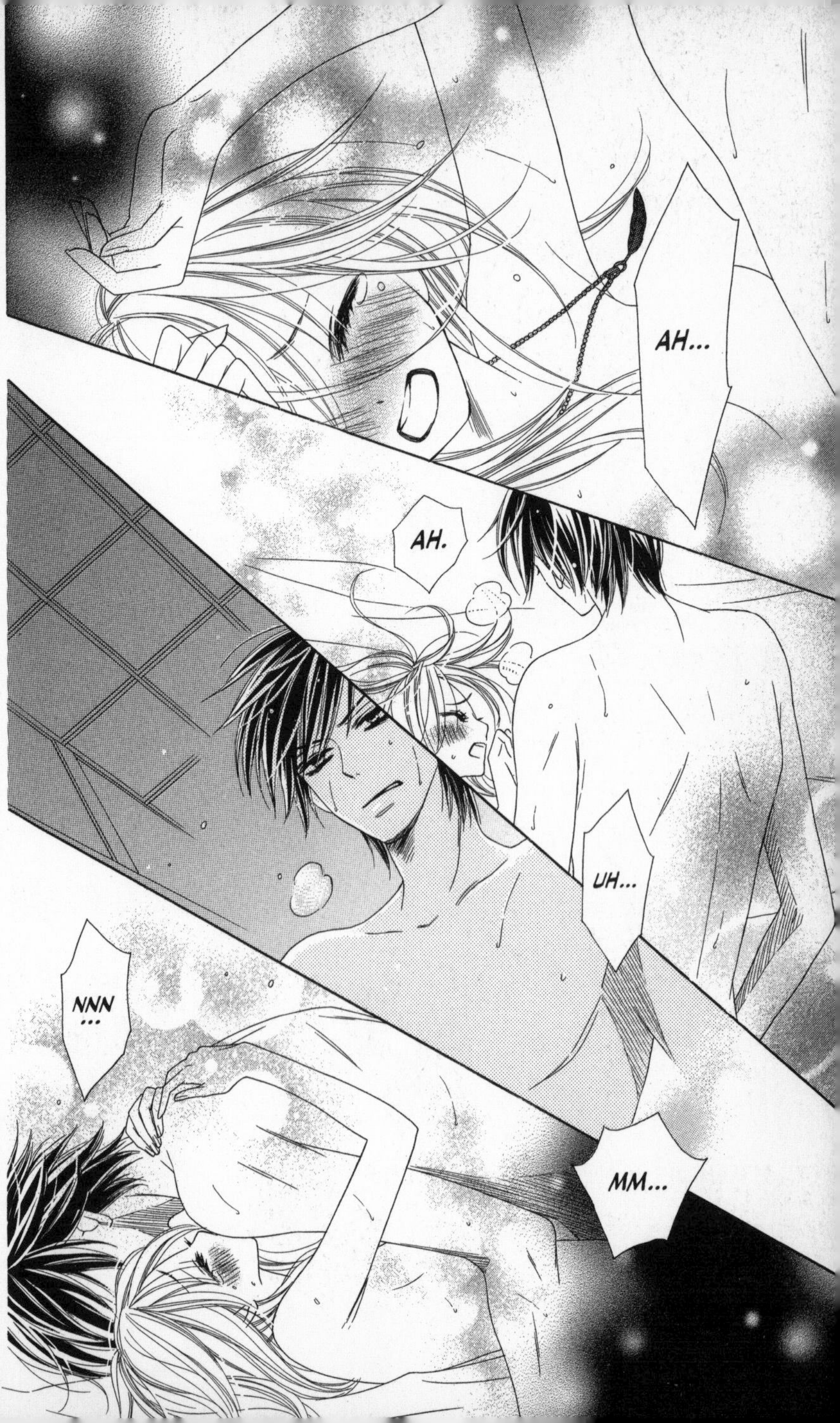
AH...
AH.
UH...
MM...
NNN ...

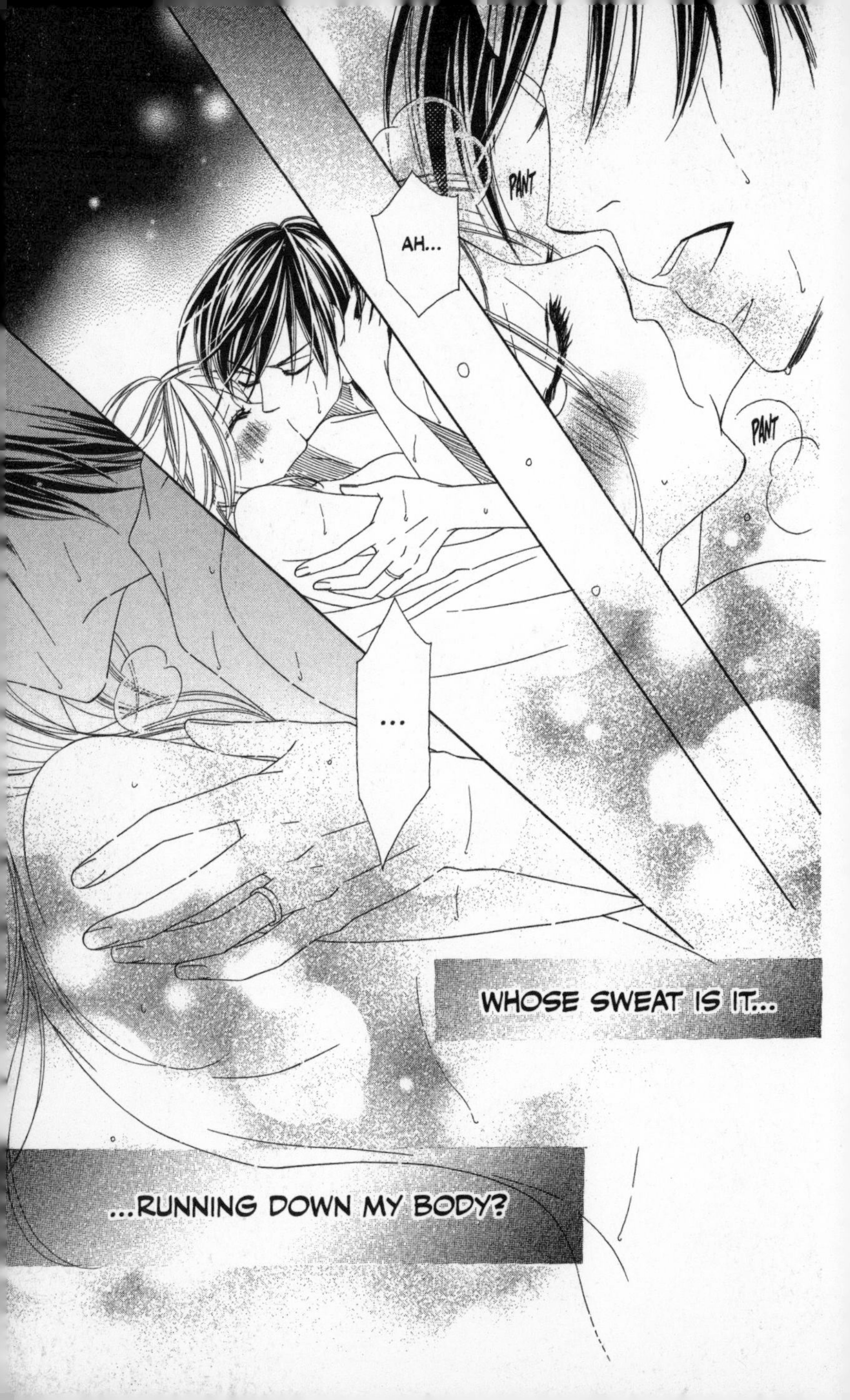
PANT
PANT
AH...
...
WHOSE SWEAT IS IT...
...RUNNING DOWN MY BODY?

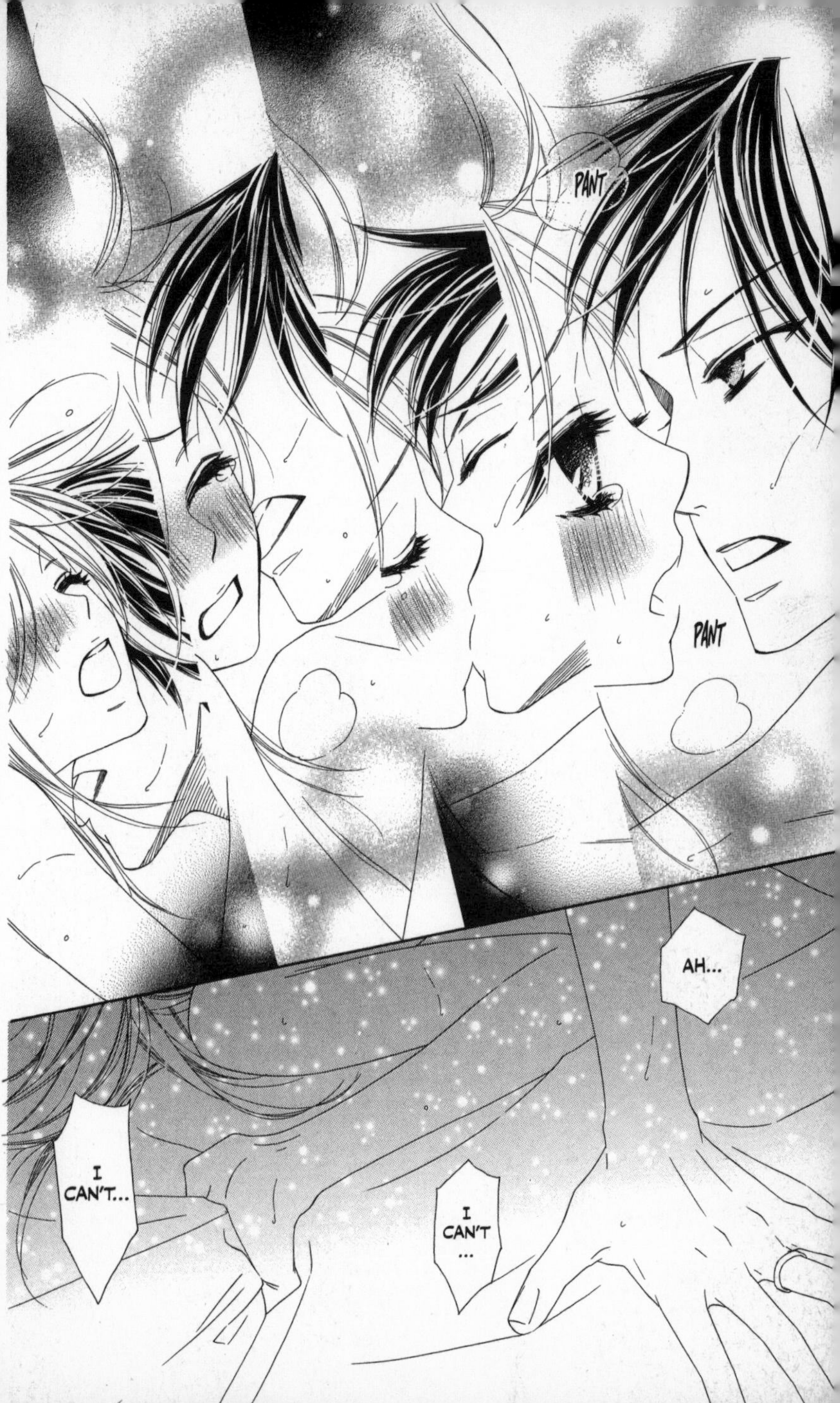
PANT
PANT
AH...
I CAN'T
...
I CAN'T...

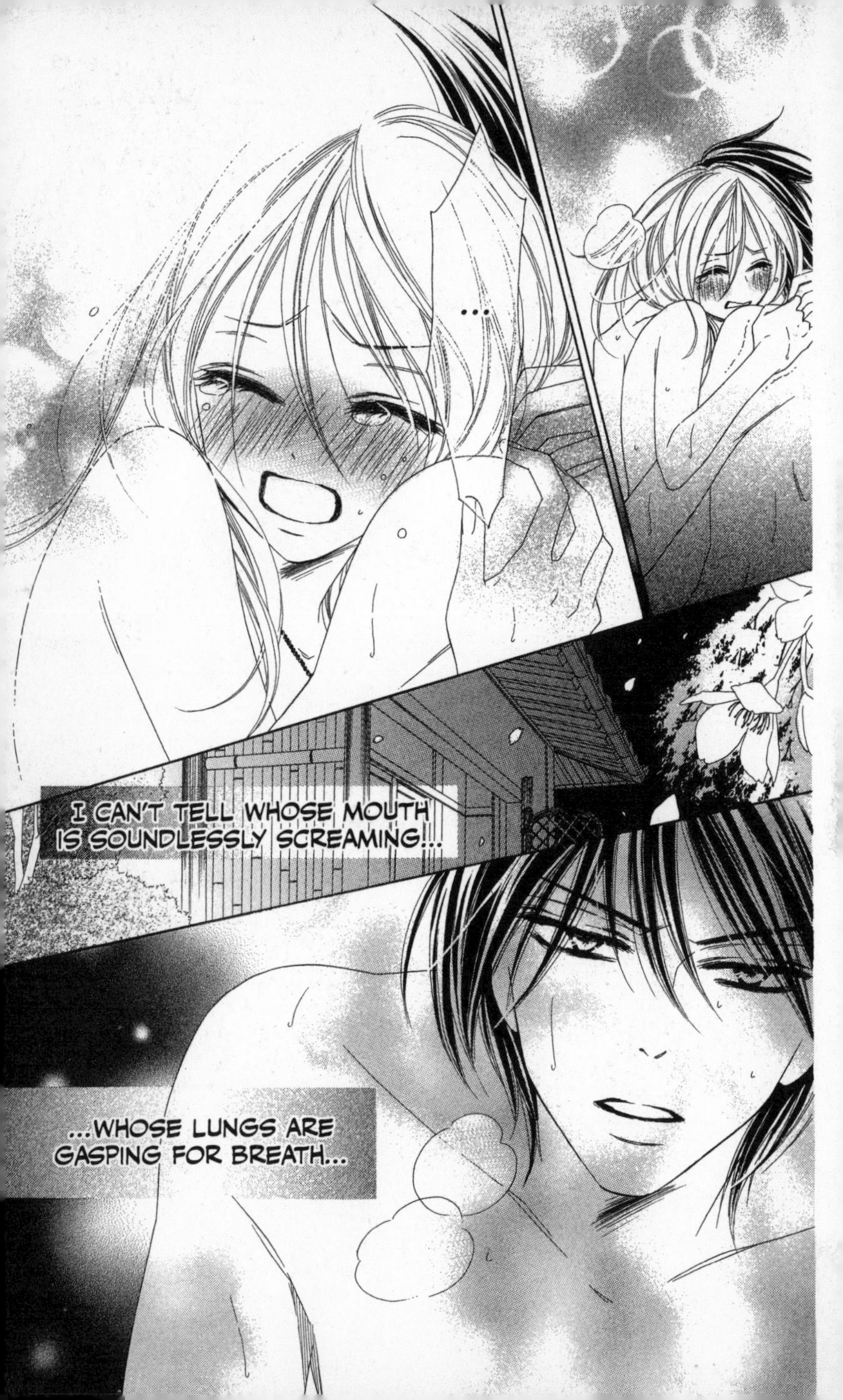
...
I CAN'T TELL WHOSE MOUTH IS SOUNDLESSLY SCREAMING...
...WHOSE LUNGS ARE GASPING FOR BREATH...

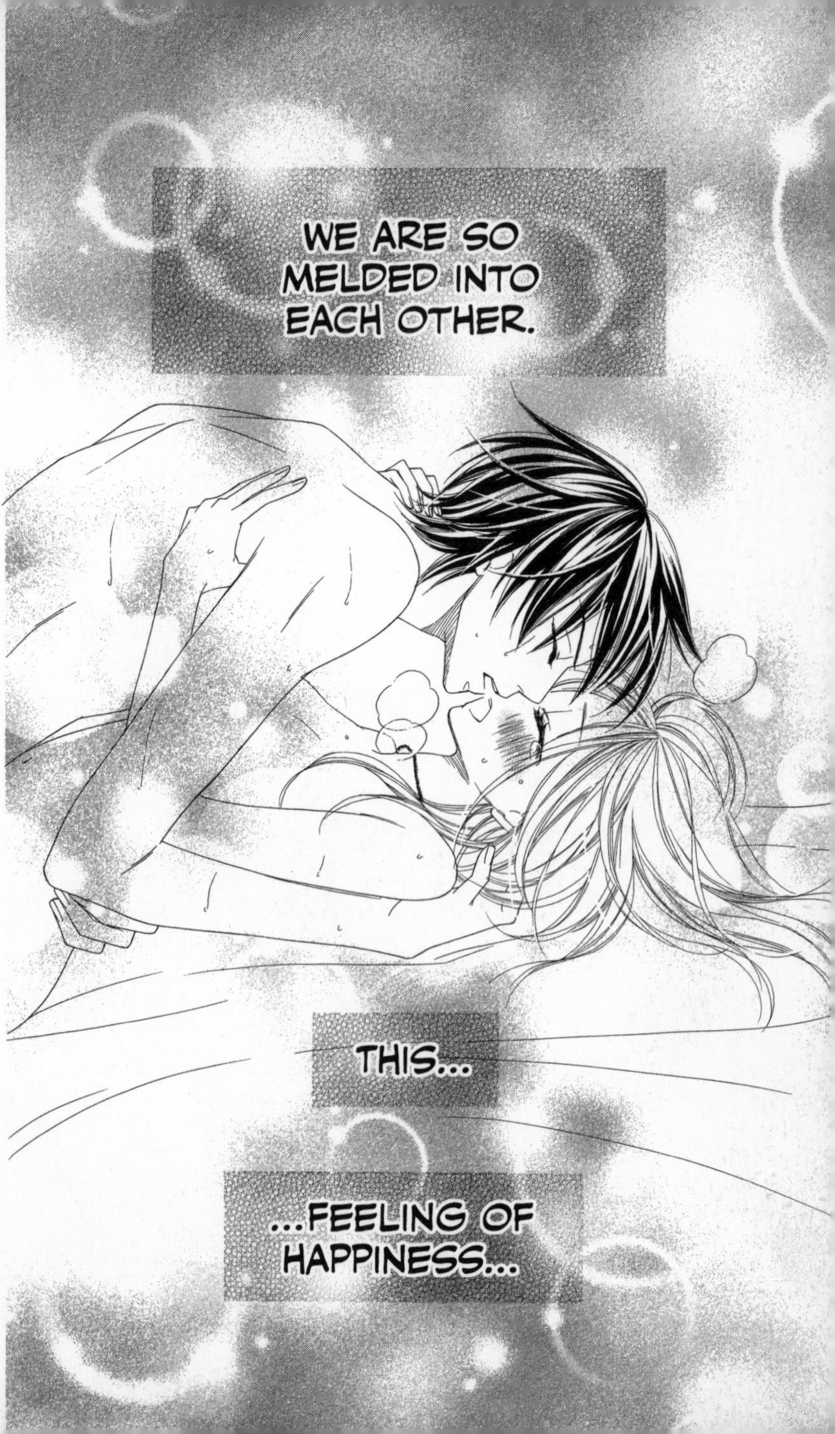
WE ARE SO MELDED INTO EACH OTHER.
THIS...
...FEELING OF HAPPINESS...

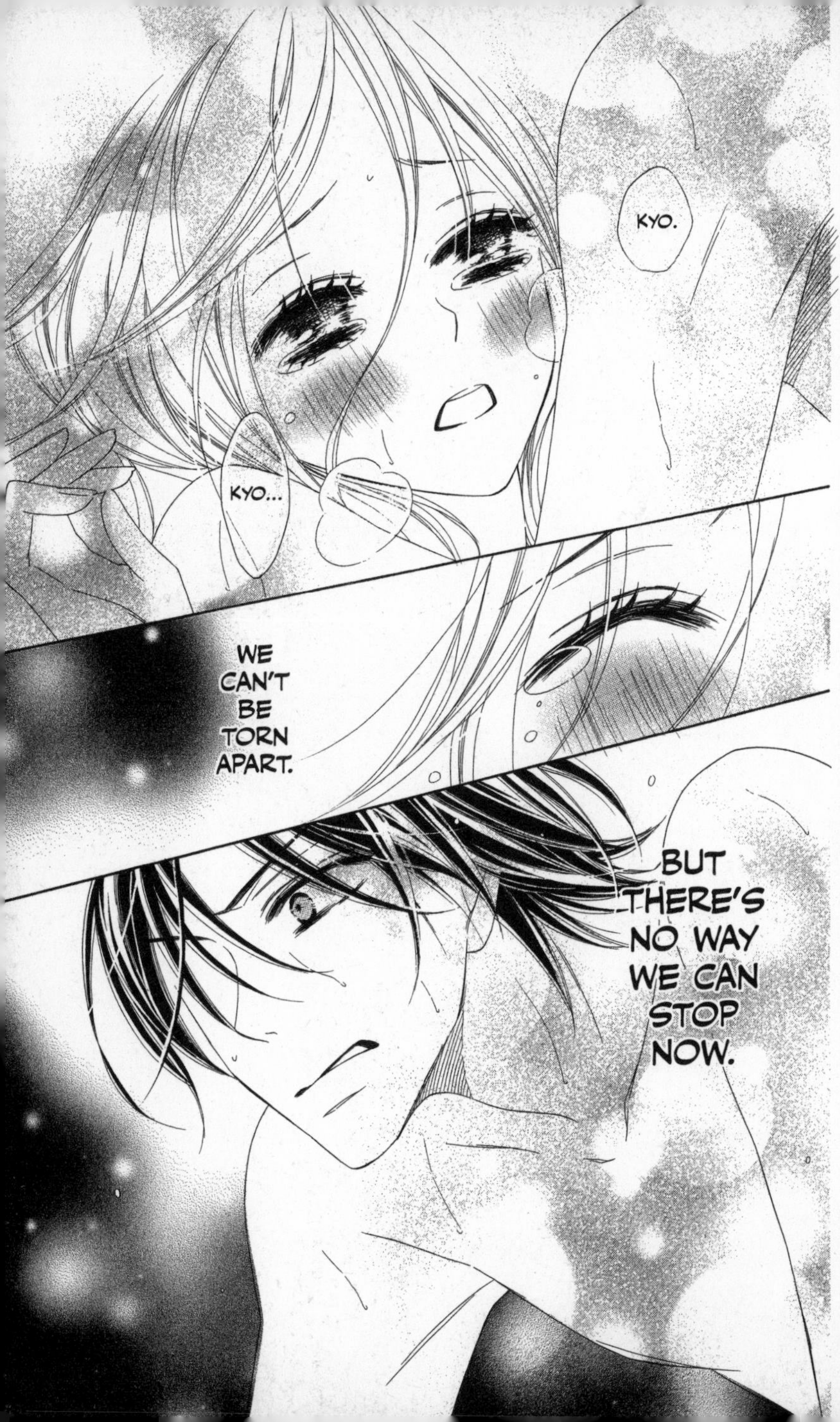
KYO.
KYO...
WE CAN'T BE TORN APART.
BUT THERE'S NO WAY WE CAN STOP NOW.

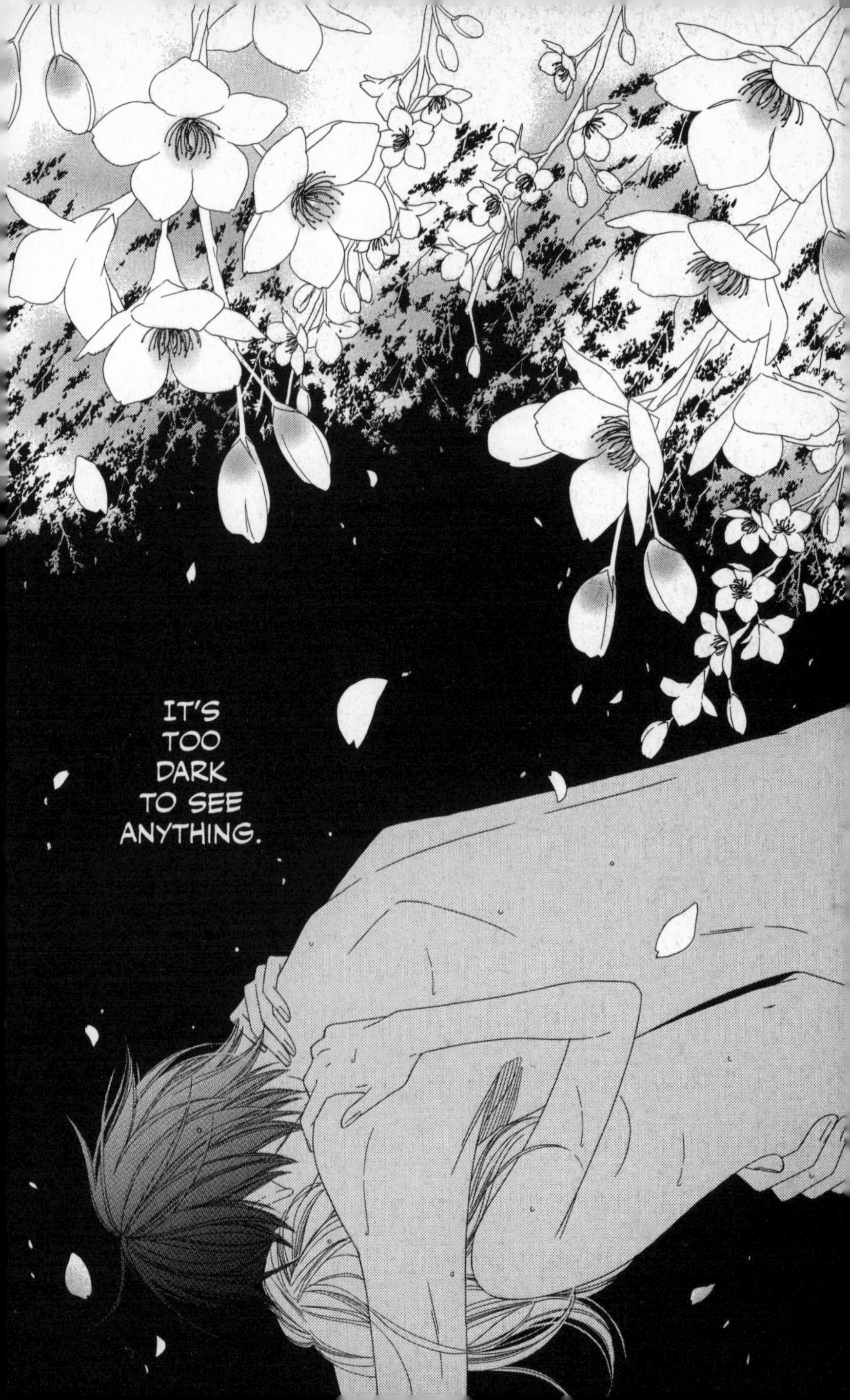
IT'S TOO DARK TO SEE ANYTHING.

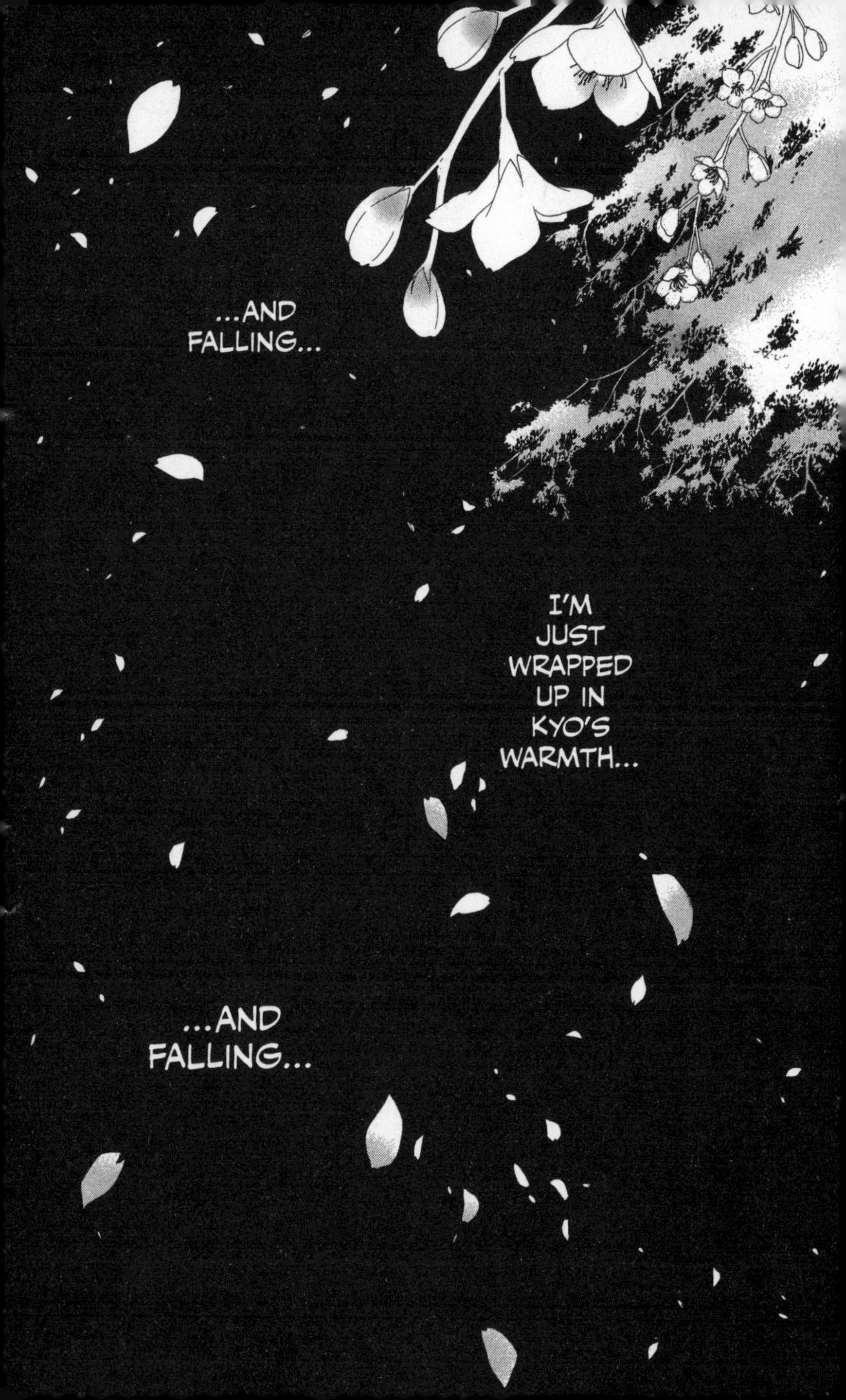
...AND FALLING...
I'M JUST WRAPPED UP IN KYO'S WARMTH...
...AND FALLING...

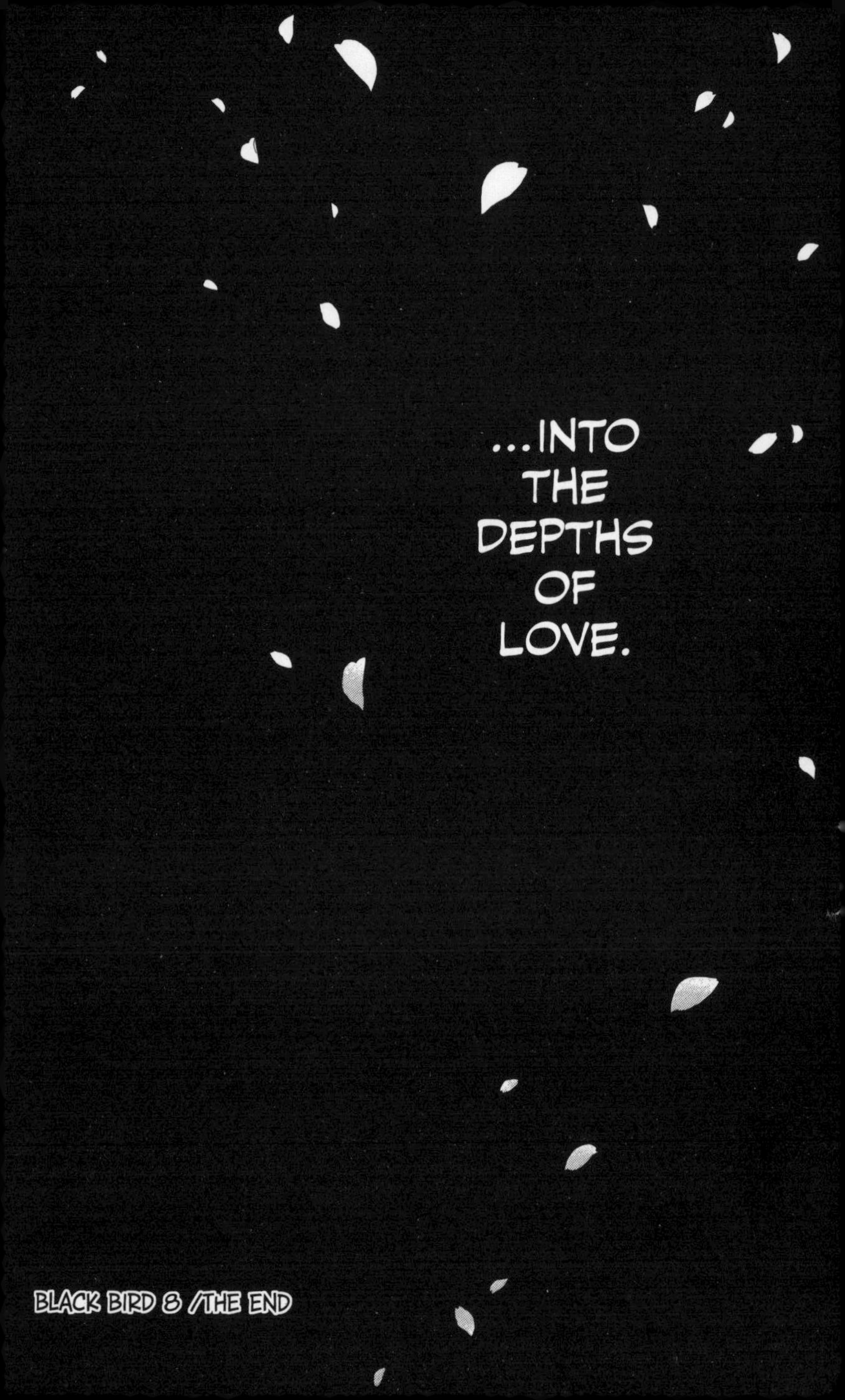
...INTO THE DEPTHS OF LOVE.
BLACK BIRD 8 /THE END

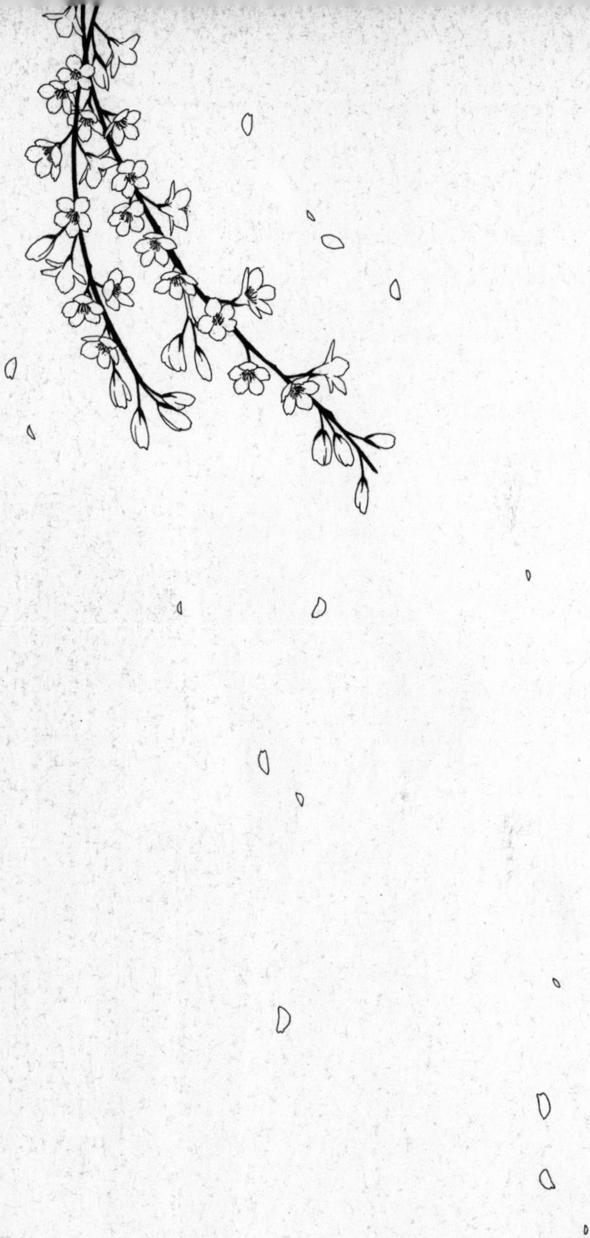

Illustration Request Extra

"Sagami and Ayame on a Date in Western Clothes"

Because of the nature of Sagami's character, and his hair, I can't imagine what sort of Western clothes he'd look good in. I can only give him this hairstyle because it's a fantasy...

But what sort of holiday are they on?

In the first volume, there are signs of trial and error with Kyo, but starting in volume 2, the Western clothing he wears has nothing to do with trends...

←This special that follows was published as a supplement to the New Year's issue. It came with a funny "fill in the face" picture of Kyo.

Arashi fans, please forgive me.

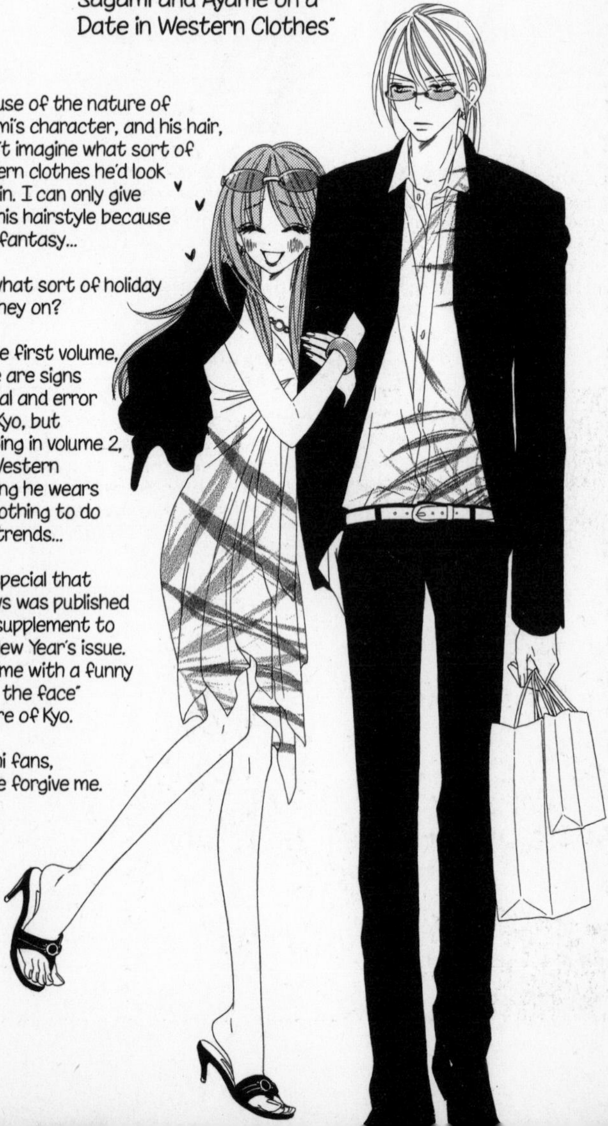

Nightmare

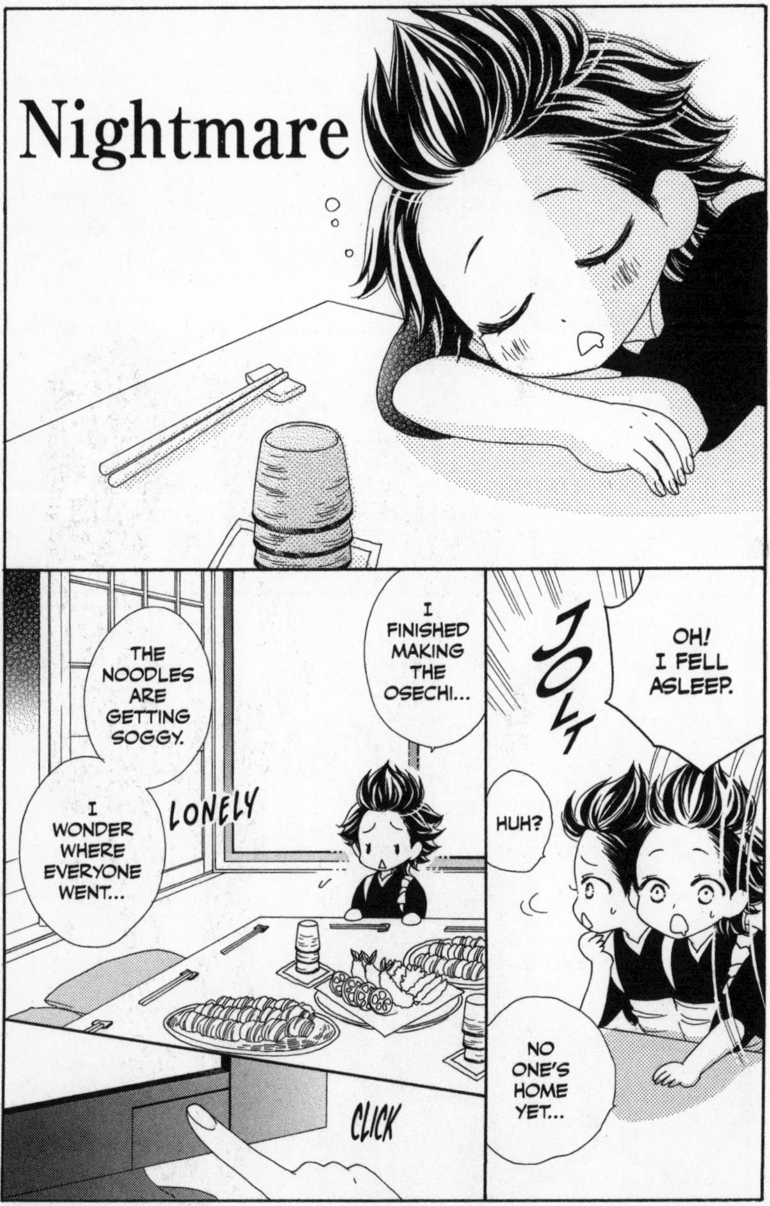

JOLT
OH! I FELL ASLEEP.
HUH?
NO ONE'S HOME YET...
I FINISHED MAKING THE OSECHI...
THE NOODLES ARE GETTING SOGGY.
LONELY
I WONDER WHERE EVERYONE WENT...
CLICK

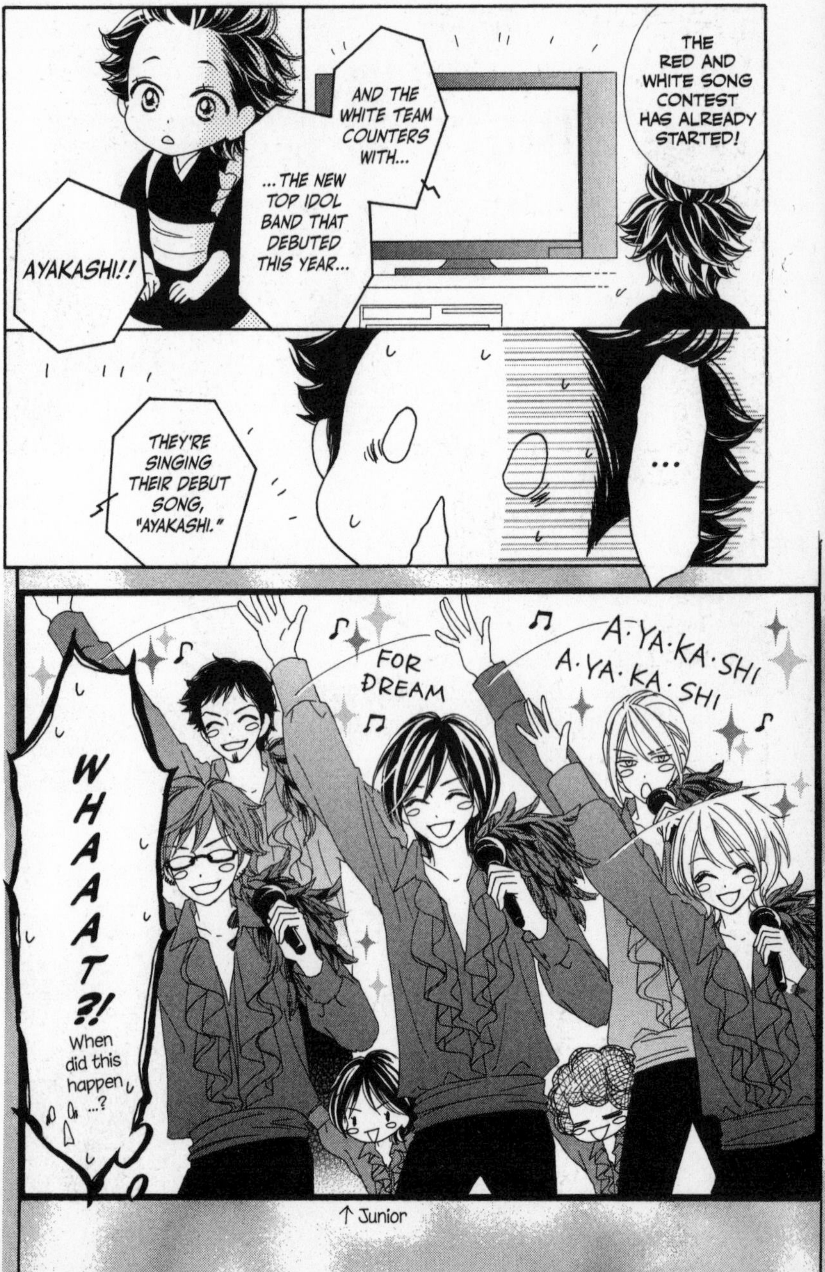
THE RED AND WHITE SONG CONTEST HAS ALREADY STARTED!
AND THE WHITE TEAM COUNTERS WITH...
...THE NEW TOP IDOL BAND THAT DEBUTED THIS YEAR...
AYAKASHI!!
...
THEY'RE SINGING THEIR DEBUT SONG, "AYAKASHI."
A·YA·KA·SHI A·YA·KA·SHI
FOR DREAM
WHAAAAT?!
When did this happen ...?
↑ Junior

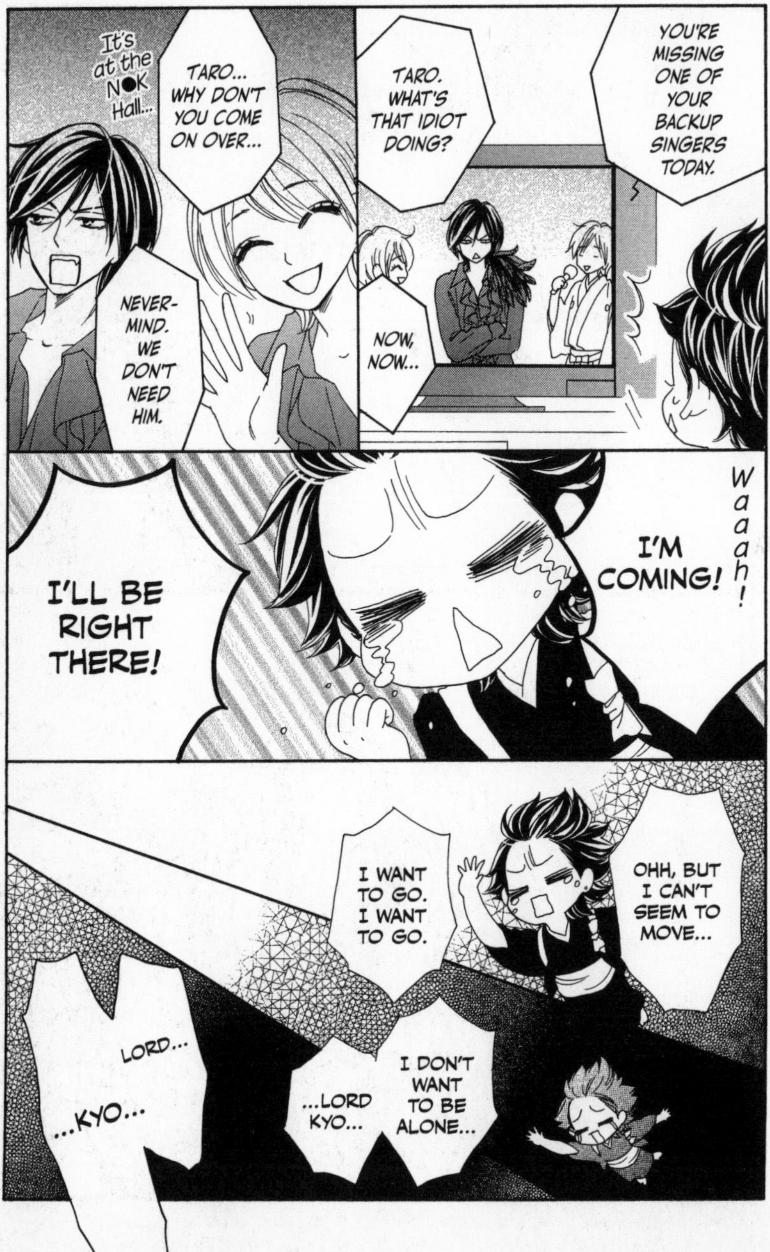
YOU'RE MISSING ONE OF YOUR BACKUP SINGERS TODAY.
TARO. WHAT'S THAT IDIOT DOING?
NOW, NOW...
TARO... WHY DON'T YOU COME ON OVER...
It's at the N●K Hall...
NEVER-MIND. WE DON'T NEED HIM.
Waaaah!
I'M COMING!
I'LL BE RIGHT THERE!
OHH, BUT I CAN'T SEEM TO MOVE...
I WANT TO GO. I WANT TO GO.
I DON'T WANT TO BE ALONE...
...LORD KYO...
LORD...
...KYO...

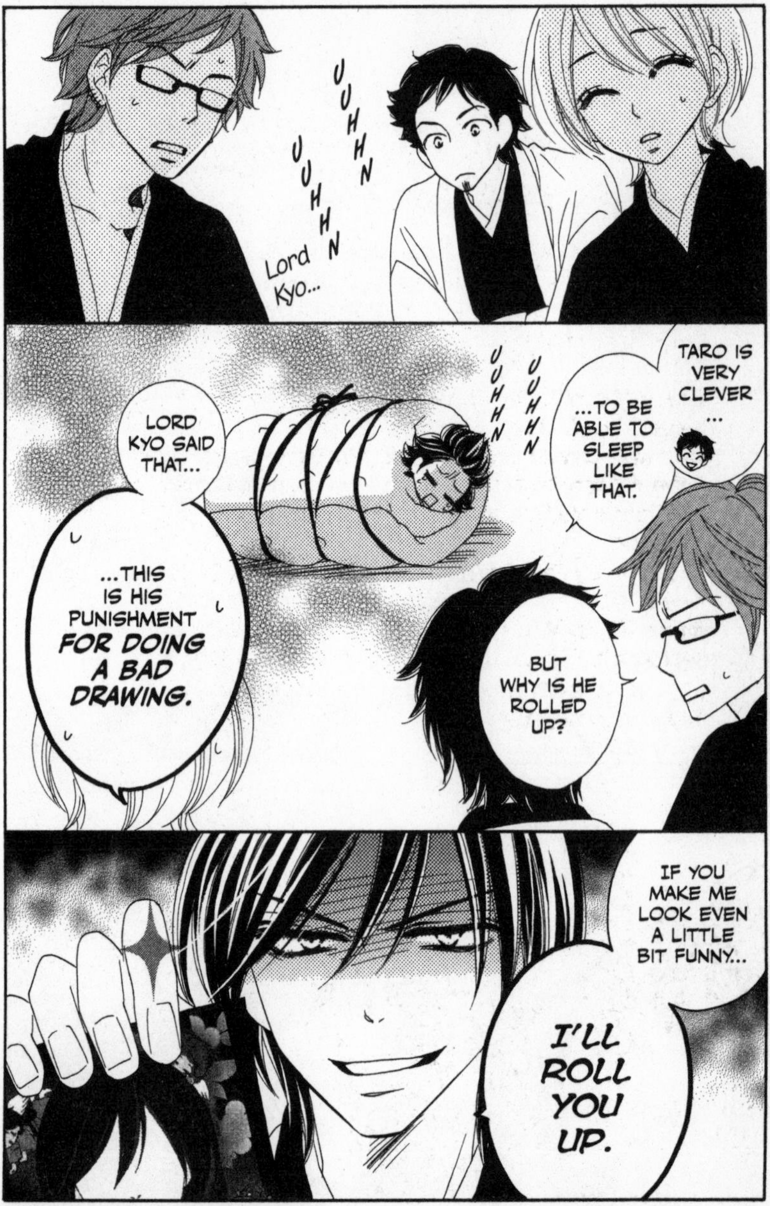
UUHHN
UUHHN
Lord Kyo...
TARO IS VERY CLEVER ...
...TO BE ABLE TO SLEEP LIKE THAT.
UUHHN
UUHHN
LORD KYO SAID THAT...
...THIS IS HIS PUNISHMENT FOR DOING A BAD DRAWING.
BUT WHY IS HE ROLLED UP?
IF YOU MAKE ME LOOK EVEN A LITTLE BIT FUNNY...
I'LL ROLL YOU UP.

NIGHTMARE / THE END *BETSUCOMI* 2009 JANUARY ISSUE SUPPLEMENT.

Hello, everyone. ♥ I'm Kanoko Sakurakoji.

In volume 7, I wrote about the miracle of the *Black Bird* drama CD production. The miracles continue as *Black Bird* has been awarded the 54th Annual Shogakukan Manga Award (in the Shojo Category).

I never thought I would ever see the day in my manga career when I would receive such an award. I have found that when a person becomes the recipient of so many wonderful honors that surpass her wildest dreams, her emotional circuits seem to short out. I am still in a daze.

From the day that I received word of the award, I have received so many congratulatory messages from my editor, my assistants, my friends and family, and from my readers. Of course, I was happy to receive the award, but I was much happier to receive everyone's blessings. Thank you very much!
  ← Continued

Now that I have been made aware that I am living my life with the support of many, many people, all I can offer are my words of thanks. I think the only way I can show you my gratitude is by doing my best to make this manga one that will be loved by everyone. I will work hard, without becoming *a tengu!* (I just realized that at the awards ceremony the other day I was going to use this expression but forgot. I feel better now.) I hope to have your continued support. ♥

Based on the picture below ↓ it looks like this might be the final volume, but it isn't! There's more! This story continues.....?

I hope to see you in the next volume...

An Auspicious Day, April 2009   Kanoko Sakurakoji

GLOSSARY

PAGE 22, PANEL 1: *Dojigiri Yasutsuna*
A sword by this name actually exists. The name *Dojigiri* comes from the legend that the general Minamoto no Yorimitsu (948-1021 CE) decapitated Shuten Doji, the leader of the ogres, with this sword.

PAGE 22, PANEL 2: *Kozuka*
Small blades that fit on the sheaths of samurai swords. They were used as all-purpose blades.

PAGE 184, AUTHOR NOTE:
Fill in the face
Part of a game called *fukuwarai* (happy laughter), where the players are blindfolded and try to place features like eyes, ears, nose and mouth on a picture of a blank face. It is traditionally played on New Year's to make people laugh, since laughter is believed to bring good luck.

PAGE 184, AUTHOR NOTE: *ARASHI*
A Japanese pop group that consists of five male members.

PAGE 185, PANEL 3: *OSECHI*
Traditional New Year's dishes.

PAGE 185, PANEL 3: *Noodles*
New Year's Eve noodles are called *toshikoshii* soba, which means "year crossing noodles."

PAGE 186, PANEL 1: *Red and White Song Contest*
Kohaku Uta Gassen. A gala televised event in Japan on New Year's Eve. The year's most popular musicians compete on either the red (female) or white (male) team.

PAGE 186, PANEL 2: *Ayakashi*
One of the Japanese words for "demon" or "spirit."

PAGE 190, AUTHOR NOTE:
Becoming a tengu
Tengu ni naru in the original Japanese. In Japan, this saying describes someone who is becoming too proud.

Kanoko Sakurakoji was born in downtown
Tokyo, and her hobbies include reading,
watching plays, traveling and shopping. Her
debut title, *Raibu ga Hanetara*, ran in *Bessatsu
Shojo Comic* (currently called *Bestucomi)* in
2000, and her 2004 *Bestucomi* title *Backstage
Prince* was serialized in VIZ Media's
Shojo Beat magazine. She won the 54th
Shogakukan Manga Award for *Black Bird*.

BLACK BIRD
VOL. 8
Shojo Beat Edition

Story and Art by KANOKO SAKURAKOUJI

Original Japanese edition "BLACK BIRD" published by SHOGAKUKAN Inc.

TRANSLATION JN Productions
TOUCH-UP ART & LETTERING Gia Cam Luc
DESIGN Amy Martin
EDITOR Pancha Diaz

Printed in the U.S.A.

Published by VIZ Media, LLC
P.O. Box 77010
San Francisco, CA 94107

10 9 8 7 6 5 4 3 2 1
First printing, May 2011

www.shojobeat.com
www.viz.com

RATED T+ FOR OLDER TEEN

PARENTAL ADVISORY
BLACK BIRD is rated T+ for Older Teen and is recommended for ages 16 and up. This volume contains violence and adult situations.
ratings.viz.com

TOKYO BOYS & GIRLS

By Miki Aihara, the creator of *Hot Gimmick*

Mimori's dream comes true when she's accepted to Meidai Attached High School, especially since she'll get to wear their super-fashionable uniform! Freshman year's bound to be exciting, but as Mimori soon discovers, looking great and feeling great don't always go hand-in-hand...

LAND OF *Fantasy*

MIAKA YÛKI IS AN ORDINARY JUNIOR-HIGH STUDENT WHO IS SUDDENLY WHISKED AWAY INTO THE WORLD OF A BOOK, *THE UNIVERSE OF THE FOUR GODS*. WILL THE BEAUTIFUL CELESTIAL BEINGS SHE ENCOUNTERS AND THE CHANCE TO BECOME A PRIESTESS DIVERT MIAKA FROM EVER RETURNING HOME?

THREE VOLUMES OF THE ORIGINAL *FUSHIGI YÛGI* SERIES COMBINED INTO A LARGER FORMAT WITH AN EXCLUSIVE COVER DESIGN AND BONUS CONTENT

EXPERIENCE THE BEAUTY OF *FUSHIGI YÛGI* WITH THE HARDCOVER ART BOOK

ALSO AVAILABLE: THE *FUSHIGI YÛGI: GENBU KAIDEN* MANGA, THE EIGHT VOLUME PREQUEL TO THIS BEST-SELLING FANTASY SERIES

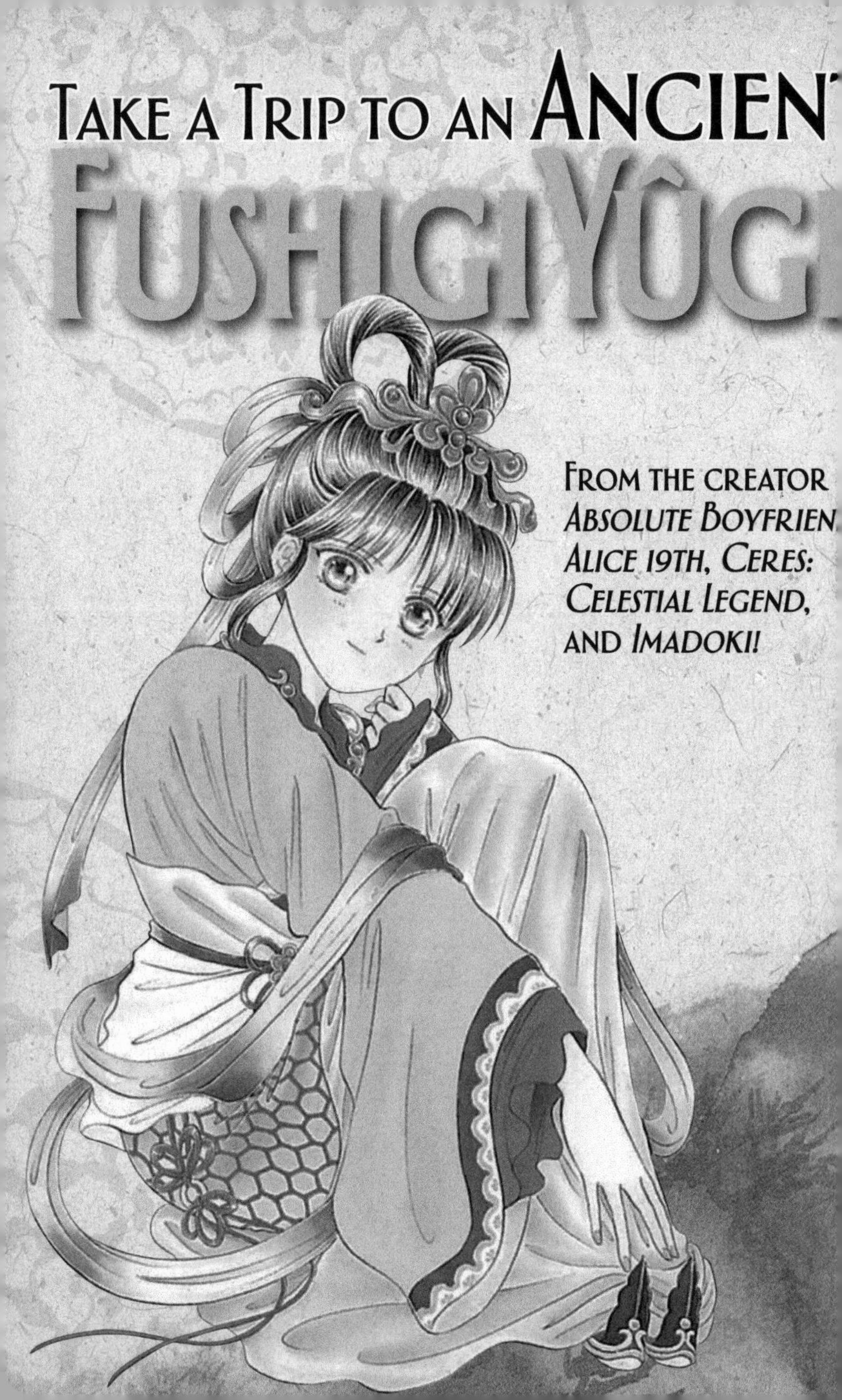
TAKE A TRIP TO AN ANCIEN
FUSHIGI YÛGI
FROM THE CREATOR
ABSOLUTE BOYFRIEN
ALICE 19TH, CERES:
CELESTIAL LEGEND,
AND IMADOKI!

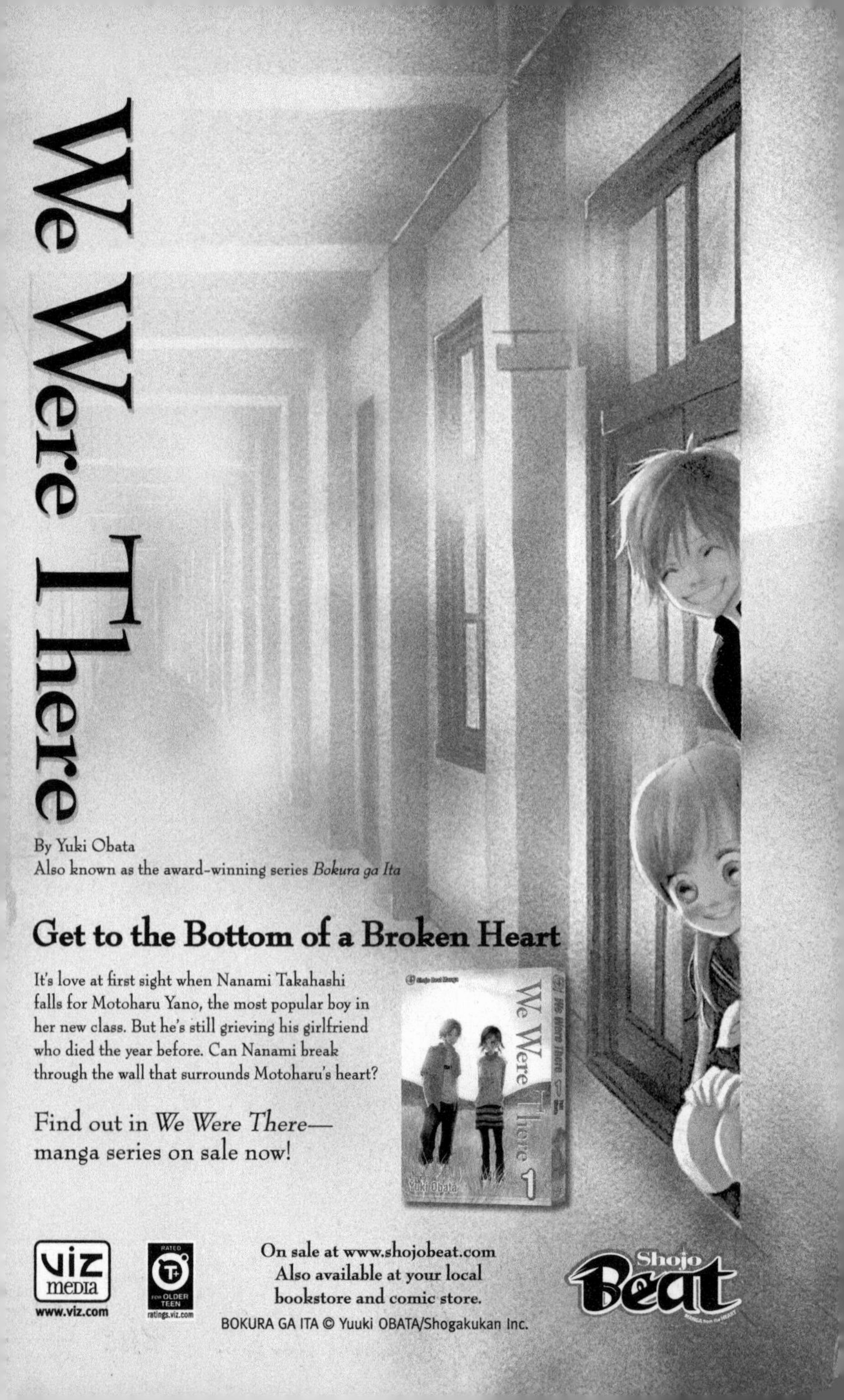
We Were There
By Yuki Obata
Also known as the award-winning series Bokura ga Ita
Get to the Bottom of a Broken Heart
It's love at first sight when Nanami Takahashi falls for Motoharu Yano, the most popular boy in her new class. But he's still grieving his girlfriend who died the year before. Can Nanami break through the wall that surrounds Motoharu's heart?
Find out in We Were There—manga series on sale now!
Shojo Beat Manga
We Were There
Yuki Obata
1
viz media
www.viz.com
RATED
T+
FOR OLDER TEEN
ratings.viz.com
On sale at www.shojobeat.com
Also available at your local bookstore and comic store.
BOKURA GA ITA © Yuuki OBATA/Shogakukan Inc.
Shojo Beat

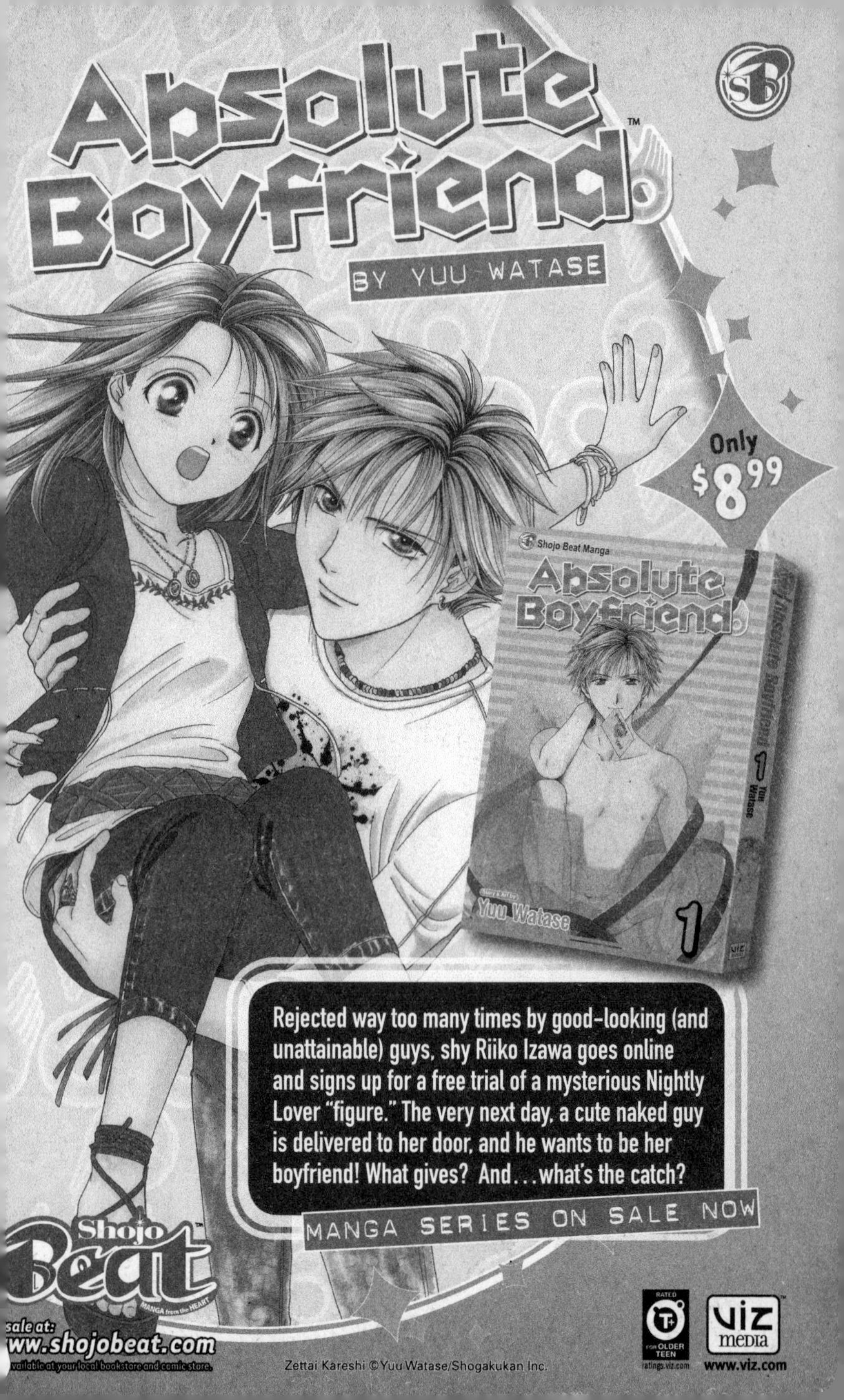
Absolute Boyfriend™
BY YUU WATASE
Only $8.99
Shojo Beat Manga
Absolute Boyfriend
Yuu Watase
1
Rejected way too many times by good-looking (and unattainable) guys, shy Riiko Izawa goes online and signs up for a free trial of a mysterious Nightly Lover "figure." The very next day, a cute naked guy is delivered to her door, and he wants to be her boyfriend! What gives? And…what's the catch?
MANGA SERIES ON SALE NOW
Shojo Beat™
MANGA from the HEART
sale at:
www.shojobeat.com
vailable at your local bookstore and comic store.
Zettai Kareshi © Yuu Watase/Shogakukan Inc.
RATED T+ FOR OLDER TEEN
ratings.viz.com
VIZ media
www.viz.com